W9-CCI-093

Law Enforcement
and the
Youthful Offender:
Juvenile Procedures

Law Enforcement and the Youthful Offender: Juvenile Procedures

Edward Eldefonso

Juvenile Probation Department
Santa Clara County, California

Department of Law Enforcement Education
Foothill College

John Wiley & Sons, Inc.   New York • London • Sydney

10 9 8 7 6 5 4

ISBN 0 471 23512 1

Library of Congress Catalog Card Number: 67-15893

Printed in the United States of America

Preface

This book is designed to cover the major aspects of police work with juveniles and, therefore, the subject matter is extensive, covering such widely diversified matters as *national and international trends, the role of law enforcement in the prevention and control of delinquency, juvenile court law, theoretical approaches to delinquency causation, police services for delinquent and neglected children,* and *special problems confronting law enforcement*; i.e., juvenile gangs, teen-age drinking, adolescent drug addiction, school drop-outs and delinquency and sexual misbehavior among adolescents.

Within the above framework, an effort has also been made to capitalize upon the student's interest in probable future police work. There is thus more material than in similar books on investigative techniques, juvenile court law, and special problems.

At the conclusion of each chapter the student will find a brief summary to serve him as a guide to the contents of that chapter, and to strengthen his memory of the prominent features after he has read it. Furthermore, at the end of each summary there are a number of questions designed to test the student's retention of textual reading.

I feel that this book provides the prospective police officer with ready access to a comprehensive, integrated, and, at the same time, authoritative textbook which embraces all aspects of police work with juveniles. This book may also be utilized by classes dealing with *Juvenile Procedures for Law Enforcement,* or any course in juvenile delinquency.

Many obligations have been incurred during the preparation of *Law Enforcement and the Youthful Offender,* some of them as impossible to identify as they are to repay. Among those persons whom it is impossible to thank, however, are two individuals who actually made it possible for me to write this text: B. Earl Lewis, Director, Department of Law Enforcement Education, Foothill College, Los Altos, California; and Robert E. Nino, Chief Juvenile Probation Officer, County of Santa Clara, San Jose, California. These men gave me an opportunity to instruct classes in Juvenile Procedures — the course for which this text was intended. I am also indebted to the following agencies for the cooperation extended in accumulating material: International Association of Chiefs of Police, specifically Nelson A. Watson, Project Supervisor, Research and Development; National Council on Crime and Delinquency; Federal Probation; Children's Bureau, U. S. Department of Health, Education, and Welfare; and the Federal Bureau of Investigation. For their individual contributions, I owe much to the following academicians: W. E. Thornton, Chief Probation Officer, County of Sacramento, California; R. E. Rice and R. B. Christensen, County of Los Angeles Probation Department, Los Angeles, California; G. Geis, Professor, California State College, Los Angeles, California; and W. C. Kvaraceus, Boston University, Boston, Massachusetts; each will recognize the points which he has contributed.

My special appreciation is extended to Naka Prastalo for her genuine enthusiasm and support and to Mildred Ann Eldefonso for reading and criticizing the manuscript—specifically the footnotes and bibliography; also, for "putting-up" with my changes of mood during the final stages of refining the manuscript. Appreciation is also extended to the several authors and publishers who gave permission to quote copyrighted material; specific acknowledgments are accorded each quotation in the text.

Edward Eldefonso

San Jose, January 1967

Contents

PART ONE

Introduction

Definitions . . . Inadequate

Cases Involving Youthful Offenders

Scope of Problem . . . National and International Trends

Prevention Is the Answer

Chapter 1

Introduction

CRIME IS NOT A NEW INVENTION; it is as old as time. Furthermore, juvenile delinquency has been its constant companion and, as such, has served as a "training school." Socrates is alleged to have declared:

> *The children now love luxury. They have bad manners, contempt for authority, they show disrespect for elders and love chatter in place of exercise. They no longer rise when their elders enter the room. They contradict their parents. Chatter before company. Gobble up dainties at the table, and tyrannize over their teachers.*

Although the problem of youthful crime is not new, current statistics indicate a development alarming enough to make it imperative we make some adjustments in our approach concerning the responsibility of juveniles for their crimes.

Just how serious is the problem?

Crime in the United States increased four times faster than the nation's population in the last five years! Serious crimes—murder, robbery, forcible rape, burglary, aggravated assault, larceny of fifty dollars or more, automobile theft—have mounted steadily since the end of World War II. According to the FBI, in 1951 criminal acts topped the one million mark, and in 1962 the two million mark was passed. There is a serious crime committed *every fifteen seconds.*

Graver still, however, is one chilling development in these statistics with respect to our most precious asset—the youth of the United States. In 1965, according to the Uniform Crime Reports, we witnessed the seventeenth consecutive year in which youthful criminality increased over the previous year! During that period, young offenders were represented in over 52 per cent of total arrests.

What social and environmental factors contribute to juvenile crime? *Who* should be responsible for the suppression and control of delinquent behavior?

So many elements must be considered with regard to the curbing and eventual control of delinquency that to give primacy to any one factor outside the home would be extremely difficult. Among other factors to consider, good—not adequate—police work is mandatory. Good law enforcement depends, to a great extent, on the quality of men selected and the effectiveness of the training they receive. Although the well-trained officer is a poor substitute for parental control, he is a vital component in effective delinquency control and prevention programs.

In almost every situation involving a delinquent act the police officer's role is a vital one, and he is *initially* involved. He sums up, in his person and his uniform, the true meaning of "Law Enforcement": *he represents the law.* Therefore, his demeanor and actions impress a lasting image in the mind of the juvenile. This image relates directly to the child's understanding of law and law enforcement and, in many instances, to his subsequent behavior.

The police officer's role in delinquency control *does not,* as many suppose, automatically end with detection and apprehension. On the contrary, Uniform Crime Reports reveal that as many juvenile cases are handled within police agencies as are referred to juvenile courts. For example, in 1965 more than 47 per cent of all juveniles taken into custody were handled on the police level with an admonishment or turned over to parents or private welfare agencies. The remainder were referred to juvenile courts, to criminal courts for trial as adults, or to other law enforcement agencies.

This may be startling to many who for the first time are shocked into an awareness of the scope of police responsibilities with relation to juveniles. The need for good judgment, bulwarked by sound training, is apparent. The police officer inescapably finds himself in a position where he must make a decision which will have its indelible effect on a young and impressionable person. The arresting officer must consider the child and the gravity of the offense. The officer must ask and answer the following questions:

Will the ends of justice and the best interests of the community and the juvenile be served merely by an oral reprimand?

Or shall the parents be advised of the offense and urged to exert closer supervision over the minor?

Or is the offense one which requires referral to juvenile court or another agency?

It is common knowledge that almost without exception the police officer is the first to approach the child in trouble. He or other members of his department make a preliminary assessment of all juvenile offenders taken into custody. Thus the police officer, in effect, sits as judge or serves as social worker in many instances. His findings determine the final disposition of almost half the cases involving juvenile offenders who are taken into custody. In order to make the correct decisions, knowledge of motivation is important. So is knowledge of juvenile court jurisdiction and procedures as well as disposition of prior cases. The progressive police officer needs to be aware of basic concepts in the social, psychiatric, and rehabilitative fields. Since much of police work relates to crime prevention, the police officer needs perception in public and human relations.

In the light of the above, it goes without saying that training is essential. Modern law enforcement, recognizing this fact, is promoting increasingly broad programs in this field. Many local training units give lengthy and detailed courses in this area of police work. From recruits and through the ranks to supervisory and command level, this aspect of police training is considered vital. Officers needed to man juvenile divisions, as a general rule, are selected with care and are given specialized training beyond that afforded other officers.

The basic responsibility of law enforcement is the protection of all people. Law enforcement officers must learn to differentiate between the apple-stealing prankster of tender years and the knife-wielding, chain-swinging hoodlum, also of tender years. There is a difference between delinquency and criminality. Certainly, the police—and the courts—must remove from circulation those who violate society's rules to the extent that they constitute a menace to the welfare of the community, regardless of their age.

Almost any aspect of police work may involve juveniles. Statistics for 1964–1965 reveal to some extent police encounters with juvenile violators of the law. Arrest of persons under 18 years of age made up more than 48 per cent of all arrests for criminal acts in cities and rural areas. The statistics presented in Chapter 3 reflect the seriousness of the problem. These statistics also indicate clearly the importance that must be attached to the problem itself and to the officer charged with the initial responsibility in the confrontation of that problem. That officer—every officer—must be adequately trained if he is to discharge his duty effectively. He must be trained in order to instruct by action, by precept, and by example.

The need for informed and well-trained police officers in combating juvenile delinquency and juvenile crime goes beyond actual apprehension and detection. Day after day, week and week, the officer who is fulfilling his task effectively is automatically helping children arrive at acceptable standards of conduct. His insistence on obedience to the law, and his firm but fair attitude in dealing with those who violate the law, assist the young child in arriving at a sound conclusion of what is acceptable and what is not. Again and again the police officer must serve as teacher, explaining the law and pointing up the inevitable retribution that follows its violation. But even the most effective law enforcement officers, putting forth their best efforts, cannot stem the tide of delinquency flowing from parental failures in growing numbers of homes.

The increase in juvenile crime (current statistics reveal that delinquency is skyrocketing by more than four times the rate of national population growth) is a continuing reason for concern. It is a sound reason for mobilizing community resources in behalf of crime-fighting agencies. It is a reason which should prompt civic-minded citizens to support a basic, progressive, continuous law enforcement training program. Unquestionably, the well-trained local law enforcement officer is a vital ingredient in crime control.

Chapter 2

Definitions . . . Inadequate

JUVENILE DELINQUENCY means different things to different people. To some, a juvenile delinquent is a boy or girl arrested for a law violation. To others, a single appearance in Juvenile Court identifies the delinquent. To many, the term covers a variety of anti-social behavior which offends them, whether or not a law is violated.

Juvenile delinquency is a blanket term which obscures rather than clarifies our understanding of human behavior. It describes a large variety of youths in trouble or on the verge of trouble. The delinquent may be anything from a normal, mischievous youngster to a youth who gets into trouble by accident. Or he may be a vicious assaultive person who is proud of his anti-social conduct. As a blanket term, delinquency is like the concept of illness. A person may be ill and have polio or measles. The illness is different, the cause is different, and the treatment is different. The same is true of delinquency. Like illness, delinquency describes many problems that develop from varied causes and require different kinds of treatment.

The number of acts by which a juvenile can be identified as a delinquent are almost limitless. In addition to the major violations defined in the criminal codes, a juvenile is described, in some jurisdictions, as delinquent for habitually disobeying parents, truancy, petty stealing, keeping late or unusual hours, running away from home, sexual misconduct, or other nonlaw violating irregularities.

In its broad general meaning delinquency includes:

Officially adjudicated offenders.

Unofficial delinquents, or those handled informally by the courts or by some designated agency.

Cases handled by the police.

Children with special behavior problems or those displaying evidence of anti-social behavior or treated by private agencies.

Children presenting evidence of anti-social conduct, whether or not they are taken before official or private agencies.

Such breadth of meaning explains why a large number of acts may constitute delinquency.

However, in a strictly legal sense, the term should be applied only to those adjudged delinquent by a juvenile court, but young offenders who become involved with the police and courts are only a part of juvenile law violators. There is no way of telling how many youngsters commit crimes and are not caught.

State laws differ as to the age which determines whether a young offender will be handled as a juvenile or as an adult criminal. Most states have age 18 as the limit, others 16 or 17. Some state laws require persons of juvenile age to be tried in an adult criminal court for certain crimes such as murder. In many states, the juvenile court can waive jurisdiction so that a juvenile is tried in an adult criminal court for offenses such as a felony.

WHAT DOES JUVENILE DELINQUENCY MEAN?

The many variations in juvenile court law are confusing. For example, in one state a child who commits a specific offense may be handled as a juvenile delinquent while one who commits the same offense in another jurisdiction may be handled as an adult criminal. This makes an accurate definition or statistical count of juvenile delinquents difficult, as Table 1 in Appendix A shows.

Today the term *juvenile* when applied to delinquency refers to a major social problem involving a specific age group defined locally by law. Until 1899, when the first juvenile court law was enacted by the Illinois legislature, all juveniles who came into contact with the law technically fell into the category of "criminals."[1]

As *Dr. Milton L. Barron* so eloquently pointed out in his book, *The Juvenile and Delinquent Society,* in terms of historical perspective there have been three dominant movements contributing to the emergence of the concept of the juvenile delinquent and the institution of the juvenile court as differentiated from crime and criminal proceedings.

The concept that *immaturity* exempts the individual from moral responsibility in choice of behavior is perhaps the earliest movement in this direction. In common law, a child up to the age of 7 has long been held to be non-responsible under the principle of *mensrea* (blame intent based on the minor's ability to distinguish right from wrong). Furthermore, common law declares that the child from 8 to 14 years of age has been presumed to be incapable of guilt, and thus irresponsible, because

[1]W. C. Kvaraceus and W. E. Ulrich, *Delinquent Behavior, Principles and Practices,* National Education Association of the U.S., Washington, D.C., 1959, p. 114.

of immaturity unless he could be shown to have sufficient intellectual capacity to perceive the difference between lawful and unlawful behavior. The second movement is reflected in current juvenile court processes.

This principle of *chancery of equity* was established by early English kings in reaction against the rigidity of the law and court as applied to minors and to those needing aid. Under the principle of *parens patriae* (father of his country) and its modern counterpart, *in loco parentis* (the state standing in place of the parent), the child's rights have been ordered in civil law in such matters as neglect, dependency, and guardianship. From this principle emerged the concept of "the ward of the state" to apply to the juvenile handicapped by lack of effective parental supervision or control.

Third and most recent—the result of certain combinations of intellectual and reform movements, notably middle-class humanitarianism and child psychology—there arose a strong tendency to protect the child from the sweatshop, whipping post, and incarceration with adult offenders. At the same time, social and psychological research combined with modern penology to stress cause of crime, diagnosis, and treatment, and ultimately to focus on prevention through individual study and therapy, especially in the case of younger offenders.[2]

These three developments led to the present-day concept of juvenile delinquency as something quite different from adult crime. The earlier concept of the young offender to whom punishment is accorded to fit the crime has been largely replaced by the concept of the juvenile as a youngster needing guidance, much as any child in need of medical assistance in the form of diagnosis and treatment. The close affiliation of the early juvenile court with the child-guidance movement, initiated by Dr. William Healy (Cook County, Illinois, 1909), illustrates this point, although the focus was exclusively on the individual and his family rather than on environment.

Thus the term *juvenile crime* represents a contradiction within a strictly legal framework since "crime," by definition, can be engaged in only by adults. Legally, the term *juvenile delinquency* includes all the youngsters between certain age limits (7 through 18 in most states) whose behavior or series of behaviors involves infractions of rules and norms in such a manner as to bring them to the attention of authorities connected with official institutions. The official institution may be in the form of the overall legal societal authority or a sub-institution such as an education facility (school).

[2]*Ibid.*, pp. 45–116.

Two major kinds of violations are included in states and federal statutes: first, those violations of law which, if committed by an adult, would be called crimes; second, those transgressions peculiar to the juvenile age group, such as truancy and incorrigibility which have special significance only for members of this group. Hence, there are in the legal concept both the linear law which includes offenses ordinarily defined as "crimes" but now, because of the age factor, handled as "delinquencies" and the special infractions which are meaningful to the younger members of the community.[3]

What does this mean? When an attorney speaks of tort, contract, or bailment, he has in mind something specific. When the police officer, probation officer, parole officer, or deputy sheriff discusses a burglary or a robbery or a rape, he speaks of crimes that have a common law meaning. He knows the elements that make up the specific crime, and generally he knows what actions come within the offense. But this is not so when someone speaks of juvenile delinquency. There are dissertations, periodicals, books, and many media which discuss juvenile delinquency and all profess to be alarmed over it, but no one can tell exactly what it is that constitutes delinquency. A noted authority on crime and delinquency, Professor Clyde B. Vedder, states that "*a very difficult problem in studying juvenile delinquency is deciding upon an exact definition of the term itself—no two authorities agree in this matter.*"

There seems to be a concerted effort on the part of the authorities to avoid labeling juveniles as delinquents. According to statistical information from the FBI Uniform Crime Reports and the Children's Bureau of the Department of Health, Education, and Welfare, law enforcement agencies handle more than two-thirds of juvenile police arrests informally. Scrutiny of statistical information from such agencies shows that more than 1,700,000 youths have had contact with various police agencies throughout the nation—but only approximately 500,000 actually appeared before juvenile courts throughout the states on petitionable offenses.

Thus it is safe to say that more than half of the juveniles taken into custody by the various law enforcement agencies throughout the country are returned home without further action. It is also safe to say that half the juveniles who are referred to juvenile courts are released without a finding of delinquency.

Who Is a Delinquent?

For purposes of further discussion throughout this book, a delinquent is defined as *any law violator under the statutory age as described by*

[3]*Ibid.*, p. 117.

the state in which he resides, whether or not he comes to the attention of the court. However, agencies such as law enforcement, school, and probation-parole officers have devised their own concepts of juvenile delinquents.

OTHER CONCEPTS

Police Concept

The police concept classifies the delinquent as the *statistical delinquent or accidental offender* and the *personality-disordered delinquent.* The statistical delinquent is a minor who, through immaturity or through impulsiveness, is involved in a delinquent act although he normally functions well. These acts usually occur during gang activities or among the "spur-of-the-moment" automobile set. However, this particular delinquent, the statistical or accidental offender, usually does not repeat and matures into a normal law-abiding citizen.

On the other hand, the personality-disordered delinquent often engages in a series of anti-social acts which necessitates an immediate referral to the juvenile probation department and, in most cases, custodial care or some type of official help appears necessary.

School Concept

This concept is rather a general one. Schools are concerned with delinquents who fall into such categories as:

1. *The academic delinquent—a minor who is not working up to full capacity in school.*
2. *The behavioral delinquent—a boy or girl who does not get along with teachers or peers in classroom or in recreational functions.*
3. *The mentally or physically retarded delinquent—a child unable to compete with his classmates due to severe emotional or physical handicaps, thereby causing him to act out in a hostile, unacceptable manner.*

Generally, the school feels that an unhappy child is a potential delinquent. As an example, the school cites the youngster who is unable to keep up with the manner of dress utilized by his peers or the youngster who will not conform to dress standards. This youngster may be teased and taunted by peers. Eventually, he is provoked into striking back. Is this a delinquent? No, but the seed is planted.

Probation Concept

The probation concept deals with the juvenile who is actually referred to the juvenile probation department by various agencies and a petition is filed in behalf of the minor, alleging the LAW VIOLATION. The probation concept contends that not all minors who appear before the juvenile court appear on a delinquency petition. Minors may appear before the juvenile court for truancy, neglect, dependency, incorrigibility, or other "predelinquent" activities.

Thus, according to the probation concept, *no juvenile is a delinquent without a court finding*. The juvenile court feels that it would be unjust to declare a juvenile delinquent at the point of his apprehension, just as the adult court does not consider an adult a criminal at his point of apprehension. The adult is presumed to be innocent until proven guilty. According to the probation concept, the juvenile should be accorded the same presumption.

As previously stated, 80 to 90 per cent of the juveniles apprehended after violating the law are released without court action adjudging them wards of the court. Therefore, there is a legal difference between a youngster being apprehended as a juvenile delinquent and being found to be a delinquent in a juvenile court proceeding. The probation concept suggests that a minor's legal rights are protected and until such time as a court of a competent jurisdiction passes upon the evidence and makes a finding that the juvenile is a delinquent from a legal point of view, the child is no more delinquent than the adult who is not a criminal until he is properly charged with an offense against the law and is found guilty as charged.

SUMMARY

Definitions of delinquency are inadequate because: (1) Experts are unable to agree on a single definition. (2) State laws differ on what is a delinquent offense, i.e., burglary, petty theft, runaway, incorrigible behavior, alcoholic beverage violations, etc. (3) State laws vary in determining the "age limits" for prosecution as an adult or handling as a delinquent.

In its broad general meaning, delinquency includes (1) officially adjudicated offenders, (2) unofficial delinquents, (3) cases handled by the police, (4) children with special behavioral problems, and (5) children presenting anti-social conduct, whether or not they are taken before official or private agencies.

Historically, there have been three dominant movements contributing to the emergence of the concept of the juvenile delinquent and the institution of the juvenile court as differentiated from crime and criminal proceedings: (1) Concept that immaturity exempts the individual from moral responsibility, (2) the principle of *parens patriae* and its modern counterpart in *loco parentis,* and (3) the tendency to protect the child from evil influences.

In this chapter we defined a delinquent as *any law violator under the statutory age as described by the state in which he resides, whether or not he comes to the attention of the court.*

Three other concepts, much more specific in nature, were also presented: (1) the police concept—a statistical or accidental offender and the personality-disordered delinquent; (2) the school concept—the academic delinquent, the behavioral delinquent, and the mentally or physically retarded delinquent; and (3) the probation concept—defining a delinquent as a minor who is adjudged as such by a court of competent jurisdiction.

QUESTIONS

1. What is meant when the statement is made that "*juvenile delinquency* is a blanket term which obscures rather than clarifies our understanding of human behavior"?
2. What are the five broad, general meanings of delinquency as indicated in the text?
3. Define *in loco parentis.*
4. What is our definition of a delinquent?
5. Discuss the school's concept of a delinquent.
6. Discuss the police concept of a delinquent.
7. Discuss the probation or juvenile court concept of a delinquent.
8. *True* or *False* . . . In California, the juvenile court may waive jurisdiction of children between 16 and 21.
9. *True* or *False* . . . In general, the juvenile court has exclusive jurisdiction over children under the age of 16 in counties of 60,000 population or over. Jurisdiction over felonies is concurrent.
10. *True* or *False* . . . In Vermont, the juvenile court has exclusive jurisdiction over children 16, except for capital offenses.

Chapter 3

Cases Involving Youthful Offenders

HERE ARE TEN SHORT CASES of juveniles whose acting-out behavior caused a great deal of concern, not only to law enforcement agencies and juvenile courts, but also to the communities in which they occurred.

Note that all these cases have been purposely selected to show two common overt symptoms—stealing behavior and assaultive behavior—and have been dealt with on a continuum. This is not to imply that stealing behavior and assaultive behavior are the only, or even the most frequent, serious forms of delinquent behavior.

One other point needs to be mentioned at this time; this particular point was touched upon by William C. Kvaraceus in his book, *The Community and the Delinquent.* According to Kvaraceus, *delinquent conduct usually takes the form of overt and aggressive behavior, which forces itself upon adult awareness; less frequently does it follow the pattern of passive or inverted conduct. Society seems to concern itself, as does this chapter, almost exclusively with those children who give evidence of their maladjustments through assaultive behavior, stealing, vandalism or other overt attacks on society.*

Kvaraceus further states that children who express emotional difficulties by quietly retreating, or evading reality, very seldom appear as delinquents. However, symptoms such as bed-wetting, nail-biting, extreme shyness, or fears show that these children have an acute need for adult attention and help, even though they may not be labeled as delinquents and do not seek attention in a *noisy* overt fashion. In societies overly concerned for the acting-out youngster, it is not unusual that the nail-biter or bed-wetter is overlooked. The community should not overlook the large group of quietly deviating children who represent an equally great hazard to themselves and society.

To return to the ten cases—these cases are the type that law enforcement agencies are most concerned about and although they do not represent the "average" delinquent case, they will serve a useful purpose by introducing the basic issues that must be faced and the fundamental principles most useful in dealing with delinquent children.

STEALING BEHAVIOR CASES[1]

1. Abe

Abe is reported missing again by his widowed mother. This time she reports that her money-box with about $20 is also gone.

Abe is a junior high school boy who has been known to the local child guidance clinic for several years. He was originally referred to the clinic as an unruly and overly aggressive behavior problem; he was having considerable difficulty with his school work and his teachers. His absences were frequent, many of them constituting truancies.

For the last four years Abe had been treated unsuccessfully for a serious scalp condition which resulted in the loss of most of his hair. His friends nicknamed him "baldy" and "cueball"—names which Abe found as repellent as his baldness. Medical prognosis as to any improvement in his scalp condition was discouraging.

During the last year Abe began to wear a black skull cap in the classroom. This was partly due to the need to cover up an unsightly condition resulting from the application of medication and partly to Abe's desire to hide his affliction from the world. However, the black skullcap only made Abe more conspicuous by accentuating his unsightly condition. He now faced the constant hazard of having his protective headgear knocked off by one of his classmates.

During his first visit to the psychiatrist, he showed considerable insight into his problem and readily proffered this remark: "The guys in my glass are always riling me and driving me nuts. I can't take it anymore and don't know what to do." This is not altogether true, however, since Abe had been building up a long list of truancies as a means of escape from the unfriendly school and the classroom. With good support from the school principal and the guidance counsellor, the psychiatrist was able to utilize the truancies for their therapeutic value. Additional medical aid was procured from a medical center in another part of the state, but the scalp condition failed to respond to further treatment. During this period, Abe established a strong bond with the psychiatrist and other clinic staff members. He felt they were his real friends and were trying to help him.

[1]Adapted with permission from: W. C. Kvaraceus, *The Community and the Delinquent*, World Book Company, Yonkers, N.Y., 1954, pp. 20–29.

At the last staff meeting, prior to Abe's latest disappearance, the psychiatrist reported that Abe has made considerable progress, that he showed himself more accepting of his physical condition, that he had voluntarily discussed the discarding of his skullcap, and the prognosis for his behavior disturbances was good, taking a longterm point of view. Now the mother reports that her son is "gone," and that he took some of her money without her consent.

When Abe is picked up by the police in a nearby city, he is found to be carrying a set of boxing gloves which he purchased in a second-hand store. The rest of the money he spent on fancy food items and on movies, so he had to sleep in hallways and cellars. He is glad to get home and appears genuinely sorry to have caused his mother so much concern. The mother is so relieved to have Abe home again that she readily forgives him and asks the authorities "not to do anything about it or to hold it against my boy." In fact, she confides to the school counsellor that she is sorry she told anyone that Abe had taken her money.

Is Abe a delinquent? Can the community do anything more for him, since he is already known to the local child guidance clinic? Has the clinic failed in its treatment of this boy? Should "harsher" or "firmer" methods be used by the appropriate authorities in the community?

2. Spontaneous Stealing

A group of neighborhood boys have hold of "a good thing" in Mr. N, a neighbor who is a heavy drinker. The boys frequently help him make his way home. They run errands for him to the local package store whenever he cannot get there under his own power. He always repays them generously for their services with whatever bill he happens to pull out of a pocket. It may be a dollar, but more often it is a five or ten. The neighborhood residents know Mr. N's affliction, but they also know "he has plenty of money." Their attitude is one of envy more than pity.

On one weekend that has almost been lost, the boys bring Mr. N home. He is already quite unsteady on his feet. He asked the boys to wait a minute; he would like them to get him several packages of cigarettes and, of course, more beer. While the boys are waiting, Mr. N goes to the telephone directory, shakes it vigorously, and some 20 or 30 green bills flutter to the floor. The boys scramble to help pick up the scattered bills. They hand some of the bills back to the owner, at the same time putting "some of the stuff" into their pockets. Mr. N is too woozy to notice. After the boys have procured the supplies and have completed their mission, Mr. N rewards them in the usual fashion.

Several days later Mrs. N reports to the police that her husband is missing about $2,000. She also thinks she knows who stole the money.

In the meantime, the boys have bought a car from a friend—without benefit of a bill of sale or a transfer of ownership. They have rented a cottage at a nearby resort and have been winning many prizes, playing every game of chance on the boardwalk. When the police catch up with the culprits, they find the boys in possession of the car, a roomful of junk won at the amusement stands, and only a few small bills. Three of the boys, who are still in high school, have good academic records. One of them has been a star football player this season and has made the "all-state team." Their only known misconduct has been the truancy involved in this monetary run-away. Two of the older boys had left school more than a year ago. Since that time, they have been employed intermittently at odd jobs. Both say they were going to enlist in the Marines. This is the first time any of them have been in any "real trouble." The boys all admit taking the money but state defensively, "We didn't know it was so much until we counted it; then, we were afraid to return it."

Mrs. N states she doesn't want "to make trouble for the boys or their families." She is interested only in getting her money back. If restitution is made, she is willing to forgive and forget, but none of the boys' families is able to raise that kind of money. So three of the boys face juvenile court hearings while two of the older boys will be arraigned in the adult court.

Are all these boys delinquents? What problems does the matter of age present to legal authorities and to society in general? Should they be treated lightly because this is their first offense? Mrs. N is interested only in restitution. If she can get her money back, she is willing to forgive and forget. Can society and the legal authorities do likewise? If restitution is not forthcoming, will it help society or the boys if they are sent to an institution for their act of delinquency or crime?

3. Well-Organized Stealing

Two boys, using a burglary kit, loot cars in a dark parking lot close to a public dance hall. Two look-outs stand at the approaches to the parking lot, ready to whistle should anyone come toward the parking area. The boys in the lot work fast and methodically. They know their business and are well equipped. They jimmie a trunk, a window, or a door, take any clothing, packages, or objects that may be on the floor, on the sets, or in the glove compartment. Each operation is quick, skillful, and systematic. Occasionally when they find an unlocked car, they almost disdain to look inside, knowing they will find little or nothing. The payoff, they have learned, is in the locked cars.

This is not the first time they have cased a location, organized the team, and carried out a job according to plan. They have no trouble getting rid of the loot to several second-hand dealers who act as fences. There is danger and adventure in this business. However, on this occasion they are caught by the police at gunpoint. The two lookout accomplices escape, but they are picked up the next morning and are placed in a local jail with their gang to await their parole workers. All of them have already spent time in the state industrial school for boys.

Sitting in the "iron house," they complain loudly about their "bad luck" and accuse each other of "botching up" the job. Two drunks who are their cellmates jeer and laugh at them. This only makes the boys "sore" and they are ready to fight. Defensively, they swear the next time they pull a job they will not get caught. Their only immediate concern is that they have run out of cigarettes. After all, they have been through this before. It is only a matter of time before they will be back in the institution. In about six months they will have worked their way out.

Is there any question whether or not these boys are delinquents? It it true that only adjudicated cases represent real delinquency? How exasperating is it for the police to tread the mill of arresting and re-arresting the same gang? The police don't mind strong-arming these loud-mouthed and brash talkers. They feel the boys are laughing at them and are taking refuge in their juvenile status when they actually are hardened criminals. These boys are headed for a life of crime. Is there anything society can do for them?

ASSAULTIVE BEHAVIOR CASES

1. Raymond

Facts

In January of 1962, 16-year-old Raymond skipped school and remained at home. After his parents and younger brother had departed, he went next door and asked to borrow a tool to repair his bicycle. The woman and her 5-year-old son accompanied Raymond to the basement to obtain the tool. While in the basement, Raymond viciously attacked and killed the woman and her son, using a hammer and a screwdriver.

Following the perpetration of the crime Raymond returned to his home by crawling over a back yard fence. He later hid his bloody clothing in a school locker. When the crime was discovered, Raymond gave the pretense of assisting police by pointing to tracks in the snow which indicated the killer had left the scene by crossing his yard. Raymond was not a suspect during the initial phases of the investigation, but confessed several days later during a routine interview by police officers. Raymond told authorities that on the day of the murder, "I was thinking about relations with women. . . . I went next door and asked for a wrench as an excuse." He added, "We went downstairs. I didn't say anything or touch her. We came back up. I asked for a screwdriver and we went to the basement again. Suddenly I hit her with the hammer."

Disposition

On being brought to trial Raymond pleaded not guilty by reason of insanity. On March 16, 1962, two state-employed psychiatrists informed the court that he was legally sane when he committed the murders. Because of his plea, a separate trial was held to determine Raymond's sanity. During the trial, three prominent psychiatrists testified that he was sane at the time of the trial as well as at the time of the perpetration of the crime. Two other psychiatrists testified that in their opinion Raymond had been suffering from a severe brain disease for the past several years and was probably incurably insane and dangerous.

After deliberating for approximately nine hours, the jury arrived at a verdict of insanity. Following this, the judge committed Raymond to a state hospital until "restored to reason." Under the state statutes involved, he can never be tried for the murders, although he can be released from the hospital at any time on a recommendation from the hospital staff.

Background

Raymond lived in a large western city all of his life with his natural parents. They were both regularly employed at the time of the crime. Raymond was enrolled in a local high school and was considered an average student. His home life was considered desirable as he got along well with his parents and teachers. His father stated he had no suspicion his son might be involved until he was arrested by the police. He added that in addition to showing no emotion, his son "has been sleeping better since the crime." The father gave his personal opinion that Raymond has suffered a mental disorder for at least fourteen years. There was no indication that his parents had ever sought competent medical advice concerning this alleged mental disorder.

Prior Criminal Activities

Prior to the commission of the above offense, Raymond had no record with juvenile authorities and was never handled by any court or probation department. His only questionable activity consisted of a report by a neighborhood acquaintance that he exhibited an avid interest in sex magazines and photographs.

COMMENTS: During Raymond's trial his father made the statement that "no grief has ever been shown over the thing he did."

Was Raymond really insane? Could the crime have been averted if competent medical advice concerning Raymond's alleged mental disorder had been solicited? What about retribution on the part of society?

2. Roger and Clifton

Facts

Just past midnight on June 14, 1962, in a large northern city, Eugene was escorting two girls to their homes. On the way, they were accosted by three youths, two of whom were later identified as Roger and Clifton. Roger made a remark directed at the girls which prompted the girls' escort to tell him to mind his own business. An argument ensued and Eugene struck Roger. The blow was warded off and Roger struck back, knocking Eugene to the sidewalk. As Eugene attempted to get up, Clifton pulled out a .38 caliber revolver and fired once, fatally wounding him. The trio then fled the scene, but were apprehended the next day.

The weapon used to perpetrate the killing was obtained on the previous day when Roger and Clifton went to the home of another youth and threatened to beat him if he did not give them a gun owned by his grandfather. The intimidated youth emptied the gun of its ammunition and gave it to the two boys, who purchased some ammunition later that day.

Disposition

On November 26, 1962, Roger and Clifton, both aged 17, entered pleas of guilty to second degree murder. On December 13, 1962, they were sentenced to serve 20 to 40 years in the state prison. The third youth was not prosecuted.

Background

CLIFTON. Clifton was the youngest of six children and born in the same city where the killing occurred. His parents were divorced and the location of his father is not known. Clifton was of average mental intelligence and was well liked both at home and school. He was in the tenth grade at the time of the killing, a member of the YMCA, and attended church regularly.

ROGER. Roger was born in a southern state, but had moved to the northern city five years prior to the commission of the crime. Although he had been termed a mischievous youth, he did get along well both at home and at school, and attended church regularly. Roger's parents and his four brothers and sisters resided in a five-room flat. His stepfather apparently did not provide any supervision for the boy, leaving the task entirely to his mother. Neither parent was employed at the time of the killing and both were on welfare.

Prior Criminal Activities

CLIFTON. Despite his favorable personal relationships, Clifton's criminal exploits during the year preceding the murder were quite frequent. In May 1961, he was arrested on two separate occasions for unarmed robbery and for breaking and entering. In August of the same year, he was arrested and charged with larceny of a bicycle and in December he was charged with unlawfully driving a car and with riding in a stolen car. In all these instances, no action was taken against him and he was referred to the Probation Department.

In April 1962, Clifton held a razor blade against the stomach of a 14-year-old youth and demanded his money. He was arrested for robbery and again referred to the Probation Department.

ROGER. Roger first came to the attention of the police during the summer of 1961, when he was involved in an argument with a girl on a street corner. He was picked up by authorities, warned, and released. In September 1961, he was charged with attempted larceny from an automobile which he and another youth were found loitering alongside. This automobile was partially stripped and was reported stolen. Roger was reported missing by his mother in August 1961, and before returning home threatened a youth with death, in an attempt to make him change his story against Roger's brother who was being tried for another crime.

COMMENTS: Approximately an hour before the killing, Roger and Clifton purchased some wine and drank it in a garage near where the shooting took place.

Both minors had been involved in numerous prior offenses—offenses which appear to have been serious. But it seems that neither youngster was institutionalized for clinical study. What possible referrals could have been made on these cases other than to the juvenile probation department?

3. Richard

Facts

Late one afternoon in June 1962, a 10-year-old boy was reported missing by his parents. Thinking there might have been foul play involved, the police questioned the youth's parents concerning possible suspects, but were unable to obtain any leads. However, when the parents were asked about suspicious people, they talked about a "nice looking boy" who had been seen in the neighborhood since school had recessed for the summer. This "nice looking boy" turned out to be Richard, age 16. The boy's parents mentioned that since Richard had been seen in the neighborhood a dog had been poisoned and a pet chicken stolen. They also reported that their home had been entered and Richard had been seen going through the yard.

The following day the body of the missing youth was found in a shallow grave on the beach across the street from his home. An autopsy revealed he had been strangled, sexually molested, and shot in the back of the head. Richard was picked up for routine questioning, and admitted he had dragged the boy to his own garage, hit him several times, choked him, and shot him in the back of his head. He also related he had taken the body across the street and buried it in the sand.

Disposition

In November 1962, Richard was found guilty of first degree murder, but because he was under 18 years of age at the time of the offense, a sentence of death could not be imposed under the state law. The judge ruled that he was insane when he committed the crime and that he was still insane and ordered him to a state hospital for an indeterminate period of time.

Background

Richard's parents were high school graduates and the father had a good job. The family lived comfortably in a good residential neighborhood and owned two automobiles. Richard was the second of three children. His father reportedly did not take much interest in his children. He did, however, coach a Little League baseball team on which his son played.

Richard was described as a "rough show-off" in high school. Although there was no indication he had actually threatened anyone, his gym teacher would not permit him to use the archery equipment or the shot-put because he was afraid Richard might "injure his fellow students."

Prior Criminal Activities

Between April 1956 and August 1958, Richard was arrested for petty theft, shoplifting, suspected tampering with the mail, and disturbance of the peace. All of these arrests were handled informally. In 1959, he was arrested for attempted burglary and placed on probation for 18 months.

The following summer Richard tried to drown a young girl and was charged with attempted murder. He was not quite 15 at the time.

There was no apparent reason for the crime and he explained his action for the crime with the comment that he had an "urge to kill." Richard was sentenced to 6 years for this crime and also spent some time in a state hospital for mental examinations. He was paroled to his parents early in 1962, although his record showed he had made little progress and their was little indication that his parents were especially anxious to have him return home.

COMMENTS: When asked whether he killed the 10-year-old boy, Richard refused to answer verbally; instead he wrote an a piece of paper, "I don't know why I did it. I am crazy."

Has the clinic (state hospital) failed in its treatment of this youth? Is the hospital indirectly responsible for the murder? What could the school have done to prevent the crime? Could they have done anything at all?

4. Lynn, Donald, James

Facts

On the night of August 2, 1962, Lynn, Donald, and James went to the apartment of a 72-year-old woman to rob her. Lynn and Donald acted as lookouts while James crawled up the fire escape to the woman's third-floor apartment. Being almost close enough to touch her through the open window, James saw her watching television from her bed. She was clad in a housedress. James crawled to the roof where he found a two-by-four-inch board with jagged metal strips nailed to one end. He returned to the open window and found the woman now wearing her nightgown. As she turned the light out, James struck through the window with his weapon and knocked her to the floor. Entering the room he beat her repeatedly while she tried to ward off the blows. He used a pillow to stifle her screams and raped her. James fled without ransacking the apartment as previously planned. He avoided his companions, stopping only briefly to remove his undershirt and wipe the woman's blood from his hands and shoes. James threw the undershirt into a trash can and then returned home.

The police, responding to a neighbor's call for help, forced open the carefully locked door and found the woman lying in a pool of blood with deep gashes in her head. While searching the area for the assailant, the police spotted Lynn and Donald less than a block from the scene of the assault. These two youths led the police to James' apartment where they found him getting ready for bed. His arms and shoes were still bloody. At the police station, James admitted beating and raping the woman. All three were charged with burglary, rape, and felonious assault.

tenement flats. His school attendance was irregular and his grades poor. He showed complete lack of parental guidance, especially from his father.

Prior Criminal Activities

ELLIS. Ellis was arrested twice in 1960, once for petty larceny and the other time for burglarizing a supermarket. The next year he was charged with breaking into parking meters, ransacking a school, and destroying private property. In 1962, his criminal activities included purse snatching, receiving stolen property, arson and attempted robbery. Following his arrest, Ellis was implicated, either through identification or by his own admission, in a number of criminal assaults and attempted criminal assaults. A woman who was raped on November 28, 1962, identified Ellis as one of her assailants.

LEON. Leon's criminal record dated back to 1956 at which time he was reported to police as being an incorrigible. The complaint stemmed from the fact that he would be given money to buy groceries for the family and would spend it on himself and stay away for several days. During the next four years he was reported on a number of occasions as a runaway. In 1960, Leon tried to charge merchandise at a drugstore but the druggist called the police and held him until they arrived. Shortly after, he admitted involvement in a purse snatch. In October 1962, he was arrested for tampering with an auto and destruction of property.

COMMENTS: An attorney involved in the case said, "This is the most atrocious crime we have had in my time."

Obviously, both youths were menaces to the community. Looking into the backgrounds of both boys, there is a common history of little or no supervision on the part of their parents. Was this lack of supervision a major cause of such violent behavior?

6. Dennis and John

On the evening of December 19, 1962, Dennis and John, both aged 16, were loitering about the streets of a large midwestern city. The two youths decided to get some money, and stealing a woman's purse seemed to be the least hazardous way. They walked through an area where a building was being remodeled and John picked up a 33-inch length of galvanized pipe which they vowed to use as a weapon only if their robbery attempt met with resistance. While in search of a victim the two youths saw an elderly woman alighting from a bus and they followed her to the front of the hospital where she was employed.

Coming up behind the woman, John grabbed her and hit her on the head with the pipe, killing her. He grabbed her purse and ran to the other side of the street where he met Dennis. Several blocks away they emptied the contents of the purse into their pockets. The two youths then walked back to where they had committed the crime and saw that their victim was still lying on the ground. Becoming frightened, John told Dennis to go for help inside the hospital and told a boy passing on a bicycle to go for the police. Since the boys were well known to a police officer answering the call, they were searched and the change purse containing $4.73 was found. Both boys readily admitted their involvement in the crime.

Disposition

John entered a plea of guilty to first degree murder and was sentenced to life imprisonment on March 1, 1963. Dennis was also convicted of first degree murder on March 17, 1963, and was sentenced to life imprisonment. He was also sentenced to two 5-year terms on two robbery charges to run concurrently with his life sentence.

Background

JOHN. John's father, a former dogcatcher, was unemployed at the time of the incident because of paralyzed nerves in both legs. He and his wife supported seven of their nine children on a municipal aid to dependent children fund and relief checks totaling $234 a month. John's oldest brother, 24, spent two years in a federal reformatory for larceny, and a sister, 13, spent time in a children's home for truancy. John, himself, was expelled from the eighth grade about a year before the perpetration of the crime. The family of nine lived in a dilapidated brick house.

DENNIS. Dennis lived with his parents, a sister, 15, and two brothers, 14 and 1, and an adopted sister, age 2. His father is an ex-convict who was released from a workhouse in 1962. Dennis's 19-year-old uncle, who lived with the family, was sentenced to five years in prison in December 1962 after being convicted of purse snatching. Another uncle, aged 24, was sentenced to prison in September 1962 for a savings and loan holdup. Dennis had started his first year in high school, but soon dropped out.

Prior Criminal Record

JOHN. John's criminal record began in 1958, when he was arrested for the destruction of church property with an air gun. He and his companions were turned over to their parents. The same year he was also arrested for arson, trespassing and damage to government property, and two counts of petty larceny involving two bicycles. In all three instances he was released to his parents. In March of 1960, John was arrested on suspicion of burglary of a local restaurant. He was again turned over to his parents and referred to juvenile court for final disposition. Shortly after, he was charged with three counts of burglary and four counts of stealing under $50. Again he was turned over to his parents and referred to juvenile court for final disposition. He was arrested ten more times that year for destruction of property, burglary, larceny, and disturbing the peace. In one instance, he took a rifle from a home which he had been watching and another time he suffered alcoholic gastritis after consuming a large amount of liquor and wine which he burglarized from a tavern. In each case he was released to his parents and referred to juvenile court for final disposition.

John's numerous referrals to juvenile court proved to be ineffective as his criminal activities continued unabated. John was finally incarcerated in a boys' home and was not released until January 1962, and was still under the home's supervision after his release. That year he continued his old ways. In March 1962, he was arrested for stealing a fur-lined jacket from an automobile. In September, he and another youth took $113.72 from an open safe in a food shop. The slaying of the elderly woman ended his brief but active career.

DENNIS. Dennis was arrested in March 1962, along with several other youths, for possession of a stolen automobile and was charged with automobile theft. In April of 1962, Dennis was arrested for burglary and theft. He was turned over to his parents for disposition of the juvenile court. In May he was arrested for auto theft, burglary, and larceny. Other offenses committed in 1962 included purse snatching, vandalism, and the turning in of a false fire alarm.

COMMENTS: Dennis and John went on their purse snatching spree in order to obtain $40 to buy an old automobile. Prior to the above incident the youths robbed two other elderly woman and obtained $9.75 which they invested in a pinball machine.

The records of both minors reveal a long history of delinquent activities. What is law enforcement's responsibility to the community when dealing with youngsters with such records? Are juvenile court procedures responsible for letting such records grow?

7. Thomas

In December 1961, Thomas walked to a shopping center in a northern state with the intention of assaulting a woman. Seeing a girl seated in a parked car, Thomas entered the car, threatened her with a knife, and told her to drive to a nearby pond. As she neared the pond, the car got stuck in the sand. Thomas then told her to get out of the car and walk down a dirt road toward the pond. After reaching the water's edge, which was frozen, the girl turned and attempted to retrace her steps. At this point Thomas struck her on the head with a piece of wood and then cut her throat. He removed her clothing because he wanted "to see what she looked like." Following this, Thomas dragged her out on to the ice, broke a hole in it, and pushed the body through.

Thomas returned to the pond a week later and removed the body from under the ice and stabbed it several times. He then pushed the body under the ice again. In March 1962, the body was found floating in the pond.

In January 1963, two years later, while driving around in the family car, Thomas saw a woman driving to her home and followed her. She was alone and he entered the house and confronted her, claiming he just wanted her money. The woman began to struggle with Thomas and he received a cut on his finger. Thomas stabbed her in the chest and forced her into the bedroom and made her partially disrobe. He was about to rape her when she fled from the room. He chased her and stabbed her several more times, killing her. Before returning home, Thomas disposed of his clothes in a wooded area.

After the body was discovered and during the ensuing investigation, information was developed that a youth was seen leaving the woman's residence and entering a 1958 blue Chevrolet. A policeman recalled that Thomas' family owned such a car. Thomas was subsequently apprehended and confessed to these two brutal murders.

Disposition

The court, after hearing the testimony of two doctors, committed Thomas to a mental institution for an indefinite period.

Background

Thomas came from a good home with respectable parents and attended church regularly. He was the youngest of three children and had a good school record, including participation in athletics. He was, however, described as a "loner" and had no noticeable friends.

Thomas was subject to strange moods, especially after looking at certain popular magazines which frequently contain pictures of nude or nearly nude women. Thomas admitted that he had feelings come over him and could tell two or three hours in advance that he was going to do something.

Prior Criminal Activities

In 1959, Thomas had been charged with two counts of breaking and entering. Two years later three similar charges were made against him, and he was placed on probation for six months. Early in 1962, he was charged with assault with a dangerous weapon after he attacked a girl with a knife. He was admitted to a hospital for mental examination, but was released a short time later. An examining doctor classed him as a probably aggressive schizophrenic who should be put on probation under psychiatric care for five years or committed to a mental hospital for at least three months if there were other unlawful acts.

COMMENTS: During the court hearing Thomas said, "I'm glad you got me before I do it again."

There is always a possibility that Thomas may be released from the mental institution as "cured." What procedure should be taken by law enforcement to ensure the protection of the community (i.e., fingerprints, registration, etc.)?

The lack of personal background data concerning the ten cases of youthful offenders makes the task of arriving at any valid conclusions of contributory or causative factors almost impossible. Attempts to explain delinquent behavior, whether the act be of serious (aggravated assault) or minor (petty theft) nature, cannot be done simply or briefly. These cases have been brought to the reader's attention in order to raise certain valid issues which will be discussed in the remaining chapters of this book.

Chapter 4

Scope of Problem . . . National and International Trends

THE BROAD INTERPRETATION of criminal and delinquent behavior holds that such actions are not in and of themselves the "problem," and that crime is a product of various social and psychological problems. Just as certain maladjusted persons turn to alcohol, suicide, or narcotics, others manifest the symptoms of their disorganization through behavior which brings loss or injury to others.[1] Research projects by psychiatrists, sociologists, and psychologists, reveal that some individuals in all societies and in all classes of society respond to economic, social, and psychological pressures by perpetrating crimes.

Economic necessity or problems fostered by racial, religious, or national prejudice may lie at the base of such criminal and delinquent behavior. The failure of parents to teach their offspring society's code of conduct may also serve to develop youngsters who have no real knowledge of, or appreciation for, those social standards.[2]

Therefore, many law-enforcement agencies are designed to deal with the crime problem by giving due considerations to underlying causes. However, although the police *cannot* ignore the causes of crime, in terms of *performing* their appointed task of law enforcement, police officers must dismiss many causative factors.

For the police, the "problem" of juvenile delinquency and youth crime is one of either minimizing those known delinquent-breeding conditions and opportunities, or identifying and apprehending those who violate the law.

Delinquency—as we have come to label the criminal conduct of persons of a fixed statutory age—consists of those forms of behavior which we would call crime if engaged in by adults, and those non-criminal but symptomatic behavioral patterns which many persons believe tend

[1]G. W. O'Connor and N. A. Watson, *Juvenile Delinquency and Youth Crime: The Police Role*, International Association of Chiefs of Police, Washington, D.C., 1964, p. 14.

[2]*Ibid.*, p. 14.

to direct the child into anti-social channels. Smoking, truancy, incorrigibility, curfew violations, and the like, although not strictly criminal acts, are part of a special class of legislative definitions of behavior which are considered unhealthy for the development of the child.[3]

Simple answers are not available to such complex problems, but it is certain that few answers will come from the development of and adherence to a single theory of causation or treatment. If we were to subscribe to a particular belief, common factors might be identified, but still each individual delinquent or criminal would stand apart as a testament to the diversity of human behavior.

MEASURING DELINQUENCY

The quantitative analysis of juvenile and adult criminal behavior necessarily is based upon those measuring devices which are currently available. Statistical studies of social problems often suffer from our inability to account properly for the many diverse factors which may affect the validity and the comparability of various sets of data. It may be assumed that crime-reporting procedures within a group of police departments remained static during the study period, but the facts may well be contrary to that assumption and the resulting conclusions are invalid. Therefore, any attempt to analyze crime statistics, and to derive valid and meaningful conclusions must be carried out with utmost care. Failure to do this will result in the development of programs based upon fiction rather than fact.[4]

The Scope of the Problem

In evaluating the size of the delinquency problem, statistics utilized must, of necessity, be limited to reports on children coming to the attention of law-enforcement agencies and courts. As we already know, such statistics denote only a portion of all children whose anti-social behavior could, if detected, be dealt with by law. Optimistically speaking, they reflect trends in the numbers and characteristics of the entire groups. The police arrest data collected by the *Federal Bureau of Investigation* and the juvenile court delinquency data collected by the *Children's Bureau* are the two sources of national statistical information most frequently cited. It is felt that these agencies provide statistics which, although not perfect measures of delinquency, are considered valid. The U.S. Children's Bureau and the Uniform Crime Reports shed light not only on the volume and trend of delinquency, but also

[3] *Ibid.*, p. 15.
[4] *Ibid.*, p. 21.

on the types of offenses committed and the characteristics of the juvenile offenders by sex, age, and place of abode.

Although the Uniform Crime Reports and the juvenile court's statistics as presented by the Children's Bureau are, as previously stated, not the exact measures of delinquent activity, they do include children whose acts were considered serious enough to bring the minor to the attention of the arresting agency and a referral to juvenile court. Law-enforcement arrests of juvenile and court delinquency data, while different in definitions, extent of coverage, geographic representation, and other factors, nevertheless show a remarkable similarity in trends.

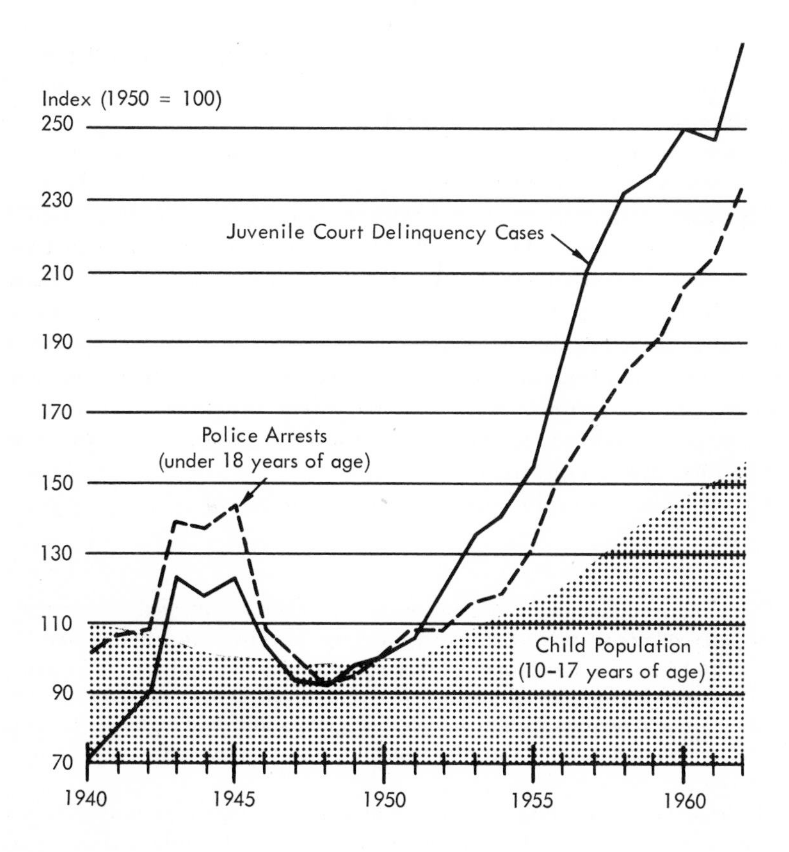

Figure 1 The indicators of delinquency (police arrests and court cases) have increased much faster than the population. (*Sources*: Children's Bureau, Federal Bureau of Investigation, and Bureau of the Census.)

Following a sharp increase due to World War II, both arrests and court cases dropped abruptly until 1948; from then on until 1960 there was a steady increase in both series of data.

Police arrests continued to climb in 1961, but delinquency cases heard by juvenile courts decreased slightly in that year for the first time since 1948. In 1964, however, both police arrests and juvenile court cases again increased over the previous year—13 and 14 per cent, respectively.[5]

Note that there is a striking similarity between the trends in these two series of data (Children's Bureau and Uniform Crime Reports), suggesting that they may each be influenced by some common determining factor that perhaps is "delinquency."

The acceleration of delinquency and crime is just about as urgent as a problem can get. Mountains of statistics coming from police files, court records, and correctional institutions from coast to coast tell a shocking story. Each statistic represents a human tragedy.

As previously indicated, in the opinion of many experts, the only reliable statistical information regarding arrests is collected by the Federal Bureau of Investigation and represents police arrests of juveniles throughout the nation. This statistical division was established in 1930 and by 1964 more than 4,000 city and county law-enforcement agencies serving over 124.2 million persons—66.2 per cent of the U.S. population—were reporting arrest data to it. These reports reveal that over 2.0 million youngsters under 18 years of age were arrested in 1964, excluding traffic violations, except driving while intoxicated. In all, approximately 442,000 youngsters came to the attention of various juvenile traffic courts throughout the nation.

Other statistics compiled by the *Federal Bureau of Investigation* for 1964 are:

1. The most frequent offense of juveniles was larceny, followed by burglary. Property offenses, such as robbery, burglary, larceny, auto theft, embezzlement and fraud, stolen property (buying, receiving, possessing), and forgery and counterfeiting, constituted 41 per cent of all arrests of juveniles. Offenses against persons such as murder (neglect and manslaughter), forcible rape, aggravated assault, and other assaults (non-aggravated) totaled only 9 per cent.
2. Alcoholic beverage control violations and drunkenness represented 11 per cent of the arrests of persons under 18 years of age. Disorderly conduct accounted for 11 per cent and sex offenses accounted for less than 3 per cent

[5] R. I. Perlman, "Antisocial Behavior of the Minor in the United States," *Federal Probation*, Vol. XXVIII, No. 4, December, 1964, p. 27.

of the arrests and narcotic drug violations were less than one-half of one per cent.

3. The Federal Bureau of Investigation Uniform Crime Reports for 1964 also show that delinquency among children is skyrocketing at more than four times the rate of national population growth.

The Uniform Crime Reports were designed primarily for adult offenses and do not specifically identify such juvenile offenses as runaway, truancy, and violation of curfew. It is noteworthy that 27 per cent of juvenile arrests are lumped in the "all other offense" category where many offenses such as juvenile misbehavior rather than crime are grouped. Nearly half of the arrests of girls are placed in the "all other offenses" category, compared to less than one-third of the arrests of boys. Younger children are also usually classified in this category.

Other areas of interest as compiled by the Federal Bureau of Investigation Uniform Crime Reports of 1964 are as follows:

1. Over one-fourth of the girls but more than two-fifths of the boys were arrested for property offenses. As already noted, the most frequent single offense for both boys and girls was larceny. However, girls were infrequently arrested for burglary and automobile theft as compared to boys.
2. Regarding murder and manslaughter by negligence, such incidents were rare for both boys and girls—less frequent for girls.
3. Promiscuity among girls was quite prevalent in that girls accounted for over 4 per cent of sexual offenses other than forcible rape as compared to 1.5 of the boys arrested.
4. Over 50 per cent of the girls and over 19 per cent of the boys arrested were in the area of liquor law violations, drunkenness, and driving while intoxicated, disorderly conduct, vagrancy, and gambling.

Offenses against persons (murder, manslaughter by negligence, forcible rape, and assaults), although comprising a small proportion of total offenses, increased in frequency with age, in both urban and rural areas. Certain property offenses (robbery, fraud, and forgery or counterfeiting) increased slightly but progressively with age, whereas arrests for burglary sharply decreased with age, and more often for boys than for girls. Larceny arrests also decreased progressively with age, particularly in the cities. Arrests for auto theft peaked at 15 years of age.[6]

An interesting point to be aware of is the fact that burglary and property offenses in general, as well as liquor violations, represented greater proportions of arrests in rural areas than in the cities.[7] Significant also, after closer scrutiny of these reports, is the fact that city youngsters were

[6] *Ibid.*, p. 24.
[7] *Ibid.*, p. 24.

more often arrested for disruptive behavior—such as disturbing the peace and offenses against persons—than were their rural peers.

As stated earlier, whereas the Federal Bureau of Investigation Uniform Crime Reports compile statistics only on youngsters who are taken into custody, the *Children's Bureau* is the source of *juvenile court* statistics. The Children's Bureau initiated a plan for uniform reporting of a few essential statistics by juvenile courts in 1926, and since then the content and reporting procedures have been modified several times. Presently, the Children's Bureau is compiling data from a national representative sample of 502 juvenile courts to provide a basis for national estimates that have a known degree of reliability. The procedure is quite simple—delinquency data collected are limited to a simple count of cases by sex of the child. Although traffic cases are also reported, they are kept separate from other delinquency cases.

Since the Uniform Crime Reports do not take into consideration the unofficial cases—cases handled by the police without referral to the courts—statistical information from the Children's Bureau approximates more closely the definition of those who consider a child delinquent only when the courts have so adjudicated. These exclusions from the Uniform Crime Reports comprise almost one-half of the police arrests and are primarily for minor offenses. In other words, about half of the cases handled by police departments are adjusted unofficially and the youngsters are not referred to juvenile courts.

The Children's Bureau of the Department of Health, Education, and Welfare also reports that in 1964:

1. 686,000 juvenile delinquency cases (excluding traffic cases) were processed by juvenile courts in the United States. These children represent 2.0 per cent of all children age 10 through 17 in the country.
2. Juvenile court delinquency cases continued to be primarily a problem of boys who were referred to court more than four times as often as girls.
3. Based on reports serving very large cities, boys were referred to court for considerably different reasons than girls. More than half of the offenses committed by girls were for violation of laws applicable to juveniles only—runaway, truancy, curfew violations, ungovernable behavior, etc. Only one-fifth of the boys sent to court were involved in offenses of this nature, whereas over half of the boys were referred for offenses against property—larceny, auto theft, vandalism, robbery, and burglary; only about a sixth of girls were involved in such cases. These data are similar to those compiled by the Federal Bureau of Investigation Uniform Crime Reports.
4. There was a high proportion of dismissals in cases appearing before the juvenile court; of the 686,000 cases appearing before the courts, roughly two-fifths of the cases originating in large cities were dismissed with warning or adjustment.

5. Fifty per cent of the delinquency cases petitioned resulted in the child being placed on probation; in almost one-fifth of the cases the child was committed to an institution or an agency. Where petitions were not filed, more than one-half of the youngsters were returned to "status quo" without services provided by the court. Such cases, handled unofficially by the court—without filing any petition—comprised almost half of the court delinquency cases of 1964.

Trends in Juvenile Delinquency Arrests in California, 1960-1964

As has been pointed out, the relationship of juvenile delinquency to crime in general offers a great deal of difficulty to all who are concerned with developing accurate measurements of law-breaking. Offenses are committed by both adults and juveniles and there is little information available describing the proportion of different types of offenses committed by juveniles alone. One simple study made in a California county for a full year indicated about 30 per cent of the seven major offenses of felony crimes were cleared by the arrests of juveniles. The data indicated that about 60 per cent of the auto theft and 30 per cent of the burglaries that were cleared involved juveniles.

The law-enforcement agencies of California have, on the whole, developed reliable and comprehensive record systems for reporting arrests. This reporting has been extended to cover juvenile arrests almost as completely as adult arrests. From a law-enforcement standpoint, juveniles are considered in California to be persons under 18 years of age. Arrested persons between the years of 18 and 21 can be processed as juveniles, but usually they are handled as adults. In the development of arrests-reporting, a separate accounting has been made for arrested juveniles under the age of 18.

Juvenile arrests are recorded for the same Penal Code violations as are adult arrests. In addition, under the Welfare and Institutions Code, youths can be charged with delinquency for reasons other than Penal Code violations. This includes such behavior indicated in the Welfare and Institutions Code as incorrigibility, runaways, waywardness, improper associations, truancy, and many other activities of this nature. In the statistical summary of juveniles arrested, these charges have been grouped under a heading of delinquent tendencies as or posed to charges which are Penal Code violations. The delinquent tendency grouped under a heading of delinquent tendencies as opposed to disturbing the peace, and liquor violations which would appear to be violations of Penal Code sections. However, the use of these reasons for arrest with respect to juveniles is so broad that it seems more appropriate to include them under the delinquency tendency group.

In the report on juvenile arrests in the classification called "law violations," the distinction has been made between major and minor violations. The former includes homicide, robbery, aggravated assault, burglary, grand theft, auto theft, forcible rape, and narcotics laws—all categories which would be considered as felony arrests if applied to adults. Seven other groups have been included in the minor law series: other assaults, petty theft, other sex, weapons laws, drunk driving, hit-and-run auto, and arson. Obviously, some of these offenses when committed by adults would be classified as felonies. Because of the much more flexible attitude of the law toward juveniles, it is generally accepted by officers who work in the juvenile field in law enforcement and probation that these seven categories are comparable to the misdemeanor level of offenses chargable against adults. (See Table 2 in Appendix A.)

From 1960 to 1964 juvenile delinquency arrests based on population in the 10 to 17 age group in California have increased 17.3 per cent. (See Table 2 in Appendix A.) Except for a slight decrease in 1961, increased rates have been noted for each year. Most of these increases have been in the delinquency tendency area where a 19.1 per cent rise was recorded. This rise corresponds quite closely to the 18.8 per cent increase shown for minor law violations during the same period. The more serious felony types of offenses included in the major law violations group showed a rate rise of only 9.4 per cent in the last four years, about half the increase noted for minor offenses.

The total number of juvenile arrests reported for 1963-1964 and the rate per 100,000 population, age 10-17, revealed that the only decrease among the major offense groups was in aggravated assaults: 3.6 per cent less in 1964 than 1963. Auto theft arrests which totaled over 15,000 for 1964 showed a rate increase of 12.3 per cent. Burglary, as usual, was a major offense having the greatest number of arrests, 22,772, which is over 2,000 more than the previous year, resulting in a 4.6 per cent raise. Narcotics arrests by far showed the greatest increase of any offense group: a rate increase of 41.3 per cent.

Of the 269,584 juveniles arrested in 1964, 217,611 or 80.7 per cent were boys and 51,973 or 19.3 per cent were girls. The ratio of boys arrested to girls arrested based on rates per 100,000 population age 10 to 17 years is as follows:

The number of boys arrested in California in 1964 was 6.3 per cent higher than in 1963. (See Table 3 in Appendix A.) The 1964 total of girls arrested was 10 per cent above 1963. The percentage change in rate, based on the state population for the 10 to 17 year-old group for each sex, was 3.9 per cent for boys and 7.5 per cent for girls.

NATIONALLY—HOW BAD IS JUVENILE DELINQUENCY?

When we look back far enough it appears that there have been tremendous increases in delinquency. For example, let us examine the statistics compiled by Dr. Negley Teeters and his associate, David Matza, as far back as 1918. These antiquated statistics were presented by *Roul Tunley* in his book, *Kids, Crime and Chaos,* while describing conditions as they were almost 50 years ago in only one specific locality—Cuyahoga County, Ohio—but they are interesting because they include a large metropolitan area, the city of Cleveland.

In 1919, after World War I ended, the figures showed a delinquency rate of 65.9 per 1,000 children. By 1920, the figure had dropped to 52, and by 1939, when the country was beginning to climb out of the Depression, the figure was down to 21.0. In 1957, however, the delinquency rate had swelled to 33.5, an increase of 70 per cent over the 1939 figure, a period when our current statistics also began to soar. Unfortunately, such figures do not exist for the country as a whole, and as Roul Tunley stated, "If such figures did exist we might easily find that all our comparisons are made with periods of low delinquency."

A few other factors also have helped to push up our present statistical peak. There are infinitely more automobiles around today than a generation ago—more autos to steal and to use both before and after violating the laws. With more money available, guns are more freely bought and used. Furthermore, there is a tendency in certain quarters to include more and more youths in the same charge. A newspaper story will state, "Twenty youths charged with carrying firearms" when only one of them actually possessed a gun. "Fifty-seven youths charged with homicide," was a headline recently, but it involved only one murder.[8]

But the question of whether juvenile delinquency is more violent or widespread today than ever before should not obscure the fact that a serious problem does exist and that it can be controlled to a far greater extent than is being done at the present time. When all the figures and charts are weighted, discounted, corrected, adjusted, and dissected, the fact remains that an extraordinary large number of adolescent males are arrested, come before courts, and are labeled "juvenile delinquents."[9] Although less than 3 per cent of our juvenile population (including traffic violators) become annual statistics, the number takes on more

[8]R. Tunley, *Kids, Crime and Chaos*, Harper and Row, New York, 1964, p. 51.
[9]*Ibid.*, p. 53.

importance when we consider the percentage of youngsters who become court cases at least once during their period of adolescence (estimated as eight years). Looked at from this direction, it appears that *12 per cent of our children are liable to become delinquents during their teens.*[10] According to statistics compiled by the U.S. Children's Bureau, the greatest increase in our population during the 1960's will be in the age group most vulnerable to delinquency and youth crime. This is shown in the Bureau's projected population increases for the various age groups during 1960–70. (See Table 4 in the Appendix A.)

This is quite startling in that the problem will definitely become more serious if the present trend continues. The best statistical indicators of anti-social behavior of minors in the United States—police arrests and juvenile court cases—show a general upward trend, beginning in 1949. Even after a decade or more of these annual increases, however, only 4 per cent (1.1 million) of the juveniles aged 10 through 17 were arrested by the police, only 1.8 per cent (478,000) were referred to juvenile courts for delinquent behavior, and only 0.2 per cent (65,000) were committed to institutions for delinquent children.[11]

The trend toward greater delinquent activities could conceivably means that under our present jurisdictional set-up, the male juvenile—if the female delinquent is excluded from our statistics—has one chance in five of appearing in court as a juvenile offender.

RELATION OF THE TRENDS TO DELINQUENCY[12]

The impact of these social and economic trends—population growth, increasing urbanization, youth unemployment, and school dropouts—on our society as a whole is already being felt. Their direct influence on the delinquency problem in the future remains in the area of speculation, although there are some ominous signs.

Delinquency in the past decade increased faster than did the child population. Will we see a repeat performance in the coming decade? Not necessarily, but a sense of urgency is created by the predicted growth of the youth population in the 1960's with its concomitant problems. During that period, it is estimated that 7½ million young people will enter the job market without finishing high school and 2 million of them will not even have finished grammar school.

[10] *Ibid.*, p. 53.

[11] Perlman, *op. cit.*, p. 29.

[12] I. R. Perlman, *Juvenile Delinquency and Some Social and Economic Trends*, Children's Bureau, Department of Health, Education, and Welfare, Washington, D.C., 1963, pp. 19–20.

This will occur at a time when automation will be creating some drastic changes in our total economy. Although in the long run the demand may not be far fewer workers, there probably will be less room for unskilled workers; more and more jobs will require special knowledge and skills. This situation will affect the whole labor market, but its effect on young people, whose unemployment rate is already about twice that of adults, will be especially harsh. Those who drop out of school before completing high school are even worse off. Studies indicate that they are the last to be employed and the first to be fired; they change jobs more frequently, earn less, and are out of work for longer periods of time than those who complete high school. What will be the prospects of the poorly educated and poorly trained when competition for jobs increases? How will they react?

Youths in minority groups face even greater employment problems than other young workers. In 1964, about one out of every four of these teenagers in the labor force was unemployed, compared with about one out of every eight other teenagers. Since 1955, the jobless rate among minority teenagers (both boys and girls) has risen faster than among majority teenagers—up about 60 per cent among minority groups compared with 30 per cent among others. Non-white girls have a much higher unemployment rate than any other group in the entire labor force. Non-white youths, both graduates of high school and dropouts, are primarily employed in low-paying service occupations and in farm labor jobs. Even when minority youths have high school diplomas, their unemployment rate is about double that for white graduates.

Another ominous sign is that the country is becoming more and more urbanized. There are many positive aspects of urban living—more abundant educational opportunities, more health and welfare services, more cultural activities, more diverse job opportunities. But for some people, especially minority groups, urbanization brings with it a host of problems. They are compelled by poverty and discrimination to live in slum areas. Many young people drop out of school from sheer economic necessity. Others drop out because of lack of adult example and precept in taking advantage of educational opportunities. Faced with frustrations, lack of training, and lack of legitimate opportunities for success, many youths acquire the sense of hopelessness that infects a large part of their adult community. Too often they try to find their answers through unlawful means.

Delinquency rates are about three times higher in urban than in rural areas. Will increasing urbanization compound the unfavorable conditions that already exist in many urban areas and spawn further delinquency?

Certainly not all children who drop out of school, or who are unemployed, or who live in slum areas, become delinquent. Nor do those who have studied the situation carefully claim that providing full employment for youth in the large cities would automatically banish juvenile delinquency. Statistics on the interrelationship among these factors are not abundant and when available are often contradictory. A recent intensive study by B. M. Fleisher, "The Effect of Unemployment on Juvenile Delinquency," indicated that the effect of unemployment on juvenile delinquency is positive and significant. Another study, "Juvenile Delinquency Control Act," showed that delinquency increased as employment increased. These contradictions probably result in part from the fact each of the general terms used—delinquency, employment, school dropout—has diverse meanings. Delinquency, for example, includes a wide range of behavior. Employment could be scaled from poor-paying, unsatisfactory jobs to high-paying, high-status, interesting, and highly satisfying jobs. Nor do school dropouts form a neat homogeneous group. The complexity of these concepts emphasizes the need for research that will break down the categories into more concrete subgroupings to clarify and refine interrelationships.

Nevertheless, we know that slum areas produce disproportionately high rates of delinquency and that the problems of school dropouts and youth unemployment are particularly acute in such areas. In a study by J. B. Conant, *Slums and Suburbs,* of a slum area of 125,000 people, mostly Negro, a sampling of the youth population showed that roughly 70 per cent of the boys and girls aged 16 to 21 were out of school and unemployed. We know, too, that a high proportion of delinquents have had a history of school retardation and truancy—characteristics which describe many school dropouts. So even in the absence of conclusive research on the relation of school dropouts and unemployment to delinquency, some danger signals are evident. It almost seems axiomatic that a youth out of school and out of work is a likely candidate for getting into trouble.

The future direction of these social and economic trends—population growth, increasing urbanization, youth unemployment, and school dropouts—is predictable, although their precise effect on the delinquency problem remains in the area of speculation. The federal government, as well as many state and local governments, agencies, and organizations have undertaken action programs to forestall some of the more likely consequences. These action programs include "back-to-school" drives, urban renewal programs, slum clearance, youth employment-training programs, and research and demonstration projects in the prevention and control of delinquency. The ultimate purpose of these programs is to provide for every child, whether potentially delinquent or not, every opportunity to utilize his full capacities.

While many theories have been advanced to explain juvenile delinquency in general, the baffling question is why delinquency continues to rise in so prosperous a country as the United States. According to Perlman, among the factors cited as possible explanations are:[13]

"1. Post-war prosperity with success being increasingly emphasized in material terms. This emphasis coupled with the lack of opportunities for achieving success by legitimate means, brings increasing pressure toward deviant behavior.

"2. Poor housing conditions, primarily in central cities, where recent waves of in-migration have caused over-crowding.

"3. Increasing breakdown of traditional controls and families and neighborhoods and transfer of the control to the formal law-enforcement agencies.

"4. Growing numbers of employed mothers.

"5. Expanding influence of mass media with strong emphasis on violence, toughness, glitter, and false values.

"6. Impending threats of war and annihilation, producing attitudes of irresponsibility and normlessness.

"None of these factors alone is sufficient to explain the increased delinquency, nor has the degree of casual influence always been proved. The theories are often based on logic rather than facts. It is, however, universally recognized that juvenile delinquency is an enormously complicated, many-faceted problem and that many factors interact to produce it.

"More and more, though, it is realized that the rising tide of delinquency cannot be understood in isolation from other youth problems. Whether these problems, like the ones mentioned above, are casual or merely concomitant, there is too frequently an unhappy connection between high rates of delinquency and conditions of social and economic deprivation. Most disturbing to us in the United States are the forecasts of social and economic trends which will make it increasingly difficult for young people, especially those living in slum areas, to achieve their goals of success. Some of the trends—population growth, increasing urbanization, youth unemployment, and school dropouts—exert their heaviest pressures against youths at the bottom of the social and economic ladder who, when caught in a web of problems, will be the most likely candidates for the police blotter. Each of the trends constitutes a problem of major dimensions and statistics regarding them are important to the future outlook regarding anti-social behavior of minors."

Occasionally an "expert" puts all the blame for social evils on the American culture, explaining delinquency as solely an American problem—as part of the decadence of a capitalistic economy, or as symbolic of a developing but still immature culture, or as the product of a

[13]Perlman, *op. cit.*, pp. 27–28.

sophisticated, overdeveloped affluent society. This particular claim "that delinquency is uniquely an American problem" is without foundation. There are many countries which also have serious problems with juveniles.

Comparative statistics compiled by UNESCO indicate the extent of juvenile crime around the world. Cities such as Tokyo, Melbourne, Amsterdam, Stockholm, Johannesburg, and Tel Aviv are confronted with juvenile gangs who cause just as much concern as they do in America. Delinquent activities in Moscow are increasing at an alarming rate, even within the youth ranks of the Communist party. The problems have, on occasion, come to the attention of the "outside" world via the newspaper media and visitors who have spent some time in the city of Moscow. Harrison Salisbury, *The New York Times* correspondent, formerly in Moscow, has written that "few countries have had so much delinquency as the Soviet Union in its 40-year existence."

Almost every language in the world now yields a phrase labeling those youngsters of many nations whose behavior or tastes are different enough to excite suspicion if not alarm. They are the *teddy boys* (more recently referred to as *mods*) in England, the *nozem* in Netherlands, the *raggare* in Sweden, the *blousons noirs* in France, the *tsotsis* in South Africa, the *bodgies* in Australia, the *halbstarken* in Austria and Germany, the *taipve* in Taiwan, the *mambo boys* or *taiyozuku* in Japan, the *tapkaroschi* in Yugoslavia, the *vitellomi* in Italy, the *hooligans* in Poland, and the *stiliagyi* in U.S.S.R.[14]

Russia does not offer statistics regarding their problems with youngsters who have "adopted that capitalistic way of life" and the problem that goes along with it—anti-social behavior. As previously stated, Moscow's delinquents are called *stiliagyi* and incidents are mentioned publicly only when the government attempts to make a point. Their attack may be against rock 'n' roll music, buying foreign currency, espionage, wearing western-styled clothes, use of intoxicating beverages (such a use by youths in Russia is extensive), etc. In making these points, however, the Soviets reveal the extent of the juvenile misbehavior, whether it be robbing telephone boxes, selling heroin, muggings, gang fights, beating up police officers, drunkeness, or just plain unwillingness to work.

Consider a world report on juvenile delinquency by *Roul Tunley*, a free-lance writer, who relates the following:[15]

[14]W. C. Kvaraceus, "Juvenile Delinquency: A Problem for the Modern World," *Federal Probation*, Vol. XXXIII, No. 3, September 1964, p. 12.

[15]R. Tunley, *Kids, Crime and Chaos*, Harper and Row, New York, N.Y., 1964, pp. 38–41.

"Checking into official figures, I was surprised to find that Sweden probably has the highest juvenile delinquency rate in the world, higher than ours. According to Karl Erik Granath, Director of the Child-Welfare Counsel in Stockholm, three percent of Sweden's teenage youth go through their courts. This compares with 1.8 per cent in this country (or 2.3 percent if traffic violations are included). Furthermore, Sweden with the second highest number of autos per capita of any country in the world (we are first), can boast of the highest per centage of car thefts by juveniles, thus putting our young auto-snatching hoodlums still further in the shade.

"Turning from Sweden to Japan, the traveller finds conditions almost as astonishing. In this oriental country, before World War II, children were said to be among the most obedient and law-abiding of any nation on earth. Obviously, things have changed.

"Even before looking into the statistics, the unwary visitor, fed on a poster diet of dainty Japanese girls in flowering kimonas moving along obediently behind their men, is apt to get a shock as he walks down the Ginza. *Here, teenagers*, in skin-tight bluejeans and dyed red hair, cigarettes dangling from their lips, can be seen walking along with their arms around their boyfriends. This unsettling picture, it turns out, is a suitable prelude to a look at the official figures. Although Japan's rate of delinquents brought before her courts is still lower than ours (1.2 percent), the rate of crime has far outstripped ours.

"What's more, the ratio of crime committed by Japanese youngsters when compared with adults is out of all proportion to ours, showing juveniles acting far more lawlessly, compared with their elders, than ours do. For example, in Japan, teenagers commit a shocking 21 per cent of all the country's crime. Ours commit about 12 per cent. Take one category—violent sex. In our country juveniles account for 19 per cent of the total rapes. In Japan they're in the majority—52 per cent.

"Consider, then, the case of a 17-year-old Japanese who wandered into a ladies' restroom in a restaurant by mistake not long ago. When a woman attempted to admonish him for his behavior, he simply took out a knife and hacked her to death on the spot.

"We tend to think we have a monopoly on misbehaving youngsters—a view encouraged by many foreigners envious of our material well-being. But such a 'monopoly' does not square with the facts. The sweep of juvenile crime in certain places can match, or even top, our own brand. It is not true of all countries, of course, as we shall see. In some places, juvenile delinquency is under control, or even going down. But what interested me particularly was in many countries abroad, even those with lower rates, there was a new and alarming pattern of misbehavior. It indicated a purpose and organization which our youngsters lack. In fact, there were times I wondered if our delinquents weren't a little backward.

"Most of us remember, for example, that in the spring of 1960 a riot in Istanbul by a group of students mostly in their teens, resulted in the fall of the Menderes government in Turkey.

"At about the same time in Tokyo the delinquent behavior of 76,000 students, rioting wildly outside the Diet Building forced President Eisenhower to cancel his visit to Japan. One may argue that such students were not strictly delinquents, but certainly similar behavior by teenagers in front of our capitol in Washington would have been labeled delinquent. In any event, not long after the riots, a 17-year-old boy, who had a two-year record of violence, stabbed and killed the Socialist party chairman, Inejiro Asanuma, and caused another upheaval in the government.

"While our young students were doing such things as rolling beds, rocking streetcars, stealing girls' panties, or (at Harvard) demonstrating to keep their diplomas in Latin rather than English, their violent South Korean counterparts were toppling the long-standing government of President Rhee."

To be sure, juvenile delinquency in America may express itself in bigger (though hardly better) ways than in most parts of the world. But keep one fact in mind: **delinquency is by no means an exclusively American commodity.** If delinquency is not a disease that has spread rapidly about the world like a virus, then at least it is symptomatic of a profound disease, an unrest among the youth who may be aptly described as an explosive generation in a revolutionary world.

SUMMARY

The experts agree that the two series of national data most frequently cited are: (1) the police arrest data collected by the Federal Bureau of Investigation, and (2) the juvenile court delinquency data collected by the Children's Bureau. Both collections of data focus not only on the volume of delinquency, but also on the types of offenses committed and on the characteristics of the juvenile offenders.

Delinquency continues to rise due to:

Post-war prosperity with "success" being increasingly emphasized in material terms.

Slum conditions; deteriorated housing—mostly in the urban areas where there is considerable overcrowding due to in-migration.

Breakdown in traditional family and community control.

Attitudes of irresponsibility due to the continual threats of major war.

Increasing numbers of employed mothers.

The use of mass media to emphasize vice, violence, crime, and false values.

Anti-social behavior on the part of minors is not strictly an American innovation. Other countries are also having their problems with youthful misbehavior. In Sweden for instance, their delinquent ratio is higher than the United States. Automobile thefts are just as prevalent in Sweden as in the United States, Russia, Japan, Germany, the Netherlands, Italy, England, Taiwan, Yugoslavia, Austria, South Africa, Poland and France, to name a few. All countries are having "problems" with their youths. Therefore, delinquency is not strictly American and confined to the United States.

QUESTIONS

1. Delinquency—as we have come to label the criminal conduct of persons of a fixed statutory age—consists of: . . . List.
2. Any attempts to analyze crime statistics, and to derive valid and meaningful conclusions, must be carried out with utmost care. Why?
3. What two agencies compile statistical information which are most frequently cited?
4. *True* or *False* . . . The most frequent offense, according to FBI statistical information, is aggravated assault.
5. *True* or *False* . . . FBI reports reveal that delinquency among children is decreasing—when the national population growth is taken into consideration.
6. *True* or *False* . . . Girls offenses, according to FBI statistical computations, are generally in the area of automobile thefts and burglaries.
7. Discuss Chapter 1.
8. Why does delinquency continue to rise in the United States? Cite the factors pertaining to "post-war prosperity," etc.
9. Discuss the many countries who are having serious problems with juveniles—cite the phrases or language these countries use to label their delinquents.
10. Is delinquency purely an American dilemma? If not, discuss problems in Tokyo and Istanbul.

Chapter 5

Prevention Is the Answer

THE WAY TO SOLVE the delinquency problem is to prevent boys and girls from becoming delinquents in the first place. Society is not solving that problem because the emphasis is not placed on that all-important job: *Prevention*. Morevor, it appears that society is blocked by a psychological "Chinese Wall" of fallacies which keep us busy with impractical plans that are doomed to fail right from the start. The correctional program in the United States seemed to be content to treat individual delinquents (after they have already committed delinquent acts), while overlooking almost entirely the factors which create them. There is too much reliance on conventional recreation programs to prevent delinquency and they never can! The little preventive work that has been attempted such as the practice of not giving the culprit an arrest record and referring him to a social agency for "straightening out," commendable as it is, is not solving the problem.

Society must find a way to correct the faulty home and environment *before* the child becomes a police case. It is both unfair and impractical to rely on the really few private agencies to do this large scale, complex public job. Very little is done the improve the environment and to clean up the social slum which breeds delinquency. If the child is expected to "conform to society," then most certainly there is an obligation to see to it that the highly delinquent society in the United States becomes a better example for the child. Young children learn what they see, they live with what they learn, and society usually receives the delinquency which it unwittingly generates and deserves.

The biggest gap in our treatment of delinquent children is our failure to get into the highly maladjusted home before serious problems start to develop. School authorities, probation, police, family casework agencies, and neighbors are often aware of these situations, but frequently they do nothing about them because of apathy or because there appears to be no particular way of entering the picture until some drastic official action must be taken. Some methods must be found to do this kind of preventive work on the community level!

Responsibility for the prevention of delinquency should remain with local communities. The state can and must provide leadership for a prevention program, but the ultimate responsibility for taking corrective action must remain at the local level. A good prevention program requires the cooperative effort of many citizens and organizations. The agencies mentioned above must coordinate these efforts. A system of case referrals and responsibility must be developed.

Some preventive work can be attempted with groups of children. Some require individual social case work. Gang activities present a challenge to the entire community, and special group members should work with law enforcement agencies and school officials to identify these gangs, study them at first hand, gain the confidence of the gang leaders, and then guide their activities into constructive channels.

Almost all communities have areas that present special hazards to children. These require constant surveillance. Sufficient trained juvenile officers must be provided to supervise these areas and provide assistance to the adult leaders or other responsible individuals to further maintenance of order. This assistance should be provided before there is destructive activity by the juveniles.

WHAT IS PREVENTION?

All over the land private and public agencies call meetings to discuss the prevention of delinquency, and invaribly most of the plans and action center around the saving of boys and girls who are already delinquent and in trouble with the law. From the first time a boy commits a delinquent act and is picked up by a patrolman or has a complaint filed against him, whether he is arrested or referred to a social agency for handling, *the best society can hope for is to attempt to rehabilitate this recalcitrant youth so that he does not recidivate. This is a correctional approach—not preventive.*[1]

Of course, all of this is excellent work. It is bound to rehabilitate many youngsters for a decent life. But no amount of this good work, whether it is the Juvenile Aid Bureau practice of avoiding arrest and referring the youngster to a social agency, the very finest probation work, or excellent and successful programs of training in a juvenile institution—none of this will effect the preventive phases of this whole problem. The main problem of reducing delinquency is concerned with those children who are personally weak and highly vulnerable to

[1]B. Solomon, "Why We Have Not Solved the Delinquency Problem," *Federal Probation*, Vol. XXVII, Nov. 4, December 1953, p. 15.

the hazards and pressures of their environment, but who have *not* yet committed serious delinquencies or come in conflict with the law.[2]

Juvenile Aid Bureau work, juvenile court handling, detention, probation, commitment to institutions, excellent programs of recreation, education, and vocational training in these institutions, and parole—no matter how good they all are and no matter how successful—will have very little effect on the overall juvenile delinquency problem. *The reasons for this ineffectiveness are (1) because the majority of institutionalized delinquents repeat their offenses and, more importantly, (2) because every year more than four million new babies are born and a whole new army of potential juvenile delinquents grows up, giving each committee the job to do over and over again.* Even if the assumption is made that excellent rehabilitation facilities are successful in saving a third of the community youngsters for a decent life, that is an extremely small total compared with the many millions with whom preventive work should and must be carried on year after year.

Although preventive work can also be carried on after a child is committed to a correctional institution, such prevention is applied to criminals of any age in the hope of preventing them from repeating their criminal acts. But according to a noted authority in the field, Ben Solomon, who has written numerous articles in *Federal Probation,* "Such treatment can hardly be called or classified as basic 'Prevention.' The line between 'Prevention' and 'Correction' in all correctional work is very clear and very definite." Solomon is of the opinion that a simple definition of delinquency prevention is concerned mainly with all programs that affect a child's life *before he commits delinquent acts serious enough to warrant commitment to a correctional institution.*[3]

Therefore, if we subscribe to Solomon's thinking, it follows logically that correction starts where prevention ends. Such programs of correction (rehabilitation), of course, include treatment which aims to "prevent" the offender from repeating his offense.

AREAS OF CONCERN

There are many areas of importance in a preventive program, but we will discuss only those which are predominant.

Causes versus Cases. It is not unusual in planning for delinquency prevention to place a great deal of stress on finding and listing causes, and making lengthy, exhaustive, and expensive studies and surveys, but very often the results of such studies are blithely ignored, giving nearly

[2]*Ibid.*, p. 15.
Ibid., p. 15

all the attention to cases, individual boys and girls who have already become serious delinquents. Furthermore work is done almost exclusively on the individual cases and very little, if anything, is done about the causes, the contributing factors, and the environmental pressures which create these cases in the first place. In a typhoid epidemic the physicians do work on the individual cases, of course, but at the same time a major effort is made to find the polluted water or the carrier—the source of the epidemic—and to remove or alleviate some of the causative factors. Very little, if any, of this type of work is attempted in delinquency prevention.[4]

The Home. In preventive work, there should be a great deal of stress in the area of the quality of a child's parents, especially the mother, because to a large extent the first five or six years of a child's training are the most important. Very little research is done in this area, and a great deal of attention should be placed on more programs to service the needs of the less privileged girls, 5 to 10 years of age, the mothers of tomorrow, for whom very little is provided in communities throughout the United States. These children need special training in homemaking and family-rearing skills in the hope that they will select their husbands by higher standards and become better mothers and better homemakers.[5]

In speaking of the *quality* of parents, this term does not refer to finances. Obviously, some parents of very high quality have low income, and some parents of very low quality have plenty of money. Preventive work is concerned with the type of home a child has, whether such a home has a decent place to sleep and adequate and regular meals, whether he is surrounded with affection, and whether he is accorded supervision and guidance commensurate with his needs, and has a sense of being wanted and appreciated.

Another area of concern in preventive work is the neighborhood the minor resides in; often it is a slum area, ramshackle, ugly and filthy, or vice-ridden. The number of taverns and other negative influences in the community certainly should also be considered. Are there any recreational facilities and youth-serving agencies? The type of school where the minor is enrolled is probably the most important factor in prevention work. Is the child being subjected to emotionally unstable teachers, or is he being forced through an inflexible academic curriculum that is beyond his needs or abilities?[6]

Besides the already mentioned areas, a preventive program should be

[4]*Ibid.*, p. 16.
[5]*Ibid.*, p. 16.
[6]*Ibid.*, p. 16.

very much concerned with the pressures and hazards of the neighborhood and what can be done about them.

The Individual. The main concern in a prevention program is, of course, the individual. If, in the final analysis, the juvenile is weak physically, mentally, emotionally, or socially, the ability to resist temptations and to fight the pressures of the negative influences within his community may be slight. The ascertainment of the traits of the individual child and the immediate strengthening of any weakness before he gets into trouble with the law is good preventive work.

The area of the individual is where prevention programs have most often failed.[7] The physical and psychological examination of a highly emotional child should be standard procedure in any prevention program. If treatment is necessary, such treatment should be for an extensive period of time in hopes that the minor, upon reaching maturity, may be able to withstand negative influences and make better choices in life.

The Neighborhood. When a child spends a large part of his youth in a slum neighborhood, it is important to do something about the threatening environment, the apathy that created the epidemic in the first place. In order to do so, it is necessary that liason be maintained not only with the family, but also with the neighborhood, the school, and the church. Here again prevention has often failed miserably and it seems that the only time concern is displayed with environment is after a delinquent is committed to an institution. At this time there is a concerted effort to see that the juvenile receive the care, supervision, training, and recreation that he should have had before he was institutionalized. To make matters worse, after the juvenile is released from the training school, he usually returns to the same detrimental environment from which he was removed.[8]

The Weakest Link. The weakest link in all efforts to solve this whole delinquency problem seems to be our inability to get into the highly maladjusted home before a complaint is filed or an actual case develops. Very often these homes are unfit places for children, but usually society can't do much to change these homes until it is too late. Unfortunately, these homes often have large families and all the children, especially the very young, are in real danger of developing delinquent patterns. Yet these homes are rather easy to find—school officials, public welfare department investigators, police, neighbors, and family casework agencies generally know them—but we have no practical way of

[7]*Ibid.*, pp. 16–17.
[8]*Ibid.*, p. 17.

inspecting and correcting these homes until they become court cases.[9] Every state has laws relating to adults contributing to the delinquency or dependency of minors in or outside the home circle, but little can be done to really enforce these laws before court cases develop. This inability to "take the offensive and attack the problem" needs much thought, and probably some legislative revisions will be required to make preventive measures more effective.

A PREVENTION PROGRAM

As we have seen, authorities in the field agree that there is no single cause of delinquency. Any effective prevention program must, therefore, be many-sided. Here are some suggestions for developing a more comprehensive blue-print for action.

Special Services in Schools

The schools' major contribution toward the control and prevention of delinquency is made by helping children and youths to grow into competent and responsible adults. Most people want to meet the expectations set for them by their families, their schools, and their communities, and most people do so with reasonable success. The person who achieves whatever is expected of him is not likely to become a delinquent. However, a certain proportion find difficulty in making the transition from childhood to adulthood. These are the potential delinquents. Therefore, the schools must be prepared to take certain actions to help such people avoid trouble. These actions should include:

1. Identifying potential problem pupils at the earliest possible age.
2. Providing sufficient flexibility in the school program to permit adjustments for these pupils.
3. Providing intensive work with individual pupils who present special social and emotional problems.
4. Accepting the responsibility for cooperation with other community agencies and organizations in providing and using needed services.

Jobs for Youth

Job opportunities for young people, particularly the school dropout and the delinquency prone, need to be made available in increasing numbers. Many young people get into difficulty because their failure in school is reflected by their later failures to secure satisfactory employment. Existing and additional youth employment committees should

[9] *Ibid.*, p. 17.

be encouraged, involving representation from labor, management, the schools, and State Departments of Employment.

These committees should continue to concern themselves with developing summer-time and part-time employment for children still in school and full-time jobs for those young people who end their schooling with graduation from high school. Consideration should be given to some kind of employment internship program that would involve selecting terminal students in high school and junior college to begin work one year prior to graduating, while taking appropriate skill courses for school credit.

Mental Health Services

Because good mental health is a by-product of other favorable factors, individuals look to the area of every day social activity to build their defenses against mental breakdown. This includes the home, school, church, jobs, and recreation, public health and safety, and economic security.

The provision for basic health and welfare services effectively administered serves as a deterrent to disturbed behavior. Additional and better co-ordinated services providing early identification, diagnosis, and treatment are essential to a comprehensive program of prevention.

Modern psychiatric approaches demand that children and their families receive early treatment with as little dislocation as possible from their home, school, or community. To do this, psychiatric services must be located in the local community so that there is a minimal disruption of the patient's community ties and relationships.

To achieve the degree and quality of services required for mental health, responsibility must be shared among federal, state, and local public and private agencies. The potential of such citizen participation should be encouraged to the fullest by vigorously furthering this partnership.

Assistance Programs

Strengthening a child's own home is the most effective way to prevent juvenile delinquency. An examination of delinquent case histories shows that disorganization in the family is frequently the forerunner of overt delinquent acts.

The contributions that can be made by the social welfare services to the prevention of delinquency lie mainly in the area of:

Mitigating the negative effects of deprivation faced by underprivileged families whose earnings are neither stable nor adequate enough to afford a decent standard of living. This refers to those who ordinarily lack opportunities enough to afford decent housing and the basic needs of health, recreation, education, etc. It also refers to those who lack the protection afforded by coverage under programs for survivors, disability and unemployment insurance.

To some extent the general assistance programs of the various counties throughout the United States function to this purpose, but are too varied and too limited to do more than support people at a standard which cannot possibly support stable and wholesome living conditions.

The Aid to Federally Dependent Children Program also has as its basic purpose the strengthening of family life. Moreover, it includes many of the most deprived, and hence high delinquency risk, children. In numbers it affects more children in home interviews than any other social welfare program. These children are in families where major family breakdown has already occurred, e.g., incarceration, death, disability, desertion.

Providing social services in addition to financial aid to these families to prevent further disintegration and to rehabilitate them if possible.

Role of Voluntary Social Welfare Agencies

Voluntary social welfare agencies have an important contribution to make in the prevention and treatment of delinquency, both individually and in cooperation with public agencies. They have professional family service programs, child-care institutions, foster-care services, day-care centers, and group work activities that reach many thousands of families and children yearly. But they must develop the means to reach many more families and children in trouble and provide treatment for them. They must continue to encourage the boards of directors of volunteer groups, representing as they do a broad cross-section of our communities, to be concerned with the welfare of *all* citizens; to engage in experimental programs, demonstration projects, and basic research in the behavioral sciences.

In recent years, more and more private social agencies have been caught in a squeeze of spiraling costs and shrinking income from the volunteer dollars, and frequently they have been forced to emergency retrenchment. Thus an extra burden has been thrust upon tax-supported agencies. Also, and consequently, the low cost and greater diversification of private agency programs are lost to the public agencies. Therefore, special incentives should be provided the voluntary agencies to give additional family and child welfare services to pre-delinquent and delinquent children and their families both in their own home and while the youngsters are away from home in foster care.

Probation Services

Probation departments must be encouraged to develop more preventive services. Only two counties have developed procedures for the discovery and treatment of delinquency-prone children. Little has been done by probation agencies to utilize volunteer groups and citizen action committees engaged in preventive work.

Increased emphasis needs to be placed on the treatment of delinquents in their local communities where family relationships can be strengthened. The state institutions should be reserved for the delinquent children and youths and those who are so emotionally and mentally disturbed that they cannot be treated properly in local facilities.

Police Services for Juveniles

Law enforcement has a positive role to play in delinquency prevention. Trained juvenile officers, alert to happenings in the adolescent's world, can frequently avert trouble before it develops. Proper surveillance of hazardous areas can prevent unwitting youngsters from becoming accomplices in criminal activities. Close cooperation of community agencies with law enforcement officers would help spotlight community needs in the field of delinquency prevention. This would often permit effective action to be taken before trouble begins.

This brings us to the question: *Is the police role in prevention a proper one?*

Some criticism has been noted as to the propriety of the police engaging in what might be termed the "treatment" field in reference to combating delinquency. Certainly the police are qualified for the most part, to enter this field, although admittedly there are many elements of treatment in this approach. In fact, the official contact between a child and a police officer is, in a sense, a phase of treatment. The officer's attitude and conduct toward the child may have a decided effect on the child's outlook and feeling toward those in authority.

A reply to this criticism may be found in the answers to two simple questions: "Is crime prevention a police responsibility?" and "Is delinquency prevention, crime prevention?"

It is obvious that crime prevention is a police responsibility, and it logically follows that if most of the adult criminals were juvenile delinquents, preventing delinquency is crime prevention. To apply intelligently these fairly new concepts in law enforcement by trained personnel for the purpose of delinquency prevention is, without question, a proper function of a police department as part of its responsibility to a community.[10]

In their efforts to control and prevent delinquency, the police are exposed to sociological, psychological, socio-psycholgical, and biological theories. The police, as such, have not participated extensively in many conferences that have been held in various sections of the country. In approaching the problem from realistic and practical standpoints, police officials believe that there are three major factors in delinquency control:[11]

First the Home. Unquestionably, the opinion that unsuitable, unstable, or inadequate home situations are paramount in analyzing delinquent causation is shared by practically all those having a knowledge of conditions and factors.

Second, the Church. How lack of spiritual guidance effects the whole delinquency picture is not clear. It is significant, however, that many delinquent children have had little or no religious instruction. It can be assumed that families which perpetuate delinquents are usually not a part of the church-going population. Here, then, is a need and a challenge for churches to expand their activities to develop missionary types of endeavors. There is a need to reach the unreached.

Third, the School. Next to home, the school is the great training ground. It is here that the early detection of the problem child and recognition of delinquency in the home structure become apparent. There is a need for schools to be staffed with specially trained personnel, not only to be alert to such conditions, but qualified to diagnose and refer those cases that need follow-up treatment.

A preventive activity that clearly falls within an acceptable function of the police is to act to control or suppress conditions in the community that might lead to delinquency or crime. These conditions are generally part of certain types of group activities, such as:

1. The pool room, bowling alley, or roller rinks in or around which children are allowed to loiter to an unreasonably late hour and where the very young may be allowed to smoke and to purchase cigarettes, and the upper-age minors to drink beer or liquor.
2. The dance hall, bar, or "smoke shops" in which young girls learn to drink and solicit for immoral purposes.
3. The candy stores, magazine and gift shops, or other such establishments that sell pornography.

[10] J. E. Winters, "The Role of the Police in the Prevention and Control of Delinquency," *Federal Probation*, Vol. XXI, No. 2, June 1957, p. 5.
[11] *Ibid.*, p. 6.

4. The various entertainment establishments that attract children during school hours and thereby encourage truancy.

During normal patrol of a city, police officers become aware of such danger areas. It is obviously a reasonable performance of their duty to see that the laws regulating such businesses are being observed by the proprietors. Sometimes, of course, a business may be operated within the letter of the law and still have an undesirable atmosphere about it, insofar as the welfare of children is concerned. It is advantageous then, in all cases, for the police officer to become well acquainted with the proprietors of businesses of this nature and to enlist their help in protecting and contributing to the welfare of young people. Such an approach may in the long run produce better results than the constant use of or threat of "action."[12]

However, there may be cases where sympathetic appeals, warnings, and threats are all to no avail. In such instances, the police may have to take court action or appeal to a licensing agency that issues permits to do business. A civil court injunction is often an effective solution. And, of course, the prospect of losing his license will ordinarily make a proprietor more cooperative.[13]

In areas and situations where undesirable conditions exist through no fault of a particular establishment or person, the police should call the matter to the attention of some community planning body. In many cities cooperation between the police and the youth-serving agencies has resulted in various projects to combat such situations. For example, information provided by the police on delinquency areas and on gang activities has led to the establishment of new recreational facilities and to the use of "detached workers" by social agencies in an effort to convert the gangs into social clubs.

The police are, of course, tremendously interested in efforts to create a better environment for juveniles and to lead them away from delinquency, but often there is some question as to the extent to which they should participate in such efforts. For example, it is questionable whether a police officer should attempt to work with a gang in the same manner that detached workers from social agencies do. However, in some other areas of this work there are indications that police officers can be very effective without prejudice to their responsibilities as law-enforcement agents. This is particularly true in the case of recreational activities.[14]

[12]*Police Services for Juveniles*, Children's Bureau, U.S. Department of Health, Welfare, and Education, Washington, D.C., 1954.

[13]*Ibid.*, p. 52.

[14]*Ibid.*, p. 53.

Certain organizations, particularly agencies exclusively concerned with leisure-time activities and recreation, have questioned the appropriateness of recreational programs conducted under police auspices. In response to such critics, proponents of police recreation programs have pointed out that:

Insufficient recreational facilities force the police into these programs to meet crucial needs.

Actual experience in some communities has shown that the police can be very effective in work with so-called "pre-delinquents," that is, children in underprivileged areas who are not interested in the programs of conventional recreational activities. Only the police seem to speak the language of these youngsters and seem to understand their motivation and aspirations.

Such programs are invaluable in impressing children with the concept of the police officer as a friend.

Strong as such arguments may be, many people still hold that they do not justify police participation in such programs. They ask whether the police would countenance recreational agencies engaging in police functions on the grounds that the police department's performance is inadequate. These critics of police also contend that the development of the child's concept of police officers should come about through the child's observation of officers engaged in their proper duties, and through standard educational techniques. This desirable goal, it is pointed out, can be obtained without permitting the police to perform functions that are said not to be properly theirs.

In recent years, a number of organizations have considered this question and have taken a somewhat middle-of-the-road point of view. They have emphasized the importance of calling the attention of the community to recreational needs. They have seen police engaged in these programs only as a lost resort. They have called for police recreation programs that employ trained recreational personnel and meet the standards of national recreational organizations.

Considering these arguments, it is clear that there are *four points that should be reviewed prior to police undertaking recreational programs.* These points are:

The police have the responsibility to keep the community informed of recreational needs particularly in underprivileged areas.

All communities should provide recreation based on community needs and develop facilities through broad community programs involving leisure-time activities.

Police participation in providing recreational service should be determined through joint community planning.

Recreation supervisors should be trained in the field of recreation and recreation programs should meet recognized standards.[15]

Traffic safety is another area of prevention in which the police play a significant role. In nearly every community, police handle juveniles who violate traffic rules and regulations in the same manner as they handle adults. Quite often the enforcement of traffic laws is the responsibility of the special traffic division, but no distinction is made between juveniles and adults; a citation is simply issued for the violator to appear before the appropriate judicial agency.

However, in connection with this traffic question, the police do regard juveniles differently from adults in one respect. They see the juvenile driver eventually as an adult driver, and they would like that juvenile to become and remain a safe driver. For this reason, police departments in many communities have undertaken certain traffic safety programs for young automobile drivers. Bicycle safety education and junior safety patrol programs have also been set up. These three programs cover most of the police activity in traffic safety.[16]

Those departments that have traffic divisions usually entrust these programs to that unit as being best qualified for such work.

Here are some of the activities that are found in these programs:

1. *Traffic Safety for Young Automobile Drivers.*
   This includes:
   a. Planning and assisting with driver education and training in the schools.
   b. Using every public education medium available to impress upon juveniles, as well as adults, the need for safe driving.
   c. Sponsoring or operating traffic schools for juvenile operators.
2. *Bicycle Safety Education.*
   This follows the same general pattern for automobile drivers, but is directed to a younger age group with the principal approach through the school.
3. *Junior Safety Patrol.*
   This is carried out in cooperation with the schools and the Parent-Teacher Associations. This program gives the police an opportunity to develop an extensive safety education program in the schools, as well as to promote good relations with juveniles.

As in the case of other preventive activities, there is generally complete approval of traffic safety programs, but there may be objection to certain types of programs being conducted by the police. It is apparent that the need for such programs should be defined and the agency best

[15]*Ibid.*, p. 55.
[16]*Ibid.*, p. 56.

qualified and most appropriate for the task should be entrusted with it. In any case, police interested and their cooperation in these programs cannot be dispensed with.[17]

SUMMARY

There is only one way to solve the delinquent problem and that is to prevent boys and girls from becoming delinquents in the first place. Thus far, this important job is being relegated to second position as compared to corrections. Once a youngster has committed a delinquent act and is apprehended, the "machinery" of the correctional field moves into high gear. However, this is not prevention, just correction. It is becoming increasingly clear that prevention programs should take precedence over correction, and that such preventative programs should be increased.

Prevention is concerned with many areas, including (1) causes versus cases, (2) the home, (3) the individual, (4) the inability to act before cases develop, and (5) the neighborhood.

A prevention program should include the following: (1) jobs for youth, (2) mental health services, (3) assistance programs, (4) voluntary social welfare agencies, (5) probation services, and (6) police services for juveniles.

Regarding law enforcement, there is no doubt that police should be actively involved in prevention programs. They must be in a position to avert trouble before it develops. Close cooperation with community agencies will help to ascertain community needs in the field of delinquency prevention and thereby eliminate trouble before it starts.

Police officials feel that there are three practical and major factors in delinquency control; (1) the home, (2) the church, and (3) the school.

A preventive activity that clearly falls within police jurisdiction is to act to control or suppress conditions in the community that lead to delinquency and crime. These conditions generally are: (1) pool halls, bowling alleys, or roller rinks where children loiter to an unreasonable late hour; (2) poorly supervised dance halls and bars; (3) candy stores, magazine and gift shops, or other such establishments that trade in pornographic materials; (4) various entertainment establishments that attract children during school hours.

Police should enter the recreational field only after: (1) the community is informed about recreational needs, particularly in underdeprivileged areas, and such information is ignored; (2) police partici-

[17]*Ibid.*, pp. 56–57.

pation in providing recreational services has been determined through joint community planning; (3) recreational facilities are developed through broad community programs involving leisure time activities; and (4) police recreational leaders are trained in the field of recreation and programs meet recognized standards.

QUESTIONS

1. *True* or *False* . . . Police should not enter the field of recreation.
2. *True* or *False* . . . Prevention is in the treatment field and should start immediately after the minor is *apprehended*.
3. *True* or *False* . . . Prevention programs should be under the control of state and not local communities.
4. Discuss the main areas of concern in prevention.
5. Outline a prevention program.
6. Discuss the role of probation services in a prevention program.
7. Why should the police become involved in prevention programs?
8. What points should be considered by police prior to becoming involved in recreational programs?
9. Discuss *Traffic Safety* programs.
10. What are some of the activities that may be found in traffic safety programs?

PART TWO

Factors Related to Juvenile Delinquency and Theories

Police Services for Juveniles

Police Services for Neglected Children

Police Relationship With Other Agencies

Legal and Social Components of Probation and Parole

Chapter 6

Factors Related to Juvenile Delinquency and Theories

WHY DOES DELINQUENCY OCCUR, and why does it increase at a rapid rate? On many occasions, the assumption is made that a clear knowledge and understanding of the causes leading to delinquency can lead naturally to a clear understanding of how to control and prevent delinquency.

This type of reasoning is based on the frequent experience of successfully solving a problem after the causes have been determined. Some conquests of infectious diseases have followed this sequence of solution. The problems, so to speak, of infectious diseases, flood control, and highway construction have been solved in this manner—by understanding and forming a clear picture of the causes. However, it should be noted that in such instances the causes are relatively simple and, although not usually singular, small in number. This is certainly not the case when dealing with human behavior.

Knowledge of causes does not always result in the ability to control a problem when the causes are both extremely complex and numerous. For example, much is known about the causes of many cardiac diseases, such as those in the cardio-vascular and metabolic areas, without a corresponding ability to control or prevent these illnesses. In some such instances the causes themselves are very complex and not subject to control. Causation of delinquency has more in common with this latter circumstance than it does to the more simple and hopeful relationship described from many infectious diseases and the threats of natural environmental forces.

It should be noted that although control of problems may be aided by the knowledge of causes, it is not always completely dependent on full understanding of causation. Medicine has many instances of the development of successful treatments, and even of preventive methods, before the causes of some illnesses were known. Similarily, efforts to control or prevent delinquency need not and must not, in fact, await a comprehensive statement of causes.

A number of factors associated with delinquency have been identified in a fairly complete way. Many factors are part of broad social and economic problems which are, themselves, as difficult to control as is delinquency. These statements are not made to indicate any attitude of defeatism, but only to indicate the complexity of the problems of delinquency and the limitations of the advantages that can be expected from a delineation of the factors which relate to juvenile behavior.

It is not illogical for the person engaged in prevention and treatment to be concerned with factors related to juvenile delinquency; he is better prepared to treat, prevent, or rehabilitate if he knows what causes such anti-social behavior. Yet it is astounding what a wide variety of answers you will get—even from the experts—to a simple question like: what factors make a kid misbehave?

For the purpose of teaching, the author classified the answers to this question in three brief *general* groups of categories of factors relating to juvenile crime: the Sociological (social), the Psychological, and the Physiological (biological). Extensive treatment of the aforementioned categories in the succeeding pages will be made by presenting various *Theoretical Approaches to Delinquency Causation.*

SOCIOLOGICAL (SOCIAL) FACTORS

From time to time, various factors have been found or supposed to relate to juvenile behavior. Unless a specific theory is discussed, it is preferable to speak on related factors rather than casual factors. For casual factors implies a simple set of relations that do not exist. Delinquent behavior, like other forms of behavior, is responsive to social and economic conditions, and other dominant features of society. There has been deviate behavior ever since there have been laws and moral codes. City life, population mobility, divergency in values, in life styles, and in opportunities of social and economic advancement, family instability, the lure of quick wealth and social success and activities on the fringe of conventional society—these characteristics of modern society are not in themselves necessarily the causes of delinquency, but they are contributory factors. Such characteristics provide the context within which patterns of delinquent behavior arise and are transmitted. They make more difficult the operation of informal social control, which has always been more important than formal legal controls in maintaining the moral order of society.

A part of the increased rate of delinquency is related to an increased tendency to use the police and the courts to settle minor disputes, which formerly would have been considered private matters. For effective control of delinquency, then, it becomes necessary to seek modes of compensating for our counteractions which either encourage or foster deviate behavior.

As we have seen, many studies of juvenile delinquency suggest that the rates of delinquency are highest in the deteriorated areas of our larger cities. These are the areas in which the most recently arrived low-income immigrants have settled. Also, existing in such areas are those who have drifted there because of failure to compete successfully for more desirable living space (because of lack of skills, disease, or other disability), and persons who have located in those districts because of a desire for freedom from conventional restraints. These neighborhoods are characterized not only by physical deterioration, but by their great heterogenity of background and moral standards, the lack of neighborhood solidarity, the lack of opportunities for youth to participate, meaningfully, in the kinds of activities that are available to children in more favored neighborhoods, and by the presence of "successful" members of the underworld, who are regarded as heroes by the youths. These circumstances of life are often associated with unstable families, and a high incidence of illegitimacy and desertion, leading to both marginal employment, with inadequate supervision for the needs of children, and the absence of a father figure with whom the child can identify and look to for supervision, guidance, and affection.

Delinquent behavior has been found to be particularly high among the children of minority groups or second generation immigrants (children of foreigners who have settled in the United States) due to conflicts of American customs with the culture of their parents. Such children are often disorganized personally, and this personal disorganization frequently contributes to delinquent behavior patterns.

A high proportion of delinquents and criminals come from homes which have been broken by deaths, desertion, or divorce. The importance of the family in the development of personalities is well known. Homes characterized by marital conflict, or by absences of an important member, understandably contribute more than their share to delinquency and crime. However, it is important to recognize the fact that not all children from broken homes become criminals; therefore, this can hardly be considered the sole factor.

Still another social process is claimed to be operative in some forms of delinquent behavior. The *street corner* group or delinquent gang represents the adolescent version of lower-class culture. This sub-culture places a high value on masculine "toughness," "sharpness," and other traits. Rebellion against middle-class norms may be a by-product rather than a major factor in the unlawful delinquent behavior. Undoubtedly, different constellations or factors can produce delinquency under various conditions. Much more needs to be learned about how these factors are grouped and with what frequency and to what places.

In under-privileged environments, delinquency may not be so much an expression of economic need, but more of individual maladjustment, as a patent, behaviorial expression of basic conflicts that confront the child and the adolescent. It must be added that neither the basic conflict of values nor delinquency is by any means confined to the urban slums. They find their most favorite expression in such an atmosphere, but they are also found in larger society.

Children learn from what they see around them, not merely from what they are told. Some elements of delinquency are widespread in the moral pattern of our society, as has been indicated by some of our most thoughtful citizens of the contemporary scene.

Another aspect of the contemporary environment, significantly involved in the problem, arises from the very high premium put upon certain forms of success and the preoccupation of many parents with their own social and occupational success. When this is coupled with the freedom that adolescence can achieve from parental restriction, the family as a source of sound values and mechanism of social control is further weakened. There is evidence that middle-class youths emulate for "kicks" many of the behavioral patterns that have their origins in relatively deprived areas. These expressions of rebellion from parents are likely to appear where parental standards are inconsistent, or too stringently applied to the adolescent and not wholly manifested in parental behavior.

There have been major fluctuations in the amounts of delinquency which appeared to be associated with major social and economic changes. At least in recent years, delinquency has increased in times of economic properity, marked by hedonistic (life of pleasure) values in many circles, such as the 1920's, the 1950's, and the 1960's, and has fallen in times of depression. We do not yet know about the factors which mediate between these broad changes and delinquent behavior. Detailed studies along these lines and other areas mentioned above should be most enlightening.

PSYCHOLOGICAL FACTORS

Psychological factors relate primarily to an individual psychological pathology, some forms of which are pre-disposed to delinquent behavior. Psychological factors contend that inner-tensions and emotions, unresolved conflicts and unsatisfied needs of the individual underlie antisocial behavior. It should be noted that many of the factors described above as productive of delinquency also contribute to psychological pathology. However, personality disturbances can occur in any section of society, whereas sociological factors such as deteriorated neighborhoods are confined to identifiable areas. Occurrence of delinquent behavior by one or a few youths in generally non-delinquent areas frequently reflects personality disorders rather than the existence of a widespread delinquent culture. It should also be noted that the conditions of family life in underprivileged areas operate to increase the probability of psychological disorder among children. The end results, therefore, are that in delinquent areas children with personality disorders tend to be numerous and there is a ready arena of delinquent culture in which to act out their problems. In less delinquent areas, however, psychological disturbance upon the part of a few children may still be expressed through delinquent behavior, and they may even be able to recruit other youths who might otherwise not show this behavior. Such relationships further illustrate the extreme complexities of the factors related to delinquency.

Many psychiatrically orientated psychologists consider delinquency and criminology to be products of personality maladjustments. The socialization process is regarded as producing either healthy or unhealthy personalities, and delinquency is considered a correlate of the latter.

Psychiatrists have, on the whole, amended an earlier convention that the criminal or delinquent is essentially a psychotic person. However, other schools of criminology have not yet entirely ruled out psychosis as a factor related to crime and delinquency. They have largely concentrated their focus on one psychosis, namely, schizophrenia, which appears to be directly related to criminology; they have also devoted a great deal of attention to the relationship between the "psychopathic personality" and crime. However, if schizophrenia is the most frequent psychosis found among prisoners or delinquents in institutional facilities, it is also the most frequent in society. The rates of schizophrenic symptoms are higher in the deteriorated sectors where criminal and delinquent behavior is at its maximum.

Psychologically oriented students of delinquency, on the other hand, tend to emphasize the personality attributes which distinquish delinquent from the non-delinquent.

Research studies found, for instance, that the average delinquent boy is more psychopathic manic than the average non-delinquent boy. Psychologists think the source of personality deviation among delinquents is lack of acceptance and affection for a child by his parent. The aforementioned psychological explanation advocates that feelings of insecurity, inadequacy, withdrawal, frustration, and rebellion develop in the child.

PHYSIOLOGICAL (BIOLOGICAL) FACTORS

If juvenile delinquency was due to a sole physical factor, and that factor was a wart on the end of one's nose, then it would be a simple matter to collect all delinquents with warts on the ends of their noses and remove them by surgery—thereby eliminating delinquency. However, as we well know, the physical factors in juvenile delinquency are more subtle and complex than any other factor. In fact, there may be many who would question any physiological basis for delinquency. Most investigators feel that health and disease play a rather minor role. But let us briefly examine what we call physiological factors and attempt to ascertain their importance in understanding juvenile delinquency.

Factors such as body build, intelligence, sex, race, general appearance, and the presence or absence of congenital defects are some of the physiological factors which may or may not have a direct relationship to delinquent behavior. In the past such factors were given impetus by numerous studies, especially genetic studies of family groups such as the "Jukes" by Dudgale and the "Kallikak" by Henry Goddard, which showed that long lines of members of the same families committed crimes of all sorts and were dangerous social misfits. Out of these studies came the idea that defective heredity played a major role in delinquent behavior. This particular belief continued until 1930 when further studies revealed that most mentally retarded children do not become delinquents, and those who do become delinquents are gullible and easily led. Furthermore, although feeeblemindednes has long been associated with criminal and delinquent behavior, the validity of such studies is weakened by the fact that the extent of feeblemindedness in the non-delinquent population is not precisely known, and that a larger proportion of the more intelligent delinquents elude the law. While it is true that physiological factors may play a minor role in the over-all picture of delinquency, some factors require closer thought and scrutiny. What is the significance of the high percentage of abnormal electroencephalograms among delinquents? How much do we really know of the birth of the delinquent and that all important first fifteen minutes of life? The picture is confused and until answers are found to the above mentioned questions, and many others, there can be little hope that the student of delinquency will be enlightened in the near future.

THEORETICAL APPROACHES TO DELINQUENCY

In many penal institutions doctors, lawyers, editors, engineers, and public officials swing into line with fellow convicts when the bell rings for meals or lock-up time. But still crime marches on. Murder, robbery, assault, kidnapping, and the like continue to flourish in all parts of the world.

Mistakenly, the uninformed public believes that it has the solution to the paramount problem of crime and delinquency.

Stop gambling was one of the earliest suggestions, and laws were accordingly passed prohibiting gambling in almost every state.

Close houses of prostitution and get rid of dope peddlers were additional remedies offered by well-intentioned but ill-informed persons.

Equally convincing was the contention years ago, and even today, that if every child were given a fair chance to obtain an education, his criminal tendencies would be restrained and crime could be greatly diminshed.

Playgrounds have been established in most of the towns and cities of America, but still crime and delinquency spread alarming.

For every situation arising in connection with crime and delinquency which captures the attention of the public for the moment, ignorant persons mistakenly believe that they have the one and only answer to the perplexing problem.[1]

Many criminologists have stopped trying to find a single theory that will explain crime and delinquency. They find particular factors which often repeat themselves in many cases, for example, factors of gang membership, lack of status in constructive groups, tensions in homes, and, perhaps, a sense of failure in competition.

However, Harry Elmer Barnes and Negley K. Teeters[2] make the following flat statements:

"No physical abnormality, no degree or type of insanity, no extent of mental retardation, no extremity of poor health, no degree of physical deprivation, no extreme of poverty, no filth of slum life, no lack of recreation, no stimulation of press, movie, radio or television, no hysteria or crime wave, no family discord or broken home, will surely and without exception produce crime. A crime is committed only when a peculiar combination of personal and social factors comes into juxtaposition with an utterly unique physical structure of a human being, to create a specified crime situation. And, viewed in a merely external fashion, the same apparent constellation of factors might not produce

[1]A. Vollmer, *The Criminal,* The Foundation Press, Inc., Brooklyn, 1949, p. 18.

[2]H. E. Barnes and N. K. Teeters, *New Horizons in Criminology,* 3rd ed., Prentice Hall, Inc., Englewood Cliffs, N.J., 1959, p. 116.

a crime the next time they merge simply because that precise sameness can never absolutely reoccur."

In general, attempts to formulate more satisfactory theories of human behavior constitute the principal content of the whole group of "human behavior" sciences, namely, biology, physiology, medicine, psychiatry, psychology, social psychology, and sociology.[3] But these various theories can be viewed only in relation to some intellectual or cultural frame of reference because the specialist tends to theorize in his field.[4]

The rest of this chapter examines the principal types of explanations of crime and delinquency propounded by the various disciplines. No attempt his been made to be all inclusive. All that has been attempted is the examination of one or two illustrations of each type or kind of explanation that has been offered by the various disciplines. The various theories are presented in a sentence-structured outline form in order to present a more concise statement covering the substance or main points of each theory. Such a condensed version would afford the student a better opportunity to digest the material.

I. *The Anthropological Approach*
   A. Attempts to discover whether the criminal is significantly different in his physical structure from the non-criminal. It examines the physical traits of behavior.
      1. Cesare Lombroso (an Italian army physician)
         a. In his writing he affirmed the atavistic origin of the born criminal and suggested a close relationship between crime, epilepsy, insanity, and degeneracy, as a whole—in other words, a type of man more primitive and savage than his civilized counterpart.
            (i) He studied a series of 383 skulls of criminals and recorded the percentage frequency of a considerable list of forehead, and other cranial features which he studied.
            (ii) Comparison with savage and prehistoric skulls led him to emphasize the born criminal as a physical type characterizing primitive man and even animals.[5]
      2. Earnest Hooton (a Harvard anthropologist)
         a. Hooton contends criminals are organically inferior. Crime is the resultant of the impact of environment upon low-grade human organism. It follows that the elimination of crime can be effected only by elimination of the physically, mentally, and morally unfit; or by their complete segregation in a socially aseptic environment.[6]

[3]G. B. Vold, *Theoretical Criminology*, Oxford University Press, New York, 1958, p. 3.
[4]*Ibid.*, p. 28.
[5]D. R. Taft, *Criminology*, 3rd ed., Macmillan, New York, 1956, p. 79.
[6]Vold, *op. cit.*, p. 59.

(i) His conclusions:
  (a) Criminals are inferior to non-criminals in nearly all their bodily measurements.
  (b) Physical inferiority is significant principally because it is associated with mental inferiority.
  (c) The basic cause of the inferiority is due to heredity and to situation or circumstance.
  (d) Dark eyes and blue eyes are deficient in criminals, and blue-gray and mixed eyes are in excess.[7]
  (e) Tattooing is more common among criminals than civilians.
  (f) Long and sloping foreheads, long, thin necks, and sloping shoulders are similarly in excess among criminals, in comparison with civilians.

3. William H. Sheldon
   a. Technique of applying body type to individual delinquents—three basic body types:
      (i) The *endomorph*—having a predominance of visceral and fatty tissue.
      (ii) The *mesomorph*—having a predominance of muscle, bone, and connective tissue.
      (iii) The *ectomorph*—predominance of skin and nervous tissue.
   b. According to Sheldon, each body type is characterized by specific traits of temperament and personality.
      (i) *Endormorph*—fat (rolly-poly) and characterized as a slow-moving individual who is warm and affectionate.
         (a) Very gregarious, enjoys comfort, soft clothes, soft food, and soft, slow music.
         (b) When irritated or confronted with a problem, the *endomorph* seeks advice from a well-stocked refrigerator.
      (ii) *Mesomorph*—the muscular boy is characterized by loud speech and laughter; excessive vigorous discharge of physical energy.
         (a) He thrives on competition and communicates more favorably with people in physical competition.
         (b) Solutions to problems are found through physical activity regardless of whether such activity is of negative or positive behavior.
         (c) In examining delinquent boys in the Boston area, William Sheldon found that they tended to cluster in the mesomorph section of his typological triangle; that is, to be more physically aggressive, muscular, and physically stronger than average.
      (iii) *Ectomorph*—tall and lean type who appears to be a "bundle

[7] *Ibid.*, p. 62.

of nerves"; continually displaying short, quick, jerky movements, strained speech, and conservation of energy.

(a) Food is viewed as a necessary nuisance and little pleasure is found in meals. He is a shy individual who prefers silence and refrains from becoming involved in close relationships or competitive endeavors.

(b) Problems are solved by withdrawing and reflecting about it.

II. *The Psychological Approach*

A. Analyzes motivation and diagnoses personality deviations. This approach holds that inner tensions and emotions, unresolved conflicts, and unsatisfied needs of the individual underlie anti-social behavior. Psychology tends to stress the individual rather than the group. Psychological research has contributed chiefly facts concerning deprivations in human needs, desires and individual deviations in personality.

1. Sheldon and Eleanor Glueck

a. Concerned themselves with the personalities of delinquents and how they differed from those of non-delinquent.

(i) The Gluecks ascertained that delinquents are more extroverted, vivacious, impulsive and less self-controlled than the non-delinquents. They are less fearful of failure or defeat than the non-delinquents. Furthermore, the Gluecks found that delinquents are less concerned about meeting conventional expectations and are more ambivalent toward or far less submissive to authority. They are, as a group, more socially assertive. To a greater extent than the control group, they express feelings of not being recognized or appreciated.[8]

2. W. I. Thomas

a. Contents that the individual needs an adequate and wholesome outlet for the expression of his psychic drives and wishes; he requires, particularly, some satisfying implemention of his social drives or "wishes." Frustration of these basic, psychological demands or the impossibility of securing socialized satisfaction may channelize them into law-violating activity. Lack of affection and security easily leads to sexual delinquency, to theft, and incorrigible behavior in children.[9]

III. *The Psychiatric Approach*

A. Originally specialized in the diagnosis of mental illness. Increasingly, however, psychiatrists have extended their activity into the analysis of all degrees of personality deviation and even of normal behavior. One

[8] S. Glueck and E. Glueck, *Unraveling Juvenile Delinquency*, Commonwealth Fund, New York, 1950, p. 102.

[9] P. W. Tappan, *Juvenile Delinquency*, McGraw-Hill Book Co., New York, 1949, p. 105.

of the major assumptions of psychiatry is that the origin of behavior difficulties is to be found in emotional tensions originating early in life in conflicts in the family. Moreover, behavior patterns established then are thought of by the psychiatrist as relatively fixed and permanent.

1. Franz Alexander
   a. Defines anti-social behavior as "meaningful substitute behavior" growing out of an individual's conflicts and deep unconscious inner urges.[10]
      (i) The only difference between the criminal or delinquent and the normal individual, states Alexander, is that the normal man partially controls his criminal drives and finds outlets for them in socially harmless activities. This power of controlling and domestication of the primitive unsocial tendencies is acquired by the individual as a result of education. In other words, criminality, generally speaking, is not a congenital defect, but a defect in the bringing up.[11]

IV. *The Psychoanalytical Approach*

A. Traces behavior deviations to the repression of basic drives. This repression is occasioned by the mores or demands of civilized life and produces a conflict between the superego or conscience and the basic drives such as sex and hunger. Another conflict is between desire for success and limited life opportunities. The source of these mental conflicts is unknown to the victim. He seeks release from conflicts either by some mental substitute such as daydreaming and other flights from reality, or by overt compensatory behavior, which may be delinquent or criminal. Thus delinquent and criminal behavior is seen as an unconscious effort to solve an emotional problem.

1. Sigmund Freud
   a. The central core of ideas involves the notion of basic mental conflicts due to certain incompatible elements of the personality with the unacceptable portions repressed into the unconscious and kept there by the censor; a term used to describe the capacity to force unity and harmony into obvious and conscious personality by repressing the undesirable elements into the subconscious.
      (i) But the repressed ideas, impulses, or complexes continue to exist, even though put out of the conscious mind, and a considerable portion of ordinary mental activity consists of the "roundabout" ways in which the repressed elements of personality seek to evade or outwit the censor and achieve some sort of indirect expression. The three basic elements of the personality that must be brought into balance are the *id*, the *ego*, and the *superego*.
   b. Delinquent and criminal behavior, under this general theoretical

[10] G. B. Vold, *op. cit.*, p. 22.
[11] *Ibid.*, p. 125.

orientation, is to be understood, simply and directly, as a substitute response, some form of symbolic release of repressed complexes. The conflict in the unconscious mind gives rise to feelings of guilt and anxiety with a consequent desire for punishment to remove the guilt feelings and restore a proper balance of good against evil. The delinquent or criminal then commits the criminal act in order to be apprehended and punished.[12]

V. *The Ecological Approach*

A. Shows the influence of the spatial distribution of men and institutions upon behavior patterns.

1. Clifford Shaw

a. Shaw indicated on spot maps the home addresses of no less than 55,998 delinquents divided into eight groups, comprising juveniles, youthful felons, adults, and delinquents of both sexes. Data from as early as 1900 and as late as 1927 were included in his first study. Shaw found that delinquency was very unevenly distributed in the city of Chicago. For example, in 1926 some areas showed no complaints of juvenile delinquents by police or probation officers, while in one area 26.6 per cent of boys of juvenile court age had been involved in some type of act which resulted in complaints to the police in that single year.

(i) Shaw found that delinquency rates varied inversely with the distance from the Loop, except where outlying industrial areas increased the rates locally. Areas where delinquency was concentrated were found to be characterized by proximity to industry and commerce, physical deterioration, decreasing population in a period when the city as a whole was growing rapidly.

b. The major explanation of the concentration of delinquency was found to be in the deterioration of the neighborhood as an agency of social control. As the city grew and became industrialized, former residential areas were invaded by industry or commercial establishments. Population became mobile. People lost interest in the appearance and moral reputation of the neighborhod because their residence was shorter. Neighborliness declined.

(i) Immigrant groups brought conflicting patterns, and conflicts between the first and second generation multiplied. The neighborhood ceased to be a primary group defining behavior and regulating it in the interest of a common standard. It became indifferent. Hence, patterns differed widely, and criminal groups could exist side by side with noncriminal. Finally, a stage was reached in some areas where

[12] *Ibid.*, p. 119.

certain types of delinquency and crime were not considered to be inappropriate.[13]

2. Frederick Thrasher
   a. Frederick Thrasher's *The Gang* involves a study of 1,313 gangs in Chicago and indicates their concentration in a twilight zone of factories and railroads radiating from the central Loop district.
   b. According to Thrasher. "Gangland represents a geographically and socially interstitial area" between the Loop and the residential districts and in other midpositions. The concept of traditional or interstitial area was important, for it suggested that crime originates on the edges of civilization and respectability and in communities imperfectly adjusted to normal conditions.
      (i) Thrasher's work called attention to the appeal of the gang for adventurous recreation, to the gang's importance as a social group, to its cultivation of an intense spirit of loyalty, and to other qualities it possesses that have social values.[14]

VI. *The Social, Sociological, and Cultural Approach*
   A. *The Social Approach* includes consideration of educational, religious, recreational, occupational, and other factors.
   B. *The Sociological Approach* is concerned with the effects of group life, social attitudes, and group patterns of behavior, as well as the influence of social status, of the role of the individual plays and his conception of it, and of various other types of social institutions and relationships.
   C. *The Cultural Approach* considers the influence of various constitutions and social values that characterize groups and social disorganization. Culture is generally considered to be the sum total of the achievements of the group; sociologists and anthropologists use the cultural approach.
      1. Edwin H. Sutherland (differential association)
         a. A person becomes a delinquent because of an excess of definitions favorable to violation of law over definitions unfavorable to violation of law. When any person becomes criminal, he does so because of contacts with criminal patterns and also because of isolation from anti-criminal patterns. Any person inevitably assimilates the surrounding culture unless other patterns are in conflict.[15]
            (i) The hypothesis which is suggested here as a substitute for the conventional theories is that white collar criminality, just as other systematic criminality, is learned; that it is learned in direct or indirect association with those who already practice the behavior; and that those who learn this

[13]C. R. Shaw and H. D. McKay, *Juvenile Delinquency in Urban Areas,* University of Chicago Press, Chicago, 1942, p. 55.

[14]H. E. Barnes and N. K. Teeters, *op. cit.,* p. 155.

[15]H. E. Barnes and N. K. Teeters, *op. cit.,* p. 159.

criminal behavior are segregated from frequent and intimate contacts with law abiding behavior.

(ii) Whether a person becomes a criminal or not is determined largely by the comparative frequency and intimacy of his contacts with the two types of behavior.

(a) This may be called the process of *differential association*. It is a genetic explanation both of white-collar criminality and lower-class criminality.

(b) Those who become white-collar criminals generally start their careers in good neighborhoods and good homes, graduate from colleges with some idealism, and, with little selection on their part, get into particular business situations in which criminality is practically a folkway and are inducted into a system of behavior just as into any other folkway.

(c) The lower-class criminals generally start their careers in deteriorated neighborhoods and families, find delinquents at hand from whom they acquire the attitudes toward, and techniques of, crime through association with delinquents and in particular segregation from law-abiding people. The essentials are the same for the two classes of criminals. This is not entirely a process of assimilation, for inventions are frequently made, perhaps more frequently in white-collar crime than in lower-class crime. The inventive geniuses for lower-class criminals are generally professional criminals, while inventive geniuses for many kinds of white-collar crime are generally lawyers.

b. A second general process is social disorganization in the community. Differential association culminates in crime because the community is not organized solidly against that behavior. The law is pressing in one direction, the other forces are pressing in the opposite direction.

(i) In business, the "rules of the game" conflict with legal rules. A business man who wants to obey the law is driven by his competitors to adopt their methods. This is well illustrated by the persistence of commercial bribery in spite of the strenuous efforts of business organizations to eliminate it. Groups and individuals are individuated; they are more concerned with their specialized group or individual interests than with the larger welfare. Consequently, it is not possible for the community to present a solid front in opposition to crime.

(ii) The Better Business Bureaus and crime commissions, composed of business and professional men, attack burglary, robbery, and cheap swindles, but often overlook the crimes of their own members. The forces which infringe on the lower-class are similarily in conflict. Social disorganization affects the two classes in similar ways.

c. The factor or process which is here suggested hypothetically as the explanation of both upper-class and lower-class crime is that the criminal behavior is learned in direct and indirect association with persons who had practiced the same behavior previously and in relative isolation from those who opposed such behavior.
   (i) In both classes a person begins his career free from criminality, learns something about the legal code which prohibits certain kinds of behavior, and also learns in variant groups that other kinds of behavior which conflict with the general code may be practiced.
   (ii) Through contact with these variant cultures he learns techniques, rationalizations, and the specific drives and motives necessary for the successful accomplishment of crimes.
      (a) If he is reared in the lower socio-economic class, he learns the techniques, rationalizations, and drives to be used in petty larceny, burglary, and robbery; while if he is reared in the upper socio-economic class and engaged in an occupation of the kind characteristic of that class, he learns techniques, rationalizations, and drives to be used in frauds and false pretenses.
      (b) The process of acquiring criminal behavior is identical in the two situations, although the contents of the patterns which are transmitted in communities differ.[16]

2. Albert K. Cohen
   a. In his analysis of the culture of the gang, he sees much delinquency flowing from a sub-culture which persists primarily in urban areas, generation after generation. He maintains that most middle-class and working-class children grow up in "significantly different social worlds" and, due to difficulty experienced by working-class boys in measuring up to the conventional materialists' standards and socially acceptable behavior norms of conduct, they tend to engage in "negativistic" delinquency.[17]

SUMMARY

The theories briefly outlined above are at best only segmented and emphasize clearly that the answer to criminal behavior is too complex to be settled by the knowledge derived from one behaviorial discipline.

[16]W. C. Reckless, *The Crime Problem*, 2nd ed., Appleton-Century-Crofts, Inc., New York, 1955, p. 224–225.

[17]A. K. Cohen, *Delinquent Boys: The Culture of the Gang*, Free Press, Glencoe, Illinois, 1955, p. 25.

Criminology presents no final conclusions today. We do not yet know all the reasons why men commit crimes. Because of this inadequacy of knowledge, each specialist tends to formulate his theory in terms of his own experiences.

The general trend in criminological research is, and has been, toward an eclectic theory—a processual analysis, if you will—which is the only sound approach to a defiant puzzle like crime causation. Some years ago Enrico Ferri, the distinguished criminologist, wrote concerning criminal causation:[18]

> "Crime is the result of manifold causes, which, although found always linked into an intricate network, can be detected, however, by means of careful study. The factors of crime can be divided into individual or anthropological, physical or natural, and social. The anthropological factors comprise of age, sex, civil status, profession, domicile, social rank, instruction, education, and the organic and psychic constitution. The physical factors are: race, climate, the fertility and disposition of the soil, the relative length of day and night, the seasons, meteoric conditions, and temperature. The social factors comprise density of population, emigration, public opinion, customs and religion, economic and industrial conditions, agriculture and industrial production, public administration of public safety, public instruction and education, public beneficence, and in general civil and penal legislation.
>
> "To these factors we could add many others without ever exhausting the supply, since they include all that the Universe contains, not omitting a word or a gesture. What we must add, however, is the fact that as a whole they determine the 'law of criminal saturation': Just as in a given volume of water, at a given temperature, we find the solution of a fixed quantity of any chemical substance, not an atom more or less, so in a given, social environment, in certain defined physical conditions of the individual, we find the commission of a fixed number of crimes."

Hitherto, the fund of possible explanations invoked, by the criminologist has been much too narrow. Ordinarily, he is content to trace it to but four or five all-powerful causes—sometimes, indeed, to no more than one. Drink, epilepsy, a defective moral sense, some outstanding feature of heredity, or some characteristic of city life, is seized upon in isolation, and made accountable for all. With the same exclusive emphasis, some solitary panacea has correspondingly been put forward. It is as if we should explain the Amazon in its flood by pointing to a rivulet in the distant Andes, which as the tributory that is farthest from the final outflow, has the honor of being called the source. Dry up the rill, and the river still flows on. Its tributories are countless, though all stream into one sea.[19]

[18]H. E. Barnes and N. K. Teeters, *op. cit.*, p. 207.
[19]*Ibid.*, p. 207.

No single theory, therefore, should be expected to provide the explanations for the many varieties of behavior involved. Research of the future may be expected to become more seriously concerned with establishing meaningful, functionally operative typologies. Then the methods and procedures applied to one type of criminal behavior problem would be recognized as of only limited applicability to other kinds of problems. Thus, for example, the exhaustive attention given in the past to establishing individual differences in traits and characteristics of criminals and delinquents will be recognized as appropriate for only certain, specific kinds of problems or situations. Other problems and situations will need to develop other techniques and methods, different from those utilized in the analysis of the individual.[20]

It must be abundantly clear from this discussion that explanations of why crime occurs are both varied and contradictory. It has appeared that crime is a varied phenomenon that may be approached from many points of view. Each particular "theory" represents primarily a possible approach and reflects some special point of view rather than any full-blown unitary accounting for all crime in all societies for all times. Even as there is no generally satisfactory or completely adequate theory of human behavior in general, so there is no entirely adequate or generally accepted theory of criminal behavior.

QUESTIONS

1. Discuss the *Sociological (social) factors.*
2. Discuss the *Psychological factors.*
3. Discuss the *Physiological (biological) factors.*
4. *True* or *False* . . . Franz Alexander, utilizing the anthropological approach, attempted to discover whether the criminal was significantly different in his physical structure from the non-criminal.
5. *True* or *False* . . . Earnest Hootan, in his theory, contended that criminals are organically inferior.
6. *True* or *False* . . . Sheldon and Eleanor Glueck concerned themselves with the psychological approach and to personalities of delinquents.
7. Discuss William H. Sheldon's theory.
8. Discuss the social, sociological, and cultural approach–i.e., Edwin H. Sutherland's Differential Association.
9. The general trend in criminological research is, and has been, toward an eclectic theory. Why?
10. Indicate the theoretical approach which you find the most valid and cite reasons why.

[20]G. B. Vold, *op. cit.*, p. 314.

Chapter 7

Police Services for Juveniles[1]

THE PRIMARY RESPONSIBILITY of law enforcement is the control and prevention of crime and delinquency through the enforcement of laws defining conduct considered detrimental to the good order of society. Since many criminal acts are committed by minors under the age of 18 years, a large proportion of police work involves the detection, investigation, apprehension, and referral of these juveniles. In addition, law enforcement agencies are concerned with minors who come to their attention for non-criminal reasons. The initial handling of neglected children, for example, is often a police matter; and peace officers also have the responsibility of dealing with runaway, incorrigible, and wayward youngsters.

Law enforcement officials have always been concerned with the control of juvenile crime; however, within the last two decades, police organizations began placing particular emphasis on their work with juveniles, and a definite trend in the development of specialized juvenile police services has been established. While the growth of the delinquency programs throughout the nation contributed to the increased emphasis on juvenile police work, other factors were probably equally responsible. The policeman who walked a beat 30 years ago had a greater opportunity to know more intimately the inhabitants and social institutions in the area he patrolled and could easily resolve minor law enforcement problems, but the replacement of the foot officer by motorized patrol units reduced personal contact between the police and the inhabitants of their areas.

At the same time, within the last several decades, there has been an apparent decrease in the effectiveness of family controls. As a result, police and other public agencies have been compelled to assume greater

[1]Much of the material in this chapter and Chapter 8 appears in *Police Services for Juveniles*, Department of Health, Education, and Welfare, Children's Bureau, Washington, D.C., 1954.

responsibility in containing juvenile anti-social behavior. Public demand for more activity in the field of juvenile control, and a growing realization that apprehension and punishment alone are not sufficient to stand the tide of delinquency, also contributed to the increasing emphasis on juvenile policework.

The Awareness of the Police

Law-enforcement officers, although generally aware of the primary factors which go to produce criminal behavior, are not basically concerned with the "why" of human behavior. They are employed, trained, and directed to find the answers of *"what, how, when, who, and where." The police officer must fruitfully use the analysis of motive and the causation as an investigative aid in his search for the perpetrator of a crime; however, his immediate primary goal is to detect, identify, and apprehend the individual.*[2] It is incumbent upon the police administrator to expend his efforts and his resources as effectively as possible so as to minimize the opportunities for crime. The "problem" of delinquency for the police administrator is not one of probing the philosophical and political roots of our social and economic systems. Nor is it the police administrator's obligation to engage in the longitudinal or cross-sectional psychological evaluations of the delinquent. The American citizen, by and large, has not indicated that the police should do more than protect their persons and their property. The concept of the thief-catcher remains. It has been solely through the works of the police officers themselves that duties beyond the traditional ones have been adopted—despite the public.

It is clear that the law-enforcement arm of our various governmental executives has been developed to protect the community by reducing the opportunity for criminal behavior. The job has been made more difficult because of the vast social changes during the past half century. Changes such as population density, mobility, social deprivation, communication media bombardment with status-oriented advertising, and other social innovations have increased both the desires and the opportunities for crime.

Police Techniques Versus Delinquency

The juvenile delinquency problem confronting every law-enforcement agency consists primarily of the need to develop and apply pro-

[2]G. W. O'Connor and N. A. Watson, *Juvenile Delinquency and Youth Crime; The Police Role,* International Association of Chiefs of Police, Washington, D.C., 1964, p. 17.

cedures for dealing with youths which reflect an awareness of, and an appreciation for, the unique legal system which is invoked. Realistically, police officers gather information from persons and from things in every criminal case which they handle. *The techniques for such processes are not amenable to variations according to age of the suspect; therefore, in the area of routine crime investigation, few if any differences are noted between cases involving adult suspects and those involving youths.*[3]

Although the investigative techniques pertaining to juveniles and adults are quite similar, there are psychological and legal theoretical concepts which dictate the need for diversity of action in the areas of case preparation, disposition, and prevention.

The diversity of action, however, occurs only after the identity of the suspect has been determined. Once the age of the suspect has been determined, the application of different techniques is appropriate. The changes in procedure are dictated primarily by statute and the local juvenile court. The rules against photographing, fingerprinting, and record-keeping do not originate from within the police establishment. Such departmental orders as exist simply translate legal dicta into terms appropriate to departmental procedures. Although the factors which affect the juvenile, and which may be said to be causes of his delinquent behavior, are not unlike those which affect the adult, society has said quite loudly and clearly that children are not to be held criminally responsible for their acts. Society is of the opinion, and rightfully so, that the chances of redirecting a wayward youth are greater—because of his flexible nature and changing personality structure—than are those of changing an adult who has become more established in his ways.

Another concept which directs law-enforcement agencies into dealing with youth is the one which holds that juveniles do not understand and have not internalized the social, moral, and legal codes of our culture. Obviously, the use of chronological age as the basis of defining criminal responsibility is unreal although easily administered. However, the statutes in all states utilize chronological age and law-enforcement agencies have no alternative but to adhere to the juvenile court law. The fallacies of such a procedure are clearly recognized by individual officers and this recognition produces a reaction against the system of juvenile justice which spreads and tends to create dissatisfaction.

[3]*Ibid.*, p. 17.

IMPORTANCE OF POLICE ROLE

What should a police officer do with a child he has taken into custody for committing a delinquent act?

What action should an officer take when his attention is called to a child who is suffering from neglect or abuse?

What exactly is the role to be played by the police officer in a community's program to control juvenile delinquency and to protect and further the welfare of young people?

These are important questions for citizens and law-enforcement officers concerned with the problems of youth. Their importance is readily understood. Every day the police have contact with large numbers of children. In the case of each of these meetings, the police officer's behavior may have a far-reaching effect, for good or bad, upon the youngster's response to authority and to the efforts made to help him. The police-juvenile relationship is evidently a matter that requires careful consideration and planning in every community.

Primary among the factors affecting police services for juveniles in any community is the authority the police force has over juveniles, and also the functions assumed by the police department in regard to juveniles.

The extent of local police authority and responsibility, and the manner in which local forces exercise them, depend on both the particular powers given a local police force by law, and as affected by judicial interpretation, and on the limitations provided for by law. The attitude and policy of the department head may also have an effect to some degree. As a result of these variables, the number and types of functions carried out by the police department in one community may exceed, or differ from, those undertaken in another.

Two functions, however, are the main concern of all police departments. Stemming directly from the customary legislative mandate that the police shall be responsible for the protection of life and property and for the maintenance of law and order, these functions apply to juveniles and adults alike. They are:

1. *Control of Crime and violations of the law.* This includes apprehension and referral for prosecution, or other appropriate action, of persons who have committed crimes or other offenses.
2. *Enforcement of regulations.* This means enforcement of a vast number of restrictions imposed by law on people's day-to-day activities for the purpose of protecting the safety and rights of the general public. Traffic regulations are examples of such restrictions.

A *third function*, accepted by the police in many places, is the rendering of general assistance in a variety of cases having little relation to crime control or regulation. Some examples of these forms of assistance are: helping to locate lost or runaway children, searching for lost property and maintaining service for restoring to rightful owners lost property which has been found, and aiding persons locked out of their homes. These duties the police have accepted largely as a matter of custom.

So far as juveniles are concerned, the developments mentioned in practice apply principally to known or suspected delinquents, or to children who are neglected. Police interest in juveniles has not been limited, however, to those already in need. A *fourth* function, now engaged in by many police departments to varying degrees, is the prevention of delinquency and crime. Thus we find that in many communities the police act to prevent delinquency by enforcing laws, ordinances, or regulations. Quite frequently, too, it is the policy of the police to act protectively toward children who are found wandering the streets late at night, or under circumstances that might be harmful to them. In these cases, the police return the child to his home and possibly counsel the parents or guardian on the need to give more supervisory care.

In addition to pursuing these more or less customary preventive activities, some police departments have now extended their work to include recreation and character-building programs, safety-education programs, and counseling service. The counseling service is directed toward children and young people who have come to the attention of the police because of behavior which suggests that they are particularly vulnerable to delinquency.

A considerable number of communities have made definite progress toward giving sharper definition to what police service for juveniles should be and how this should be carried out. To summarize some of these local developments, many police departments are now giving greater attention to training their officers in those modern concepts of law enforcement that emphasize protection, treatment, and rehabilitation of the child. In many places, officers have been appointed to work especially with children. In a considerable number of communities, special units or divisions have been established to carry on the work with juveniles. Special procedures have likewise been devised that are aimed at contributing to rehabilitation, and, at the same time, sparing the juvenile wrong-doer the public exposure and shame so often visited upon the adult. Finally, in those communities that have given particular attention to the problem of young people, the relation of the police to other community agencies has been strengthened and clarified, so that the police have a better understanding of what can, and should be, done for children through the use of other resources in the community.

Naturally, some of these activities of the police in regard to children, and particularly the "preventive" activities, have not gone unquestioned. For example, the issue has been raised by many citizens and by some police officers themselves as to whether programs involving such matters as recreation and unofficial probation are not beyond the proper scope of police work and more the obligation of other agencies. Also, in regard to procedures affecting known delinquents, the opinion has been expressed in some quarters that the police should simply turn all children directly over to the juvenile court authorities, without undertaking further service for them.[4]

In every community, then, police services for juveniles depend on the functions assigned to, or assumed by, the police department and on how these functions are carried out. One of the chief aims in the rest of this chapter will be to outline various types of practice in regard to these functions so far as they affect children; to offer opinion as to how certain of the functions might best be carried out, and to help determine whether in certain instances a particular function is a proper concern of the police.

Juveniles and Police Philosophy

Nowhere in police philosophy is there anything about punishment by the police. Nowhere is there anything about rehabilitation or reforming the offender. These are not police functions. Moreover, nowhere is there anything specific about juveniles in this philosophy. *Juveniles are not exempt from the enforcement of the law.* They must be held to answer for their wrongs against society. Tender years, immaturity, irresponsibility are not *excuses* for theft, vandalism, or violence. The fact that a person is an adult does not permit police always to use force in arresting him; nor does the fact that one is a juvenile, per se, require that no force be used. What is unnecessary or excessive force is determined by the extent of the circumstances, of which age is but one factor. This is not to say that there are no differences in handling juveniles and adults. However, insofar as the realization of basic objectives is concerned—the vigorous and successful completion of the job given the police by society—there are no fundamental philosophical or policy differences. There are adaptations of the philosophical con-

[4]*Police Services for Juveniles,* Children's Bureau, Department of Health, Education, and Welfare, Washington, D.C., 1954, p. 3.

cepts which, while they do not in any way modify the basic objectives, result in procedural differences in the handling of juveniles as compared to adults.[5]

This is not to say that the law-enforcement agencies throughout the nation are not concerned about rehabilitation. The police department, of course, subscribes to the public policy generally throughout the nation which dictates that the primary objective of programs for dealing with juvenile delinquents and youthful criminals is rehabilitation; law-enforcement programs, practices, and procedures are devised to implement that policy.

The objective sought by the police in handling juvenile offenders, then, even those guilty of serious crimes, is protection and rehabilitation. To this end, the police are willing and anxious to cooperate with other community agencies, both public and private. Stark realism based upon first-hand experience impels police agencies to assert that there are some young people who prove to be incorrigible and irrevocably committed to criminal ways. It must be admitted, however, that it is impossible to tell in advance which ones there are. Therefore, the arresting officer must so conduct himself in all cases as to promote and encourage reform, and nothing must be done that would tend to cause a juvenile to continue his criminal behavior.[6]

INVESTIGATION OF JUVENILE OFFENSES

All juvenile offenses should be as thoroughly and completely investigated as possible. Some police officers are said to show a tendency to neglect certain facts in the investigation of juvenile offenses on the assumption that the juvenile court does not need or require detailed facts and evidence. This assumption is not correct. *Full information concerning the case is always needed to sustain petitions.*

The techniques utilized in the investigation of offenses will be those developed by police science, as taught in the best police academies and treated in standard texts on police investigation. A discussion of such techniques is beyond the scope of this chapter.

In addition to investigating the facts surrounding the offense, a police officer working on a juvenile case very often needs to secure information about the child himself. He must be concerned with the offender as well as the offense.

The conditions under which a child may be taken into custody will generally be found in a state's juvenile court law.

[5]O'Connor and Watson, *op. cit.*, p. 33.
[6]*Ibid.*, p. 34.

Many state juvenile court laws contain the provision that "any child found violating any law or ordinance, or whose surroundings are such as to endanger his welfare, may be taken into custody without a warrant."

This particular provision pertaining to apprehension without warrant, as quoted from the *Standard Juvenile Act*, is certainly broad enough to meet all practical contingencies.

Only a relatively small proportion of the total number of delinquent children with whom the police have contact need to be taken into custody. The majority of this group give the police no particular trouble other than concern for their welfare and where they can best be held. But there is a small group of adolescent delinquents—generally to be found in the upper-age limits of the juvenile court jurisdiction—whose behavior can give the police a great deal of trouble and make the process of taking them into custody a serious matter.

The question may arise: What is the matter with the word, *arrest*? Why "take into custody"? This change in language reflects a change in concept that may be embodied in the statutes in order to carry out the intent of the juvenile court laws. Practically all such laws state that the adjudication of a child as a delinquent is not a criminal conviction. It is intended that even the adjudicated delinquent should enter adulthood with a clean slate. At the present time, however, a person is obligated to reply *yes* to the question, "have you ever been arrested?" if he was ever "arrested" by a police officer as a juvenile. This has sometimes had unfortunate consequences for the person when he is applying for a certain kind of employment, trying to enter the armed forces, or in other such circumstances. Therefore, statutes covering juveniles should clearly state that a juvenile is not "arrested," but is "taken into custody."

The change in language suggested does not mean, however, that a police officer should not have the same protection when taking a child into custody as he has in the case of arresting an adult. Laws to use reasonable force should be granted the officer in "taking into custody" just as it is in "arresting."

If a child is taken into custody, it should be the duty of the police officer to locate the parents or guardian or custodian of the child as soon as possible thereafter. For this purpose, and this alone, the child may be held by the police temporarily.

Whenever possible, the officer should then return the child to his parents, with a notice to them that the child's and their presence may be required by the juvenile probation department. However, if the parents cannot be found within a reasonable period of time, or if after consulting with the parents, the officer is of the opinion that the interests of the child or the safety of the community warrant the child's detention, the child should be taken to the place of detention or shelter designated by the court in accordance with agreed written procedures.

Degree of Proof

When juvenile courts were originally established in this country, the intent of the founders was to create a clear break from the traditional criminal court trial procedure. Juvenile court proceedings were marked by a degree of informality which made it readily apparent that the concern of the court was for the welfare of the child. Rules of evidence and the need for obtaining counsel, as are normally found in the adversary hearings of criminal courts were minimized in order to accomplish the effect of a treatment-oriented hearing. The variations between juvenile and adult courts have been such that many police officers have expressed dissatisfaction with what they felt was a lack of concern for the facts of the incident. Such dissatisfaction has not been justified in all jurisdictions. The juvenile court has virtually restricted its concern to the offender, whereas the adult court is mainly concerned with the offense. In keeping with the juvenile court philosophy, such restriction pertaining to concern with the offender was thought to be a necessary procedure.[7]

However, in recent years, greater and greater attention has been directed to the apparent disregard of the constitutional rights of the youth appearing before the juvenile court. As a result, it seems that many courts are gradually restoring the various procedures and safeguards of the traditional criminal court hearing. Counsel for the defense are not uncommon today in juvenile court cases.

Sensitivity to rules of evidence, issues, and facts of the case in adversary hearings in juvenile court cases are becoming more predominant and the nonadversary atmosphere which once prevailed is quickly disappearing. From the viewpoint of the police, the juvenile court hearing should remain informal so long as that hearing can adequately establish the fact that the youth did, in fact, commit the offense for which he was taken into custody. This particular view advocates that the juvenile court hearing should first establish the minor's involvement in the particular offense, and then specify the corrective action appropriate for the individual. It is felt that probation services or treatment must not be ordered for youths who have not been adjudged delinquent on the basis of demonstrable evidence.

[7]*Ibid.*, p. 53.

The procedures which a police agency follows in gathering evidence of an offense involving a juvenile should be *identical* with those used in the investigation of *cases involving adult suspects.* The degree of proof required is no less for juveniles than for adults, and every care must be exercised to assure the rights of the child as those rights serve to protect him from unwarranted treatment or correction.[8]

Methods of Interview

Undoubtedly the most important means that the police officer has for carrying out his investigation is *interviewing.* This method of investigation is used not only in dealing with the child himself, but also in securing information from parents, witnesses, complainants, correctional workers, educators, and other interested persons. Interviewing is particularly important because it involves close personal contact between the police officer and these various people. The reputation of the department, as well as the effectiveness of the police officer's work, may depend on how well he conducts interviews.[9]

The aim of the police officer in interviews is to learn as much as possible about the facts of the offense and, when appropriate, about the child who is believed to have committed the offense—all knowledge that will help him to dispose of the case in the best interests of the community and the child.

It should be pointed out that interviewing methods will vary from case to case. *Interviewing methods found suitable for a sophisticated 17-year-old delinquent experienced in assault, robbery, or rape will not be the same as those utilized with an 11-year-old boy caught stealing fruit from a vendor's wagon.*

Officers must become adept in the art of interviewing if they are to succeed in solving cases. There has been much concern expressed in various quarters about police methods of interrogation. The official policy of the I.A.C.P. (International Association of Chiefs of Police) condemns the use of so-called "third degree" methods and denial of the fundamental rights of any person. Every enlightened and experienced executive knows that "third degree" or "star-chamber" procedures are not only fundamentally wrong, but also self defeating. Increasing proportions of police training time are devoted to the "rights" question and police are sensitive to it.

With specific reference to questioning suspects in criminal cases, there are several restrictions which have been placed on police in this vitally important area. Whether these restrictions are safeguards against

[8] *Ibid.*, p. 54.
[9] *Police Services for Juveniles, op. cit.*, p. 11.

the "overzealousness" with which some critics charge the police, or whether they are a well-meaning, but unrealistic erosion of necessary police authority is still a moot question. The practical result is a serious curtailment of the effectiveness of interrogation as a police technique in many cases, especially with suspects who are, in fact, guilty and who have learned to rely upon these restrictions for protection from punishment. In many cases the police cannot prove guilt through physical evidence, such as fingerprints, or through witnesses simply because there are none. Under these circumstances, it is necessary to question the suspect and to check out what he says. His alibi and any discrepancies in his answers may be the only sources of proof of guilt short of a confession. If he cannot be interviewed adequately, even this source of proof is cut off. Moreover, if he is innocent, he is denied opportunity to prove it without being formally charged. It is the people and not the police who are the ultimate victims of this system. Police do not seek the privilege of denying suspects their rights, but they do feel that some realistic balance between rights and cooperative responsibilities must be achieved in the public interest.

On numerous occasions, police officers have been confronted with comments from juveniles, such as "You can't do anything to me, I'm a juvenile." These youngsters usually have arrived at the point where they are above the average delinquent and cannot be considered as still in that category. These sophisticated delinquents "have been through the mill," either in person or vicariously with friends, and are cognizant of the fact that they cannot be held by the police. Furthermore, such youngsters are often of the opinion that if they do go to court, nothing very drastic will occur. Carrying this one step further, many of these youngsters seemingly are not concerned about probation, feeling that it is quite painless. Some of them are well educated by their peers and others on how to thwart the machinery of justice and "come out relatively unscarred." Only the naive would describe these children as "unfortunate youngsters who have made *one* mistake" just because of the innocence of immaturity.

Swinging the pendulum in the other direction, there are many juveniles who are genuinely concerned by their first confrontation with the law and are sorry for what they have done. These youngsters are usually amenable to correction through some counseling and can usually be redirected with good prospects for future acceptable behavior.

The policeman meets all kinds, from the scared youngster to the big, arrogant bully. Sometimes the officer does not know what he has until he gets the person under control and asks a few questions. In fact, occasionally he does not know that the boy is a juvenile until subsequent investigation discloses that information.

Police experience reveals that, on the whole, questioning juveniles is easier and more productive of the true facts in a shorter period of time than questioning adults. This does not mean that juveniles are necessarily more cooperative than adult offenders; it means that they are less resistive. Police recognize that the greater suggestibility and pliability of youths mandate certain self-imposed restraints in questioning them. The standard interview prohibits making promises and threats. *Abusive language, epithets, sarcasm,* and *harsh tones* are no more justified (and no more useful) then physical punishment. Excessively prolonged interrogation of the juvenile is likewise contrary to proper police practice.

The interrogation should be so constructed that all possible relevant facts bearing on the incident may be obtained, whether leading to the establishment of responsibility of the alleged offender, or favoring his innocence, or minimizing his participation. It must be borne in mind that such information and any discrepancies noted are ultimately to be included in the report to the court, and will serve as a guide to the probation department in preparation for a court appearance.

Interviews with the youth, if conducted properly, can be and often are of value in relieving him of tension, apprehension, and guilt feelings and in preparing him for the probation and court process. If the minor's confidence is gained, much can be learned about the offense in question and his relationship with his parents and other members of the family and their attitude toward him. An attitude of understanding by the investigating officer, rather than one of sitting in judgment, is essential toward the successful development of the investigative process.

Questioning regarding misconduct often presents the investigating officer with the problem of how far the procedure should be carried in obtaining a complete story. The welfare of the minor and the plan for assistance in his problems demand that, insofar as possible, there should be revealed all past and current misconduct, even if the other of his associates are implicated through his disclosure. An adjustment is difficult and often impossible for the minor who leaves a juvenile court hearing carrying on his conscience other offenses which may continue to trouble him. The possibility always exists that, at sometime in the future, these misdeeds may be disclosed by others and may result in his arrest and further hearing. On occasion, also, the subject may reveal during the court hearing facts withheld from the arresting officer or the juvenile probation officer, thus causing confusion or delay in the disposition.

Because there are instances in which the offender changes his story to minimize his misconduct during the court hearing, or because he or his parents decide to offer a contest, it is essential that the investigating police officer take utmost care in constructing an intelligent, readable offense report. If possible, statements by the minor should be included in the offense report. This will ensure that the juvenile probation officer assigned to the minor's case will be properly prepared to testify in court.

There are certain attitudes and types of behavior which every police officer should avoid in interviewing, since they destroy respect for law enforcement and accomplish no good whatsoever. These can be listed as: *(1) using profanity or obscenity; (2) branding the children with such epithets as "thief," "liar," or "tramp"; (3) losing temper; (4) telling falsehoods; (5) using physical force; and (6) making promises that cannot be kept.*

Here are a number of other approaches that have been found useful by police officers in their dealings with the large majority of young people with whom they have contact, and with their parents.

All necessary information should be obtained with tact and patience. A certain amount of resistance is to be expected. The child should be encouraged to tell his own story, and it is always wise for the police officer to obtain as much information as he can about the offense prior to his interview. If the child's story differs considerably from the known facts, he should not be accused of lying, but should be given a chance to review what he has said and thereby "save face." Some young people respond more freely if given a chance to write down their story.

The officer should put his questions in simple language, being sure that the child understands clearly what is asked. It is better if questions are phrased in a manner which encourages more than a mere *yes* or *no* answer.

After the facts about the particular offense have been cleared up, an encouraging reminder that it is best to clean the slate for a new start may lead the child to tell about other offenses which he has committed. It often helps a juvenile delinquent to know that the police are not shocked by the facts of law violations and that they understand why people violate laws.

When the police officer feels that a more inclusive investigation is called for, he should attempt to make the youngster feel that he really wants to help him. The child who violates the law is generally the child with problems. This may be the first opportunity he has ever had to talk about his troubles. The police officer should attempt to cover the various phases of adjustment—in the home, at school, and in the community. It is important in such discussions that the police officer be tolerant of any strong feelings the child may express about his parents, teachers, or other persons in authority.

A single interview may close a case; in fact, it generally does. Therefore, some consideration should be given here to the use of the interview for disposition, though the general topic of disposition is treated more fully later in this chapter.

If referral is made to another agency, the agency's methods, procedures, and services should be explained in an understandable manner. Whether it is a casework agency, a detention home, the juvenile court, or a probation department, an explanation will help prepare the child for new relationships and thus contribute to their effectiveness. Whatever the disposition, the reasons for it should be explained, and the fact that the plan was arrived at for the welfare of the child and the community should be emphasized.

Setting for the Interview

The setting for an interview can often be the determining factor in the solution of a case.[10] The location of the interview will necessarily depend on the seriousness of the offense, the age of the juvenile, the time of day, and other such factors. Younger children should ordinarily be interviewed in their own homes. The following conditions have been found to increase the effectiveness of office interviews:[11]

1. *Privacy, so that there will be no unnecessary interruptions.*
2. *Proper light and temperature for comfort.*
3. *Furnishings consisting of only the necessary chairs and desk without distracting extraneous items, not even a telephone.*
4. *Location of the office apart from other departmental units.*
5. *Provisions for satisfying the child's needs for food, drink, or clothing, and so on, prior to the interview.*

When interviewing in schools, welfare offices, or other neighborhood facilities, the investigating officer should take particular care to ensure privacy in the interview, and the police officer concerned should be in plain clothes.

The presence of other persons during the police interview with a child may be of particular importance in certain cases. The following material, extracted from new standards for specialized courts, prepared

[10]*Ibid.*, p. 11.
[11]*Ibid.*, p. 12.

by the Children's Bureau, in cooperation with the National Probation and Parole Association and the National Council of Juvenile Court Judges, is submitted here for its relevance to this question:[12]

> "A police officer's interview with a child in the course of an investigation into the commission of a delinquent act differs markedly from an investigation with respect to an adult suspected of committing a crime, in that, because of the child's presumed immaturity, special safeguards should be thrown around the interview. It must be remembered that in certain situations, dependent upon the age of the child and the act committed, waiver to criminal court may be a possibility. Therefore, at the end of the interview it is not known whether or not the court specializing in children's cases will retain jurisdiction over the case if a petition is filed, or will waive its jurisdiction and permit the child to be tried in criminal court. It cannot always be assumed, therefore, that the police interview can lead only to a non-criminal proceeding."

Therefore, whenever possible, and especially in the case of younger children, police interviews with juveniles should be conducted in such a manner as to protect the rights and best interests of the minor. The interview should take place in the presence of the parents or guardian of the minor, except when the parents or their presence would interfere with the officer's duty to obtain the facts surrounding the alleged offense, or where the parents or guardian have themselves participated in or contributed to the conduct of the minor being investigated. It is the police officer's duty to protect the guaranty of rights and best interests of the minor, but it is also his duty to learn the truth. There may well be instances in which the presence of the parents will tend to "block" or impede the investigation; in such cases the officer may refuse the parents the right to be present at the interview. The officer, however, must always remember that he may be charged with having obtained a statement from a minor by means of duress or by the infringement of the minor's guaranteed rights.

Various reactions pertaining to methods of interviewing juveniles by law-enforcement officers show that this is a subject that needs further consideration and is beyond the scope of this chapter. However, in reviewing various policy guides of law enforcement agencies throughout the country, the following should be stressed when interviewing juveniles:[13]

1. During the interrogation, whether of juveniles or adults, officers must scrupulously avoid practices which would make it likely that an innocent person would confess.

[12]*Ibid.*, p. 22.
[13]*Ibid.*, p. 23.

2. During the interrogation, as in all police procedures, officers must be sensitive to, and have respect for, the basic legal as well as human rights of all persons, adults and juveniles alike.
3. In questioning juveniles, harsh, abusive language, epithets, profanity, and other vulgarities must never be used.
4. Police should always give consideration to having the parents present during the investigative interrogation and to the advisability of conducting such interviews in the home, but the decisions in these matters are to be made by the police, in light of the totality of the circumstances in each specific case.
5. Initial interrogation of juveniles should be done by the uniformed patrolman who makes the original contact to the same extent that he would question an adult. Follow-up investigation, including interrogation, should be handled by the detectives or juvenile officers, depending on the department's organization.

FACTORS IN TOTAL INVESTIGATION

It must be recognized that it is not the function of police officers to do case work and that they do not make comprehensive case studies. The social information they do secure must be limited to that needed for a general understanding of a youngster's situation so that he may be referred to the proper source for help. In other words, getting this information is part of a screening process to determine whether the child should be: *(a) returned or left at home without other action; (b) referred to a health, welfare, educational, or recreational agency;* or *(c) referred to the juvenile court.*

As a practical matter, whether the officer should secure additional social information, as well as the extent of such information, depends primarily on the seriousness of the offense, and the child's past offenses, if any. Children who are allegedly implicated in serious offenses, or who are known to be chronic offenders, should be referred to the juvenile court upon being taken into custody. In such instances, there would be no need for gathering social information. The probation department would make its own thorough social study.

In instances in which a child denies participation in a delinquent act, the officer should not make an attempt to secure social information from persons other than the child or his family. It does not seem fair to mark a juvenile as a delinquent when his delinquency has not been established. *In any case in which the child denies participation and the officer believes that: (a) the act is serious enough to warrant action; and (b) there is sufficient evidence for referral to court, the child should be referred to the court immediately.*

In addition to the two categories of cases described above, there is a third category in which the officer would probably not wish to gather social data. They are the cases involving minor offenses or non-serious first offenses that demand minimum police activity and usually lead simply to the release of the child to his parents.

The following are circumstances in which the investigating officers should obtain only such social information about the child, that is in addition to the facts about the offense, as would be necessary "to determine whether the child needs to be referred to the court":

1. When the act, if committed by an adult, is a felony.
2. When the act is a minor offense, but the child has committed previous offenses that establish a pattern.
3. When the act is a single minor offense, but the child's reactions to the act and other associated factors clearly indicate that he requires the assistance of the court.
4. When a child denies the act, but there is probably cause for the officer to believe that he may have committed the act, notwithstanding the denial.

The cases calling for gathering of more extensive information by the police are generally those that fall between the extremes of serious and minor cases, or of a long pattern of offenses and a first offense. These are borderline cases. They require study by the police officer before he can decide what is the best disposition. The study should be concerned with the adjustment of the child within his family, at school, and within the community.

In studying the juvenile's place within the family, an effort should be made to reveal both the positive and negative factors. Appraisal of the parents' ability to handle the situation without the help of a community agency is of particular importance.

Unsatisfying experiences at school may lead to delinquent behavior. On the other hand, poor adjustment in school may indicate the presence of other serious difficulties for the child. It is desirable, therefore, to have the child's opinion of his school adjustment and information from the school showing their opinion of the child. Information that a police officer would obtain from school officials might include the child's school achievement, his classroom behavior, and his attendance record.

In a number of instances, then, the police officer must undertake the full investigation of a case. The following are suggested as factors that should be included in such an investigation:

Circumstances of the offense, including all details necessary to sustain a petition in court.

Record of any previous police action.

Record of any previous court or social agency action.

Attitudes of the child, his parents, and the complaint in the offense toward the act.

Adjustment of the child at home, at school, and in the community.

Any variety of methods is used by the police agencies in reporting the offenses to and communicating with the probation department. Generally, in delivering a minor to the department, they submit a cursory report, providing essential details, and follow up a day or two later with a full written report. Some agencies send juvenile officers to complete the investigation, and they then report orally to the investigating probation officer.

The quality and completeness of work by the police on a given case varies from excellent and complete to sketchy and inadequate. How adequate the work may be depends on the talent and the number of personnel in a given department, on its policies, and the volume of work at a given time. The existence of a police juvenile bureau charged with exclusive responsibility for investigation of all juvenile offenders is important to this question.

In any event, there inevitably will remain the deputy probation officer's responsibility of substantial inquiry as to the offense, ranging from interviewing the minor and his parents, to seeking and interviewing witnesses. This should not be construed, however, as meaning that the deputy investigating the case will spend a significant amount of time in the field doing work that is essentially police investigation.

GUIDELINES FOR POLICE DISPOSITION

After a police officer has made a thorough investigation of a delinquency case, he is ready to make a choice of disposition. But it must be recognized that an officer does not always have complete freedom of choice in this matter. His course of action may be more or less dictated by law, the policies of the police department itself, the extent of community services available, and the policies of agencies offering the services. However, with all these possible limitations, he still has considerable latitude and, accordingly, considerable responsibility.

The following are some of the ways in which an officer may dispose of a delinquency case. What each *has* to be, or *might* appropriately be chosen as the disposition is discussed, as well as what such disposition involves.

Referral to the Juvenile Court

The criteria for referral to the juvenile court are as follows:[14]

1. The particular offense committed by the child is of a serious nature.
2. The child is known, or has in the past been known, to the juvenile court.
3. The child has a record of repeated delinquency extending over a period of time.
4. The child and his parents have shown themselves unable or unwilling to cooperate with agencies of a non-authoritative character.
5. Case work with the child by a non-authoritative agency has failed in the past.
6. Treatment services needed by the child can be obtained only through the court and its probation department.
7. The child denies the offense, but the officer believes judicial determination is called for and that there is sufficient evidence to warrant referral, or the officer believes that the child and his family are in need of aid.
8. There is apparent need for treatment.

Whatever criteria are agreed upon in a particular community for the referral of a case to a juvenile court, definite policies should be established for such referral by agreement between the juvenile court officials and the police department. These policies should preferably be put in writing. They should be flexible, in order to meet needs of changing conditions, and they should be re-evaluated periodically to make certain of their effectiveness in meeting the needs of children, their families, and the community.

Among the specific items that such an agreement or policy should cover is the information the officer will supply the court. Such information should include:

Facts of the offense which give the juvenile court jurisdiction over the case, *and personal data* about the juvenile.

Information about any co-delinquent or the complainant, including a statement regarding injuries or damages.

Any reasons for requesting juvenile court action other than, or in addition to, the specific offense.

A brief summary of any significant factors revealed in the investigation.

Every police officer has an obligation to familiarize himself thoroughly with the juvenile court philosophy and procedures so that he may interpret them to the child he refers to the court and to the child's parents.

However, the officer should *avoid* giving any suggestion as to what

[14] *Ibid.*, p. 20.

the probation department study will lead to or what the court disposition may be, since these are matters outside his jurisdiction.[15] If the local court situation warrants the statement, the police officer should assure the child and his family that the study made by the probation department will help the judge to make a disposition that will not be punitive, but that will be in the best interests of the child, the family, and the community.

Release to Parents or Guardians without Referral

Generally speaking, a delinquent's own home is the best place for him, whether or not he is referred to any agency in the community for treatment. Before releasing a child to his own home without other referral, however, a police officer should look for evidence of the parents' interest in the welfare of their child and of the family's ability to meet his problems. Certain criteria that might lead a police officer to select this disposition for a delinquent case are as follows:[16]

1. The offense is minor in nature, and there is no apparent need for treatment.
2. The child shows no habitual delinquency pattern.
3. The family situation is stable.
4. The relationship between the child and the parents is good. The parents seem aware of the child's problems and able to cope with them.
5. Adequate help is being given by public or voluntary agency in the community.

In actual practice, release to parents without referral is probably the disposition most frequently made by the police officers in regard to delinquency cases. There is some question, however, as to whether this disposition should be used as often as it is. Release to parents might be more successful if child and parents were referred to another agency in the community for help. Local follow-up studies might throw a light on this question.

Release to Parents with Referral to Non-Authoritative Treatment Resources

Among the non-authoritative agencies to which police officers may refer delinquent children for treatment are family service agencies, child guidance clinics, mental hygiene clinics, public agencies serving families and children, visiting teaching services, church groups, and other similar organizations. *It must be understood, however, that a police officer should never force a child or his family to accept such help*

[15] *Ibid.*, p. 20.
[16] *Ibid.*, p. 21.

by threatening court action if they do not comply with his wishes. If they are unwilling to accept help, the referral will probably be of little or no value.

There are indications that police officers do not use non-authoritative treatment resources to the maximum advantage. In a special juvenile delinquent project conducted by the International Association of Chiefs of Police, a survey revealed that only about half of the police departments reporting use referral to such an agency in disposing of delinquent cases.[17] It is true that in many communities such resources are either limited or nonexistent, but it seems likely that in many places these resources are not used more than they are because of the failure on the part of the police or of the agencies or of both to work out a more cooperative and mutually helpful relationship.

The delinquent who would be most appropriately referred to a special social agency is a child who is not referred to the juvenile court, but whose delinquency is sufficiently serious to demand professional attention that he cannot receive from his parents. This is the child whose misconduct is just beginning rather than one whose pattern of antisocial behavior is serious and well established. In many cases the family of such a juvenile might also be referred to an agency.

In order to make a referral to the appropriate agency, a police officer must know about the needs of the child and his family and also about their willingness to ask help of such treatment resource.

In preparing a child and his family for referral, the officer should do a constructive job of explaining the functions of the agency. He should describe the special skills of the workers employed in the agency and explain how they are able to help children and parents with specific problems. The officer should make it clear that problems can be solved only through the joint efforts of the agency and the child or his parents, and that the agency canont undertake to help them without their active interest and participation.

The officer should also provide specific information as to the name and address of the agency, the telephone number, and the person to contact. This information should be written on a card for the child and his parents. Once they have expressed their desire for help, the officer may telephone the agency to explain the case and, in certain instances, to make an appointment for them. A brief written summary of the case, as seen by the officer, may also be of value to the agency.

A police officer will usually have many opportunities to refer children to recreational and other group-work agencies. If the officer be-

[17]*Ibid.*, p. 22.

lieves that the primary cause of the child's antisocial behavior is a lack of constructive leisure-time activities, such a referral is entirely appropriate. Groups like the Boy Scouts, Y.M.C.A., Y.W.C.A., settlement house, and other organizations offering supervised youth programs contribute a great deal to helping a boy or girl make a personal and social adjustment. It is evident, however, that the activities sponsored by these organizations are not a cure-all for delinquency. Many juveniles with emotional problems really need skilled case work treatment before they can participate in such activities to advantage. Police officers, therefore, should not indiscriminately refer all delinquent cases to these agencies.

Agency referrals can be made in a number of ways:[18]

By the police themselves, either by an individual officer, or by special referral unit.

Through the intake division of the probation department of the juvenile court.

By an information and referral division of the community welfare council or council of social agencies. In some communities, this referral unit is a case conference committee coordinating counsel.

Transfer to Home Community (Runaways)

Occasionally a police officer will take a child from another community into custody and decide not to refer him to the juvenile court, but to return him to his own home. Many such children are runaways who may or may not be delinquents, depending on the state juvenile court law.

The following steps are usually involved when a police officer does decide to return the child to his home:[19]

Ascertaining True Residence. In order to check the child's story about where he actually lives, the officer will want to contact the police department or some other agency in the child's community for verification of facts and for advice as to disposition. Information obtained in this process might alter the officer's decision to return the child to his own home and prompt a referral to the juvenile court.

Actually Returning the Child. If the child is to go home, the means of transportation will probably be determined by the distance involved and wishes of the child's parents. Sometimes the parents can and will call for the child. Sometimes the police in one community or the other

[18]*Ibid.*, p. 23.
[19]*Ibid.*, p. 39.

arrange for transportation. If the distance is great, the child may be returned by public transportation. The ticket may be purchased by his parents, by voluntary agency, or by a public agency. If public transportation is used, some arrangement must be made to provide sufficient supervision so that the child is cared for en route and actually reaches his destination.

The act of running away is seldom harmful in and of itself so far as the protection of the community is concerned, but it is often serious for the child. Such behavior is frequently evidence of a difficulty that the youngster is facing at home or in the community. It is, therefore, extremely important that the police department in the child's home community, in addition to participating in arranging for the child's return, also secure sufficient information to determine whether the case is one that should be referred to the court or to some other agency in the community.

SPECIALIZATION

There have been many opinions expressed as to the role of the police in programs designed to control and prevent juvenile delinquency. Modern police thinking accepts the theory of rehabilitation as being a realistic approach in most cases, and police departments have adopted techniques and methods designed to further that purpose.

Special training units within the police department, participation in community efforts, and official stress on prevention rather than arrest and prosecution are some of the measures being devised and implemented throughout the country. It is generally agreed that these activities constitute a major police role in the prevention and control of juvenile delinquency.[20]

Law enforcement agencies, recognizing the growing challenge of juvenile delinquency, have expanded their activities to meet this challenge and its effect upon the welfare of the community and its citizens. Police departments have organized special units within the structure of the department, staffed with personnel having qualifications in this particular field. Special training of the personnel has been inaugurated to stress the importance of rehabilitation of youthful offenders rather than just taking punitive action in all cases.

The purpose of such a unit is concentration on the understanding control, and suppression of juvenile delinquency; the elimination of

[20]J. E. Winters, "The Role of the Police in Prevention and Control of Delinquency," *Federal Probation*, Vol. XXI, No. 2, June 1957, p. 3.

detrimental influences; and the protection of delinquent, dependent, neglected, and mistreated minors. Generally speaking, these special units have the same objectives as the entire department. However, in view of the fact that the juvenile court laws are essentially protective and rehabilitative, it is frequently necessary to modify the procedures established for the handling of adults by law enforcement when dealing with juveniles.[21]

Whether or not to assign officers to specialized study in connection with juvenile cases, the extent and degree of specialization, and the duties and responsibilities of the specialists are important questions for police administrators. The decision to specialize is based on the theory that a specialist, because of superior knowledge and more intimate acquaintance with the problems, can do a better job. In large, more complex communities, the need for specialization is generally conceded to be more pressing. Specialization in large police departments is probably both essential and inevitable. Therefore, the question is not whether to specialize, but just what added duties should the specialists assume and what should they take away from other personnel.

There are some dangers in specialization. Danger exists in that there may be a tendency for non-specialized personnel to ignore matters which they really should handle. Overemphasis on specialization may produce inhibitions to effective communication, and may also generate morale problems. Remarks by a patrolman, such as "Forget it—that's a job for the Diaper Dicks," are not entirely fictitious. Another potentially dangerous situation is the overdependence of the executive policy maker on the naturally biased viewpoint of the specialist to whom he turns for guidance. Such policy decisions are likely to perpetrate difficulties by subordinating general objectives to those of the specialty.

Despite the potential "dangerous problems" some specialization is necessary. One reason is that the formula for handling juvenile cases arising from provisions of the law and juvenile court procedures would, in many instances, take officers away from their regular duties too frequently and too long, whereas this follow-up work can be performed economically by specialists. Even if every officer could be trained to do the job well, it would be administratively unsound to have every man try to handle to completion all details of every job. Then, too, without some specialization there would be some desirable programs that would never get off the ground. Only someone with a special interest and the necessary background can take the initiative to "spark plug" such programs.

[21]*Ibid.*, p. 5.

The initial investigation of cases involving juveniles is invariably conducted by regular patrol officers. It is the man in the field who is in the best position to spot law violations and initially investigate reported offenses. As a result, the "beat" officer is more than likely the first official to contact the delinquent juvenile. The decision to arrest or not to arrest is, in many instances, completely in his hands, and his decisions, as well as his use of investigative skills, can be one of the most important steps in the entire juvenile control process. *A poor approach or an unwise arrest or detention decision at this point may nullify any future corrective action, as well as vitally affect the minor's later behavior.*

The initial investigation is basically an inquiry as to whether there is sufficient evidence to show that the juvenile comes within the jurisdiction of the juvenile court law and, if so, whether the minor should be taken into custody. It may also be used to determine whether the circumstances require more than just a warning or, if a citation system is in effect, if it is appropriate to refer the minor to the probation department without detaining him.

Most departments with special juvenile officers generally assign all cases involving juveniles to such officers for investigation and disposition. This includes cases in which the juvenile is the victim as well as those in which he is the perpetrator of the delinquent act. Even when a juvenile is released by the arresting officer, a report of the incident is usually submitted to the juvenile bureau to permit the case to be reviewed and the necessary further action to be taken.

On receiving the referral, the juvenile officer further investigates the facts of the offense and, if necessary, obtains such other background material as he believes necessary to make an appropriate disposition. He must determine whether further referral is warranted and the method of referral.

Although the present juvenile court law in *some states* is not very specific regarding the notification of parents of minors who are taken into custody, virtually all departments routinely notify parents, usually within a few hours after a child is taken into custody.

Certain administrative problems are concomitant with the decision to specialize. The first of these is how and on what basis to select the specialists. Other problems concern the training, duties, and pay of such people. These questions, like the others, have no simple and universally applicable answers. What is good and proper in one community could be quite out of line in another.

The source of personnel for special assignments and promotions is ultimately the patrol division. The very nature of police organization makes this inevitable. We have here what is at once a paradox and a dilemma. The patrol division is generally conceded to be the backbone of the police organization. As such, it should be strong and dynamic. Police officers should seek ways to make the patrol more efficient and effective. Siphoning off the cream of the personnel to handle specialist duties defeats this aim to a degree. The dilemma results from the fact that the best people possible for specialized assignments are usually selected, but in so doing police agencies run the risk of leaving in the patrol force the least qualified men. This process can have an unfortunate psychological effect in that the patrol division comes to be regarded as the part of the organization in which to begin and which to get out of as quickly as possible. It is looked upon as only a stepping stone to better things, the least desirable of police assignments since the so-called "best men" do not stay there. The only solution is better selection procedures, with emphasis on upgrading the entire police operation. In fact, ultimate licensing of men for police jobs on the basis of education and other qualifications is a desirable goal for the future. Improvement in beginning salaries and in working conditions are matters which must receive simultaneous favorable attention in order to attract suitable candidates.

In summary, then, it can be said that the decision to establish a separate functional unit which is responsible for matters relating to juveniles must be based on demonstrated need for more effective ultilization of departmental manpower. Need may be evaluated in a number of ways, such as:

1. Inability of regular investigators to clear cases involving juveniles.
2. Juvenile case processing removes patrolmen from their beats for an extended period of time.
3. Community insistence on police involvement in non-police youth programs.
4. Desirability of assigning a juvenile court officer to present cases.
5. The extent to which the department is required to provide social background data to the juvenile court.

As previously indicated, juvenile officers must be selected from the group of experienced line officers. Their selection should be open and competitive to assure that the best-suited men are chosen from all those available. Juvenile officers should be assigned rather than appointed. Pre-service training should be required to assure adequacy of knowledge and skills required in the new position.

Finally, except in the very largest departments, the juvenile unit should be a subsidiary of the criminal investigation unit and juvenile unit responsibilities should center about providing follow-up investigation and staff assistance functions.

POLICEWOMEN AND JUVENILES

It is not quite fair to say that a policewoman was the originator of the idea of crime prevention as a regular police function. From the beginning, there have been individual policemen who, usually on their own time and at their own expense, did exactly the same sort of things for boys and girls as police do today. However, in the distant past such activity was strictly "extra-curricular" and was usually considered "welfare stuff—not police work."

The first officially recognized and sponsored police participation in this type of work was in 1905 when Mrs. Lola Baldwin was appointed to do protective work with girls at the Lewis and Clark Centennial Exposition in Portland, Oregon. She was not called a policewoman, however. The first woman in the world to hold that title was Alice Stebbins Wells of Los Angeles who was appointed to do this type of work in 1910. Portland again took the lead by establishing the first Juvenile Bureau in America a few years later.

Between that time and 1922, when the International Association of Chiefs of Police officially and formally accepted crime prevention as a major function, declaring that policewomen were essential to a modern police department and setting up minimum qualification standards, the growth of the preventive movement was nationwide but spotty. It is a little hard to say whether the increasing number of policewomen—usually in the early days appointed at the insistence of women's clubs—"sold" the idea of crime prevention to law enforcement administrators, or whether the growing conviction of law enforcement officers that they must and could "do something" about this problem led to the appointment of more and more women.

Be that as it may, by 1911 the theory was officially established and the practice already set up in many large cities of America. Until this time, and indeed for some time after this, the policewoman was the only member of the force to do official crime prevention work, so the Woman's Bureau idea became established because the early leaders feared that a scattering of women throughout the departments would result in loss of appreciation of their special services in preventive and protective work. Thus at this stage in the history of the development of this newest police function, it might be well to pause and examine more carefully just what it is that policewomen have done and can do to make their services of such proved value as today's world-wide acceptance would indicate.

The next advance in police technique came with the establishment of the Juvenile Bureau staffed by both men and women trained in the particular techniques of work in this field, with every member of the force given a minimum "conditioning" course to insure the all-important cooperation necessary. Although the role of policewomen is still in a stage of transition, the above brief history brings the reader up-to-date.

Job Analysis

First, it should be recognized that women's value to law enforcement is not limited to the juvenile field. Women as "undercover" agents have had a wide vogue in fiction and some small counterpart in reality. Their best future in the crime detection field of police work may, however, be largely, as trained technicians in crime detection laboratories. It is even possible that in the field of traffic control which is essentially an engineering problem, women engineers can be of great help to the police. Most progressive police administrators are also finding that there is a great place for women in the "functional" operations of a police department—stenographic, clerical, records, communications, and radio, to mention a few. Furthermore, some state laws require the presence of a woman in certain specific instances where women and juveniles are concerned; hence, the matrons. As a matter of fact, the matron was really the first woman in this whole field, having been originally appointed in 1886.

The major contribution of the policewoman to law enforcement is in "preventing crime," as a juvenile officer. In this analysis of her work, the policewoman's job can be considered under two main headings: her case work and her control of community causal factors.

Case Work. What cases should she be responsible for? Should she handle cases of all juveniles up to 12? Up to 18? Both boys and girls? Should she handle all cases of girls and women? How does her community and police department define delinquency, and how early does law enforcement come into the picture? Does she work with the "pre-delinquent" and what is meant by that term?

These are questions which a community has to answer in relation to local factors. The general practice, however, in a modern police department with a juvenile bureau staffed by adequately trained men and women is to have the policewomen handle both boys and girls up to 12, and all girls and women. In general also, the term *delinquent* is socially rather than legally defined so that many "troublesome" children as well as those who have violated ordinances or laws come to the bureau. There are few cities in which the police attempt specific case work with the "pre-delinquent." They are considered, however, to have a definite responsibility to encourage the schools, social agencies, and child guidance clinics to undertake this responsibility, and where there is no adequate local program to promote its establishment.

DISCOVERY. Where does the policewoman get her cases? Some, of course, she discovers herself through her patrol of commercial amusements and questionable neighborhoods, but the great majority of her cases are referred to her. These come from various sources. In the first place, every member of her own department not only turns over to her boys and girls contacted in line of regular duty, but actually has an eye specifically open for the type of child to which the juvenile officer can be helpful. In the second place, many boys and girls and women are referred to the policewoman by other law enforcement agencies. In the third place, workers from social agencies, both public and private, *if the policewoman is of a caliber to merit their cooperation,* refer many cases. Finally, the public in general—usually desperate and distracted parents or irritated neighbors—ask for her help. In some communities, where the policewoman or juvenile officer has established such a record of effective square-dealing and helpful understanding as to merit it, and through an enlightened public relations policy that has "sold" the idea to them, the kids themselves come to the bureau asking for help.

INVESTIGATION. The policy regarding the extent of investigation varies in different communities. In those cities in which the policewoman is thoroughly trained, once the case is before her from whatever source she goes to work to find out not only the *what* but the *why* of the matter. In many cases, she not only must make a social case investigation that goes into family background, school and work histories, aptitudes, aversions, recreation, and all the rest of it, but when circumstances warrant she must also secure examinations by experts. For example, when girl cases are concerned with sex, a woman physician must be consulted for examinations. Before a satisfactory disposition can be attempted, many cases will also require both psychological and psychiatric examinations.

When all the facts are gathered, it is customary for the policewoman to present her findings at a case conference and the proper disposition for that particular case decided upon. The more common pattern, where the standards for the selection of the policewoman are not so high, is for her to refer all such cases—with a discovery report—to a casework agency.

DISPOSITION. What happens to these youngsters may be roughly classified under five headings:

1. There are those cases in which the policewoman requests that a petition be filed for the court.

2. There are many cases of minor infractions of not very serious social implications where the child is released to the parents, after appropriate interviews and suggestions.

3. Cases referred to other jurisdictions. These include a large number of runaways, particularly among the girls. These youngsters, many of them in their early teens, may have followed "boy friends" in the services from coast to coast. Whenever possible, they are sent back to the proper agencies in their own communities or to their homes.

4. Cases that the policewoman refers to appropriate social agencies for more prolonged study and treatment. In general, police juvenile bureaus are not geared to carry out social case treatment and probably should not attempt to expand their services in this direction. Here again, if there is no public or private local agency in this field, the policewoman should help sell the need to the public.

5. There will still be left a large group of boys and girls needing more than the mere release to parents, but whose cases are not serious enough to require either referral to social agencies or juvenile hall. They will greatly benefit by a type of "voluntary" probation. This is worked out in various ways in many communities. Sometimes the policewoman herself acts as an unofficial counselor and friend to her girls. Sometimes, she will volunteer help to look after individual cases. Often it is organized to some degree as when a service club or a woman's club or church will undertake the responsibility for finding "big brothers" or "sisters" to such youngsters. In general, the men to whom the policewoman might refer cases should not be limited to members of fraternal or business clubs (or to their wives in cases of girls). However, the tremendous interest of such organizations deserves the fullest recognition of law enforcement officials because no conflict of lay and professional prerogatives and functions need arise if both are clearly understood.

To sum up the result of the case-work function of the policewoman, if she does all of these things successfully, the policewoman helps to prevent crime through cutting down the stream of boys and girls who otherwise would go on into juvenile court.

Control of Community Casual Factors. What are the "moral hazards" in a community, how does the policewoman discover them, and what can she do about them?

DISCOVERY. The policewoman must have the background (perhaps through the training program) to recognize a "moral hazard" when she meets it—whether it be a degenerate hanging around a schoolground, the lack of proper playground facilities in an overcrowded district, or ons in places of commercial amusement, to mention a may discover personally through her regular patrol or al assignments. The *second* way in which she will discover mental causes of antisocial behavior will be through her causal factors in the cases that she herself is handling. There stablished techniques that help in this discovery and evaluation, n as use of the "spot map" and other methods of proved social research. Through proper study and evaluation, she will soon know pretty well what is wrong with the community and where the lacks are.

ACTION. What can she do? It is right here that the modern policewoman has the greatest potential value to law enforcement in preventing crime today. This is because she—even more than a policeman, no matter how well trained, as a juvenile officer—has at hand the strong backing of the community groups which are essential if the problems involved in controlling or removing community "moral hazards" are to be met. Fortunately, earlier policewoman sold the value of this movement to all the greater national organizations of women well over a quarter of a century ago.

There is in every community a great and well-organized weapon of public opinion ready to act. Moreover, the policewoman is an officer trained in case work as well as police work. Consequently, she will have the respect and full cooperation of the other social agencies in town, as well as women's and civic groups. All of this the police will need if they are to overcome the organized pressure on the other side by those profiting by present conditions. Public pressure may help in cleaning up and keeping clean the commercial amusements, the sale of liquor and salacious literature, and the like. There is a tremendous public concern in this area.

AREAS OF CONTROVERSY[22]

The use of records, fingerprints, and photographs in police work with juveniles often gives rise to controversy. There is, of course, room for differences of opinion about certain aspects of these subjects. But very often they are approached in a one-sided manner, either with unrealistic sentimentality, or with a complete lack of understanding and sympathy for the goal of rehabilitation for delinquent youth. Between these two extremes there must be a fairly clear line of procedure that can be laid out and marked equally by recognition of the practical need to protect the community and by full consideration for the welfare of the individual youth.

[22]*Police Services for Juveniles, op. cit.*, pp. 27–31.

Adequate records relating to children alleged or known to be delinquent should certainly be maintained by the police. There are several reasons for such records:

1. To provide information, for the police themselves, the court, and other interested agencies, on all police contacts, past and present, with a given juvenile.
2. To define delinquency areas.
3. To throw light on community conditions that may contribute to delinquency.
4. For use in evaluating a delinquency-prevention program.

Such records as are maintained should be as brief as practicable and to the point. For example, a patrol officer's report form for taking a child into custody should cover all the facts needed, but should be simple and brief enough to insure the officer's cooperative participation in the report system.

There is little question that records should be maintained on all cases wherein a bona fide complaint is received, an investigation made, or a child taken into custody; in other words, on any case involving a child that requires action and disposition by the police.

The records on an offense committed by a child should include a record of the complaint and of its clearance; if the child is taken into custody, there would also be a booking entry.

There would also be a record of the investigation in a juvenile case, including any social information gathered. It has been suggested that this record should be made available only to the juvenile court and probation department and to social agencies having a legitimate interest in a case.

There should be complete understanding and formal agreement among the various agencies affected as to the use that may be made of the information from police records.

The question of which method should be used for maintaining juvenile records often gives police departments difficulty. Generally, all police records should be integrated in a single centralized system. However, in providing for segmentation of juvenile records within the centralized system if the department has a juvenile division, there are great advantages in permitting that unit to maintain specialized records. For example, a case of a missing child reported in one precinct station and found in another could probably be cleared more promptly through separate juvenile unit files than it could be through central record systems.

A cleared entry on the complaint or offense record for a case involving a juvenile should refer to the juvenile's file by code, including only such additional information, exclusive of his name, as may be needed for adequate cross reference.

Another perplexing issue, in the handling of juveniles by police, is that of determining operational standards for applying the identification processes to arrested youths. This question is not limited to cases involving juveniles. However, the need for clarity in policy is far more apparent at the youth level.

Perhaps in no other areas are there strong feelings such as those in relation to fingerprinting and photographing. Many arguments have been advanced by both proponents and opponents. Some of these arguments are based on emotion while others appear to center about factual case histories which are cited to prove or disprove the value of prints and photographs.

Regardless of the arguments advanced against the fingerprinting of juveniles, there is no question as to the validity or reliability of identification based on fingerprints. Certainly, no other form of personal identification has yet been developed which can be recorded, classified, filed, and searched with such high degrees of reliability and ease. In fact, recent electronic data-processing advances make this procedure even more attractive because of speed of retrieval.

Some state laws forbid both fingerprinting and photographing of children, except by order of the juvenile court. Elsewhere the practice is determined by the policy of the police department; it varies from fingerprinting of all children taken into custody and suspected of an offense, to fingerprinting of only those children suspected of serious offenses. Photographing is less widespread than fingerprinting, but practice follows a similar policy.

Those who oppose fingerprinting juveniles point out that it stigmatizes the youngster, simply because of its association in the public mind with criminal procedure. They maintain that fingerprinting is contrary to the principles of the juvenile court, which seeks to avoid treatment of the juvenile as a criminal. They also hold that the psychological effect of fingerprinting is harmful to the delinquent child. Already prone to the "tough-guy" complex, they argue that he may be pushed further in this direction if he is fingerprinted. Although juvenile court laws do not specifically forbid fingerprinting, the practice violates the spirit of legislation and, it is said, other means are usually sufficient for identification.[23]

Probably the most formidable argument against fingerprinting is the fact that print records may be misused by agencies having access to

[23]Judge V. B. Wylegaig, "Juvenile Offenders Should Not be Fingerprinted," *Federal Probation*, Vol. XI, No. 1, January-March 1947, p. 16.

them for personal purposes. If the records are improperly interpreted, they may greatly handicap an individual in later life. There have been instances in which public and private employers, branches of the armed forces, and state and federal governments have discriminated against individuals because of a juvenile record uncovered by means of fingerprinting files.

Those in favor of fingerprinting children point out that it is the most accurate method of identification. It detects the offender and protects the innocent. It gives a complete record. Furthermore, they say, the "tough-guy" aura of fingerprinting is rapidly being dissipated; it has become more common practice in industry and government to fingerprint all employees, both for identification purposes and for security reasons.[24] It is also maintained that putting a child's fingerprints on file is sometimes very effective in preventing future offenses.

Law enforcement's experience has been that the argument pertaining to fingerprinting as a degrading or traumatic process is without merit. Furthermore, the rather common belief that only criminals are fingerprinted is incorrect. Shame or embarrassment attached to being fingerprinted springs largely from the fact of the arrest, rather than from the technique used to firmly establish identity.

The factor to be considered is the need for positive identification, and this should be the major consideration in the development and implementation of a policy for fingerprinting. Thus a person whose identity is verified by parents immediately after a minor arrest need not be printed unless there is evidentiary material for which comparison prints are needed. On the other hand, a youngster who has been caught in a burglary should be printed so that latent prints from future and past burglary scenes may be compared against a single or complete file of known offenders. The organization of fingerprints in this fashion is considered by law-enforcement agencies as a vital investigative aide and the age of the burglar cannot reasonably be offered as the basis for using or excluding such a technique. The psychological and emotional trauma of the burglary itself is what really counts rather than any supposedly associated with the arrest and ensuing identification procedures.

Extensive examination of the "fingerprinting issue" reveals that the use of fingerprints in a particular investigation does not form the heart of the issue as it presently exists. Those who oppose the fingerprinting of the youth seem to do so as a means of expressing their belief that the consequences of childhood transgressions should not linger and haunt the rehabilitated individual in later life. There is merit to this concept,

[24]C. L. Schilder, "Juvenile Offenders Should be Fingerprinted," *Federal Probation*, Vol. XI, No. 1, January-March 1947, p. 46.

and the way in which police maintain security over identification records stands as the essential point of dispute. Therefore, it is incumbent upon law-enforcement agencies to formulate a policy on fingerprinting which will adequately consider the individual circumstances surrounding each juvenile delinquent. Obviously, some persons' fingerprint records should forever remain in active files. Equally as obvious is the concept that some persons should never be printed to begin with.

Some rules suggested by those *who favor* the use of fingerprinting for identification, but who want to *protect* the child from injury, are as follows:

1. Fingerprinting should be permitted only on the authorization of the juvenile court. Appropriate legislation should be adopted by each state to make such judicial authorization a legal requirement.
2. Authorization for fingerprinting would be appropriate for identification purposes in the following types of situations:
   a. The juvenile has been taken into custody as the suspected or known committer of a serious offense such as robbery, rape, homicide, manslaughter, or burglary of serious consequences.
   b. The juvenile has a long history of delinquency, involving numerous violations of the law, and there is reasonable ground to assume that this pattern of behavior may continue.
   c. The juvenile is a runaway and refuses to reveal his identity.
3. If it is found by the police or the court that a juvenile who has been fingerprinted was not really involved in the case in question, all prints should be returned to the court for destruction.
4. If fingerprints are taken and filed in local, state, or federal systems, they should be given a non-criminal status and maintained on a civil identification file with no information that would disclose the reason or circumstances for which the prints were taken.

The same safeguards that apply to other records on juveniles apply with special force to fingerprints, which are basically a form of record. No juvenile fingerprints should be recorded in a criminal section of any central fingerprint registry. Because of the connotations of criminality associated with fingerprinting in the minds of many people, the use of prints should be held to occasions where identification hinges upon evidence available only through their use, and where sanctioned by law or juvenile court policies. In many jurisdictions, the consent of the juvenile court must be obtained before such procedures are utilized. This author is of the opinion that such a consent should not be necessary; however, policy should be formulated with juvenile agencies in order to ensure complete cooperation and consistent coordination between agencies.

As to the question of photographs of juveniles, presumably the requirements relating to the use and safeguarding of fingerprint records would also apply to photographs. In any case, photographs are rarely found necessary in police work with juveniles.

SUMMARY

The primary responsibility of law enforcement is the control of crime and delinquency through the enforcement of laws defining conduct considered detrimental to the good order of society. Since many criminal acts are committed by minors under the age of 18 years, a large proportion of police work involves the detection, investigation, apprehending, and referral of these juveniles.

Techniques of investigation do not vary with age. Therefore, in the area of routine crime investigation, few if any differences are noted between cases involving adult suspects and those involving youths. Although the investigative techniques pertaining to juvenile and adults are quite similar, these are psychological and legal theoretical concepts which dictate the need for diversity of action in the areas of case preparation, and prevention. The diversity of action, however, occurs only after the identity of the suspect has been determined. Once the age of the suspect is known, the application of different techniques is appropriate. The changes in procedures are dictated primarily by statute and the local juvenile court.

The extent of local police authority and responsibility, and the manner in which local forces exercised them, depend both on the particular powers given a local police force by law and as affected by judicial interpretation, and on the limitations provided for by law. The attitude and policy of the department head may also have an effect to some degree. As a result of these variables, the number and types of functions carried out by the police department in one community may exceed or differ from those undertaken in another.

Two functions, however, are the main concern of all police departments: (1) control of crime and violations of law and, (2) enforcement of regulations. A *third function* accepted by the police in most places is the rendering of general assistance in a variety of cases having little relation to crime control or regulation. Some examples of these forms of assistance are: helping to locate lost or runaway children; searching for lost property and, when found, maintaining service for restoring lost propery to its rightful owners; and assisting persons locked out of their homes. A *fourth function* now engaged in by many police departments to varying degrees is the prevention of delinquency and crime.

Law enforcement is not a rehabilitation or punishing agency. These are not police functions. Moreover, nowhere is there anything special about juveniles in this philosophy. *Juveniles are not exempt from the enforcement of the law.* They must be held to answer for their wrongs against society. Tender years, immaturity, and irresponsibility are not excuses for anti-social behavior. The fact that one is an adult does not permit police to use unnecessary force in arresting him; Nor does the fact that one is a juvenile, per se, require the use of less force. This is not to say that there are no differences in the handling of juveniles and adults. However, insofar as the realization of basic objectives is concerned—the vigorous and successful completion of the job given us by society—there are no philosophical or policy differences.

The most important "tool" the police officer has for carrying out his investigation is *interviewing*. The aim of the police officer in the interview is to learn as much as possible about the facts of the offense and, when appropriate, about the child who is believed to have committed the offense—all knowledge which will help the officer to dispose of the case in the best interests of the community and the child. The standard interview procedure prohibits making promises and threats; abusive language, epithets, sarcasm, and harsh tones are no more justified (and no more useful) than physical punishment. Excessively prolonged interrogation of the juvenile is likewise contrary to proper police practice.

There is a great deal of controvery over the use of fingerprints, records, and photographs in police work with children. Adequate records relating to children alleged or known to be delinquent should certainly be maintained by the police. Such records are invaluable and provide information for the police themselves, the court, and other interested agencies on all police contacts, past and present, with a given juvenile. Furthermore, such records define delinquency areas, "throw light" on community conditions that may contribute to delinquency, and are used in evaluating problems in prevention.

The validity and reliability of identification based upon fingerprints have never been an issue regardless of the arguments advanced. Some state laws forbid both fingerprinting and photographing of children, except by the order of the juvenile court.

QUESTIONS

1. What is the primary responsibility of law enforcement?
2. Discuss juveniles and police philosophy as "treated" in the text.

3. Discuss the question of the word "arrest" in relation to "take into custody?"
4. List the "don'ts" in interviewing.
5. List the conditions which have been found to increase the effectiveness of office interviews.
6. Discuss the areas of controversy.
7. What are the guidelines for *police referral to the juvenile court*?
8. What are the guidelines for a release to parents with *referral to a non-authoritative treatment agency?*
9. The officer investigating an offense should supply the court with information pertaining to the offense. List what such information might include.
10. What are the guidelines for *releasing the minor to his parents without further action*?
11. Discuss the "steps" involved in referring runaways to their community?
12. What is the purpose of a specialized unit working with juveniles?
13. What are some of the dangers in specialization?
14. Discuss the history of policewomen and juveniles.

Chapter 8

Police Services for Neglected Children

NEGLECT IS A COMPLICATED SOCIAL AND LEGAL PROBLEM. When a child's home environment is seriously detrimental to his normal development, the intervention of the social and legal agencies may be essential for the protection of the child.

The conditions which separately or collectively indicate the need for action include:

Lack of physical care and protection.
Lack of supervision, guidance, and discipline.
Exploitation of children.
Lack of protection from degrading conditions.
Abuse and physical cruelty.

Dependency and neglect cases in the United States totaled 150,000 in 1964. These cases increased by 3 per cent between 1963 and 1964.[1] This upward trend began in 1951 and continued in each subsequent year, except 1956. The increases in the last four years, however, have barely exceeded the percentage increases in the population. Thus the rate of juvenile court dependency and neglect cases has remained relatively constant during that period; about 21 cases per 10,000 child population under 18 years of age. Other than those reaching a court, additional cases were dealt with by certain community agencies without referral to court.[2] (See Tables 6, 7, and 8 in the Appendix.)

There is certainly no disagreement regarding the fact that police departments have an important function in protecting children who are neglected, abused, or become involved in dependency status. However, in most communities there has been no agreement, by either police de-

[1]*Juvenile Court Statistics*, 1964 Statistical Series No. 83, Children's Bureau, Department of Health, Education, and Welfare, Washington, D.C., 1964, p. 6.
[2]L. D. Swanson, "Role of the Police in Protection of Children From Neglect and Abuse," *Federal Probation*, Vol. XXI, No. 1, March, 1961, p. 43.

partments or community agencies, as to the appropriate role of the police. Nor has there been effective coordination of police activities with activities of other agencies.

Because the role of the police in this area of community services has not been clearly defined, many questions arise. Should police officers receive and respond to complaints about neglected children? Are investigations of these complaints an appropriate function of the police? What constitutes an "evaluation" by the police? What should be the role of the police in taking children into custody and in using shelter care facilities? How can the police and community agencies work together in planning services for neglected and abused children?[3]

Many different factors are involved in evaluating a neglect situation and arriving at decisions for appropriate action. This chapter is intended to clarify these factors and to discuss certain aspects of neglect raised by these questions and to help clarify the role of the police in the community network of agencies working together to protect children from neglect and abuse. These areas take into consideration the needs of the parents, children, and families in relation to the child's well-being, and the steps that may be taken to meet these needs. The areas to be discussed include: the investigation of neglect cases, referrals to community agencies, taking children into custody, use of shelter care, and areas in which social services can help families change hazardous conditions and areas in which the court and legal agencies carry responsibility.

WHO ARE THE NEGLECTED CHILDREN?

Childhood is a successful period for most youngsters, in the sense that they have from their parents, relatives, and family enough care and protection to enable them to grow up to be reasonably competent adults. However, the childhood of some youngsters is severely marred by parental failure or inadequacy. Family failure may be bizarre and obvious, such as for the child who is completely deserted or who is physically hurt by angry or violent parents, or it may be undramatic and corroding, as for the child who feels unwanted at home and confused in his family relationships, so that he loses his motivation and drive. Experience has shown that children who are being short-changed through parental neglect or family inadequacy can be helped in many ways, particularly if their troubles are recognized at an early date and if sensitive, appropriate help is made available to the family and the child

[3] *Ibid.*, p. 44.

in a way that is adapted to the needs of the individual situation.

These neglected children become visible to the community in a variety of ways, as is shown by the following examples:

1. *Michael, age six, is a source of great concern to his grandmother because of cruel and erratic treatment by his mother who beats him excessivly for minor wrongdoings and then showers him with presents.* The grandmother believes that his serious difficulties at school are the results of his fears and uncertainty, and reports to the police that he has twice run away to her house, pleading to be allowed to stay there.
2. *The social worker, who is providing financial assistance to Mrs. Jones and her four youngsters, notices that Mrs. Jones is becoming increasingly listless, depressed and discouraged.* Mrs. Jones recounts that on two recent occasions she cried uncontrollably for three consecutive hours and was so sick the next day that she couldn't get up and had to keep eight-year-old Mary home from school to care for the younger children.
3. *Susie, at the age of eight months, is brought to the hospital with body bruises and a broken arm, which her mother explains resulted from a fall from her high chair.* X-rays reveal an earlier partially healed break which the mother does not mention, and the examining doctor strongly suspects that these injuries may not be accidental.
4. *Most days when Johnny comes to school, he and his clothing are dirty. Frequently, he does not come to school at all.*The school representative who visited the home was appalled by the odor caused by filth and generally low housekeeping standards. She observed that the two preschool children were eating left-over unheated food directly from the tin cans in which it came.
5. *Mrs. Brown committed suicide two months ago, leaving her husband overwhelmed with the responsibility of caring for their four children.* He is determined that they should not be placed and has had a succession of several inadequate housekeepers. Finally, after one woman badly mistreated the children, he stayed at home himself to care for the children and has applied to the Welfare Department for financial assistance.
6. *Three small children are stranded with their parents in a broken-down car in a service station. The station manager contacted the police department because the children looked so poorly cared for and he had overheard the father offering to give the youngest one to a station employee.*

These are examples of how neglected children in any community may become visible to different persons in different ways. The problems of these children arise from various kinds of parental failures and parental inadequacies. Some of the children have parents who are desperately trying to live up to the demands of being a parent, and who can and will make use of help from any agency to improve their work as parents. Others have parents who are so preoccupied with their own problems and their own needs that they cannot carry the responsibility for children and, in these cases, alternative plans must be made for the children's own good.[4]

The inability of parents to provide a physical setting that is reasonably clean, safe, and comfortable is common in neglect situations. The inability of the mother regularly to provide food that is nourishing and well prepared is another facet of breakdown in child nurture. The inability to provide comfortable and reasonably becoming clothes, suitable for school and play, summer and winter, and to keep them clean and mended so that the child's appearance does not embarrass him or set him apart from his group is frequently another part of the parents' failure.

The lack of established, orderly daily routines is usually a symptom of family breakdown. These are disorganized households. Meals are irregular. The house is in disarray. It is dirty, sometimes filthy. Broken windows or stairs and rough or splintered floors are a constant source of physical danger to children. Beds are broken, springs sag, mattresses and bedclothes, if indeed there are any, are not clean. The plumbing leaks; frequently it is out of order. Body cleanliness for children, as well as for adults, is often neglected and may lead to skin or scalp infections that isolate and embarrass children.

In the great majority of households that lack physical care and protection for children, two factors are present: *poverty* and *inadequate housing*. Such situations are particularly pertinent to large family groups.

The following statement is quoted from a case record: "The family of ten is living in two rooms. The plaster is falling down; window panes were out. The plumbing leaked. The wind howled through the cracks and it was bitterly cold." Two young children with frostbitten hands and feet were removed from this home to a hospital.

In the total picture of neglect, the percentage of abused children is small. Parents who are physically cruel to children are usually suffering from pathological conditions.

Physical punishment is a common form of child discipline. The practice differs among cultural groups. What may appear severe to some is not considered so by others. Brutal treatment is, at times, associated with fanaticism and rigid, unreasonable behavior standards. Beatings are administered with self-righteous fervor. Both physical and psychological damage to the child can be severe and may have far-reaching consequences.

[4]"Planning For The Protection And Care Of Neglected Children in California," preliminary report of a study by National Study Service, New York, 1964, p.p. 1–2.

Characteristically, abuse of children is not related to a child's misbehavior. Parents frequently describe some trivial annoyance that led to cruel treatment. Physical cruelty sometimes is associated with alcoholism or drug addiction, with a resulting loss of a parent's good judgment.

Medical and social work literature, in the last few years, has reported on the phenomenon of physical abuse inflicted on infants and young children by their parents. This is commonly referred to as the "Battered-Child Syndrome." The children sustain serious injuries to bone and soft tissues that result in permanent crippling or in death. A national survey of hospitals in 1961 indicated the admission of 302 such cases. Of them, 85 suffered permanent brain damage and 33 infants died.[5]

Currently, only superficial facts are available about parents who inflict such injuries. Actual experience indicates that: *(1) adults who inflict injuries on children are likely to repeat the attack; (2) the adult is not reacting to specific behavior but to his own feelings; (3) police warning, court action, and probationary status have been ineffective as deterrents. In these circumstances, young children are dependent on the social, medical, and legal agencies for protection.*

Reports of abusive treatment from any source, or the observation by police officers of bruises and injuries suffered by the child, are sufficient reasons to make a thorough investigation of the family situation, to seek medical opinion and, where available and indicated, psychatric advice. Parents are likely to be evasive in discussing their relationship to a child, and suspicious of agency action. Occasionally, parents are relieved to express their true feelings about the child and to participate in planning for his care outside the home. Frequently, an expression fo severe hostility is directed to one particular child in a family group, while other children are given adequate care.

THE POLICE ROLE IN CASES OF NEGLECT

Generally, the role of the police in cases of neglect can be broken down into receiving and investigating, verifying, evaluating, and disposing of complaints.

Receiving and Investigating Complaints

Situations involving neglect of children usually are brought to the attention of the police by someone other than the parents. Sometimes instances of neglect are observed by police while responding to other

[5]H. C. Kempe, "The Battered-Child Syndrome," *Journal of the American Medical Association*, Vol. CLXXXI, No. 1, July 7, 1962, pp. 17–24.

complaints, such as domestic disturbances. Many of these complaints concern children caught in the middle of family crises, such as destitution, loss of the home, violent fights of parents, and parents who threaten suicide. These crises often lead to children being left alone, locked in closets, undernourished, or severely beaten. The following examples are typical of the many complaints received each year by the police throughout the country:[6]

Responded to a complaint concerning three children, ages two to six, left alone in a parked car for several hours. Observation indicated that the children were dirty and unkempt, cold and hungry, poorly clothed, and in need of medical care.

Responded to a domestic disturbance, where drinking parents had been fighting. Children were frightened and appeared to be abused by parents. The home was in disorder.

Responded to a complaint about several children, ages three to seven, left alone in a small apartment for several hours. Complaint indicated that this situation was not new, but was being reported to an official agency for the first time.

A variety of sources point out the authority and the responsibility of the police for receiving and responding to complaints of the types illustrated.

These authorities[7] see the police department as an appropriate agency for investigating complaints of this type, filing petitions for court hearings, and referring cases to community welfare agencies. They contend that recognized police procedures in cases of neglect are, in many respects, similar to those used in cases of delinquency and that the investigation of offenses is primarily a police function. Another authority states that the police are permanently in the field of child protection since no other community service is organized to perform all of the functions of the police in relation to neglect and abuse.[8]

In some communities, one or more social agencies may have by statute

[6]Swanson, *op. cit.*, p. 44.

[7]*Standards for Specialized Courts Dealing with Children*, Children's Bureau Publication No. 346, Washington, D.C., 1954, p. 11; *Child Welfare Services*, Children's Bureau Publication No. 359, Washington, D.C., 1957, p. 11; J. P. Kenny and D. G. Pursuit, *Police Work with Juveniles*, 2nd ed., Charles C Thomas, Springfield, Ill., 1959, p. 260; *Municipal Police Administration*, 4th ed., International City Managers Association, Chicago, 1954, p. 1.

[8]"Neglect, Social Deviance, and Community Action," *National Probation Parole Association*, New York, January 1960, p. 22.

or charter a responsibility for providing protective services in behalf of children who are neglected or abused. Therefore, it is incumbent upon each agency involved to plan in a cooperative manner and coordinate their efforts in responding to complaints about neglect and abuse.

This is not to say that overlapping will not exist regarding law-enforcement agencies and community agencies receiving and responding to complaints of neglect. Such overlapping is essential when we consider the fact that the police department or any other community agency cannot by itself handle all complaints of neglect which arise in a community. Although the police department is in the best position to accord immediate response to emergency complaints regarding neglectful situations, the brunt of receiving and investigating complaints should not fall solely on the law-enforcement agency. If, however, a private or public agency responds to a complaint regarding a case of neglect, the responding agency should be cognizant of the fact that if the children are in immediate danger, the police department should be called into the situation during the initial phase of the investigation.

A police officer who is called in on the case of a neglected child should first make a thorough investigation of the facts and circumstances of the case. He can then decide whether the case requires further action and, if so, whether there should be court action or adjustment through a non-authoritative agency. If court action is warranted, the officer must decide whether it should be on behalf of the child or directed at the adult involved in the case. It is often difficult for the police officer to make an investigation of a neglect case. The child concerned may be too young to give an accurate account of what has happened, or might be afraid to tell the officer the true story. The very neighbor who called the case to the attention of the police may later be reluctant to testify against the parents of the child. Under such conditions, the police officer is often hard-pressed to make an adequate investigation.

In his contacts with reporting or complaining neighbors, the officer will have to persuade them that they should cooperate with the authorities in order to protect the child concerned. Whenever possible, he should promise them that their names will not be involved in further action on the case unless they are needed to legally prove the neglect or contributing charge.

In dealing with the parents of an allegedly neglected child, the officer investigating the case must keep in mind the many pressures that may have caused the parents to be guilty of neglect. It may be helpful if the officer lets the parents know that he understands about such pressures and encourages them to talk about their problems as they see them.

In this way, the officer may be able to see possible strengths in the family that could be drawn upon to bring about an adjustment.

The officer should also be certain to learn whether the present instance of neglect is an isolated incident or whether it is part of a long-time pattern of neglect that would call for court action.

It may be necessary in some cases for the police officer to arrange for pictures to be taken within the home. This would be to provide visual proof that undesirable conditions exist. Calling appropriate persons to witness such conditions is sometimes also advisable. In a case where cruelty on the part of a parent toward a child is indicated, a licensed physician should be asked to make a physical examination of the child so that he can testify in court about the child's condition.

Verifying Complaints

The initial question which should concern the police in responding to reported complaints of abuse or neglect of a child is: Does neglect or abuse exist? This fact should be established by a proficient police investigation, based on a knowledge of the law and of the offenses governed by law, rules of evidence, and previous police experience in handling such complaints. Methods of gathering evidence include statements of witnesses and complainant, interviews with parents and children, and general observation.[9]

Evaluating Complaints

After observing and investigating home conditions and discussing the case with the family and witnesses, an evaluation of the situation is made by the police officer. This evaluation should include those aspects of the case regarded as legally and socially significant: the seriousness of the situation, the need for immediate protection of the child, observations concerning the physical conditions of the child, attitudes of parents, statement of witnesses, and general conditions of the home. This evaluation is not a social history, since it differs in purpose, scope, and degree, but is simply a process for arriving at police disposition.[10]

Disposing of the Case

A number of cases can be closed by a warning or a reprimand. As mentioned before, in dealing with neglect situations it is important for the police officer to be aware of the many pressures that may cause parents to neglect their children. Rather than being willful, the neglect may simply be a symptom of the fact that these pressures have mounted

[9]Swanson, *op. cit.*, p. 45.
[10]*Ibid.*, p. 45.

beyond control. In such cases, the police officer may find it more suitable to refer the parents to a social agency for help. Through such means as good interviewing techniques, the police officer should try to differentiate between those who want to be and can be helped by a social agncy, and those who have shown, by willful neglect of their children, that they need the authoritative service of the court.

A police officer should be informed about the community agencies that can be of service in neglect cases. Definite policies for referral should be arranged between the police and such agencies. Smoothly working relations with the agencies will enable the police department to explain their services to parents in need of referral.

Minor instances of neglect or misconduct by parents toward their children may most appropriately be dealt with by a reprimand regarding the matter and a warning of the possible consequencies if the act is repeated. For example, a police officer may be dispatched in response to neighbors' reports that a child is being beaten. Upon investigating, the officer may find no conclusive evidence that the beating is beyond the normal discipline within parental prerogatives. However, *if the facts warrant it,* the officer may want to make it clear to the parents that under certain circumstances such an incident could lead to further action by the police in behalf of the child.

On the other hand, there are instances where the officer, before disposing of certain cases, should check the records of the police department and other community agencies to determine whether the family has been known previously. In any event, adequate records should be maintained regarding the complaint, normal facts of the investigation, and the police disposition.

Court action involving the neglect of children is called for when:

> *The alleged neglect constitutes an immediate danger to the health and welfare of the child and the facts on hand are sufficient to support a petition.*
>
> *The alleged neglect does not constitute immediate danger to the health and welfare of the child, but there is reason to believe that court action or service is needed to protect or aid the child and the facts on hand are sufficient to support a petition.*

If these conditions do not strictly apply, as previously mentioned, the police may first try other dispositions, if the department policy and agreement with the local courts permit such steps. Policies relative to court action against adults should be worked out jointly by the police department, the juvenile court, other courts that might be involved, and the prosecuting attorney's office.

TAKING CHILDREN INTO CUSTODY

Taking children into custody is primarily a police function. By law, the police have the responsibility and authority to take immediate custody of children in danger of violence or serious injury. This authority may also be vested in other administrative agencies, such as a society for prevention of cruelty to children. Usually, such an agency is granted this authority by law.[11]

When questions arise as to the need to take a child into custody, the police, if possible, should consult with special agencies about the desirability of such action. Distinction should be made between the desirability of taking children into custody and statutory grounds for such action. The police cannot take children into custody merely upon the request of an individual or a social agency. They must determine whether sufficient grounds exist for such action. Since the police have the responsibility and authority, the final action to take children into custody must rest with them. Where another community agency has such powers under the law, that agency may, of course, also take such action.

Not all children taken into custody by the police must come under the jurisdiction of the court. Exceptions are lost children and children left alone because of emergency family situations, such as hospitalization of one or both parents. Such children may be held temporarily pending arrangements by the parents for permanent care or return home.

The lack of adequate shelter care facilities for neglected children presents just about as great a problem for the police as the lack of detention facilities for children needing secure custody. Often the only shelter care offered is the facility used for delinquents.

In those communities where specific facilities for the shelter care of neglected or abandoned children do not exist, they are usually supplied by public or private social agencies. The police should develop a close working relationship with such organizations. Arrangements should also be made whereby police officers can have access to the shelter at any time of the day or night. In communities where no adequate or separate facilities exist, it is the obvious responsibility of the police to work vigorously with other groups in an effort to bring about the establishment of such facilities.

The police should put a neglected child in shelter only when absolutely necessary—that is, when the health and welfare of the child is in immediate danger. Otherwise, the child should be allowed to remain with the parents, pending further consideration of the case by the authorities, or study and recommendation by the social agencies called in.

The police should be certain to let the juvenile court and the parents know when a child is being placed in shelter. If school is in session, the school authorities should also be notified, either by the parents, the court, or the police.

Statutes of some states provide certain safeguards governing the process by which children are placed in shelter care. For example, a number of state juvenile court statutes, similar to the *Standard Family and Juvenile Court Acts*, provide that no child shall be held in detention or shelter care longer than 48 hours, excluding Sundays and holidays, unless a petition has been filed.

SUMMARY

The conditions which separately or collectively indicate the need for police action pertaining to neglected children are: (1) lack of physical care and protection; (2) lack of supervision, guidance, and discipline; (3) exploitation of children; (4) lack of protection from degrading conditions; and (5) abuse and physical cruelty.

Dependency and *neglect* cases in the United States totaled 150,000, in 1964. Further statistical studies reveal that there is an upward trend in neglect cases. On numerous occasions, these cases do not reach the court and are settled by private agencies or handled informally by police agencies.

The problems of neglected children arise from various kinds of parental failures and inadequacies. Some of these children have parents who are desperately trying to live up to the demands of being a parent. Therefore, public and private agencies are consulted and the serious-minded parents prove to be cooperative. Some children have parents who are so preoccupied with their own problems and their own needs that they cannot carry out the responsibility for children, and in these cases plans must be made for the removal of the child from the home.

Two factors are present in those homes that lack physical care and protection for children: (1) poverty and (2) inadequate housing. The above situations are particularly true in the large family groups.

Characteristically, abuse of children is not related to a child's behavior. Furthermore, in numerous cases, only one child in the entire family may be "singled out" and physically or emotionally abused. Current experience indicates that: (1) adults who inflict injuries on children are likely to repeat the attack; (2) the adult is not reacting to specific behavior but to his own feelings; (3) private and public agencies have been ineffective as deterrents; that is, probationary status, police warning, and court action have not been successful.

The police role in cases of neglect can be broken down into receiving and investigating, verifying, evaluating, and disposing of complaints.

Court action should be initiated when there is concern, about the immediate danger to the health and welfare of the child, and information on hand will support a petition. Also, there is reason to believe that the services of the court are needed to protect or aid the child when the facts on hand are sufficient to support a petition.

Although, by law, the taking of a child into custody is primarily a police function, the police when possible should consult with special agencies about the desirability of such action. Consultation of this sort is needed because taking a child into custody may be more harmful to the child than requesting assistance from a specialized protective services agency which will attempt to work out the problem within the family constellation.

QUESTIONS

1. List the neglect conditions which separately or collectively indicate a need for police action.
2. Dependency and neglect cases totaled 150,000, in 1964. How much of an increase was there between 1963–1964?
3. Discuss the following cases of neglect: *Michael, age 6; Mrs. Jones and her four youngsters; Susie, age eight months; three small children stranded in a broken-down car at a service station.*
4. List the two factors that are present in a great majority of households that lack physical care and protection for children.
5. *True* or *False* . . . Characteristically, abuse of children is not related to a child's misbehavior.
6. *True* or *False* . . . Adults who inflict injuries on children are not likely to repeat the attack after police action in the form of verbal warnings.
7. *True or False* . . . *Frequently,* an expression of severe hostility is directed against only *one* child in the family constellation, while other children are accorded adequate care.
8. Generally, the role of the police in cases of neglect can be broken down into four categories. List them.
9. When is *court action* regarding neglect of children indicated?
10. Is the responsibility of taking children into custody primarily a police function? If affirmative, *explain.*

Chapter 9

Police Relationships with Other Agencies

IN ALMOST EVERY ASPECT of their work with juveniles, the police must have contact with at least one other agency in the community. It must be recognized that the police services are only a part of the total community effort to promote the welfare of children and young people. For police services to be made more effective, then, they must be planned in relationship to the over-all community program as well as to the services offered by individual agencies.

COMMUNITY PLANNING

Experience has shown the public and private agencies in communities that they can do a much more effective and economical job in meeting the social needs of people if they plan and coordinate their efforts. Therefore, in many communities the agencies have gotten together to form community planning bodies, known by such names as "Health and Welfare Council," "Council of Social Agencies," "Community Council," and the like.

As a major public service in the community, the police department should take part in this community planning and be a member of any coordinating council that may exist. *The Special Juvenile Delinquency Project—International Association of Chiefs of Police* query on police services revealed that 48 per cent of the police departments responding were not represented on community planning bodies. Of course, it is possible that in many communities there were no such planning bodies to which the police could belong. Where this is the case the police should join with other interested agencies and persons to establish a council. Consultative services for this purpose are available from Community Chest and Council of America, Inc., The National Council on Crime and Delinquency, and from various state departments.

Insofar as services to children are concerned, the police department might bring to the attention of the planning bodies such matters as:[1]

1. The delinquency rate.
2. Focal points of delinquency and crime in the community.
3. Various services needed for families and children which are lacking.
4. Inadequacy of detention or shelter care facilities.
5. Need for new laws or revision or repeal of existing laws.
6. Need for greater interpretation to the public of existing laws.
7. Need for additional personnel to serve juveniles.
8. Need for assistance in conducting community programs.

The community planning meetings are also the place to work out problems as to which agency can best conduct programs to meet the various community needs.

Association with the community planning body thus gives the police an opportunity to understand better their own position in the composite picture of services to the community; to bring the services and their needs to the attention of other agencies and the public; and to learn what resources can be called upon for assistance when needed.

WORKING RELATIONSHIPS WITH INDIVIDUAL AGENCIES

Although police officers, and particularly special juvenile officers, should be familar with the contribution and operation of all agencies in the community (an up-to-date directory of agencies can be of great value), it is clear that the major part of their work with children will involve contact with only a limited number of agencies. This contact should normally be close and continuous and, therefore, the relationship should be based on a clear understanding and amicable acceptance of the role of each of the participants.

The agencies with which the police have most frequent contact are the juvenile court and its probation department, public welfare department, recreation and other such group-work agencies, private family and childrens' agencies, and the public schools. There will be specific matters about which the police will have to reach agreement with each of these agencies. In every case, however, a few fundamental arrangements will apply, among which are the following:[2]

One or more representatives of the police department should meet with the executive and other key administrative personnel of the other

[1]*Police Services for Juveniles*, Children's Bureau, U.S. Department of Health, Education, and Welfare, Washington, D.C., 1954, pp. 44–45.
[2]*Ibid.*, pp. 45–46.

agency to plan jointly how the two agencies can work together to serve juveniles and their families.

Agreements resulting from such joint planning should be put in writing whenever possible so that they will be available to members of the police department and of the other agency who did not attend the meeting.

The police department and the other agency should arrange for a guest speaker from each of them to appear before staff members of the other to explain his own agency's functions and what it can contribute to the work of the other.

The police should invite speakers from the social case-work field and from recreation work to appear before conferences of law enforcement agencies.

As stated earlier, special problems will have to be worked out with the individual agencies concerned, as in the following instances.

With the Juvenile Court (Including the Probation Department)

A number of matters call for meeting and agreement by the police and juvenile court. Some examples are:

1. Each should interpret to the other the framework of administrative policy and procedure within which it operates. Organization charts are useful for this. Legal provisions controlling functions and programs should be thoroughly explained.
2. The specific functions of the police and of the court should be carefully defined, with particular attention given to the extent of the police investigation and the type of report to be submitted to the probation department.
3. Definite policies governing detention and shelter care should be worked out, covering both delinquent and neglected children.
4. An arrangement should be made so that the police officers do not need to attend juvenile court hearings to testify, *except when the facts in the case are disputed.*
5. A method should be worked out for the juvenile court to inform the police about the final disposition of cases initiated by the police.

With Case-Work Agencies[3]

Some of the important areas that should be clarified in the police-social work agencies are:

1. Definite agreement should be reached as to the types of cases that the police are to refer to the treatment agency.
2. Methods of referral should be agreed upon.

[3] *Ibid.*, p. 47.

3. Police officers should become well acquainted with the agency's intake workers, with whom they will work on most cases. Understanding between the worker and the police officer will make it easier for the police to get questions and problems settled.

With the Schools[4]

The schools and the police department frequently have occasion to work together in the case of juveniles who are in need of special types of help from community agencies. Policies must be jointly formulated to:

1. Define the role of the police in relation to truants, clarifying the relationship between attendance officers and police officers.
2. Specify the violations of law within the school building that school officials will report to the police for investigation.
3. Specify procedures that an officer will follow in taking a child into custody at school or interviewing a youngster at school.
4. Establish police responsibility for the protection of children from adults loitering around school grounds with unlawful intent.
5. Specify the extent to which school records will be made available to police officers and police records to school personnel.
6. Set forth police responsibility for regulating juvenile pedestrian traffic to and from school, and for aiding in traffic safety education.
7. Provide for police services in handling large crowds at athletic meets and social functions.

With Recreation and Other Group-Work Agencies[5]

In meeting with executives and appropriate employees of individual leisure-time agencies, the police should try to reach an agreement on a number of matters. For example:

1. The type of cases to be referred to the leisure-time agency.
2. The use of leisure-time agencies' facilities for police interview purposes.
3. Arrangements for the police officer to visit the leisure-time agency as a friend interested in observing its constructive activities.
4. The procedures that an officer will follow in taking a child into custody at a recreational agency or in interviewing a child at a recreational facility.
5. Law violations that take place on agency property that will be reported to the police for investigation.

With Health Agencies[6]

There are many occasions when a police officer can make use of a

[4]*Ibid.*, pp. 47–48.
[5]*Ibid.*, p. 48.
[6]*Ibid.*, p. 48.

community's health facilities for serving the needs of children or their parents. City hospitals, private hospitals, specialized health clinics, county and city health departments, and emergency clinics are among the types of health facilities with which the police should be well acquainted. To insure proper use of health facilities:

1. A police officer should be thoroughly familiar with the intake policies of both public and private hospitals and out-patient clinics, so that he can make appropriate referrals to these facilities.
2. Agreement should be worked out regarding the use of hospital and health agency records by the police. The availability of such records or any interpretation of them can be very helpful in police investigations.

With State Agencies[7]

Police departments need to develop a working relationship with appropriate state agencies, particularly those concerned with:

1. Licensing business establishments.
2. Licensing foster homes and institutions for children.
3. Institutional care of emotionally disturbed and mentally retarded children.
4. The correctional program for delinquents in training schools and on placement or parole.
5. Highway traffic.
6. Child labor laws.
7. Protection of constitutional rights and interpretation of statutes.

SUMMARY

Community opinion as to the enforcement of laws relating to vice is invariably divided. The majority of the community, and it is usually a very large majority, appears to be indifferent to the problem. This division of public opinion makes the police task even more difficult. The police are nearly powerless without the support of the large majority who all too frequently are content in their passive role.

The law-enforcement officer should also be cognizant that there will always be a certain amount of natural resentment on the part of the public, and such resentment should be accepted. In order to improve community relations, every peace officer must accept as a personal challenge the winning of public support and respect. Lip service to this goal is readily obtained; however, failure to follow through is legion. The factors which are considered basic, if the police are to establish and maintain acceptance are: (1) attitude, (2) demeanor while on traf-

[7] *Ibid.*, pp. 49–50.

fic patrol, (3) courtesy, (4) appearance, and (5) proper use of the telephone.

The agencies with which the police have most frequent contact are the juvenile court and its probation department, the public welfare department, the recreation and other such group-work agencies, private family and children's agencies, and the public schools. In dealing with agencies, the police should endeavor to make a few fundamental arrangements and arrive at procedural agreements.

QUESTIONS

1. A number of factors call for meeting and arriving at an agreement by the police and the juvenile court. List five examples.
2. Why should the police take part in community planning?
3. List "matters" which the police should bring to the attention of community planning bodies.
4. List the fundamental arrangements which should be agreed upon by the police and agencies such as the juvenile probation department, public welfare departments, schools, and other agencies dealing with children.

Chapter 10

*Legal and Social Components of Probation and Parole**

As POINTED OUT EARLIER, in the nineteenth century probation was frequently defined as a suspension of sentence, with the understanding that further delinquency would result in punishment. Today probation is more likely to be defined as "a consciously planned treatment process"; "a helping process that changes a law violator into a law abider"; "a new and therapeutic experience with authority"; or "psychotherapy aimed at changing distorted or unrealistic attitudes."

The experts in the field who use these definitions also view probation as having a different meaning to the delinquent and to the general public. The probationer himself may see the probation officer as a person in authority who checks on him and who has the authority to send him away. It is not uncommon for the delinquent to picture the probation officer as hostile or at least unfriendly; the probation officer, however, sees himself as a helping person, one who is treating the delinquent. The general public considers probation as a second chance; if the delinquent can change his behavior, he need not lose his liberty.

The Children's Bureau in Washington defines probation as "a legal status in which a child, following adjudication in a delinquent case, is permitted to remain in the community, subject to supervision by the court through the court's probation department or an agency designated by the court, and subject to being returned to the court at any time during probation."[1]

In each of these definitions there is a recognition that the court sees the need for the delinquent to change. Having violated the code of the community, he is given the opportunity to change; if he does not, then other measures are to be taken by the court. According to this view, the

*For further information on legal and social components of probation, see a workshop report compiled by the Department of Health, Education, and Welfare in 1962: "Training for Juvenile Probation Officers."

[1]*Standard for Specialized Courts Dealing With Children*, Children's Bureau, Department of Health, Education, and Welfare, Washington, D.C., 1954, p. 18.

delinquent who does not need to change because his behavior was atypical for him, should not be placed on probation, and admonishment and warning from the court regarding his own responsibility for his action should be sufficient.

But when the court, through its study of the adolescent and his family, finds that change is necessary, several dispositions are possible. Generally, they are limited to: (1) probation and/or placement in a relative's home or a foster family home, or (2) commitment to a suitable institution or agency for treatment. Whatever the disposition, all the parties concerned should recognize that the court believes that the delinquent needs a change and as a result of its study has selected this way as the most likely path. The disposition is designed both to aid the adolescent and to protect the community, as the court has the joint responsibility of serving both.

The court's disposition which perceives the need for change and provides the method to be used to accomplish it, is frequently regarded as punishment by the probationer. Having done wrong, the individual must make up for it. On some occasions, the delinquent may regard the disposition of probation as "getting away" with law-breaking, and may react to probation rules with contempt. Such responses have lent credence to the cry of "mollycoddling" by those who have no faith in probation as a method of changing the individual's attitudes and behavior. From another viewpoint, the court's disposition is regarded as an expression of the community's recognition that the delinquent needs to be helped with his social problems. For example, a boy was referred to court for participating in a car theft. He was not the instigator, but had followed the lead of the other boys, lest he be considered "chicken." Investigation revealed that this was an isolated incident and that generally he could be relied upon to use good judgment. The judge, knowing this, could effectively point out the responsibility of each boy for his behavior and the fallacy of trying to prove one's manhood through delinquent behavior.

THE GOALS OF PROBATION

Because of the differing needs of individual delinquents, the goals of probation vary from immediate to long-range, from limited to broad, from mere stopping of the delinquent behavior to rehabilitation of the individual. The minimum goal of stopping delinquent behavior is generally accepted. Should goals be higher? Should the goals be to help the delinquent achieve his highest potential? Should probation continue until the delinquent has made an adequate social adjustment in the community, perhaps through careful planning regarding his life situation? Phrasing this another way, should probation terminate when the youth is considered law-abiding or should it continue in order to resolve other social or emotional problems?

If the answer is that the probation officer should assist with only those problems that are related to delinquent behavior, the question arises how this separation of problems can be determined. Can we delineate which areas of the client's life are the concern of the probation officer and which are not? Would the probation officer work with a delinquent youth with his dating problems, for example? Or would this be overreaching?

It is felt that the following factors affect the goals of probation:

1. The situation and capacity of the client.
2. The culture and environment of the youth and his family.
3. The concept of probation held by the judge and the probation staff.
4. The quality and quanity of staff, as they affect the service available to the youth and his family.
5. The court's situation in the community and the availability of community resources.

The Probation Plan

To meet the goals of probation, the probation plan needs to be tailored to the individual and to have within it the elements of change required by the court. Stereotype rules and conditions should be eliminated. The philosophy of the juvenile court movement is based upon the individual child. Falling back on standard probation conditions for all delinquents denies the uniqueness of the individual approach necessary for successful probation.

How the probation plan is arrived at will be discussed in the next section. However, the probation officer is responsible for formulating the plan; the judge may approve it, modify it, or disapprove it. It is the probation officer who has the responsibility for carrying out the details of the plan, along with the delinquent.

Some courts set down rules of probation, but it seems better to leave the details of limitations of activities to the supervisory authority vested in the probation officer. For example, matters such as keeping probation appointments, attending school, and the limiting of travel should be left to the authority of the probation officer.[2]

Although the general treatment plan may be agreed upon at the time of the hearing, it would be unwise to make this a part of the court

[2] *Ibid.*, pp. 18–19.

order, since the plan may need to be modified as treatment progresses. The probation officer should be permitted to take such action within the scope of his authority.

As referred to earlier, the probation plan is subject to different interpretations by the delinquent and court personnel. It can be considered by the delinquent as the punishment allotted for wrong-doing, or as the frame work within which social treatment can be accomplished as envisioned by the court. It can also be interpreted as neither punishment nor rehabilitation, but a social plan focused on the welfare of the adolescent and the community. This plan requires that the youth control his behavior in specific ways, and is designed to help him effect an adequate adjustment with the help of the probation officer.

THE ROLE OF THE PROBATION OFFICER

The juvenile probation officer has two roles, and there must be no conflict between these roles. The juvenile probation officer must be considered, first, as a court officer or "arm of the court" and secondly, a correctional social worker.

As a Court Officer

As an officer of the juvenile court the probation officer:

Is a creature of the statute and must work only within those limitations. He is only an agent of the court and has no authority to change orders of the court or to disregard those orders.

Makes investigations and determines whether a child should appear before the court by filing a petition.

Makes factual objective reports to the court, so that the court may arrive at an intelligent decision.

Makes suggestions and recommendations to the court.

Keeps the court informed as to the progress made with the court's wards.

Is a legal representative of the juvenile court.

As a Correctional Social Worker

The probation officer performs the following functions in his capacity as a correctional social worker:

Conducts a social investigation, makes a subjective analysis, and works out a realistic plan for each case he presents to the court.

Makes certain that no child is placed on probation until a specific plan has been formulated.

Supervises and accords consultation and guidance to both the ward and his family. There is little point in granting probation unless a plan is prepared and adequate supervision is continued until the child no longer needs such supervision.

Represents the child's best interests to the court.

As a Social Diagnostician

From the time the adolescent and his parents come to the attention of the court, the probation officer is assessing them as individuals and as members of a family and members of the community. The social study made by the probation officer is designed to: *(1) identify and evaluate the factors causing the delinquent behavior, and (2) develop and recommend a necessary program which will eliminate or alleviate these factors.*

During the interval that the probation officer is making the social study for the court's use, he is also preparing the delinquent and his parents for the hearing. He tries to learn the meaning of his total experience to the youth and at the same time convey to him the purpose of the court and the functions of the staff members who will deal with him. In some cases, the social study will reveal that the delinquent does not need the services of the court—that there are other community agencies available to meet his needs.[3] In these situations, the role of the probation officer is to enable the delinquent to accept the referral—and to give the agency, to which he is referred, adequate information regarding him so that the referral will be accomplished.

In stiIl other cases, the study will point out that the referral will be accomplished.

In still other cases, the study will point out that the delinquent does not need any social services. His behavior was atypical; social control can be maintained without relying on probation or other measures. In these situations, the judge can use the social study prepared by the probation officer as a way of making the hearing a positive experience for this child. Here again, the point is that the court's purpose is to serve the child; it can do this best if the remarks made by the judge to the child are based on an understanding of that child.

The material obtained by the social study comes from many sources, including the delinquent himself, his parents or relatives, the school, the police, social agencies, professional personnel such as doctors and ministers, and other interested and informed people concerned with the delinquent. Selection of what material goes into the report in order to give a clear picture of this youth is at the core of the probation officer's

[3] *Ibid.*, p. 97.

job. Information from these sources needs to be blended and evaluated. When reports have been received from other professional people, these should be incorporated into the study in order to formulate the probation plan. This method offers the judge a unified, comprehensive report rather than a set of reports which may need consolidating.

As the person responsible for the social study, the probation officer needs to be able to work with ease and confidence with the people providing information. He needs to know when to refer the delinquent for psychological testing or for psychiatric study, and how to use the information obtained from these sources. His evaluation of the material in the social study is the basis of the probation plan which defines the means of helping the delinquent to achieve responsible behavior.

It is commonly agreed that although the probation officer should not be exclusively a psychotherapist, the degree to which he is involved depends on the nature of the case. It is generally agreed that the probation officer is a correctional social worker whose function is to provide treatment consistent with the philosophy of social work as practiced today. It is concluded that the probation officer should not engage in psychotherapy, but should only ask questions, make statements, and require conduct on the part of the delinquent as is defined in the legal description of the probation officer's duties. However, the probation officer in his use of social case work should be able to build on the strength of his relationship with the delinquent in order to work out a sound probation plan. There are other descriptions of the probation officer's function, however, and all point out that he should use all his skills and knowledge in the appropriate social work method (case work, group work, community organization) to assist the delinquent.

As a Controlling Person in the Delinquent's Life

When the need for the delinquent to change has been recognized and approval has been given to the probation plan, both the delinquent and the probation officer are responsible for implementing the plan.

The limitations set by the court for the delinquent youth are restraints that are appropriate and often essential facets of the plan to assist the youth and protect the community. The probation officer is present to help the delinquent to understand and comply with the probation plan; he is also available to help the client with problems, as they relate to delinquent behavior. The goal of both is to restore the delinquent from his restricted supervised status to legal freedom. Until it is safe to do this, the probation officer is expected to provide the necessary special controls and relationship resources.

The question often arises as to whether the probation officer can be both a controlling and helping person. Some people believe that control exerted over the probationer is anti-therapeutic because it is resented by the probationer. Others hold that there is necessarily authority in the helping relationship. It can be a positive force; when the probation officer abrogates his authority, he misses giving the delinquent the opportunity to deal with the problems he has regarding authority within his own personal and social relationship.

But how far does the control or the help function go? Does the probation officer have the right to tell the probationer to shave off his mustache or cut his hair? Can you require him to wear non-pointed shoes?

The answers to these questions lie in the goal that is set when the probation plan is made. In general, this goal will be to help the client develop socially acceptable standards and adequate personal and social controls. In the process of developing these, they cannot be at any point too alien to him. The probation officer and the delinquent need to find a comfortable way of working together—one within the cultural system of the delinquent.[4] If the attempt is made by the probation officer to get the client to adopt a different set of culture values, then the probation officer's plan becomes a form of coercion against which the delinquent will rebel. The plan should be designated to assist, not to trap, the probationer.

The most common problems of probation are those involving social relationships. Should the probation officer control the delinquent's selection of friends, or his association with other probationers? Should certain hangouts be permitted? Are there times when the probation officer takes over the authority of the parent? Here again, the answers lie in understanding what is the individual goal of probation. The effort is to assist the delinquent in establishing a more satisfactory and acceptable pattern of behavior. How far can he himself go along his social relationships? Does he need control for a period of time, or is guidance enough so that he develops the control needed?

There are certain legal boundaries to which the delinquent is held by the probation officer. One of these is school attendance. If the delinquent is of school age and in good health, he must attend school. The efforts of the probation officer are again twofold: to help the youth accept school and gain interest in it, and to assist the school in understanding and planning to meet the needs of the youth. In some cases, the court may help the community evaluate school attendance requirements as they affect the youth of the community.

The control plan for the delinquent is set up to help him achieve

[4]*Ibid.*, p. 66.

good citizenship. He must live within the law. The probation officer identifies with the mores of the community and with the law. He represents the law-abiding citizen. For example, if the probationer admits that he has been shoplifting, the probation officer handles this in an appropriate manner—by re-referral to the court for another disposition, by forcing the delinquent to return the merchandise, or by purchase of the articles taken. The manner in which this is done can be therapeutic or can convince the youth that (1) he can outsmart the adults when he is caught, or (2) no one will understand him. In no case can the probation officer ignore the delinquent. The delinquent needs to know that there are adults that he can't seduce into delinquency as silent partners.

In some courts, a new petition is filed for each delinquent act. In others, the supervising probation officer is consulted before a new petition is filed. It is generally believed that when a new petition is being considered, the supervision probation officer should be consulted. Based on his understanding of the delinquent, the supervising probation officer often can contribute important knowledge in making this decision.

As an Agent of Change

Concern with change, the most characteristic common element of the methods of social work, is also at the core of the probation officer's job. Change must be planned and the plan must be followed thoughtfully. Both the delinquent and the probation officer need to understand and agree on the goals toward which they are striving. *The process of positive change may come about through:*[5]

1. *Interaction* between the delinquent and the probation officer, through the help given directly to the delinquent and/or members of his family.
2. *Referral* of the delinquent to other resources and the help he receives through these services. The knowledge of other resources and the ability to help the delinquent use them makes the probation officer more effective.
3. *Creation of new resources* to enable the individual to solve his problems.

The probation officer also serves as a change agent in relation to both the court and the total community. Where he observes that policies or procedures of the court need revision, it is his obligation to work for constructive change. Within the community, he should point out what additional services are needed for the youth. Generally, he should work through the channels provided by the court, rather than independently.

[5]W. W. Boehm, "Objectives of the Social Work Curriculum of the Future," *Social Work Curriculum Study*, Vol. 1, Council on Social Education, New York, 1959, p. 131.

This idea of the probation officer as a change agent raises many questions, such as:

If the family is the basic problem, does the probation officer work with them, or refer them to a social agency?

Is probation child-centered to the exclusion of the parents?

If the delinquency involved is group participation, should the probation officer take the responsibility for intervention with the group when not all members of the group are under court jurisdiction?

To what extent should the probation officer function as a community change agent? Should he organize and lead a youth group?

In dealing with the question of family, the Children's Bureau in its publication, *Standards for Specialized Courts Dealing with Children*, states:

> "In certain situations, much of the work of the probation officer may have to be done with parents. Although the parents of a child on probation are not themselves on probation or under supervision, they should be aware of the fact that their behavior and ability to help and control the child may have a bearing on the success of the service. If, for example, the parents are interfering with the probation officer or are failing to abide by a restraining order of the court, the probation officer may have to bring the case back to court."

The question of group participation has often triggered discussions by experts in the field pertaining to the responsibility for probation of individuals not officially under court jurisdiction. Naturally, there are many sharp differences as to the use of official versus unofficial probation. Throughout many workshops in the country, it is agreed by participants that regardless of the kind of intervention the probation officer attempts, he must have the knowledge to identify the kind of problems and the appropriate way to deal with the problems; for example, intervention with the family, with the peer group, or with the community.

The question of the probation officer as a community organizer drew the attention of workshop participants at *Haven's Hill Lodge, Michigan, in 1960*. Some of the participants meeting under the auspices of the Children's Bureau, viewed the probation officer's role as being limited to the case-work function of overcoming the distortions in the attitudes of clients. Others viewed his role as that of a social worker who deals with many aspects of the community, as a way of meeting the treatment needs of the delinquent. This latter group believed that the probation officer must ally himself with groups seeking the solution to those community problems which are causative factors in the delinquent's behavior resulting in referral to court. One person reasoned that if we understand, as the result of a careful study, the various factors which lead to the poor adjustment of the delinquent within the community, the probation officer then has the responsibility of dealing with those pressures as they impinge on the behavior of the youngster and as they impinge on the activities of other youngsters, who at this point may or may not have come to the attention of the court.

Does this indicate that the probation officer should take responsibility for any and all problems that the delinquent might have? The consensus of the above group was that it is within the function of the probation officer to provide community leadership which would be aimed at the encouraging and helping the community to develop resources to deal with such problems. For example, the probation officer might attend meetings of community organizations and encourage their interest in various problems faced by the youth in the community—such as the need for organized social activities for teenagers, or the problem of employment during summer vacations.

It has been pointed out that *"the court is in a particularly good position to see the gaps in services which exist in the community, to bring these gaps to the attention of planning groups in the community, and to work with them to secure more adequate services."*[6]

The size of the probation staff, the resources of the community, and the policies of the given court determine how much of a community organizer the probation officer will be. Juvenile courts, along with other community agencies, have the responsibility for bringing about wholesome changes in the community. Each individual probation officer should be assigned his part of that responsibility in a way that will not dissipate his effectiveness in meeting the demands of his case load.

The question of how circumscribed or how broad the community organization role should be in the aspect of the probation task needs to be given more thought because of the wide divergence of opinion in the field.

ADMINISTRATIVE-MANAGEMENT ASPECTS

An indispensable precondition to effective probation services is an effective working relationship with the judge and the probation officer. Each must have a clear understanding of his role in the process. This

[6]*Standard Family Court Act*, National Probation and Parole Association, New York, 1959, pp. 28–29. *Standard Juvenile Court Act*, 6th ed., National Council on Crime and Delinquency, New York, 1959, pp. 31–32. *Standards for Specialized Courts Dealing with Children, op. cit.*, pp. 43–44.

means that all channels of communication should be open between the judge and the probation officer in order to provide a free exchange of ideas.

It is frequently pointed out that, on occasion, the probation officers do not respect the right of the judge to be the final decision maker regarding the plan set up by the court for the delinquent. This refers to those instances where the decision of a judge disagrees with the recommendation of a probation officer. In such situations, both the judge and the probation officer need to look for ways to collaborate effectively. In some instances, the judge may need help in accepting knowledgeable recommendations based on a thorough study of the delinquent; in others, the probation officer may need to understand that the judge has taken other factors into consideration in making his decision. It should be remembered that in deciding a case a judge must take into consideration the protection of the community. Also some judges, in certain types of cases, may be motivated by community reaction. As the judge and the probation officer work together, the judge tends to become more "case-conscious" and the probation officer becomes more "community-conscious." Thus the occasions of differences between the recommendation of the probation officer and the plan accepted by the judge diminish and boil down to those cases where legal principle dictates something other than the recommendation made to the judge by the probation officer.

This discussion leads into a question of whether or not probation officers should let families know of their recommendations before such recommendations are presented to the judge. Most authorities in the field agree that the family should know what recommendation was made and also that the judge has the authority to follow, modify, or reject it. It is recognized that both the judge and the probation officer have knowledge to bring to bear on the plan set up by the court. The judge is held accountable for the plan by the community, but this does not make the probation officer any less responsible than the judge for the kind of plan that is developed.

When the statutes spell out the jurisdiction of the court, they are often general in nature and do not detail the functions, procedures, or duties of the various personnel attached to the court. Such details, therefore, are left to administrative decision.

The probation officer, because of the pressures of a large case load, needs to determine how he can best use his time. How can he cut corners? How can he select the most important job to be done? Are there different levels of treatment so that there can be a redivision of labor?

From the history of other professions, the indication is that more than one level of professional confidence usually develops at a point when measures to deal with the personnel shortage coincide with the achievement of clarity about basic professional functions.[7] If there are functions that can be performed by agency-trained personnel, then the professionally trained (graduate) probation officers can be utilized for those tasks requiring their special knowledge and skills.

Research on this redivision of labor, or on the differential use of personnel, is in progress. This was necessitated by the fact that it was impossible to produce the number of graduate social workers needed, and the fact that some of the largest and most crucial social welfare services are being staffed primarily by persons without professional education in any field.[8] Other professions, such as medicine, teaching, nursing, and dentistry, have analyzed their functions and, compiling them in new ways, have developed auxiliary personnel to achieve a more efficient work pattern.

Returning to the earlier question—How can the probation officer do an adequate job under the pressure of numerous cases?—one expedient suggested by experts in the field and participants in the workshops was the use of a treatment unit for more complex cases. This has been countered by the suggestion that such complex cases, requiring both ample time and professional skill, probably should be referred to other community resources. It was also pointed out that the use of a special treatment unit in the court might focus skilled help on a few and result in a casual handling of the many.

In all case loads there are delinquents with various needs. The probation officer needs to recognize these and plan his time accordingly. The number of treatment hours available are limited; how they are used is the problem in management.

Regarding the administrative aspects of his work, the probation officer must understand the framework in which he works and recognize how procedures affect practice goals. Administration is a process in itself which requires thoughtful scrutiny to make it most effective. One of the key personnel in an administration in contributing to the quality of service is the supervisor.

How the job can be defined and divided is the research task. There are certain knowledge, skills, and attitudes necessary for effective performance. The knowledge, skills, and attitudes enumerated below are those considered by the experts in the field to be the most important. An effort has been made to list them in the order of their importance.

[7]Boehm, *op. cit.*, p. 63.

[8]Advisory Committee on Social Welfare Education, *Social Workers for California*, Regents of the University of California, Los Angeles, 1960, p. 34.

Function of the Juvenile Court

The function of the juvenile court is to determine when society has the right to enter into a child's life and, when such is the case, to deal with him on an individualized basis.

Law

Knowledge of the law is a prerequisite for the adequate functioning of the probation officer. He needs to have an understanding of the philosophy and role of law in society. The principles, strengths, and weaknesses of the law and the legal system need to be understood in order to apply social-work knowledge in the court. With respect for the law should come an improvement in the relationships between the lawyers and probation officers. In the language of the social worker, the court is the legal system. The probation officer must see himself in relation to law. While much of the knowledge of law must come through service training, the basic respect for law should be taught by the universities to all social-work students.

Human Growth and Change

Knowledge of the dynamics of human behavior and of personality development enables the probation officer to understand the reasons behind a youth's actions. Knowledge of psychopathology aids in the recognition of disturbed youths and parents. There are many delinquents in the probation officer's case load who lack the social and personal resources needed to adjust without help. Many become delinquent because of situational factors and then react defiantly to the process of being taken into custody and appearing in the juvenile court. The behavior of some others is due to neurotic conflicts of psychosis. A still greater number suffer from behavioral disorders characterized by poor impulse control, sometimes termed "acting-out" behavior.

Understanding the behavior and attitudes of this variety of persons requires both sociological and psychological knowledge. In some cases it is important to have sufficient recognition of pathology so that the probation officer does not attempt to deal with an emotionally ill person, but rather can refer him to other professional resources.

Sociology and Delinquency

Knowledge of social phenomenon, class values, cultural patterns, and economic influences is needed as background to understand the behavior patterns of many youths. Knowledge of earlier efforts to deal with delinquency, or the role of the police, of the background, philosophy, and structure of the juvenile court, of the uses made of detention and of training schools, of the efforts to prevent delinquency, of the treatment agencies such as child guidance clinics, and of the extent of the current problem—all such knowledge is needed by the probation officer.

The Community

Knowledge of the power structure of the community, of its social resources, how it reacts to various types of delinquent behavior, and what methods of social action can be gained in securing new resources for youth—these fields should also be familiar to the probation officer seeking to serve delinquency. Knowledge of the power structure and of the economic and bureaucratic organization of the community offers an understanding of how these determine what can be accomplished.

Self

In probation work, the officer himself helps the adolescent modify his behavior. It is the relationship with the delinquent that is the major treatment tool. The better the probation officer understands his own attitudes and beliefs, the better he can manage to discipline himself and to use the developing relationship in a professional way. Knowledge of self mitigates against the probation officer working out his personal conflicts through his clients.

Rules of Other Personnel

To avoid a conflict of approach to the delinquent and his family, the roles of other persons serving him need to be clearly defined and understood. Knowledge of the proper role of the police and of juvenile bureaus and of information regarding detention facilities and the appropriate use of the detention, and the contribution to be expected from detention personnel are all needed by the probation officer. In order to integrate the functions of the court with the functions of the other agencies in the community, knowledge of the various roles of these agencies is essential.

Authority

Knowledge of authority—its use and misuse—must be emphasized in this chapter as one of the keys to effective probation. Although the professional literature offers many definitions of authority, referring to both its sociological and psychological aspects, perhaps the dictionary version offers an adequate frame of reference.

Authority is: (1) The right to command and to enforce obedience;

the right to act by virtue of office. (2) The power derived from intellectual or moral superiority, from reputation, or from whatever else commands influence, respect, or esteem; as the authority of wisdom.

Persons coming before the court generally know its power to restrain the delinquent or remove him from his home, and commit him to an institution or appropriate facility. Knowledge of the proper application of social controls determines whether the delinquent can benefit from the court experience or not.

Records and Their Use

How and why records are kept is essential knowledge. The probation officer should be both student and critic of his own practice, and recording what he does gives him this opportunity. Each court will determine the social record that suits its needs. Often the probation officers are impatient with the amount of time needed for recording, but few would eliminate it. The case record serves as a protection to the client, as a possible resource, and as a way to develop skill and to gain new knowledge. The chief function of the record itself is to describe the situation, what the delinquent is doing about it, and the suggested plan for assisting him.

There are many other factors that should be considered when discussing the role of the probation officer. Attitudes and personality factors, such as sensitivity to client needs, objectivity, non-judgemental attitude, personal integrity, motivation to learn, developing into a well-rounded person, and a commitment to serve the delinquent, are all important, but they are beyond the scope of this chapter.

SUMMARY

There are numerous definitions of probation, but perhaps the most acceptable is the definition proposed by the Children's Bureau: probation is "a legal status in which a child, following adjudication in a delinquent case, is permitted to remain in the community, subject to supervision by the court through the court's probation department or an agency designated by the court, and subject to being returned to the court at any time during probation."

The goals of probation vary, obviously, because of the distinct needs of individual delinquents. However, all such variations should lead to the minimum goal of stopping delinquent behavior.

The following factors affect the goals of probation: (1) the situation and capacity of the client; (2) the culture and environment of the youth and his family; (3) the concept of probation help by the judge and the probation staff; (4) the quality and quantity of the staff, as they affect the service available to the youth and his family, and finally; (5) the court's situation in the community and the availability of community resources.

The juvenile probation officer has two roles, and there must be no conflict between these roles. The juvenile probation officer must be considered, first, as a court officer or "arm of the court," and second, as a correctional social worker.

As a *Social Diagnostician,* the probation officer must (1) identify and evaluate factors causing the delinquent behavior, and (2) develop and recommend a necessary program which will eliminate or alleviate these factors.

As an *Agent of Change,* the most characteristic common elements of positive change may come about through (1) interaction between the delinquent and the probation officer; (2) referral of the delinquent to other resources and the help he receives from these services; and (3) creation of new resources.

An indispensable pre-condition to effective probation services is an effective working relationship between the judge and the probation officer. Each must have a clear understanding of his role in the process. This means that all channels of communication should be open between the judge and the probation officer in order to provide a free exchange of ideas.

In order to be effective, the probation officer must have knowledge of: (1) function of the juvenile court; (2) of criminal law; (3) human growth and change; (4) sociology and delinquency; (5) the community; (6) self; (7) roles of the other personnel; (8) authority; and, finally, (9) records and their use.

QUESTIONS

1. What is the definition of probation as utilized by the Children's Bureau?
2. What is the minimum goal of probation?
3. List the factors which affect the goals of probation.
4. Discuss the goals of probation . . . in particular, the need to "tailor the plan according to the individual."
5. What are the *two* roles of the probation officer?
6. As a *social diagnostician,* the probation officer must make a *social study.* What is this study designed to do?
7. *True* or *False* . . . When the need for delinquent to change has been recognized and approval has been given to the probation plan, the *probation officer alone* is responsible for implementing the plan.

8. *True* or *False* . . . If a probationer commits a law violation (shoplifting, etc.), the probation officer should, for therapeutic purposes, ignore the delinquent or violation.
9. List the three factors that may bring about the process of positive change.
10. Should the probation officer make the families cognizant of the recommendations before such recommendations are presented to the judge?

PART THREE

History, Philosophy, and Function of the Juvenile Court

Legal Aspects of the Juvenile Court

Federal Laws Relating to Juveniles

Rights and Liabilities of Minors

Special Problems

Chapter 11

History, Philosophy, and Function of the Juvenile Court

IT HAS BEEN DIFFICULT to trace the historical developments of the juvenile court which, according to research, commenced in English law. Such research reveals that persons under a certain age were subject to differential treatment in many instances, and that the early English courts, of necessity, often made special provisions for young persons. Investigation also reveals that the juvenile court in the United States represented nothing more than a mild extension of English "common-law practices regarding juveniles." In fact, it was nothing more than a modern application of established principles, perhaps expanded more in the United States than anywhere else.

FACTORS ACCOUNTING FOR JUVENILE COURTS IN THE UNITED STATES

About the middle of the nineteenth century, a definite movement began in the United States for protecting young offenders in criminal proceedings. Dunham has explained this innovation:[1]

> "A development anticipating the juvenile court was the inauguration of probation as a device of dealing with offenders. This practice, initiated in Boston in 1841, highlighted some of the special protections that a child needed when brought before a court of law."

What was wrong with permitting a child to appear before a criminal court alone? We need only to visit a criminal court proceeding in order to get a concept of the cold and punitive nature of its atmosphere, and it would seem even more frightening to have that proceeding directed toward one's self. How much more frightening would the experience be for a child?

[1]W. H. Dunham, "Juvenile Court: Contradiction in Processing Offenders," *Law and Contemporary Problems, Summer, 1958*, pp. 509–510.

There were other important social forces which speeded the growing concern for juvenile handling. According to Lou:[2]

> "The history of modern treatment of juvenile offenders had its rise during the period of the industrial revolution and of the religious and moral revival at the beginning of the Nineteenth Century. It is more or less directly connected with the factory legislation in favor of women and children."

But the first legislation recognizing the need for special handling of offenders separately from adults came from foreign countries. England's first recognition came in the Juvenile Offender Act of 1847. However, the systematic development of the idea of the juvenile court took place in the United States. In 1869, a Massachusetts law provided for the presence of an agent or officer of the State Board of Charity in all criminal proceedings against a child under 16 to "protect their interest." In 1877, another Massachusetts law provided for the use of the term "Session for juvenile offenders" wherein a separate record and docket should be kept. In 1877 a New York law, supported by the Society for the Prevention of Cruelty to Children in New York City, prohibited mixing of juveniles with adults in prisons or places of confinement. Furthermore, the Boards of Children's Guardians Law of Indiana, passed in 1891 and amended in 1893, authorized the Board of Children's Guardians to file a petition in the Circuit Court if it should have probable cause to believe that only a child under 15 years of age was one whom we usually designate now as a dependent, neglected, truant, incorrigible, and sometimes delinquent. If the findings of the court were true, the child should be committed to the custody and control of the Board of Children's Guardians until such child should become of age.[3]

This was an interesting and progressive rule toward the improvement of juvenile justice. Very clearly, it expresses a belief that certain young children were in need of protection of the state rather than punishment for their offenses, at least before a certain age of responsibility.

From this brief review it is evident that the juvenile court was established essentially as a response to a social problem—society's concern over the callous, indifferent treatment of children accused of criminal activity. Lou summarizes the precipitating factors of the juvenile court and calls attention to the work of private agencies:[4]

> "The juvenile court movement was started principally as a protest against

[2]H. H. Lou, *Juvenile Courts in the United States*, Oxford University Press, London, 1927, p. 14.
[3]*Ibid.*, p. 18.
[4]*Ibid.*, p. 13.

the inhuman attitude of the criminal law, and the court that administers it, toward offending children, and only incidentally as a protest against the unorganized charity work of private agencies and the unsatisfactory state provision for the care of neglected and dependent or destitute children."

HISTORICAL PERSPECTIVE

It should be pointed out at this time that the juvenile court and probation have been developed to a fuller extent in the United States than elsewhere, but they are not American inventions. Both are derived from the practice in early English courts of releasing minor offenders on their own recognizance, with or without sureties. As early as 1763 the courts of England were already referring or citing precedence back to the days of the last half of the seventeenth century, 200 years before Chicago was even a trading post (origin of the first juvenile court) among the Indians in the wildness. Lord Redesdale in 1828 stated:[5]

> "Now, upon what does Lord Somers, upon what does Lord Nottingham, upon what does Lord Hardwich, upon what ground does every Chancellor who has been sitting on a bench, in a court of chancery since that time, place the jurisdiction? They all say that it is a right which devolves to the Crown, *in parens pariae*, and it is the duty of the Crown to see that the child is properly taken care of."

This particular case pertained to the custody of children of the Duke of Wellesley who, history shows, was denied the right of custody of his children because of his reckless extravagance and morally depraved character. The children were subsequently removed from the Duke of Wellesley in their best interests.

The above doctrine (*parens patriae* is the Latin phrase) has for many years been utilized to epitomize the legal and social philosophy underlying the juvenile court. *Parens patriae* describes a doctrine of the English Court of Chancery, by which the king, through his chancellors, assumed the general protection of all infants in the realm. The theory, as was pointed out in the Wellesley versus Wellesley case, was that the sovereign, as a *pater patriae*, possessed an obligation to oversee the welfare of the children in his kingdom, who, because of the frailties intrinsic to the minority, might be abused, neglected, or abandoned by their parents or other guardians. The king, through his Court of Chancery, could thereby step in and provide the requisite parental protection and care.

Although there appeared to be a great deal of latitude suggested by the broad criterion of a child's welfare, the Chancery Court very rarely

[5] *Wellesley v. Wellesley*, II Bligh, N.S. 124; 4 Engl. Rep. 1078, 1828.

performed this duty. The jurisdiction was a "delicate one" to be "exercised only when plainly demanded as a means of securing the infant's present and future well-being."[6] One reason for this reluctance was principally due to the English common-law which imposed a duty on the parents toward their children and also created a presumption that they would live up to it. Therefore, although the Chancery Court would interfere under appropriate circumstances, it was necessary that a strong case be constructed to demonstrate a completely negative situation detrimental to the child. Second, the Court was cautious about interfering, not from want of jurisdiction, but rather from absence of the means by which to effectuate care and custody; in practice, for many generations, it limited its parental duty to the supervision of wealthy minors. Finally, the court was mainly concerned with the welfare of the child (a limitation which is of interest with respect to later American developments of the doctrine of *parens patriae*). Therefore, taking this into consideration, neither the punishment of the parents nor the protection of society was a relevant criterion for judicial intervention.[7]

In the United States, the transplanting of the general English judicial system meant that the states and the federal government took the place of the Crown. Courts all but universally upheld the plenary powers and parental obligations implicit in the doctrine of *parens patriae*. However, the common-law presumption that the parents would properly perform their natural duty, and later the Fourteenth Amendment to the U.S. Constitution (which has consistently been interpreted to protect the natural right of a parent to the custody of his child from state intervention without due process of law), tended during the eighteenth and nineteenth centuries, to restrict the courts' assumption of custody to cases where it was clearly necessary in order to prevent injury to the child. The focus remained on the protection of the health, morals, and welfare of the child, rather than the protection of society, but the absence of property was no longer a consideration.[8]

Judge Peter Thatcher used this method extensively in the Boston Municipal Court during his term of office (1823-1843), and during this period *John Augustus* began to render the volunteer and informal probation services which, a century later, caused him to be termed "The Father of American Probation."

Obviously, there has been some mild controversy about the *exact place* of origin of the first juvenile court. Various early pieces of special legis-

[6]A. Pomeroy, *Treatise on Equity Jurisprudence*, 5th ed., 1307, 1941.
[7]O. W. Ketcham, "The Unfulfilled Promise of the Juvenile Court," *National Council on Crime and Delinquency*, Vol. VII, No. 2, April 1961, p. 98.
[8]*Ibid.*, pp. 98–99.

lation bore resemblance to the latter-day juvenile court. It seems clear, however, that the first juvenile court as we understand the institution today, was organized in the United States during 1899, and most authorities agree that Illinois deserves credit for fathering the juvenile court movement.[9]

Although Judge Benjamin Barr Lindsey's use of *Colorado's school law* for handling of juvenile offenders was enacted several months before the Illinois law, research indicates the Illinois Juvenile Court was provided with a solid foundation of legislative cement by the passage, on July 1, 1889, of an *Act to Regulate Treatment and Control of Dependent, Neglected, and Delinquent Children.* This is the Act upon which most subsequent legislation was based, and, in regard to Colorado's claim, it is a matter of record that Colorado's Legislature did not specifically organize the State's Juvenile Court Law until 1903.[10]

Therefore, it is a generally accepted fact that the first juvenile court law, not only in the United States, but in the world, began on July 1, 1899, with the establishment of the Chicago Juvenile Court, technically called the Juvenile Court of Cook County.

From the beginning, the juvenile court movement was given impetus in Chicago through an outgrowth of the work of a brilliant and dedicated group of social workers centered in the city. The movement also had the cooperation of the Bar Association of the State of Illinois. Furthermore, the movement was influenced by the juvenile court philosophy, and ideology sponsored chiefly by The Women's Club of Chicago, as early as 1895, and other humanitarians, social scientists, and a sprinkling of judges. The philosophy placed emphasis on treatment rather than on behavior circumstances, the prevailing viewpoint of the criminal court. Initially, a great deal of conflict arose in the legal profession as to whether or not the proposed policy of the juvenile court philosophy would violate the child offender's constitutional rights. Because of this conflict (and also because of the limited facilities of most juvenile courts), this philosophy has never fully materialized. Many criminologists now believe that the juvenile court is the principal experimental proving ground for changes in the entire crime-control system.[11]

Consistent with the concern of the greatest good for society, this first court represented a synthesis of developments (started earlier), toward

[9]G. Geis, "Publicity and the Juvenile Court Proceedings," *Fact and Facets*, Children's Bureau, Department of Health, Education, and Welfare, Washington, D.C., 1962, p. 1.

[10]*Ibid.*, p. 4.

[11]C. B. Vedder, *Juvenile Offenders*, Charles C Thomas, Springfield, Illinois, 1963, p. 143.

such objectives as separate hearings, lesser punishments for children, segregated facilities, and probation. The above was quite significant because legislation was being considered to initiate these goals, and the effect was to establish into law a philosophy of guidance, protection, and care. Furthermore, with this court as a model for the states and other countries, justice for juveniles was to become a world-wide concern.

Although the Illinois law set up a state-wide system with juvenile courts; actually only Cook County initially had both the population and facilities to operate a court. The law applied to children under the age of 16, and restricted the definition of a *delinquent child to a person under the age who violated any law of the state, or any city, or village ordinance.* At least one judge from the Circuit Court was to be designated to hear juvenile cases in a special courtroom, labeled the *Juvenile Court Room.* The Act also eliminated arrests of children by a warrant, the use of indictment, and many other forms of criminal procedure. It provided separate records and informal proceedings. It aimed to make the court's *care, custody, and discipline of a child approximate as nearly as possible that which should be given by his parents.*[12]

The Juvenile Court movement initially steered an erratic pioneer course and the first five years of its existence were largely a period of experimentation, of sentiment, and of missionary work by individuals.

However, by 1904, eleven states had enacted juvenile court legislation and eight years later there were twenty-two states with juvenile court laws. By 1927, all states but Maine and Wyoming had juvenile court acts. Wyoming was the last to join the movement, finally inaugurating the juvenile court system in 1945. California, in 1903, passed a juvenile court act.

During the beginning of the juvenile court movement in the first quarter of the nineteenth century, society began to see the juvenile offender as a child needing treatment different from that of an adult criminal. The movement to provide separate institutions for child offenders started prior to 1898 with the openings of such institutions as The House of Refuge for Children in New York City, and the first state institution in Massachusetts, but these separate institutions for minors were more concerned with the treatment of youthful offenders after their crime, than with prevention or rehabilitation. Programs in the area of counseling, vocational rehabilitation, psychological testing, or other forms of therapy were unknown. These institutions essentially were prisons, places of confinement, rather than forces for rehabilitation. Such institutions represented society's way of getting the problem of delinquency out of view—and even out of mind. The emphasis was

[12]*Illinois Laws, 1899*, p. 157.

on hard work and rigid discipline. But, although hopelessly inadequate by present-day standards, they were better than the jails and prisons formerly used for these youngsters and represented a major forward step at that time.

As social and medical knowledge advanced, the emphasis shifted from concern with the symptoms to the study of causes. Lying, stealing, truancy, reflectatory behavior, and sexual offenses—the principal manifestations of delinquency—were placed in "test tubes" and studied.

This, the clinical approach to juvenile delinquency was initiated by Dr. Wililam Healy, in a laboratory established for the Chicago Juvenile Court, in 1909. Dr. Healy suggested that a combination of factors was associated with delinquency and that the combination varies with individual cases. Subsequently, child guidance clinics were organized in all the large cities of the United States. They served as diagnostic and consultation centers for both individuals and courts. This philosophy has spread and influenced the development of clinics associated with hospitals and universities, adult education centers, and child care and parental responsibility in various welfare agencies. To this day, this particular area is still expanding.

The passage of the Social Security Act, in 1935, stimulated the rapid development of diagnostic and consultation centers throughout the states. Of particular significance in relation to juvenile delinquency were the grants authorized under this Act to assist public welfare agencies in establishing, extending, and strengthening public welfare services for children, including those in danger of becoming delinquent.

Gradually, under the provisions of this Act and other legislation, a variety of resources for services and care for children have developed. The Social Security Act gave impetus to the Social Insurance Programs, public assistance, child welfare services, public health services, maternal and child-health services, and other services of this nature, all of which are basic in providing conditions conducive to the well-being of children and youth. The Public Health Service Act in 1948 was amended to authorize grants to the states for extending and improving community health services. Federal funds for demonstration projects in mental services were authorized after the Health Service Act was further amended to provide funds from the government.

Measures aimed at juvenile delinquency in perspective have been closely interwoven with the development of measures for the well-being of people. However, although historically the provisions for delinquent youth are very old, they have not kept pace with modern knowledge and understanding of human behavior. Furthermore, they have failed to keep up with the change in patterns of our fast-moving urban society. There is still a great deal to be done in the area of prevention, treatment, and control of juvenile delinquency before it can be said that the full potential of society has been utilized.

MODIFICATIONS SINCE 1899

Historically, the guiding principle underlying the juvenile court since its founding in Cook County, Illinois, in 1899, was to inquire whether or not the juvenile manifested a condition—the condition of being delinquent—not whether he committed an offense. If it was established that he manifested the condition of delinquency, the assumption was that this was due to reasons beyond his control. The remedy, then, was not to punish him, but to remove the condition or to neutralize its effects. This called for careful study, various forms of therapy, and guidance, rather than the imposition of penalties. Historically, too, proceedings in the juvenile court were civil, not criminal. There was a hearing, not a trial. The formal trappings of the criminal court were replaced by informality. The rules of evidence were modified since the issue was not one of fact, but went to the problem of how to sway the weapons of treatment in the juvenile's behalf.

Since 1899, there have been extensive modifications in these earlier views as to how the juvenile court is to function. While jurisdictions vary, it is safe to say that today, in most parts of the United States, there is a greater concern with elements of proof than there used to be. While the rules of evidence have been relaxed, they have not been waived. While the concept of delinquency has survived as a condition somewhat difficult to define, and beyond the capacity of the juvenile to control in all instances, most juvenile courts have required more precision in defining this term and in dealing with its forms than was true some decades ago. The earlier courts required an investigation into the background of the juvenile before making disposition of him, and this practice has been continued and improved upon. Some functions have been added to the court. It is not uncommon for courts in these days, through their probation departments, to operate institutional facilities such as detention halls, camps, ranches, and shelters, whereas this was not thought of initially. Courts vary in the jurisdiction they exercise over traffic cases involving juveniles, over issues of dependency and neglect, over adults who contribute to the delinquency or dependency of a minor, over truancy, and over parallel matters going to the health and welfare of the young.

Nevertheless, the basic concern of the juvenile court with the growth and development of juveniles and youths, and with the hazards to which they may be exposed, still remains today as strong as it was 66 years ago, perhaps even stronger if that is possible. Hence, the court still inclines in the direction of primary concern with what has damaged the juvenile.

PHILOSOPHY

The juvenile court system was founded by society on the basic assumption—and a radical one if the tenets of the centuries that preceded its acceptance are considered—that there was one factor, the factor of age, of youth alone, which overcame the previously assumed notion of the complete and total responsibility of the non-insane child for all his acts. This assumption of partial responsibility was predicated on the fact of the child's immaturity and that there were conditions inherent in the immature state which made it impossible for the child to act as a responsible adult being should act. Now, as soon as this assumption was established, there followed the absolute necessity that some instrument or instruments would have to be instituted in order to determine the nature and the extent of the maturity or immaturity present in the child before the court. Logically, this led to the demand that each child should be looked upon as an individual and that all his assets and liabilities would have to be determined and evaluated before the extent of his maturity—and, hence, responsibility—could be formulated. This idea of the *individualization of treatment* for the delinquent child was the first and basic theoretical construct that Dr. William Healy enunciated directly following his association with the children before the juvenile court. It is still the underlying motivation of all work with children, delinquent or otherwise, and it is still society's ideal for the future.[13]

When the juvenile court movement began in 1899 the Committee of the Chicago Bar Association (which sponsored the act creating this court) summed up the purposes of the new law:[14]

> *"The fundamental idea of the juvenile court law is that the state must step in and exercise guardianship over a child found under such adverse social or individual conditions as to develop crime. . . . If proposes a plan whereby he may be treated, not as a criminal, or legally charged with crime, but as a ward of the state, to receive practically the care, custody, and discipline that are accorded the neglected and dependent child, and which, as the act states, shall approximate as nearly as may be that which should be given by its parents."*

[13] G. E. Gardner, "The Juvenile Court as a Child Care Institution," *Federal Probation*, Vol. XVI, No. 2, June 1952, p. 8.

[14] R. Pound, "The Juvenile Court and the Law," *National Probation Parole Association Yearbook*, New York, 1944, p. 13.

The essential philosophy, then, of the juvenile court, and of other specialized courts handling juveniles' cases, has been called "individualized justice."[15] This in essence means that the court "recognizes the individuality of a child and adapts its orders accordingly,"[16] that it is a "legal tribunal where law and science, especially the science of medicine, and those sciences which deal with human behavior, such as biology, sociology, and psychology, work side by side,"[17] and that its purpose is remedial and, to a degree, preventive, rather than punitive.

The specialized court owes its origin to the humanitarian impulse and initiative of many lawyers, social workers, ministers, and others who had become increasingly troubled by the treatment of children under the criminal law and whose efforts to correct this condition resulted in the establishment of the world's first juvenile court in 1899.

Individualized justice is not, however, easy to achieve. In order for a court to become a fully effective and fair tribunal operating for the general welfare, there must be:

1. A judge and a staff identified with, and capable of carrying out, a non-punitive and individualized service.
2. Sufficient facilities available in the court and the community to insure:
   a. that the dispositions of the court are based on the best available knowledge of the child;
   b. that the child, if he needs care and treatment, receives these through facilities adapted to his needs and from persons properly qualified and empowered to give them;
   c. that the community receives adequate protection.
3. Procedures that are designed to insure that two objectives are kept constantly in mind, these being:
   a. the individualization of the child and his situation;
   b. the protection of the legal and constitutional rights of both parents and child.

write

Some courts have been able to meet the above criteria. Others, particularly those in rural areas, have not been able to find or create the necessary facilities.[18] Others still have not fully grasped the concepts of a non-punitive justice and some have not been able to keep in balance the two-fold objective set forth under (3) above. If more attention is paid in this preliminary discussion to the maintenance of this balance

[15]R. Pound, "Society's Stake in the Offender," *National Probation Parole Association Yearbook*, New York, 1947, p. 6.

[16]G. L. Schramm, "Philosophy of the Juvenile Court," *The Annals of the American Academy of Political and Social Science*, 261-101-108, 1949, p. 101.

[17]H. H. Lou, *Juvenile Courts in the United States*, The University of North Carolina Press, Chapel Hill, N.C., 1927, p. 2.

[18]L. J. Carr, "Most Courts Have to be Substandard!" *Federal Probation*, Vol. XIII, No. 29, Nov. 29, 1949, p. 33.

and to the protection of the individual's rights than to the problem of those courts whose procedures and philosophies are still punitive in nature, it is because the shortcomings of a punitive court have been pretty generally recognized, while there has been less concern, especially outside the legal profession, about the protection of individual rights in these courts.

The question of the proper balance between the discretion of the court and the rights of the individual is partly historical.[19] Some early writers, for instance, reacting against the early assumption that parental rights were inalienable, tended to consider these rights as "merely a privilege or a duty conferred upon the parent in the exercise of the police power of the state."[20] The state, it was contended, through its courts could therefore disregard or derogate from these rights by bringing the child before the court without the use of any process at all. Some support for this position was given by the broadness of the language used in certain decisions of higher courts. "To save a child from becoming a criminal," says one decision, ". . . the legislature surely may provide for a salvation of such a child . . . by bringing it into one of the courts of the state without any process at all. . . . The act is but an exercise by the state of its supreme power over the welfare of its children under which it can take a child from its father and let it go where it will . . . if the welfare of the child . . . can be thus promoted."[21]

In fact, the first juvenile court act in Illinois did not require that the parents be notified of the court's proceedings,[22] although this fault was soon remedied. Similarly, some early courts developed what must have been a most comforting theory, that to commit a child to an institution was an act designed entirely for the child's own interest and, therefore, involved no element of restraint or loss of freedom.[23]

Early juvenile courts struggled against a weight of tradition to establish new ideas. In the eyes of many, including some of the leading members of the bar, the law had become, by the end of the nineteenth century, something of a mechanized procedure unequal to the administration of justice.[24] Furthermore, there was little understanding of the

[19]R. Pound, "The Juvenile Court in the Service State" in *Current Approaches to Delinquency, 1949 Yearbook*, National Probation Parole Association, New York, 1950, p. 27.

[20]Lou, *op. cit.*, p. 8.

[21]*Commonwealth v. Fisher*, 213, Pa. 48, 62 Alt. 198, 200, 1905.

[22]S. P. Breckenridge, *Social Work in the Courts*, Chicago University Press, Chicago, 1934, p. 197.

[23]*Ex Parte Sharp*, 15 Idaho 120, 96 Pae, 563, 1908.

[24]R. Pound, "Jurisprudence," *Encyclopedia of the Social Sciences*, The Macmillan Co., **8**:477-490, 1935.

complexity of the problems involved. A good environment and a good education were often thought of as the whole answer to the problem of delinquency and neglect. It also created what today would be an entirely unacceptable distinction between responsible citizens on the one hand, and the poor and uneducated on the other.[25]

Despite these tendencies, which were largely a product of the age, these pioneers did much to establish a non-punitive philosophy for juvenile courts. The spirit of their concepts must be maintained. In recognizing the importance of maintaining a balance between individualization and the protection of legal rights, any suggestion must be avoided of a return to a mechanized, routine application of "automatic" justice, which would be no justice at all, and which would deny one of the most vital functions of a specialized court, that of giving the authoritative support needed to assure to all children the help, the care, and the treatment they need. The administration of justice need not become routinized. Current criticism, as well as recent improvements in the handling of cases in other areas, for instance, in the criminal courts, shows a desire to improve standards of individualization without sacrificing basic rights of individuals. The situation has, indeed, changed in the last fifty years. The principle that a child involved in delinquency is in need of treatment rather than retributive punishment, for instance, is far more widely accepted today. Juvenile courts and treatment agencies no longer have to fight for their very existence. Their concepts, although not as well understood as they might be, are not unknown to the general public. The complexities of the job to be done, a fuller appreciation of the importance of family relationships, the greater possibility today of disagreements between experts as to the best handling of the case, a knowledge that anti-social behavior, in adults as well as children, is not solely a matter of ignorance or perversity, and a keener appreciation of the rights of all people to live their lives as fully as possible, suggest a need for a reevaluation of some of the earlier approaches and attitudes.

Society does not want to lose sight of the basic principle underlying the philosophy of specialized courts dealing with children, which states that any child under the jurisdiction of the court is subject to the discipline and entitled to the protection of the state. *The proceedings on behalf of the children in these courts are not adversary in nature and the court must be permitted to operate with informality and flexibility, as far as possible, consistent with the protection of the rights of the indi-*

[25]S. P. Breckenridge and E. Abbott, *The Delinquent Child and the Home*, Charities Publication Committee, New York, 1912, p. 185.

viduals coming before it. Failure to permit this would negate the basic principles underlying the philosophy of these courts. On the other hand, although proceedings on behalf of children are not adversary in nature, basic rights of both parent and child are involved.

The rights of parents to care for their children and to exercise their discretion in meeting the needs of their children are basic to society as a whole. Equally basic are the rights of children to maintain a personal liberty, free from other than parental or normal community restraint, to live with their parents, and to have someone legally responsible for protecting their interests. Modern psychology, in emphasizing the importance to the child of his own parents, has only confirmed what tradition, religion, and common sense have long known to be true.

The following are six major points reflecting the constitutional rights of minors as advocated in the 1954 publication, *Standard for Specialized Courts Dealing With Children*, of the National Council of Crime and Delinquency:

1. Due process of law is as applicable to the procedures in a juvenile court as it is in any other court.
2. The powers of the court should not be drastically limited or removed.
3. Unlimited discretion should not be placed in any officer to do as he sees fit with any child.
4. All parties coming before the court have the right to know the facts on which the court makes its decision.
5. The parent and the child have the right to legal counsel in juvenile court.
6. An administrative agency should be able to take some actions with respect to a child placed in its custody without further recourse to court order.

For purposes of simplification, it may be said that the philosophy of the juvenile court, as distinguished from that of the criminal court, is based upon two principles:

That a child in the juvenile court is not regarded as responsible for criminal acts until he has attained a much greater age than was applied under the preexisting law.

That under the jurisdiction of the juvenile court, the child is not accused of crime and suffers no conviction.

The juvenile court, then, concerns itself with children who are dependent or children whose conduct or circumstances otherwise suggest a need for custody and discipline not supplied by their parents. Therefore, the state, acting through its court, intervenes as guardian of such children offering protection and guidance instead of punishment.

FUNCTION OF THE COURT*

Since their inception, juvenile courts have often found themselves without community resources with which to make their judgments effective. For example, in a community without proper facilities, a child who required foster home care might be left in a damaging home situation, be "committed" to an institution, or be placed in a substandard facility. None of these solutions would have met the child's needs. Because of such lack of necessary resources within the community, many courts find themselves forced to develop child-care facilities within their own administrative structures, much against their will and principles. The courts, believing that the administration of some of these child-care facilities was an appropriate role for the court to play, developed such facilities with a great deal less reluctance. Still others have simply accepted the lack of proper facilities without taking any action.

There are different ways of looking at this development. At one extreme are those authorities who believe that the court should itself administer most of the child-care and treatment facilities, such as have been developed by voluntary and, more recently, public agencies. In their view, the court would thus become the primary public child-care agency in the community. At the opposite extreme are those who would limit the court's function more drastically by transferring its powers of disposition to an administrative panel or tribunal as has been done in some European countries.[26]

In the United States, there would be serious question as to the constitutionality of such an administrative tribunal. Such a tribunal would be making decisions that would deprive parents of the custody of their child or a child of his freedom.[27] An administrative tribunal made up of experts in the social sciences, as the proponents of such a tribunal usually conceive it to be, is not necessarily trained to protect the rights of people coming before it. Moreover, an administrative tribunal would be no more likely than a judge to come to decisions that are sound for the child. Like the judge, the tribunal must rely for its decision on the

**Function of the Court,* Department of Health, Education, and Welfare, Washington, D.C., 1966 (Revised), pp. 9–15.

[26] P. Lejins, "Is the Youth Authority Really Paying Off?" *Proceedings of the National Conference of Juvenile Agencies,* Forty-Seventh Annual Meeting, 1950, pp. 87–93.

[27] K. F. Linroot, "Should the Protection of Neglected and Morally Abandoned Children be Secured by a Judicial Authority or by a Nonjudicial body? Should the Courts for Delinquent Children and Juveniles be Maintained?" *Twelfth International Penal and Penitentiary Congress, 1950,* The Hague, Administration of Prisons, Vol. IV, 1950, 8 pp.

study made by the probation staff, with the help of medical, psychiatric, and community resources. The members of the panel cannot themselves make social studies, nor should they, if they are to act in a judicial capacity.

On the other hand, it does not seem desirable to center all child-care services in a court. The kind of detailed planning, for instance, involved in the day-to-day care of residential treatment of children should not be a matter of judicial decision, nor should a court review its own acts as it well might be called upon to do in such a situation. An agency providing specialized child-care services should be part of the executive branch of government or a voluntary agency, and should be under the direction of an executive trained in social work. It should not be a part of the judicial branch of government and should not be under the direction of a person whose primary qualification for the job is legal training. Also, the court ought not to be burdened with the details of administration or policy that such an agency requires. A question of duplication is also of importance. Many social agencies that render excellent service to children entrusted to their care by courts are privately supported. Others, although publicly supported, may need also to provide care for children who have not come to them through the courts. A parent who needs and wants care for his child, not requiring a change in legal status, should not be compelled to go through a court. To create two public services, one in the court and one outside, giving the same type of care would seem unnecessary.

Neither extreme point of view would, therefore, seem to meet the stiuation. A point of view which places some services in the court and others in an agency in the executive branch of government or a volunteer agency would seem to be more practical and to be in line with the American tradition regarding the separation of powers. What services should be administratively subject to each must depend on the essential nature of their contribution to the total process. To say that the court should undertake the judicial function and the agency the administrative, although basically sound, is an oversimplification of the problem and should not be taken too literally. Actually, there is no agreement as to what is "administrative" and what is "judicial," nor can the two processes always be separated in relation to court process. Instead, it may have to be said that the court should have control over the services which are necessary or closely related to its judicial function. Services which do not fall into this category should be administered by an agency in the executive branch of government or by a voluntary agency. Even then, it will be found that some services are so closely related to both functions that the choice may have to depend on pragmatic or incidental factors.

For example, in the case of neglect or delinquency the process by which the state assumes partial authority over the upbringing of a child and implements this authority can be divided into eight steps:

1. Investigation of Complaint and Filing of Petition. Investigation as used here is the action required to secure the facts necessary to determine whether an act of delinquency has actually been committed or a condition of neglect actually exists. The individual or agency which received the complaint, made the investigation, and sought authorization from the court to file a petition is responsible for providing the evidence to support the allegations made in the petition. It seems clear that investigation, as defined here, and the filing of the petition are not appropriate functions of the court. A court through the use of its own staff should not be placed in the position of investigator and petitioner and also act as the tribunal deciding the validity of the allegations in the petition. Generally, therefore, investigating complaints and filing of petitions require services proper to the police or to such other administrative agency providing protective services for children as may exist and be vested by law with these functions. In certain situations, however, it may be desirable for the court, through its own personnel, to take such action, for example, in the case of a child on probation who is alleged to have committed a delinquent act.

2. Determination of the Need for and Nature of Court Action. When a situation is brought to the attention of the court for action, it should have the power to determine whether action is needed and, if so, the nature of such action. Generally, the court's intake service is primarily responsible for making a preliminary screening to determine whether the protection of the child and the community require further action. Since this is the responsibility of the court, it is appropriate that the intake service be placed within the administrative structure of the court.

3. Establishing the Fact That the Child Is within the Jurisdiction of the Court. This action, calling as it does for legal determination as to the authority of the court to act in the case, is clearly a judicial function.

4. Establishing the Facts as Alleged in the Petition. This action is similar to that of (3) above, and is clearly a judicial function.

5. Making the Social Study. The social study is made for the specific purpose of helping the court determine what treatment disposition to make. The court's determination will, of course, be based on all relevant facts presented to it, whether presented as a result of the social study or outside of such a study, through other testimony. The cardinal principle should be that the court should have before it all the facts necessary to make an intelligent decision. The judge has responsibility for making decisions and the community holds him accountable. In most cases, however, he relies to a considerable extent on the social study made by other persons in arriving at his decision. He needs, therefore, to have confidence in such persons and to be able to hold them accountable for the adequacy of the social study and general performance of their duties. In neglect or delinquency cases, it is believed that the social study is so closely related to the judicial process that it should normally, but not necessarily, be done by personnel administratively attached to the court. In other types of cases, this may or may not be so.[28] *When this service is provided by a worker in another agency, such as a child welfare worker in the public welfare department, or in a voluntary agency, the worker should be administratively responsible to the court for service performed for the court.*

6. Determining What Action Is Needed and What Rights, If Any, of the Parent or Child Should Be Limited. This action, involving possible limitations on the rights of the child or his parents or a change in the legal status of the child, is clearly judicial.

7. Providing Needed Care and Treatment. The operation of facilities for the care and treatment of children away from their homes is a function appropriate to administrative agencies. In the case of detention (secure detention), a second principle is involved. Detention involves protection of the community, as well as of the child. Detention also involves limiting the rights of the parent and child. For this reason, the court must have control over intake and release. Following this second principle, good detention has been developed under the administration of courts, particularly in the urban communities, However, it should be possible to combine the two principles by placing administration of detention facilities under an administrative agency and ensuring that the court has control over intake and release and has a part in the developing administrative policy.

The administration of shelter care facilities for children awaiting court hearing is more closely related to the general child-care functions of administrative agencies and should be provided by them.

Providing treatment in his own home to the child who has come before the court may involve two different situations, it may involve the legal status of *probation.* The status similar to the making of the social study is so closely related to the judicial process in delinquency cases

[28] *Essentials of Adoption Law and Procedure,* Children's Bureau, Department of Health, Education, and Welfare, Washington, D.C., 1949, pp. 16–18.

that it should be performed by personnel administratively under the direction of the court, or responsible to the court. Such action is especially warranted since it enables the same person who makes the study to continue to work with the child and parents during the probation period.

Treatment of a child in his own home in *neglect situations* may also involve *protective supervision.* This involves casework service to the family which is generally more closely related to that given by family or children's agencies. However, this service involves responsibilities to and by the court which require that the service be given by the court where no agency is willing to undertake this responsibility.

8. Releasing a Child from the Control of the State. This action involves removing the limitation placed on the rights of the child and parents, which were originally limited by judicial action, and may often involve a change in the legal status of the child. These seem to be actions falling clearly within the judicial functions.

SUMMARY

The concepts of the juvenile court originated from the enlightened legal decisions of English and American jurists. The changes in social philosophy made by European and American societies concerning juvenile justice profoundly influenced the growth of these principles. Several important theories are involved. Complete histories and legal documentation exist of the subject, and the main ideas are outlined here for quick review:

The state (meaning the people) may act (through its legislature) as a guardian parent for the protection and welfare of minors who need this assistance. Additional protection of society is implied.

The juvenile court plays the role of this protective guardian parent as an equitable, not criminal, court with inherent authority which has been carefully reexpressed by the juvenile court law.

The juvenile court takes jurisdiction when legal requirements, as made by the people acting through its legislature, are met. (EXAMPLE: Allegations of a petition are adjudicated according to constitutionally derived due process of law.)

Human behavior theories of treatment of the individual and social reform of social institutions have replaced the concept of universal punishment regarding the disposition of the minor's case. (EXAMPLE: Sociological theories and psychological theories.)

The chronological events which marked the growth and development of the juvenile court and juvenile probation are:

1830 Judge Thatcher of Boston placed defendants on probation. (Adults)

1841 Washington Total Abstinence Society in Boston helped the courts with alcoholics placed on probation. (Adults)

1841 to 1859 John Augustus, shoemaker, *Father of Probation*, first extensively used the word "probation." Demonstrated the value of probation with adults and children. Introduced the following basic techniques: intake case screening, court process, supervision, social history investigation, interviewing methods, visiting minors in their environment, placement out of the home, detention, cooperation with all parties concerned in the minor's welfare, such as parents, relatives, schools, police employers, and social agencies.

1869 Acts of the Commonwealth of Massachusetts provided that a representative of the Board of State Charities appear in courts when commitment to state reformatory was impending. Judge could place the child in a home of suitable family upon the Charities' recommendation.

1878 First *probation law* in the world. Mayor of Boston appointed person from the police or city to attend the criminal courts to investigate cases and recommend amenable cases to court for rehabilitation on probation.

1899 First juvenile court in the world established in Cook County, Chicago.

1901 to 1927 Judge Ben B. Lindsey, Denver Juvenile Court, leading proponent of the juvenile court movement, nationally and internationally.

The fundamental idea of the Juvenile Court Law is that the state must step in and exercise guardianship over a child found under adverse social or individual conditions which develop criminality. It proposes a plan whereby he may be treated, not as a criminal or legally charged with a crime, but as a ward of the state to receive practically the care, custody, and discipline that are accorded the neglected and dependent child, and which, as the Act states, shall approximate as nearly as possible the treatment that the wise parent could give his own child.

It may be said that the philosophy of the juvenile court, as distinguished from that of a criminal court, is based on two principles:

1. That a child in the juvenile court is not regarded as responsible for criminal acts until he has attained a much greater age than was applied under the preexisting law.
2. That, under the jurisdiction of the juvenile court, the child is not accused of crime and suffers no conviction.

The purpose of the juvenile court law is to afford a protecting hand to unfortunate boys and girls who, by reason of their own conduct, evil tendencies, or improper environment, have proven that the best interests of society, the welfare of the state, and their own good demand that the guardianship of the state be substituted for that of the natural parents.

The history of the juvenile court and probation indicates that it is not an American invention, although it has been developd to a fuller extent in the United States than anywhere else. The juvenile court system was derived from the practice in English courts for centuries of releasing minor offenders on their own recognizance, with or without sureties. The common-law concept of *parens patriae* (father of his country) therefore derives from England. According to this doctrine, the king was the protector of all incompetents; i.e., insane, feeble-minded, and minors. As such, he had inherent powers to care for their best interests. This power was later vested in the king's "right-hand-man" known as the chancellor. The chancellor soon became the judge of the courts of equity and, as such, presided over the "children's courts." The power to care for minors then became vested in English courts of equity or chancery.

QUESTIONS

1. *True* or *False* . . . John Augustus was the first judge to utilize probation services (1830), in Boston, Massachusetts.
2. *True* or *False* . . . The first juvenile court act in Illinois required that the parents be contacted as soon as possible.
3. *True* or *False* . . . By 1904, 22 states had enacted juvenile court legislation.
4. Discuss the philosophy of the juvenile court.
5. *Outline* the history of the juvenile court.
6. List the *six major points* reflecting the constitutional rights of minors as advocated in the publication, *Standards for Specialized Courts Dealing With Children,* and the *National Council on Crime and Delinquency.*
7. Discuss the concept of "individualized justice" as utilized by specialized courts handling juveniles.
8. Discuss "modifications in the juvenile court since 1899."
9. Define *parens patriae.*
10. List the process by which the state assumes partial authority over the upbringing of a child. Implementation of this authority is divided into eight steps (Function of the juvenile court).

Chapter 12

Legal Aspects of the Juvenile Court

SOCIETY HAS DETERMINED that the best way to deal with youthful criminals is to re-educate and rehabilitate them. However, existing methods of treatment and judicial procedures set up for adult criminals do not serve this rehabilitative purpose. Consequently, separate treatment facilities and a separate court have been established for youthful offenders.

Treatment methods utilized by the adult courts are incompatible with the correctional-oriented philosophy of the juvenile court for several reasons. *The criminal courts incarcerate law-breakers, not only for rehabilitative purposes but also for the purpose of protecting society from harm and to deter others from criminal acts.* In order to realize these purposes, institutionalization may be severe and long in duration, and this type of treatment is likely to make the offender even more antisocial than he was before. On the other hand, rehabilitation requires individualized treatment.[1]

The publicity which attaches to criminal conviction and punishment renders the criminal court process unsatisfactory for dealing with juvenile offenders. Such publicity renders rehabilitative "machinery" useless. The youth who potentially would be amenable to rehabilitation is vitiated by such publicity, because a serious community stigma is attached to a conviction in the criminal courts. Perhaps, even more important, rehabilitation should begin during the court hearing. As a result, juvenile court procedure itself has been altered to achieve a protective rather than an adversary atmosphere. Rules of evidence, court procedure and sterile formality have been discarded. Thus the juvenile court is informal in nature and the court, acting in the role of *parens patriae,* takes protective jurisdiction over the minor and purports to act on his behalf.

However, with the wide publicity given to the problem of juvenile

[1] "The California Juvenile Court," *Stanford Law Review,* Vol. X, No. 3, Stanford University, Stanford, California, May 1958, p. 471.

delinquency in recent years, these specialized courts have been subjected to considerable criticism. *First, it is advocated that in the interest of informality, the reformers have discarded too many of the criminal safeguards necessary to preserve the youth's right to a fair hearing. Second, it is charged that the juvenile court system has failed to achieve its rehabilitative goal because treatment facilities are inadequate, many juvenile court administrators are reluctant to abandon the punitive approach of the criminal court in favor of complete adoption of the corrective approach, and the juvenile court law itself often injects criminal sanctions into the juvenile court.*[2]

LEGAL PRINCIPLES

There is nothing magical or revolutionary about the legal principles upon which the juvenile court rests. These concepts did not spring fully matured from the brow of the Illinois legislature in 1899, as some chroniclers would have us believe. Rather, they are of ancient lineage; they had their childhood and adolescence.[3]

They were never more clearly stated than by the Supreme Court of Pennsylvania, exactly one hundred twenty years ago. Under an 1826 statute, a 14-year-old girl, Mary Ann Krouse, had been committed at the request of her mother to the House of Refuge for "vicious conduct." A habeus corpus proceeding was brought on the child's behalf, claiming she was deprived of her liberty without due process of law and without trial by jury, a claim that is still heard today in many juvenile cases. However, in holding that Mary Ann was not being deprived of her liberty and that her constitutional rights were not otherwise infringed, the court said:[4]

"The House of Refuge is not a prison but a school. Where reformation, and not punishment, is the end, it may indeed be used as a prison for juvenile convicts who else would be committed to a common goal; and in respect to these, the constitutionality of the act which incorporated it, stands clear of controversy. . . . The object of the charity is reformation by training its inmates to industry; by imbuing their minds with principles of morality and religion; by furnishing them with means to earn a living; and, above all, by separating them from the corrupting influence and improper associates, to this end may not the natural parents, when unequal to the task of education, or unworthy

[2]*Standards for Specialized Courts Dealing With Children*, Children's Bureau, Department of Health, Education, and Welfare, Washington, D.C., pp. 1–2, 1954.
[3]W. S. Fort, "The Juvenile Court Examines Itself," *National Probation Parole Association*, Vol. V, No. 4, New York, October 1959, p. 404.
[4]*Ibid.*, p. 405.

of it, be superseded by the *parens patriae*, or common guardian of the community.

"It is to be remembered that the public has a paramount interest in the virtue and knowledge of its members, and that of strict right, the business of education belongs to it. That parents are ordinarily entrusted with it is because it can seldom be entrusted to better hands; but where they are incompetent or corrupt what is there to prevent the public from withdrawing their faculties, health, as they obviously are at its sufference? The right of parental control is a natural but not an unalienable one. It is not accepted by the declaration of rights out of the subject of ordinary legislation; and it consequently remains subject to the ordinary legislative power which, if wantonly or inconveniently used, would soon be constitutionally restricted, but the competency of which as the government is constituted cannot be doubted. As to abridgement of indefeasible rights by the confinement of the person, it is no more than what is borne, to a greater or less extent, in every school; and we know of no natural right to exemption from restraints which conduce to an infant's welfare."

The legal principles there so ably announced were consistently adhered to during the nineteenth century; by 1899 they were fully accepted as a part of American jurisprudence and thus provided a firm legal foundation upon which to build the juvenile court structure.[5]

SOCIAL PRINCIPLES

What was new about the juvenile court was that it was the first true offspring of the union of law and "the public good," because it was the first court designed to deal separately and solely with the law-breaking behavior of a child and the conditions that cause it for that particular child, hence its motto, "Individualized justice." As the product of the marriage of two ancient and honored lines fundamental in the development of man, it is no bastard product illicitly conceived. The soundness of these lines is eloquently attested by the phenomenal growth and development which has attended its childhood, but it is still in its infancy. And, as is so often true with children, it is having growing pains, lots of them; it will have many more.[6]

JUVENILE COURT RESPONSIBILITIES

The responsibilities of any juvenile court are, naturally enough, both legal and social. Procedural and substantive legal rights constitute its

[5]*Ibid.*, p. 405.
[6]*Ibid.*, p. 405.

legal responsibilities. These are not mere window dressing. They are fundamental to the dignity of man and child. They provide the boundaries and framework within which the power of the state must be exercised. No man may exercise power over another individual except according to law. Naked power, no matter how well intentioned, is despotism, and despotism, however benevolent its wielder may believe himself to be, rapes the dignity of man and violates every concept of equality and right. It is the antithesis of everything which the United States stands for. The juvenile court's power comes from the law. Its duty to comply with the law is absolute, and none the less so because in the people's minds, as well as in reality, the courts are the guardians of the people's rights.

Thus there is a necessity ever present in the juvenile court: the judge must be certain that both procedural and substantive law are compiled with. This duty rests upon the court itself, and is non-delegable.[7]

Periodic, sometimes crescendo, grumblings throughout America indicate that this necessity is not always acceded to in the day-to-day administration of all of our juvenile courts. Why not?

According to *Justice William S. Fort,* Circuit Court of Oregon, there are at least four reasons for this weakness:

1. Juvenile court laws are often far from clear.
2. The interests of the persons working in court, usually including the judges, are socially directed, sometimes to the detriment of legal rights.
3. A substantial number of the judges are not trained in law; many are only part-time judges; many are neither schooled in law nor full-time judges.
4. Few courts have enough good staff to administer the law properly in either its legal or social ramifications.

Each of these four reasons poses major difficulties. Much has been written about them all. It is most important that remedial steps be taken in each of these areas, and at once.[8] Historically, the juvenile court law has failed to specify the minimum requisites of juvenile court procedures. Apart from preliminary procedures, the only direction provided by juvenile court law in most states is that the court "shall proceed to hear and dispose of the case in summary manner." This is essentially a carry-over from the earlier statutes. As a result, juvenile court proceedings are not only unstructured, but each judge makes his own ground rules. Consequently, the nature of the juvenile court hearing varies significantly from state to state. In a strict sense, it is incorrect to speak of a juvenile court or a juvenile court system as if juvenile courts

[7]*Ibid.*, p. 406.
[8]*Ibid.*, p. 406.

throughout the country were uniform in their structure, philosophy, and activities. To assume such uniformity would be to commit error. Not only is this uniformity absent throughout the country, but it is also found lacking within a single state. For example, in the first interim report of the *Special Study Commission on juvenile Justice, in the State of California, published February 2, 1959,* the following observations are made:

"There is considerable diversity in practice among the 58 counties of this State in terms of law enforcement procedures, probation functions, and juvennile court processes and decisions. As a result, whether or not a juvenile is arrested, placed in detention, or referred to the probation department, and whether or not the petition is dismissed, probation is granted, or a Youth Authority commitment is ordered by the juvenile court, seems to depend more upon the community in which the offenses is committed than upon the intrinsic merits of the individual case . . . . There is not only variation in the practices among the 58 counties, but equally varied is the nature and extent of services provided juveniles by probation, law enforcement, and juvenile court judges."

This quotation, applicable to California, must be no means be interpreted an an indictment of that state. The fact that the people of California, through their governmental officers, have seen fit to institute searching self-examination of their juvenile justice system is worthy of highest commendation. Such a searching inquiry is analogous to that which the Senate Subcommittee to Investigate Juvenile Delinquency conducted on a national level several years ago.[9]

Despite the law's silence on the question of minimum procedural requirements, investigation of juvenile court laws throughout the country reveals that several rights are enunciated. First, if the child is detained, he has a right to a hearing on his need for continued detention within 24 hours after the petition is filed; second, there is a right to notice of hearing; third, there is a right to a fair and private hearing; fourth, there is a requirement that the allegations in the petition must be substantiated before wardship can be declared; fifth, there is a right to examine the probation officer's report to the court; and, finally, there is the privilege to appeal.

The law is silent, however, in most states with regard to several other basic rights normally associated with other courts. These include such vital questions as to whether or not minors have a right to counsel, a right against self-incrimination, a right to cross-examine witnesses, a right to have allegations in the petition substantiated on the basis of

[9]T. C. Hennings, Jr., "Effectiveness of the Juvenile Court System," *Federal Probation,* Vol. XXXIII, No. 21, June 1959, p. 5.

stipulated evidentiary rules, and a right to have a court reporter present to transcribe the proceedings. In the absence of explicit statutory direction, each judge defines his own rules or procedure. Some courts, for exmple, diligently inform minors and their parents of their right to counsel, employ firm evidentiary rules, provide a court reporter, and observe the privilege against self-incrimination; many juvenile court judges, however, regard some or all of these procedures as inappropriate in the juvenile court.

The rationale offered is that since the jurisdictional issues are not contested in the vast majority of cases such procedural requirements are unnecessary. However, the fact that most cases are uncontested does not reduce the court's responsibility for respecting legal rights. As a matter of fact, only a relatively small proportion of adult cases are contested in the criminal courts, yet no strong efforts have been observed to remove legal safeguards traditionally provided in such courts. Furthermore, since some juvenile court statutes do not adequately define, in a legal sense, what constitutes incorrigibility, waywardness, and other conduct suggesting there is a danger that the child will become a delinquent, there is a real question as to whether a child can properly evaluate and appropriately admit to such behavior.

In addition, where a specific or serious offense may have been charged, it is questionable whether the child can admit to his guilt in a legally significant sense simply on the basis of his responses to an intake probation officer or an arresting officer.

It is also known that children often fail to establish legitimate defenses which might explain their actions and, on occasion, are prone to make false admissions because contesting the case might be misconstrued by the court as being uncooperative and might result in a more severe disposition.

Furthermore, not all juvenile courts are equally diligent in satisfying for themselves that the allegations in the petition are supported by competent evidence. In some courts, the jurisdictional issue becomes secondary to the judge's concern with applying remedies for the child's problems. Thus some judges interpret their judicial prerogatives in the broadest possible terms and rationalize their glossing over of the jurisdictional issue as serving the interests of the child. In other instances, when charges of specific offense cannot be substantiated, the practice is to shift the basis of the petition through the more general allegation that the child is in danger of becoming a delinquent. Thus, if a juvenile court judge feels that a court wardship is appropriate, he has several ways of adjusting the jurisdictional issues to accomplish this goal.

The need to observe legal rights in the juvenile court does not imply conflict with the court's protective philosophy; neither is it a radical concept. If it were, this view would not be sponsored by such organizations as the National Council on Crime and Delinquency, the National Council of Juvenile Court Judges, or the United States Children's Bureau, to name but a few of the leading organizations advocating more legal protections. For example, the publication, "*Guides for Juvenile Court Judges,*" jointly issued by the N.C.C.D. and the National Council of Juvenile Court Judges, emphasizes this need in the following terms:

> "Even though the proceedings are universally held to be civil.in nature, the legal rights of all parties should be strictly protected. This is especially important in the instances where the alleged delinquency is denied. In such cases, the judge should explain that the child and the parents have a right to counsel if they so desire; that at the hearing confronting witnesses may be cross-examined; and that he is entitled to have his own witnesses."

This viewpoint has also been eloquently expressed by Judge H. L. Eastman, of Cleveland, Ohio, in the October 1959, *N.P.P.A. (now N.C.C.D.) Journal*:

> "The juvenile court, like any other court, is without authority to make legally binding decisions affecting the lives of children and their parents without adequate *legal* grounds . . . if the juvenile court deprives a child of his liberty because he has a dubious record or because commitment might be good for him, it is according him less, not more, consideration that the adult courts do. True, the court is charged by law to act in the interest of the child, but the charge applies only to the interest of the child over whom the court has authority; i.e., a child legally determined to be within its jurisdiciton.
>
> "Furthermore, in making this determination the judge must insist on reasonable application of the rules of evidence. He may not conclude, and his professional training and code do not allow him to conclude, that a child must have committed the delinquent act specified in the petition simply because he had previously manifested bad behavior in general. The judge's training requires that he stand firm on this point, even if it means resisting the demands of quite naturally indignant people."

Establishment of the theory of *parens patriae* as the constitutional basis for the juvenile court in the early cases in which the constitutional issue was raised, followed as they were by long series of cases clearly establishing that the proceedings in juvenile court are not criminal in nature, has served to confuse in the minds of some the fact that certain minimum requirements of due process are constitutionally necessary to all judicial proceedings regardless of their nature. It should be quite apparent that however benign its purpose, the juvenile court is essentially a court involved in a judicial process and therefore subject to all the safeguards that, in this country at least, are required to assure that its citizens shall be fairly treated.

In addition, some of this lack of awareness of the underlying constitutional requirements of due process is caused by the failure to elaborate upon various safeguards by the type of specific statute we are accustomed to find in abundance in the criminal law and in laws of general application in other fields.

Assuming that the juvenile court is constitutionally not in the criminal field and is in the equity field, the net result is that those safeguards specifically referable by constitution or statute to the criminal law are not applicable as such, and the right to a jury trial applicable in civil cases does not apply because traditionally it is not applicable in equity cases.

The proper and specific question to determine it concerns the procedural due process requirements of a court exercising an equity jurisdiction.

Therefore, it seems important that basic procedural methods be universal rather than parochial, and that there be greater assurance of more equitable proceedings on a state-wide and national basis.

Definite guides should be established, for example, for such fundamental procedural elements as the admissibility of evidence, the nature of detention hearings, the role of counsel in juvenile court, the use of bail and referees, the handling of minor traffic cases, remanding and certification, and court continuances.

The main problem, of course, in attempting to establish acceptable juvenile court procedures is to attain a working balance between two essential objectives; first, the preservation of the minor's civil liberties and, second, the establishment of the informal court atmosphere that minimizes the potentially harmful effects of the proceedings and encourages the minor's receptivity to treatment.

The remainder of this chapter presents the *STANDARD JUVENILE COURT ACT* in a limited scale to familarize prospective law enforcement officers with the essential rudiments of the juvenile court law. Each part of this Act is analyzed to determine: (1) if sufficient protection is afforded to the youth under present procedures; and (2) if the rehabilitative theory of the juvenile court is being frustrated by inadequate facilities, improper administration, or defective laws.

STANDARD JUVENILE COURT ACT[10]

Article I. Establishment: Personnel

Construction and Purpose of Act

This Act shall be liberally construed to the end that each child coming within the jurisdiction of the court shall receive, preferably in his own home, the care, guidance, and control that will conduce to his welfare and the best interests of the state, and that when he is removed from the control of his parents the court shall secure for him care as nearly as possible equivalent to that which they should have given him.

COMMENT ON SECTION: The well-established fundamental purpose of courts dealing with children is to protect them and restore them to society as law-abiding young citizens. According to the above section, the essence of which is included in almost all juvenile court laws, the preference in disposition in both the trial and the appellate courts is to keep a child in his home. In most jurisdictions, therefore, only a small percentage of children within the court's jurisdiction are detained or committed.

Definitions

1. When used in this Act, unless the context otherwise requires:
   (a) (Local Court) *Court* means the juvenile court.
   (State Court) *Court* means the juvenile court, or a district juvenile court, according to its context.
   (b) *Judge* means judge of the juvenile court.
   (c) *Presiding judge* means the judge so chosen.
   (d) *Board* means the board of juvenile court judges.
   (e) *Child* means a person less than 18 years of age.
   (f) *Minor* means a person less than 21 years of age.
   (g) *Adult* means a person 21 years of age or older.
   (h) *Detention* means the temporary care of children who require secure custody for their own or the community's protection in physically restricting facilities pending court disposition.
   (i) *Shelter* means the temporary care of children in physically unrestricting facilities pending court disposition.
   (j) *Legal custody* means the relationship created by the court's decree which imposes on the custodian the responsibility of physical possession of the child and the duty to protect, train, and discipline him and to provide him with food, shelter, education, and ordinary medical care, all subject to residual parental rights and responsibilities and the rights and responsibilities of the guardian of the person.

[10] *Standard Juvenile Court Act*, 6th ed., National Council on Crime and Delinquency, New York, 1959.

(k) *The singular includes the plural, the plural the singular, and the masculine the feminine,* when consistent with the intent of this Act.

COMMENT ON SECTION: *Less than eighteen* has been the standard of juvenile age jurisdiction since the first publication of juvenile court standards by NPPA and the U.S. Children's Bureau, and it has been used in every revision of the Standard Juvenile Court Act. Over the years more and more states have adopted this age level, until now only a few have a lower age jurisdiction. Experience in courts with adequate resources and professional staff demonstrates the ability of juvenile courts to deal successfully with this age level of jurisdiction.

The definitions of *detention* and *shelter* underlie the provisions calculated to control detention of children.

The definition of *legal custody* is intended to clarify the respective responsibilities of custodians, guardians, and parents when a decree changes a child's status.

Legal custody represents only one aspect of the total parent-child relationship which should be considered and dealt with by the court. Other parts are dealt with in guardianship of the person and there still remain residual parental rights. *Guardianship of the person* and *residual parental* rights also should be defined in the state statutes. Since they are closely related to legal custody, and the juvenile court under this Act is given jurisdiction over the appointment of a guardian of the person, these terms should be defined in the juvenile court act if they are not defined in other state statutes.

The Children's Bureau recommends the following definition of guardianship:

"Guardianship of the person of a minor" means the duty and authority to make important decisions in matters having a permanent effect on the life and development of the minor and to be concerned about his general welfare. It shall include but shall not necessarily be limited in either number or kind to:

1. The authority to consent to marriage, to enlistment in the armed forces of the United States, or to major medical, psychiatric, and surgical treatment; to represent the minor in legal actions; to make other decisions concerning the minor of substantial legal significance.

2. The authority and duty of reasonable visitation, except to the extent that such right of visitation has been limited by court order.

3. The rights and responsibilities of legal custody when guardianship of the person is exercised by the natural or adoptive parent, except where legal custody has been vested in another individual, agency, or institution.

4. The authority to consent to the adoption of the child and to make any other decision concerning him which his parents could make, when the rights

of his parents, or only living parent, have been terminated as provided for in [statutes governing termination of parent-child relationship].

The Children's Bureau recommends the following definition of residual parental rights:

"Residual parental rights and responsibilities" means those rights and responsibilities remaining with the parent after the transfer of legal custody or guardianship of the person, including, but not necessarily limited to, the right to reasonable visitation, consent to adoption, the right to determine the child's religious affiliation, and the responsibility for support.

The Children's Bureau would prefer to include the following definitions in the Act:

" 'Commit' means to transfer legal custody."

" 'Probation' is a legal status created by court order following adjudication in a case involving a violation of law whereby a minor is permitted to remain in his home subject to supervision by the court or an agency designated by the court and subject to return to the court for violation of probation at any time during the period of probation."

" 'Protective supervision' is a legal status created by court order in proceedings not involving violations of law but where the legal custody of the child is subject to change, whereby the child is permitted to remain in his home under the supervision of the court or an agency designated by the court and subject to return to the court during the period of protective supervision."

Local Court: Appointment, Tenure, and Duties of Employees

1. Each juvenile court judge, or the senior judge where the court has more than one judge, shall appoint a chief administrative officer, who shall have the title of director of the juvenile court. (The director, with the judge's approval, or the judge or the senior judge) shall appoint a sufficient number of assistants and other employees, and may appoint physicians, psychologists, and psychiatrists, to carry on the professional, clerical, and other work of the court. Under the general supervision of the judge or the senior judge, the director shall:
   (a) direct the work of the staff in carrying out the provisions of this Act;
   (b) serve as administrative officer for the court in such matters as personnel, office management, and in-service training;
   (c) make recommendations to the judge or judges for improvement of court services;
   (d) collect statistics and furnish reports as requested by the judge and the director of the Board of Juvenile Court Judges;
   (e) perform such other duties as the judge or judges shall specify.
2. All employees shall be selected, appointed, and promoted through (a merit system as established by the Board; or, a state merit system).
3. No member of the staff may be discharged except for cause and after a

hearing before the appointing authority. An employee may be suspended pending such hearing. Discharge of employees appointed by the director shall be subject to approval by the judge; discharge of employees appointed by the judge shall be subject to approval by the Board.

4. The compensation and expenses of all employees shall be paid by the (county treasurer) upon the warrant of the (county auditor), which shall be issued when certified by the judge.

COMMENT ON SECTION: Subdivision 1 of the "local court" offers alternatives procedures for appointment of court staff—by the director or by the judge. *The Children's Bureau* and the *N.C.C.D.* prefer that staff be appointed by the director. *The National Council of Juvenile Court Judges* prefers that both plans be stated in the statute, so that some variation in practice can occur, depending on the preferences or circumstances in a district.

Although most juvenile court laws specify the appointment of a *chief probation office,* the term *director* is also used; it seems preferable and is used in this section. In courts with a large proportion of professional personnel, the term *counselor* is preferred to *probation officer;* the word *assistant* leaves the section open as to the term to be used for probation personnel, permitting each court to adopt a title that seems most appropriate.

Under proper conditions the competitive examination has proved to be invaluable in establishing the court as a specialized agency whose staff must have a high degree of training, skill, and character, and freedom from interference by partisan politics.

The last paragraph of the section is added to establish that the appointment of staff to the extent considered necessary by the judge obligates the state fiscal authorities to appropriate the necessary funds. The number of appointments and the levels of salaries should be determined by the judiciary as an independent branch of the government, not subject to veto by the legislature or fiscal authority.

Appointment of Referees: Duties

The judge, or senior judge if there is more than one, may appoint suitable persons trained in the law, to act as referees, who shall hold office during the pleasure of the judge. The judge may direct that any case, or all cases of a class or within a district to be designated by him, shall be heard in the first instance by a referee in the manner provided for the hearing of cases by the court, but any part may, upon request, have a hearing before the judge in the first instance. At the conclusion of a hearing the referee shall transmit promptly to the judge all papers relating to the case, together with his findings and recommendations in writing.

Written notice of the referee's findings and recommendations shall be given to the parent, guardian, or custodian of any child whose case has been heard by a referee, and to any other parties in interest. A hearing by the judge shall be allowed if any of them files with the court a request for review, provided that the request is filed within three days after the referee's written notice. If a hearing *de novo* is not requested by any party or ordered by the court, the hearing shall be upon the same evidence heard by the referee, provided that new evidence may be admitted in the discretion of the judge. If a hearing before the judge is not requested or the right to the review is waived, the findings and recommendations of the referee, when confirmed by an order of the judge, shall become the decree of the court.

COMMENT ON SECTION: Referees are valuable in special types of cases; in busy courts they give the judge more time for difficult cases; they secure prompter action where the jurisdiction covers a wide area.

The judge is given discretion to direct that any case, or all cases of a class designated by him, be heard in the first instance by a referee. The judge may direct that cases like the following be reserved to him: cases in which a child is likely to be removed from the custody of his parents; cases in which the parties are likely to demand a hearing before the judge; delinquency cases involving death or serious violence; cases in which the parties are represented by attorneys, unless their consent to a hearing before the referee is given; cases in which questions of law are involved.

The right of a hearing before the judge, when demanded, must be respected. The written notice is required in order to assure the parties of the adequacy of the hearing and of their rights. Without this and other provisions clearly establishing due process of law, the court rightly becomes an object of criticism for its disregard of the rights of individuals before it.

Article II. Jurisdiction

Jurisdiction: Children, Minors

Except as otherwise provided herein, the court shall have exclusive original jurisdiction in proceedings:

1. Concerning any child who is alleged to have violated any federal, state, or local law or municipal ordinance, regardless of where the violation occurred; or any minor alleged to have violated any federal, state, or local law or municipal ordinance prior to having become eighteen years of age. Such minor shall be dealt with under the provisions of this Act relating to children. Jurisdiction may be taken by the court of the district where the minor is living or found, or in which the offense is alleged to have occurred. When a minor eighteen years of age or over already under the jurisdiction of the court is alleged to have violated any federal, state, or local law or municipal

ordinance, the juvenile court shall have concurrent jurisdiction with the criminal court.

2. Concerning any child living or found within the district:

(a) who is neglected as to proper or necessary support, or education as required by law, or as to medical or other care necessary for his well-being, or who is abandoned by his parent or other custodian; or

(b) whose environment is injurious to his welfare, or whose behavior is injurious to his own or others' welfare; or

(c) who is beyond the control of his parent or other custodian.

3. To determine the custody of any child or appoint a guardian of the person of any child.

4. For the adoption of a person of any age.

5. To terminate the legal parent-child relationship.

6. For judicial consent to the marriage, employment, or enlistment of a child, when such consent is required by law.

7. For the treatment or commitment of a mentally defective or mentally ill minor.

8. Under the Interstate Compact on Juveniles.

COMMENT ON SECTION: Subdivisions 1 and 2 describe children defined as delinquent and neglected in most juvenile court laws. However, as in the *1949 and 1943 editions of the Standard Juvenile Court Act,* these subdivisions avoid using the terms "delinquency" and "neglect"; about one-third of the states similarly avoid them. The court's jurisdiction is not less definite than it was under the older form. The present form accords with the philosophy that, in dealing with the child as an individual, classifying or labeling him is always unnecessary, sometimes impracticable, and often harmful.

Several members of the committee preferred the use of "delinquency" and "neglect" as labels or pointed to cautions that must be exercised by a court in which (as in the Standard Act) these categories are not identified. They maintain that use of the labels clarifies the basis on which the court is moving into the life of a child and his family; that a parent wants to know specifically whether the child is before the court for delinquency or neglect; and that, consequently, what is perhaps the most persuasive social reason for the elimination of categories—namely, the promotion of better court-client relations—disappears.

Neither the usage adopted in this draft nor the use of the "delinquency" and "neglect" labels properly classifies those children who are more at war with themselves than with the community—children who come within subdivision 2(b) and 2(c) of this section. No term for this group is in general use. Those who preferred the use of the delinquency-neglect labels did not wish to have these children categorized as delinquents.

This Act, *like the 1949 Standard Juvenile Court Act,* does not give the court jurisdiction over dependent children who are not neglected. The court should intervene only where authoritative action is required with respect to a child or the adults responsible for his care or condition. Cases of dependency without an element of neglect, or where no change of custody is involved, should be dealt with by administrative agencies without court action.

The last sentence of subdivision 1 relates to the provision in the section, "Redemption of Jurisdiction," in which if a minor eighteen years of age or more already under juvenile court jurisdiction is convicted of a crime in a criminal court, that conviction terminates the jurisdiction of the juvenile court.

Subdivisions 3 to 8 are merely statements of jurisdictional subject matter, for which substantive and procedural requirements would be found elsewhere in the state's statutes or common law. They cover jurisdiction similar in substance to the provisions in the *1949 Standard Juvenile Court Act,* except for subdivision 8, required in the light of the recent adoption of the Interstate Juvenile Compact, and the addition in subdivision 6 of jurisdiction for judicial consent to employment or enlistment of a child when such consent is required by law.

Transfer from Other Courts

If, during the pendency of a criminal or quasi-criminal charge against a minor in another court, it shall be ascertained that he was less than eighteen years old when he allegedly committed the offense, that court shall forthwith transfer the case to the juvenile court, together with all the papers, documents, and transcripts of any testimony connected with it. If he is under 18 years of age, the court making the transfer shall order that he be taken forthwith to the place of detention designated by the juvenile court or to that court itself, or shall release him to the custody of his parent or guardian or other person legally responsible for him, to be brought before the court at a time designated by it. The court shall then proceed as provided in this Act.

Nothing contained in this Act shall deprive other courts of the right to determine the custody or guardianship of the person of children when such custody or guardianship is incidental to the determination of causes pending in those courts. Such courts, however, may certify said questions to the juvenile court for hearing and determination or recommendation.

COMMENT ON SECTION: This transfer provision is essential to protection of the jurisdiction of a court dealing with children. It is applicable to two types of situations: first, the defendant arranged in the criminal court is under eighteen (in which instance the error should be corrected by prompt transfer to the juvenile court), and second, he is eighteen or older but the act he is charged with was committed when he was under eighteen (in which instance the criminal court does not have jurisdiction and should transfer the case to the juvenile court).

Retention of Jurisdiction

Jurisdiction obtained by the court in the case of a child shall be retained by it, for the purposes of this Act, until he becomes twenty-one years of age, unless terminated prior thereto. If a minor eighteen years of age or more already under juvenile court jurisdiction is convicted of a crime in a criminal court, that conviction shall terminate the jurisdiction of the juvenile court.

COMMENT ON SECTION: The last sentence of the section provides for termination of juvenile court jurisdiction when a minor eighteen years of age or older is convicted of a crime in the criminal court. If the criminal charge is relatively insignificant, a suspended sentence or other summary disposition might be in order. In such cases it would be unwise for the juvenile court to lose its supervisory control under the proceeding it has had. For that reason, subdivision 1 of "Jurisdiction: Children and Minors" contains the provision that when a minor eighteen years of age or older, already under the jurisdiction of the court, is charged with a crime, the juvenile court shall have concurrent jurisdiction with the criminal court.

Jurisdiction: Adults

The court shall have exclusive original jurisdiction:

1. To try any offense committed against a child by his parent or guardian or by any other adult having his legal or physical custody.

2. To try any adult charged with deserting, abandoning, or failing to provide support for any person in violation of law.

If the defendant in any case within subdivision 1 or 2 is entitled to trial by jury and shall demand it, or shall not waive trial by jury as provided by law, the court may act as an examining magistrate and certify him for criminal proceedings to a court which has trial jurisdiction over the offense charged.

3. In proceedings for support, including proceedings under the (Reciprocal Non-Support Act), and to establish paternity of a child born out of wedlock.

COMMENT ON SECTION: The provision for jurisdiction in adult cases in which a child is the victim differs from some juvenile court laws in that the court's adjudication is not required. *The 1949 Standard Juvenile Court Act* took a midway position: it provided that the court would have jurisdiction if the violation by the adult caused a child "to become in need of the care and protection of the court." It is preferable to include this jurisdiction whether or not the prior proceeding relating to the child has been held.

The section authorizes the court to refer jury trials in criminal cases to the criminal division, mainly to protect the court against having to give an undue amount of time to criminal cases.

As in the *1949 Standard Juvenile Court Act,* no section on "contributing to delinquency" has been included. Where such a section exists elsewhere in the code, the juvenile court should be given jurisdiction by ampliying the language of subdivision 1 of this section. However, the efficacy of the "contributing" laws, which are frequently directed against parents, has been doubted in many quarters. It seems more desirable, from both legal and social points of view, to prosecute in such cases under a definite criminal code provision, such as assault, impairing the morals of a minor, or any of the varied statutes in existence. This act continues the provision first incorporated in the *1949 Standard Juvenile Court Act,* giving the court ancillary jurisdiction to make orders binding upon adults in children's cases, and to punish violations by contempt proceedings. See section regarding "Degree," subdivision 7.

Article III. Initiation of Cases

Complaint; Investigation; Petition

1. Except as provided in subdivision 2, whenever the court is informed by any person that a child is within the purview of this Act, it shall make a preliminary investigation to determine whether the interests of the public or of the child require that further action be taken. If so, the court may authorize the filing of a petition; or may make whatever informal adjustment is practicable without a petition, provided that the facts appear to establish prima facie jurisdiction and are admitted, and provided that consent is obtained from the parents and also from the child if he is of sufficient age and understanding. Efforts to effect informal adjustment may be continued not longer than three months without review by the judge or the director.

2. In cases of violation of a law or an ordinance relating to operation of a motor vehicle by a child, preliminary investigation and petition shall not be required, and the issuance of a traffic citation or summons shall be sufficent to invoke the jurisdiction of the court.

3. The petition and all subsequent court documents shall be entitled "In the interest of. . . , a child under eighteen years of age." The petition shall be verified and the statements may be made upon information and belief. It shall set forth plainly (a) the facts which bring the child within the purview of this Act; (b) the name, age, and residence of the child; (c) the names and residences of his parents; (d) the name and residence of his legal guardian if there be one, of the person or persons having custody or control of the child, or of the nearest known relative if not parent or guardian can be found. If any of the facts herein required are not known by the petitioner the petition shall so state.

COMMENT ON SECTION: One of the most important features of the modern juvenile court is a well-staffed intake department, receiving all complaints and conducting investigations to determine whether (a) the court or its staff should take action, and, if so, what kind of action, or (b) the matter should be referred elsewhere. A major part of the intake function is to consider whether a case may be dealt with informally; that is, without a petition, and through the efforts principally of the social casework and counseling staff rather than the judge.

This so-called "unofficial casework" or "non-judicial" handling of cases is questioned by some, and should be protected against abuse. For example, it should not be attempted unless the facts enable the court to take jurisdiction if it chooses to do so. Where the court does not have potential jurisdiction, it does not have the right to deal with the child. The court's informal action should be limited to referral to an appropriate community agency or to conferences designed to help the parties make adjustments or reach agreements that will obviate the filing of a petition. If informal adjustment in the form of continuing casework service is to be provided it should not be presented to the child and parents as an alternative to the filing of a petition. Therefore, they may withdraw from the service at any time. (See *Standard for Specialized Courts Dealing with Children,* U.S. Children's Bureau Publication No. 346, 1954, p. 45.)

For the same reason, a child may not be detained in connection with informal handling. (*See section on Detention: Release, Shelter, and Notice.*)

When a complaint or petition is made against a member of the complainant's family, the court's staff shall inquire into the interpersonal relationships of the members of the family to ascertain the causes of the conflict. They shall assist the family by extending or securing suitable measures of help and conciliation, and this aid may be extended to persons seeking it prior to the filing of formal proceedings. They shall endeavor to make whatever informal adjustment is practicable without the filing of a petition, but no person in such cases shall be deprived of the right to file a petition or complaint.

Many juvenile court laws, and the Standard Act, include some family jurisdiction (particularly non-support and paternity) to which the informal procedure could profitably be applied.

Transfer to Other Courts

If the petition in the case of a child 16 years of age or older is based on an act which would be a felony if committed by an adult, and if the court after full investigation and a hearing deems it contrary to the best interest of the child or the public to retain jurisdiction, it may in its discretion certify him to the criminal court having jurisdiction of such felones committed by adults. No child under 16 years of age at the time of commission of the act shall be so certified.

When a petition has been filed bringing a child before the court under the provisions of subdivision 1 or 2 of the section relating to jurisdiction of this Act and the child resides outside the court district but in the state, the court may, in its discretion, transfer the case to the court having jurisdiction in the district where the child resides; or in such case the court may, after a finding on the allegations in the petition, certify the case for disposition to the court where the child resides. Thereupon, the court receiving such transfer shall dispose of the case as if the petition were originally filed or the finding were originally made there. Whenever a case is so certified, the certifying court shall forward to the receiving court certified copies of all pertinent legal and social records.

When a petition has been filed a child shall not thereafter be subject to a criminal prosecution based on the facts giving rise to the petition, except as provided in this section.

COMMENT ON SECTION: The age level of juvenile jurisdiction proposed in this Act and adopted in almost all states is "under eighteen." The central part of the age jurisdiction question involves children between 16 and 18. It is true that some 16- and 17-year-olds, and even some younger, have strongly developed tendencies which render them impervious to the average juvenile or family court's services. Accordingly, it is necessary to authorize transfer to the criminal court. Of course, before such transfer is made the court should have sufficient knowledge of the situation so that discretion can be exercised on the basis of an understanding of the child and his situation.

The National Council of Juvenile Court Judges believes that the age 16 should not be the recommended floor for possible certification to the criminal court. It states:

"If the floor were fixed at fourteen it might obviate some practical difficulty or widespread objection to the Act when a particularly abominable killer who receives widespread publicity is dealt with in juvenile court. This reasoning is particularly applicable in view of the fact that the Standard Act recommends that the juvenile court have *exclusive* jurisdiction to age eighteen. Judges realize this transfer privilege is rarely exercised, but highly important in unusual cases."

Summons; Notice; Custody of Child

After a petition is filed in the interest of a child, and after investigation as the court may direct, the court shall issue a summons, unless the parties hereinafter named shall appear voluntarily, requiring the person or persons who have the custody or control of the child to appear personally and bring the child before the court at a time and place stated. If the person so summoned is not the parent or guardian of the child, then the parent or guardian or both shall also be notified, by personal service before the hearing except as hereinafter provided, of the pendency of the case and of the time and place appointed. Summons may be issued requiring the appearance of any other person whose presence, in the opinion of the judge, is necessary. If it appears that the child is in such condition or surroundings that his welfare requires taking him into custody, the judge may order, by endorsement upon the summons, that the person serving the summons shall take the child into custody at once. A parent or guardian shall be entitled to the issuance of compulsory process for the attendance of witnesses on his own behalf or on behalf of the child.

Service of summons shall be made personally by the delivery of an attested copy thereof to the person summoned, except that if the judge is satisfied that personal service of the summons or the notice provided for in the preceding section is impracticable, he may order service by registered mail addressed to the last known address, or by publication, or both. Service effected not less than 48 hours before the time fixed in the summons for the return thereof shall be sufficient to confer jurisdiction.

Service of summons, process, or notice required by this Act may be made by any suitable person under the direction of the court and upon request of the court shall be made by any peace officer. The judge may authorize the payment of necessary travel expenses incurred by persons summoned or otherwise required to appear at the hearing of a case coming within the purview of this Act and such expenses when approved by the judge shall be a charge upon the (country, for local courts; state, for state court).

COMMENT ON SECTION: It is not the child who is summoned, but the parent or custodian who is required to appear and bring the child with him, unless the welfare of the child requires that the court assume custody of him. Here again the procedure is clearly not a criminal prosecution, even when the child is alleged to have violated a penal law.

Failure to Answer Summons; Warrants

Any person summoned as herein provided who, without reasonable cause, fails to appear, may be proceeded against for contempt of court. If the summons cannot be served, or if the parties served fail to obey the summons, or if it is made to appear to the judge that serving the summons will be ineffectual or that the welfare of the child requires that he be brought forthwith into the custody of the court, a warrant or capias may be issued for the parent, the guardian, or the child.

If, after being summoned or notified to appear, a parent fails to do so, a warrant shall be issued for his appearance and the hearing shall not take place without the presence of one or both of the parents or the guardian, or, if none is present, a guardian *ad litem* appointed by the court to protect the interests of the child. The court may also appoint a guardian *ad litem*, whenever this is necessary for the welfare of the child, whether or not a parent or guardian is present.

COMMENT ON SECTION: Appointment of a guardian *ad litem* would usually be indicated where the parent or a duly qualified guardian is not present or is not represented, or when the child seems to be in conflict with his parents.

Article IV. Custody, Detention, and Shelter of Children

Taking Children into Custody; Release; Notice

A child may be taken into custody by any officer of the peace without order of the judge (a) when in the presence of the officer the child has violated a state or federal law or a county or municipal ordinance; (b) when there are reasonable grounds to believe that he has committed an act which if committed by an adult would be a felony; (c) when he is seriously endangered in his surroundings, and immediate removal appears to be necessary for his protection; (d) when there are reasonable grounds to believe that he has run away from his parents, guardian, or legal custodian. Such taking into custody shall not be deemed an arrest.

When an officer or other person takes a child into custody he shall immediately notify the parents, guardian, or custodian. The child shall be released to the care of his parent or other responsible adult unless his immediate welfare or the protection of the community requires that he be detained. If the person taking the child into custody believes it desirable, he may request the parent, guardian, or custodian to sign a written promise to bring the child to the court at the time directed by the court. If the child is not released from custody in a reasonable time, the officer or other person in charge shall promptly notify the court of intention to file a complaint.

If a parent or other responsible adult fails to produce the child in court as required by an authorized notice, or when notified by the court, a summons or a warrant may be issued for the apprehension of that person or the child or both.

COMMENT ON SECTION: Most juvenile court laws do not state in detail the situations in which a child may be taken into custody. However, it is desirable to specify situations in which the child's custody is justified, to establish clearly the rights of children and police officers, to protect children and families, and to avoid unnecessary apprehensions.

When a child is taken into custody under subdivision 1 or 2 of the section relating to jurisdiction, the parents and the court must be notified immediately. He should be released to his parents whenever possible.

Paragraph 2 requires that if the officer taking a child into custody does not release him in a reasonable time, he shall promptly notify the court of intention to file a complaint. In general there are few instances in which the police can justifiably keep custody of the child for more than an hour before release or transfer to the detention facility.

Interrogation of a child by the police should be governed by a careful regard for the right of the child and his parents and should in no case be prolonged. A child can always be interrogated further in the detention home. However:

> "Whenever possible and especially in the case of young children, no child should be interviewed except in the presence of his parents or guardian. This should always be the policy when a child is being questioned abou this participation or when a formal statement concerning the child's participation in the alleged delinquent act is being taken. The presence of a parent during the interview may be helpful to the police as the parental attitudes shown under such circumstances may help the police decide whether the case should be referred to court or to another agency. This procedure, of course, would not apply when the matter being investigated involves the child's parents. In cases where the child has freely admitted his participation in the act to the police, there appears to be nothing improper about interviewing the child to secure background information of a social nature without the parents being present. It may be equally necessary to interview the parents without the child being present to secure social information for the purpose of making a referral."

(See *Standards for Specialized Courts Dealing with Children,* U.S. Children's Bureau Publication No. 346, 1954.)

Detention; Shelter; Release; Notice

1. If the child is not released as provided above, he shall be taken without unnecessary delay to the court or to the place of detention or shelter designated by the court. Any child taken into custody who requires care away from his home but who does not require physical restriction shall be given temporary care in a foster family home or other shelter facility.

The officer or other person who brings a child to a detention or shelter facility shall at once give notice to the court, stating the legal basis therefor and the reason why the child was not released to his parents. The person in charge of the facility in which the child is placed shall promptly give notice to the court that the child is in his custody. After immediate investigation by a duly authorized officer of the court, the judge or such officer shall order the court shall order the child to be released, if possible, to the care of his parent, guardian, or custodian, or he may order the child held in the facility subject to further order or placed in some other appropriate facility.

As soon as a child is detained, his parents shall be informed, by notice in writing on forms prescribed by the court, that they may have a prompt hearing regarding release or detention. The judge may hold the hearing or may authorize the referee to hold it. A child may be released on the order of the judge or referee with or without a hearing. The director may order the release of the child if an order of detention has not been made.

2. No child shall be held in detention or shelter longer than 24 hours, excluding Sundays and holidays, unless a petition has been filed. No child may be held longer than 24 hours after the filing of a petition unless an order for such continued detention or shelter has been signed by the judge or referee.

3. No child shall be released from detention except in accordance with the provisions of this Act.

4. No child shall at any time be detained in a police station, lockup, jail, or prison, except that, by the judge's order in which the reasons therefor shall be specified, a child 16 years of age or older whose conduct or condition endangers the safety of others in the detention facility for children may be placed in some other place of confinement that the judge considers proper, including a jail or any other place of detention for adults.

5. Where a child transferred for criminal proceedings in accordance with the provisions of the section relating to transfer to other courts is detained, he shall be held in the detention facility used for persons charged with crime, unless otherwise ordered by the criminal court. When a child is ordered committed to an agency or institution, he shall be promptly transported to the place of commitment.

6. Provisions regarding bail shall not be applicable to children detained in accordance with the provisions of this Act, except that bail may be allowed when a child who should not be detained lives outside the territorial jurisdiction of the court.

7. The sheriff, warden, or other official in charge of a jail or other facility for the detention of adult offenders or persons charged with crime shall inform the juvenile court immediately when a child who is or appears to be under 18 years of age is received at the facility.

COMMENT ON SECTION: Jailing of any child under 16 should not be tolerated anywhere. With properly designed and staffed detention facilities and the use, where needed, of mental hospitals for observation and study, children between 16 and 18 need rarely, if ever, be jailed.

Before a child is admitted to a detention facility, the intake service of the probation department should hold initial interviews to determine whether release to parents or guardian is possible so that unnecessary overnight detention may be avoided. Intake policies and procedures should be incorporated in rules of the court. *Standards and Guides for the Detention of Children and Youth* NPPA, (19558, p. 23) states:

"The court's intake service should provide twenty-four hour coverage through (a) personnel employed beyond the usual office hours, (b) personnel 'on call,' (c) written agreement with law-enforcement agencies regarding the proper use of detention when the intake officers are not available, or (d) some combination of these methods."

Detention is a most serious method of control of the child, depriving the parents of his custody; as such, it may not lawfully be continued for more than a brief period without a formal proceeding initiated by the filing of a petition. Detention is not permissible in cases not dealth with formally—that is, by unofficial or non-judicial treatment, as provided in Section relating to complaint; investigation; petition.

Children Who Should Be Detained. Children apprehended for delinquency should be detained for the juvenile court when, after proper intake interviews, it appears that casework by a probation officer would not enable the parents to maintain custody and control, or would not enable the child to control his own behavior. Such children fall into the following groups:

(a) Children who are almost certain to run away during the period the court is studying their case, or between disposition and transfer to an institution or another jurisdiction.

(b) Children who are almost certain to commit an offense dangerous to themselves or to the community before court disposition or between disposition and transfer to an institution or another jurisdiction.

(c) Children who must be held for another jurisdiction; e.g., parole violators, runaways from institutions to which they were committed by a court, or certain material witnesses.

Children Who Should Not Be Detained. Children should not be detained for the juvenile court when, after proper intake interviews, it appears that case work by a probation officer would be likely to help parents maintain custody and control, or would enable the child to control his own behavior. Such children and others who should not be detained fall into the following groups:

(a) Children who are *not* almost certain to run away or commit other offenses before court disposition or between disposition and transfer to an institution or another jurisdiction.

(b) Neglected, dependent, and non-delinquent emotionally disturbed children and delinquent children who dot not require secure custody but must be removed from their homes because of physical or moral danger or because the relationship between child and parents is strained to the point of damage to the child.

(c) Children held as a means of court referral.

(d) Children held for police investigation or social investigation who do not otherwise require secure custody.

(e) Children placed or left in detention as a corrective or punitive measure.

(f) Psychotic children, and children who need clinical study and treatment and do not otherwise need detention.

(g) Children placed in detention because of school truancy.

(h) Children who are material witnesses, unless secure custody is the only way to protect them or keep them from being tampered with as witnesses.

Article V. Procedure and Decree

Procedure in Children's Cases

Cases of children in proceedings under subdivisions 1 and 2 of the section relating to jurisdiction shall be dealt with by the court at hearings separate from those for adults and without a jury. The hearings shall be conducted in an informal manner and may be adjourned from time to time.

Stenographic notes or mechanical recordings shall be required as in other civil cases in the highest court of general trial jurisdiction, unless the court otherwise orders and the parties waive the right to such record. The general public shall be excluded, and only such persons shall be admitted who are found by the judge to have a direct interest in the case or in the work of the court. The child may be excluded from the hearing at any time at the discretion of the judge.

As soon as practicable after the filing of a petition, and prior to the start of a hearing, the court shall inform the parents, guardian, or custodian, and the child when it is appropriate to do so, that they have a right to be represented by counsel at every stage of the proceeding. If any of them requests it but is found by the court to be financially unable to employ counsel, counsel shall be appointed by the court and, if necessary, compensated out of funds in the court's budget. Upon a final adverse disposition if the parent or guardian is without counsel, the court shall inform them, and the child if it is appropriate to do so, of their right to appeal as provided in the section relating to appeals.

The court may by rule establish appropriate special procedures for hearings in cases of violating of traffic laws or ordinances by children.

COMMENT ON SECTION: A juvenile court hearing has three aspects, two of them purely legal, the third sociolegal: (1) determination of jurisdiction to hear the case; (2) adjudication of the issue; and (3) determination of disposition.

It is necessary, first, to determine the jurisdictional facts; i.e., that the alleged act falls within the purview of the statutes fixing the court's jurisdiction of the subject matter, and that all necessary parties have been given due notice so that the requirements of due process have been met.

Having determined that the court has jurisdiction of both subject matter and person, the court should then proceed to determine the facts as alleged. For example, did the child steal the car as alleged? If it is found that the child did commit the act, the court should enter a finding of delinquency or its equivalent. This establishes the court's power to act; that is, the legal authority of the court to plan for the best interest of the child.

A characteristic difference between the juvenile court and the adult criminal court is the nature of the hearing. Whereas criminal court procedure is governed strictly by rules of evidence—particularly exclusionary rules for hearsay and other kinds of evidence, rules regulating the order of presentation of testimony, and so on—the hearing in the juvenile court is much more informal, with a greater flexibility governing the admission of evidence, and a far greater control by the judge over cross-examination and the order of presentation of evidence. The hearing is designated as *informal* rather than *summary* as stated in a few juvenile court acts. In addition, it is distinguished from the criminal court hearing by exclusion of the general public. The privacy of the hearing contributes to a case-work relationship, and avoidance of the spectacle of a public criminal trial is especially advantageous in children's cases. The hearing should have the character of a conference, not of a trial. Formal procedure is incompatible with the informal conference atmosphere required by the court to gain the confidence of child and parents, to elicit the pertinent facts of events, and to become familiar with the personalities of the parties, their emotional states, and the causes of the difficulty—all of which is of the utmost importance to a wise disposition of the case.

Even though the proceedings are universally held to be civil in nature, the legal rights of all parties should be strictly protected. The judge should explain that the child and the parents have a right to counsel, that the child will not be required to be a witness against himself, that he is entitled to have his own witnesses at the hearing, and that confronting witnesses may be cross-examined.

The statutory direction on informality in children's cases has been erroneously interpreted in some juvenile courts as authorization to the judge to omit the informing the persons before the court of their rights to an attorney; in some instances this misinterpretation of informality has led the court to discourage—and even prohibit—attorneys' attendance at the hearings. But the hearing is private, not secret. In a well-operated court, an attorney who is given an explanation of or who is familiar with the purpose and character of the court is not an obstruction to the court's procedure; rather, he cooperates with the court in the setting it desires and can contribute constructively to the resoluion of the issues before it. The bar's understanding and cooperation are as important to the juvenile court as the general public's. Some appellate courts have also declared firmly that in children's cases the parties have the right to be represented by counsel and should be informed of that right.

Again, as a protection to the parties, and emphasizing the fact that, despite its informal character, the hearing of a juvenile case is a regular judicial process, the parties should be informed regarding their right to appeal. It is presumed that when they are represented by counsel, this statement by the court is not necessary. In paragraph 3 the words "if necessary" refer to such a situation as the availability of a public defender to the court without the need of any other court appointment of counsel.

In the second paragraph of the section the reference to persons who "have a direct interest . . . in the work of the court" includes newspaper reporters, who should be permitted—indeed, encouraged—to attend hearings with the understanding that they will not disclose the names or other identifying data of the participants.

The juvenile court has exclusive jurisdiction over violation of traffic laws or ordinances by children, just as it has jurisdiction over violations of other laws by children within its age jurisdiction. There is no reason why the juvenile court should not deal with these violations as it does with others. Depriving the juvenile court of such jurisdiction, as is sometimes recommended, is unwarranted; procedures available to other courts, such as specialized traffic courts, can be established just as well in the juvenile court.

Although some have suggested that the juvenile court is less appropriate than the special court for adults charged with traffic violations, most juvenile courts have the jurisdiction and there is no reason why they should not. The suggested advantage of a special procedure in the adult traffic court can readily be attained by the juvenile court by instituting a specialized procedure, which may draw upon the experience of the adult court and which may also add some special features more appropriate to child violators.

Physical or Mental Examination and Treatment

The court may order that a child concerning whom a petition has been filed shall be examined by a physician, surgeon, psychiatrist, or psychologist; and it may order treatment, by them, of a child who has been adjudicated by the court. For either such examination or treatment, the court may place the child in a hospital or other suitable facility. The court, after hearing, may order examination by a physician, surgeon, psychiatrist, or psychologist, of a parent or guardian whose ability to care for a child before the court is at issue.

COMMENT ON SECTION: Because the court is set up not to punish children or crimes but to find and remove, when possible, the causes of their misconduct, it needs to learn many things, including physical and mental condition and needs, about its wards and those responsible for them. Physical and mental examinations often reveal unsuspected conditions which help to explain misbehavior. The right of the court to order examination and when necessary to arrange hospital or medical care should be made clear in the statute.

Next to the development of the probation service and use of a socialized procedure, no development in juvenile courts has been more fruitful than the increasing use of psychological and psychiatric study and treatment. Wherever such expert service is available, it has a profound influence on the disposition of cases and on the fundamental attitude of the judge and the staff toward problems of childhood and adolescence. None of the court's methods illustrates more clearly its function not to convict and punish, but to understand and help.

Since the proceeding in a juvenile court where a child's custody is involved is the concern of not only the parties but also the state, the court's appreciation of the welfare of the child is the uppermost consideration in determining custody dispositions. Accordingly, where the ability of the parent or guardian to care for the child is at issue, the court requires power to have him examined by a physician or psychologist.

Investigation Prior to Disposition

Except where the requirement is waived by the judge, no decree other than discharge shall be entered until a written report of the social investigation by an officer of the court has been presented to and considered by the judge. Where the allegations of the petition are denied, the investigation shall not be made until after the allegations have been established at the hearing. The investigation shall cover the circumstances of the offense or complaint, the social history and present condition of the child and family, and plans for the child's immediate care, as related to the decree; in cases of support, it shall include such matters as earnings, financial obligations, and employment.

COMMENT ON SECTION: The court may call for an investigation prior to the hearing on the issues, or may postpone the investigation until after the hearing, and most postpone it until after the hearing when there is a justishiable issue. However, except where he deems it unnecessary, the judge should have the benefit of the investigation before issuing a decree.

For a discussion of the content of the social study, see *Guides for Juvenile Court Judges* (NPPA, 1957) , pp. 49-56.

Decree

When a minor is found by the court to come within the provisions of the section relating to jurisdiction, the court shall so decree and in its decree shall make a finding of the facts upon which the court exercises its jurisdiction over the minor. Upon such decree the court shall, by order duly entered, proceed as follows:

1. As to a minor adjudicated under subdivision 1 of the section relating to jurisdiction.

(a) The court may place the minor on probation in his own home or in the custody of a suitable persons elsewhere, upon conditions determined by the court.

(b) The court may vest legal custody of the minor in (appropriate department or division of state government responsible for administering the state institutions serving delinquent children), in a local public agency or institution, or in any private institution or agency authorized to care for children or to place them in family homes. In committing a child to a private institution or agency, the court shall select one that is approved by the (appropriate licensing or approving state department) or, if such institution or agency is in another state, by the equivalent department of that state where approval is required by law.

(c) In cases of violation of traffic laws or ordinances the court may, in addition to any other disposition, suspend or restrict a license to drive.

2. As to a minor adjudicated under subdivision 2 of the section relating to jurisdiction.

(a) The court may place the minor under protective supervision in his own home or in the custody of a suitable person elsewhere, upon conditions determined by the court.

(b) The court may vest legal custody of the minor in a governmental or nongovernmental agency or institution licensed or approved by the state to care for minors, with the exception of an institution primarily for the care and treatment of minors committed under subdivision 1.

3. An order vesting legal custody in an individual, agency, or institution shall be for an indeterminate period but shall not remain in force or effect beyond three years from the date entered, except that the individual, institution, or agency may file a petition with the court requesting renewal of the order and the court, after notice to parties, a hearing, and finding, may renew the order if it finds such renewal necessary to safeguard the welfare of the minor or the public interest. Renewals may be made during minority, but no order shall have any force or effect beyond minority. An agency granted legal custody shall have the right to determine where and with whom the child shall live, provided that placement of the child does not remove him from the territorial jurisdiction of the court. An individual granted legal custody shall exercise the rights and responsibilities personally unless otherwise authorized by the court.

4. Whenever the court vests legal custody of a child in an institution or agency it shall transmit with the order copies of the clinical reports, social

study, and other information pertinent to the care and treatment of the child, and the institution or agency shall give to the court any information concerning the child that the court may at any time require. An institution or agency receiving a child under this subdivision shall inform the court whenever the status of the child is affected through temporary or permanent release, discharge, or transfer to other custody. An institution to which a child is committed under subdivision 1 or 2 shall not transfer custody of the child to an institution for the correction of adult offenders.

5. The court may order, for any child within its jurisdiction, whatever care or treatment is authorized by law.

6. In placing a child under the guardianship or custody of an individual or of a private agency or private institution, the court shall give primary consideration to the welfare of the child. Where a choice of equivalent services exists, the court shall, whenever practical, select a person or an agency or an institution governed by persons of the same religion as that of the parents of the child, unless otherwise requested and consented to in writing or recorded in open court by the parent or parents; or in the case of a difference in the religion of the parents, then of the same religion as that of the child, or if the religion of the child is not ascertainable, then of the religion of either of the parents or a religion acceptable to them.

7. In support of any order or decree under the section relating to jurisdiction, the court may require the parents or other persons having the custody of the child, or any other person who has been found by the court to be encouraging, causing, or contributing to the acts or conditions which bring the child within the purview of this Act and who are parties to the proceeding, to do or to omit doing any acts required or forbidden by law, when the judge deems this requirement necessary for the welfare of the child. If such persons fail to comply with the requirement, the court may proceed against them for contempt of court.

8. In support of any order or decree for support, the court may make an order of protection setting forth reasonable conditions of behavior to be observed for a specified time, binding upon husband or wife, or both. This order may require either spouse to stay away from the home or from the other spouse or children, may permit the other to visit the children at stated periods, or may require a spouse to abstain from offensive conduct against the children.

9. The court may dismiss the petition or otherwise terminate is jurisdiction at any time.

10. In any other case of which the court has jurisdiction, the court may make any order or judgment authorized by law.

11. Jurisdiction over a minor on probation or under protective supervision may be transferred to the court of any district in the state. Thereupon that court shall have the same power with respect to the child that it would have had if the petition had been initiated there.

COMMENT ON SECTION: The section includes all the usual dispositions available to courts in children's cases. The last four sentences under subdivision 4, prohibiting a children's institution from transferring custody of a child to a correctional institution for adult offenders, is a necessary and new provision, not contained heretofore in the *Standard Juvenile Court Act.* In a number of jurisdictions it is the practice, occasionally upheld by the courts, to transfer a child to an adult correctional institution, usually for some sort of misbehavior or breach of discipline in the training school. Such a transfer is a repudiation of the entire concept of special children's proceedings, which embraces not only special court procedure but the idea that specialized training facilities for children should be available and should be used for all children adjudicated by the court.

Since the court is not empowered to commit a child to an institution for the correction of adult offenders, an institution receiving legal custody of a child should not be able to transfer him to such an institution (see *White v. Read, 126 Fed. Supp. 67*). Accordingly subdivision 4 prohibits such a transfer. A child so seriously disruptive of the institution's program that transfer is essential will, in so behaving, almost always have violated some law over which the criminal court has jurisdiction. A new proceeding should be commenced on that basis, and if there is to be a commitment to an adult institution, it should be in accord with the section relating to transfer to other courts.

Adjudication of Child; Non-Criminal

No adjudication by the court of the status of any child shall be deemed a conviction; no adjudication shall impose any civil disability ordinarily resulting from conviction; no child shall be found guilty or be deemed a criminal by reason of adjudication; and no child shall be charged with crime or be convicted in any court except as provided in the section relating to transfer to other courts. The disposition made of a child, or any evidence given in the court, shall not operate to disqualify the child in any civil service or military application or appointment.

COMMENT ON SECTION: The injunction against calling the adjudications of the court "convictions" carries out the general spirit of the law. In addition, the provision is indispensable to establishing the constitutionality of the procedure. Since the procedure applicable to adults accused of crime is not utilized in children's proceedings, it would be unconstitutional for such a procedure to culminate in a criminal conviction.

Although practically all juvenile court laws have *some* provisions incorporating the substance of the above section, a juvenile court law should have *all* the protections suggested. In addition, community alertness is needed to see that the spirit as well as the letter of the law is obeyed. The military authorities sometimes treat a juvenile court adjudication of a child as though it were a conviction of crime, and sometimes police practices ignore the non-criminal nature of the disposition. The same is true for private individuals, particularly employers.

Modification of Decree; Rehearing

Except as otherwise provided by this Act, any decree or order of the court may be modified at any time.

At any time during supervision of a minor the court may issue notice or other appropriate process to the minor if he is of sufficient age to understand the nature of the process, to the parents, and to any other necessary parties to appear at a hearing on a charge of violation of the terms of supervision, for any modification of the decree or for discharge. The provisions of this Act relating to process, custody, and detention at other stages of the proceeding shall be applicable.

A parent, guardian, custodian, or next friend of any minor whose status has been adjudicated by the court, or any adult affected by a decree of the court, may at any time petition the court for a rehearing on the ground that new evidence, which was not known or not available through the exercise of due diligence at the time of the original hearing and which might affect the decree, has been discovered. Upon a showing of such evidence, the court shall order a new hearing and make such disposition of the case as the facts and the best interests of the child warrant.

A parent, guardian, or next friend of a minor whose legal custody has been transferred by the court to an institution, agency, or person may petition the court the court for modification or revocation of the decree, on the ground that such legal custodian has wrongfully denied application for the release of the minor or has failed to act upon it within a reasonable time, and has acted in an arbitrary manner not consistent with the welfare of the child or the public interest. An institution, agency, or person vested with legal custody of a minor may petition the court for a renewal, modification, or revocation of the custody order on the ground that such change is necessary for the welfare of the child or in the public interest. The court may dismiss the petition if on preliminary investigation it finds it without substance. If it is of the opinion that the decree should be reviewed, or, except where the legal custody has been transferred to a public institution or agency maintained by the state, the court on its own motion considers that its decree should be reconsidered, it shall conduct a hearing on notice to all parties concerned, and may enter an order continuing, modifying, or terminating the decree.

COMMENT ON SECTION: For the protection of the parties the court must be empowered to modify its decree when circumstances warrant it. It is presumed that public institutions are carrying out the mandate of the decree transferring legal custody. Accordingly, the court should not review such decree unless evidence to the contrary is brought to its attention by petition of parent or guardian.

Appeal

An interested party aggrieved by any order or decree of the court may appeal to the (appellate) court for review of questions of law and fact. The procedure of such an appeal shall be governed by the same provisions applicable to appeals from the (highest court of general trial jurisdiction), except that where the decree or order affects the custody of a child, the appeal shall be heard at the earliest practicable time. In children's cases the record on appeal shall be given a fictitious title, to safeguard against publication of the names of children.

The pendency of an appeal or application therefore shall not suspend the order of the court regarding a child, and it shall not discharge the child from the custody of the court or of the person, institution, or agency to whose care he has been committed, unless otherwise ordered by the appellate court on application of appellant. If the (appellate) court does not dismiss the proceedings and discharge the child, it shall affirm or modify the order of the family court and reprimand the child to the jurisdiction of the court for disposition not inconsistent with the (appellate) court's finding on the appeal.

COMMENT ON SECTION: The right of appeal is as applicable in juvenile courts as in any other court. The informality of procedure, which is desirable, should never go to the point of ignoring the basic rights of parents and children, including the right to appeal. The importance of this right is stressed by the provision in the section relating to procedure in children's cases, requiring that persons before the court be given notice of the right to appeal.

SUMMARY

Society has determined that the best way to deal with youthful offenders is to re-educate and rehabilitate them. Therefore, existing methods of treatment and judicial procedures available for adult criminals do not serve this rehabilitative purpose. As a result, separate treatment facilities and judicial procedures have been established for youthful offenders.

Because rehabilitation should begin during the court hearing, juvenile court procedures have been altered to achieve a protective, rather than adversary, atmosphere. Rules of evidence, court procedure, and sterile formality have been discarded. Thus the juvenile court is informal in nature, and the court, acting in the role of *parens patriae,* accords protective jurisdiction over the minor and purports to act in his behalf.

The legal principles, by 1899, were fully accepted as a part of American jurisprudence and, thus, provided a firm legal foundation upon which to build the juvenile court structure. Its responsibilities, naturally enough, are both legal and social. Procedural and substantive legal rights constitute its legal responsibilities. Such procedures provide the boundaries and framework within which the power of the state must be exercised. The juvenile court's power comes from the law. Its duty to comply with the law is absolute, and none the less so because in the people's minds, as well as in reality, the courts are guardians of the people's rights.

Unfortunately, juvenile court proceedings are not only unstructured, but each judge makes his own ground rules. Consequently, the nature of the juvenile court hearing varies significantly among states and counties. In a strict sense, it is incorrect to speak of a juvenile court system as if juvenile courts throughout the country were uniform in their structure, philosophy, and activities. To assume such uniformity would be to commit error. Not only is this uniformity absent throughout the country, it is often found lacking within a single state.

When the law is silent with respect to several basic rights normally associated with juvenile courts, each judge defines his own rules or court procedure. Some courts diligently inform minors and their parents of their right to counsel, employ firm evidentiary rules, provide a court reporter, and observe the privilege against self-incrimination; many juvenile court judges, however, regard some or all of these procedures as inappropriate in the juvenile court.

The need to observe legal rights in the juvenile court does not imply conflict with the court's protective philosophy; neither is it a radical concept. If it were, this view would not be sponsored by such organizations as the *National Council on Crime and Delinquency*, the *National Council of Juvenile Court Judges*, or the *United States Children's Bureau*, to name but a few of the leading organizations advocating more legal protections.

QUESTIONS

1. What are the *legal principles* of the juvenile court law?
2. Discuss the *social principles* of the juvenile court law.
3. Why is it a necessity that the judge of the juvenile court be certain that both procedural and substantive law are complied with? List the four reasons.

4. Why is there such divergency with respect to interpretation of the juvenile court law?
5. What is the construction and purpose of the *Standard Juvenile Court Act*?
6. Briefly, discuss the jurisdiction of the minor with respect to the *Standard Juvenile Court Act.*
7. What is the petitioning process in the *Standard Juvenile Court Act*?
8. The *Standard Juvenile Court Act* discusses taking children into custody; release; notice; . . . outline this section.
9. According to the *Standard Juvenile Court Act,* a child should be detained when he falls into certain categories. List three groups as indicated in the Act.
10. According to the Standard Juvenile Court Act, a child should *not* be detained when he falls into the following groups . . . List the groups as indicated in the Act.

Chapter 13

Federal Laws Relating to Juveniles

ALTHOUGH THE FIRST STATE JUVENILE COURT LAW was enacted in 1899, the federal government until 1932 was still dealing with the delinquent child about the same as it always had. The confirmed felon of long standing was still being dealt with in most penal institutions as he had been during the Civil War, and the teenage "criminal" was no exception. The minor, whether he was a 12-year-old or an 18-year-old, who committed a petty theft was subjected to the same criminal treatment as a delinquent who was sophisticated in the area of felonious offenses.

The federal government, prior to the enactment of *The Federal Juvenile Delinquency Act,* dragged its feet because it felt that the doctrine of *parens patriae* was restricted to the state and that any venture into this field would constitute an infringement of states' rights. But the need for reform on the federal level could not be suppressed. An act providing for the diversion of juveniles to state authorities (*18 U.S.C. 662a, now Section 5001*) was enacted on June 11, 1932. This act permitted federal enforcement officers to surrender to state authorities a person under 21 years of age who had committed a federal offense and was a delinquent under the laws of the state, such person to be dealt with by the authorities of the state if they were willing to assume jurisdiction. However, on occasions, the states were unwilling to assume a responsibility which they could well shirk.[1]

THE FEDERAL JUVENILE DELINQUENCY ACT

The Federal Juvenile Delinquency Act[2] *was passed by the Congress in 1938 about 40 years after the establishment of the first state juvenile court.* It is interesting to note that the Act as originally enacted provided that a juvenile defendant should be processed as a juvenile only

[1] J. F. Byerly, "Sentencing the Juvenile Offenders," *Federal Probation,* Vol. XXVI, No. 2, June 1962, p. 23.
[2] *18 USCA 5031–5037.*

if the Attorney General *so directed.* The Act was amended on June 25, 1948, 62 Stat. 857, to carry the mandate that such a juvenile defendant shall be proceeded against as a juvenile unless the Attorney General *specifically directs otherwise.* It should be noted that prior to the above enactment, only regular adult proceedings were available. The new Federal Juvenile Delinquency Act authorized noncriminal procedures. There was no question that the federal laws did not provide adequate flexibility for the type of treatment necessary for juvenile offenders. In recommending the legislation to Congress, former *Attorney General Cummings stated:*[3]

> "Students of criminology and penalogy agree that it is undesirable, from the standpoint of the community and of the individual, that all juvenile offenders be treated as criminals. Many of them can be reclaimed and made useful citizens, if they are properly treated and cared for. . . . It is likewise advisable that a juvenile delinquent should not receive the stigma of a criminal record that would be attached to him throughout life."

The federal government taking the above into consideration responded by enacting the Federal Juvenile Delinquency Act. The act gave recognition to the principle that the youthful offender needs specialized care and treatment. The special procedures provided for in the act are calculated to reclaim young offenders, so that they will become law-abiding and productive citizens.[4]

In interpreting the act, the court stated in the case of *Shroutakon vs. District of Columbia* that one of the chief aims of the act was:[5]

> "... to eliminate the formalities of a criminal proceeding which emphasizes *punishment* and *retribution* and to provide in its place a more informal procedure designed to enhance the protective and rehabilitative features which have come to be associated with modern juvenile courts."

A juvenile, as defined by 18 U.S.C. 5031, is a person who has not attained his eighteenth birthday at the time of the offense, and juvenile delinquency is a violation of the law of the United States committed by juveniles not punishable by death or life imprisonment. It is to be noted that the age at the time of the offense is the determining factor as to whether a juvenile proceedings shall prevail.[6]

In the case of the *United States vs. Fotto,* in commenting on this definition of the juvenile as one who as not as yet reached his 18th birthday, the court stated:

[3]Commitment Authority, *Deskbook for Sentencing,* IV: 1 June, 1962.
[4]S. T. Hughs, "Trial of Juvenile Delinquents in Federal Courts," *Law Enforcement and the Juvenile Offender,* Charles C Thomas, Springfield, Illinois, 1963, p. 81.
[5]Byerly, *op. cit.,* p. 23.
[6]*United States v. Fotto,* 103 Fed. Supp. 430, 1952.

"If this was not the intention of the Congress, I think it would not have failed to say what was the determinative date—the arrest, the inditement, or time of trial. In either of the later dates, the indictment of the trial might be delayed to the prejudice of the offender and the purpose of this Act possibly nullified."

Exceptions in Application of the Act

Section 5032 of the Federal Juvenile Delinquency Act is mandatory to the effect that a juvenile who has committed an act in violation of the law of the United States shall be proceeded against as a juvenile delinquent. Three exceptions to this mandate are apparent from the statute: (1) where the offense is punishable by death or by life imprisonment; (2) where the juvenile offender is diverted to state authorities; and (3) where the Attorney General, in his discretion, expressly directs adult procedure.

Where the Offense Is Punishable by Death or Life Imprisonment

Although the first exception appears to be clear, the United States attorneys should proceed with caution as the following case will exemplify; a juvenile defendant may be charged in a multiple-count indictment or information with having transported a kidnapped person in inter-state commerce in a stolen motor vehicle. Some prosecutors may be so carried away by the kidnapping charge that they do not deem it necessary to procure waiver of juvenile proceedings as to the Dyer Act charge. It has often developed that the kidnapping charge cannot be sufficiently developed for prosecution and has to be dropped. It follows that the indictment charging the Dyer Act violation must follow, in that, the necessary waiver of juvenile proceedings was not obtained from the Attorney General prior to the return of the indictment although the circumstances attached to the violation may well have warranted such waiver.[7]

Where the Juvenile Is Directed to Local Authorities

Since the enactment of the Federal Juvenile Delinquency Act in 1938, it has been the policy of the federal government to divert juvenile offenders to state authorities whenever possible. The wisdom of this policy is apparent. A juvenile, after all, is usually a tractable offender. To remove him from his home surroundings, his associates, and whatever roots he may have developed and nourished are factors that are not likely to be considered. Perhaps this was the juvenile's first conflict with the law, and the circumstances may have been such as to characterize the offense as a thoughtless whim, and an unintentional transgression

[7]Byerly, *op. cit.*, p. 24.

or a boyish prank. Surely such a youngster can be dealt with far more satisfactorily by authorities who know him, his family, and his general background. Such a boy should not be uprooted from all to which he is anchored and thrust into a department that may possibly be more harmful than helpful.[8]

Of course, there can be no set pattern to follow; each case must be weighed by its own set of facts. In other words, some first-offender juveniles may offer far better chances for rehabilitation if they are removed from their families, associates and background. However, individual states may well meet such contingencies by commitment of such a juvenile to a state institution that will fulfill his needs, by placement in a foster home, or by arranging for his care with some relative or friend who has the interest of the boy at heart. It is also stressed that the federal government has no facilities whatsoever for the care and treatment of juvenile offenders, particularly those of tender years or for female juvenile offenders.[9]

Where the Attorney General Directs Adult Procedure

In very few instances the Attorney General will specifically direct that a juvenile offender be prosecuted as an adult. Such a decision is reached only after a very careful study of the recommendation of the interested United States attorney, the report of the probation officer, the circumstances attached to the offense, the boy's past record and the prospects of successful rehabilitation under juvenile procedure. It may be of some interest to know that when a request for adult procedure against a juvenile defendant is submitted to the Attorney General, more are denied than are approved.

Procedure under the Act and Right to Counsel

Section 5033 of Title 18 clearly prescribes that any district court of the United States shall have jurisdiction of proceedings against juvenile delinquents. This statute further provides that the court may be convened at any time or at any place within the district in chambers or otherwise. On many occasions, the child is held formally in the chambers in the presence of only the U.S. attorney, the probation officer, the attorney for the juvenile—if there is one—the juvenile, and the members of his immediate family.

The juvenile charged with an offense shall, according to the Act, be fully appraised of his rights, including his right to the assistance of counsel. If the juvenile has consented to be tried as a juvenile, the U.S.

[8] *Ibid.*, p. 24.
[9] *Ibid.*, p. 24.

Attorney makes the minor cognizant of the Act and the judge fully appraises the minor as to the charge and the consequences of being found a juvenile; i.e., he will not have a record, and if found to be a delinquent he will have been adjudged guilty merely of a "status" to which no stigma is attached, such as accompanies conviction of a crime.

In *Borders vs. United States*, the court said with reference to the above:[10]

> "Congress by express provision has removed the criminal stamp from the proceedings authorized by the Act. A proceeding under the Federal Juvenile Delinquency Act results in the adjudication of a status rather than a conviction of a crime with the stigma which attaches to such conviction."

If a juvenile is accompanied by some adult member of his family, a parent or a guardian, it is incumbent upon the court to fully explain to such parties and the juvenile the consequences of his election. In most cases, if such juvenile defendant does not have the counsel of some adult who is interested in him, the court may permit him to waive the assistance of counsel if the court is convinced he is fully aware of the consequences of his act.

However, if such a defendant should fail to sign a written consent to juvenile proceedings, as required by Section 5033, the Attorney General's office would urge the court to sign counsel to represent such juvenile in order to fully appraise him of his rights and the consequences of his action.

The Federal Juvenile Delinquency Act is not a criminal act and, consequently, neither strict procedural nor substantial legal rules will prevail and the burden of proof sufficient in a civil suit rather than a criminal suit will suffice.[11]

Despite the fact that a juvenile defendant waives certain constitutional and procedural rights when he consents to juvenile procedure, it is the tendency of the courts, and certainly with the approval of the federal department, to surround such juvenile with all the safeguards that are attached to a defendant in a criminal trial. This is as it should be. Whereas the purpose of the Juvenile Delinquency Act is to rehabilitate the juvenile offender and to avoid the stigma of conviction, it should be borne in mind that once having elected such procedure the juvenile does not constitute himself a target for any unethical prosecutor.[12]

[10] *Borders vs. United States*, 154 F. Supp. 214, Afrd. 256F. 2nd 458.
[11] Byerly, *op. cit.*, p. 25.
[12] *Ibid.*, p. 25.

Sentencing the Juvenile Offender

The next step, once the judge finds the youth to be a delinquent or if he has entered the plea of juvenile delinquency, is to pronounce sentence. The sentencing procedures of the Federal Juvenile Delinquency Act are prescribed by *Section 5034* of that Act. They are brief and unequivocal. The juvenile may not be committed for a longer term than the penalty provisions of the substantive statute violated. He may, under no circumstances, be committed beyond his minority. Furthermore, he may be placed on probation, but not beyond his minority.

Regarding parole eligibility, a committed juvenile is eligible for parole consideration at any time *(18U.S.C. 5037)*. Since this is so, a committed juvenile is not amenable to the provisions of the time statute *(18 U.S.C. 4161)*. However, as inducement to rehabilitation and as an incentive to juveniles who display some real effort to take advantage of the treatment program which has been established for their benefit, the Bureau of Prisons administratively awards good time to committed juveniles at the same rate as is provided for adults.[13]

THE YOUTH CORRECTIONS ACT

We are concerned here with the Youth Corrections Act,[14] involving youth offenders under 22 years of age when convicted, approved September 30, 1950; an important amendment thereto; and the extension of its provisions in 1958 to young adult offenders 22 years of age, but under 26.[15]

Since the establishment of the first juvenile court in 1899, a specialized juvenile court procedure has evolved. It is not uniform everywhere in the United States, but its essential emphasis is, to a greater extent, in correction rather than upon custody and punishment. Such courts have informalized their procedures. Many are administered in close relationship to clinics where efforts are made to get at the cause of the juvenile's behavior so that a wiser disposition can be made which would be impossible without clinical knowledge. Clinical study and pre-hearing investigations are recognized features of juvenile courts and correctional agency programs. The purpose is to individualize treatment. Some proponents have overemphasized permissiveness. They have insisted that it is impossible to change basic attitudes or reeducate

[13] *Ibid.*, p. 25–26.
[14] *46 Stat. 1085, 1960, 18 U.S.C. 5005–5024.*
[15] *72 Stat. 846, 1958, 18 U.S.C. 4209.*

the individual unless he is given almost unlimited freedom of choice. Since re-education aims to change the system of values and beliefs of an individual to change it so as to bring it in line with society at large, one might ask whether it is logical to expect this change to be made by the subjects themselves. The fact that change in basic attitudes often occurs in the correctional setting when the individual gains insight from experiences in a controlled environment cannot be overlooked.

The youth correction division, like the above-mentioned juvenile court movement, is neither soft nor tough, but is interested in the offender as an individual and in the causes of his behavior. The need to remove the cause of his misbehavior is primary, whether society is seeking to restore to good behavior the individual who has already broken the law, or whether society is looking at the broad problem of prevention. For centuries our society recognized only one cause of anti-social behavior—willful choice by the individual. A person breaks the law solely because he chooses to do so. This theory shaped and still underlies our traditional criminal law with its fixed sentences and the concept of punishment to fit the crime. It still influences the attitude of the public toward offenders, of many parents toward their children, and of many teachers toward their pupils. Yet science has long since found this basic theory inadequate. Science explains, for instance, why some individuals begin to steal only after suffering a brain lesion, some injury, or some disease such as encephalitis. However, it fails to account for the accidental or situational offender, or the youth who is the product of a warped and twisted mind.[16]

Although there are substantial and procedural differences in the laws of the 50 states having special provisions for youth offenders, and although the Federal Youth Corrections Act has unique features of its own, there are nevertheless many common features in the total program. The Youth Authority programs in California, Wisconsin, Minnesota, Massachusetts, Texas, Washington, Kentucky, and Arizona have unique features of their own; however, each of the programs is dedicated to the idea of individual study of the offender, using up-to-date diagnostic methods. Such programs aim to provide appropriate treatment, not for a specific period of time (as in fixed sentences dealt out by criminal courts), but as individually required. Such treatment is to be accorded either in the community through contact with trained probation members, through guided utilization of community resources, or else in several types of institutions. These institutions utilize a classification and screening procedure so that criminally sophisticated

[16]G. Reed, "The Federal Youth Corrections Act in Operation," *Federal Probation*, Vol. XVIII, No. 3, September 1954, p. 10.

youths are not brought into intimate contact with a novice. In these institutions education, training, and counselling techniques are also applied only after the individual's problems and personality patterns have been fully explored and diagnostically worked-up to the extent feasible. The authorities attempt to provide a corrective program in the community rather than the more rigid, artificial atmosphere of an institution.[17]

The Federal Youths Corrections Act is the culmination of a ten-year effort by the *Judicial Congress of the United States and its committee on punishment for crime* to secure the enactment of legislation that would provide means of methods for training and treatment of federal youth offenders who are not proper subjects for probation. This is substantiated by the following statement in House Report No. 2979, August 22, 1950, accompanying S. 2609, the Bill which became the present Youth Corrections Act. The statement:[18]

> "Reliable statistics demonstrate beyond possible doubt, that the period in life between 16 and 23 years of age is the focal source of crime. It is during that period that habitual criminals are spawned. . . . They are arrested for serious crimes twice as often as adults from 30 to 34; three times as often as those from 40 to 44; and four times as often as those from 45 to 49. . . . Reliable statistics demonstrate, with reasonable certainty, that existing methods of treatment of criminally inclined youths are not solving the problem. A large percentage of those released from our reformatories and penal institutions return to anti-social conduct and often become hardened criminals. . . . The problem is to provide a successful method and means for treatment of young men between the ages of 16 and 23, who stand convicted in our federal courts and are not fit subjects for supervised probation—a method and means that will effect rehabilitation and restore normality, rather than develop the recidivist. . . . The underlying theory of the Bill (*S. 2609*) is to substitute for retributive punishment methods of training and treatment designed to correct and prevent anti-social tendencies. It departs from the more punitive idea of dealing with criminals and looks primarily to the objective idea of rehabilitation."

The philosophy which stimulated the proponents of the Act is reflected in its basic provisions authorizing a new and more flexible procedure in imposing judgment after conviction, directing intensive corrective treatment, and approving release of the youthful offender under effective supervision when he has derived the maximum benefit from treatment.[19]

[17]Byerly, *op. cit.*, p. 26.
[18]Reed, *op. cit.*, p. 11.
[19]*U. S. Code Congressional Service*—Legislative History 81st Congress, Second Session, 1950, p. 3984.

Before discussing the procedure of the Act upon conviction, the reader should be cognizant of the *relation of the Youth Corrections Act to the Juvenile Delinquency Act.* The Attorney General has stated that a juvenile who violates a federal law between his seventeenth and eighteenth birthdays may be proceeded against as a juvenile delinquent or may be prosecuted as a youthful offender under regular criminal procedure without prior approval of the Attorney General if (a) the current offense and record of the previous delinquency indicate a need for a longer period of correctional treatment than is possible under the Federal Juvenile Delinquency Act or under the statute violated, or if, for instance (b) the current offense is serious and the offender has a record of being previously committed to a penal or correctional institution.

Unlike the Federal Juvenile Delinquency Act, which provides for the special handling of the offender from the time of arrest until disposition by the court, the Youth Corrections Act contemplates regular criminal procedure. It may be invoked against all offenders under the age of 22 who have attained their seventeenth birthday.[20]

Applicability and Procedure upon Conviction

The Act, as previously stated, defines a youthful offender as being under the age of 22 at the time of conviction. Treatment is designated to protect the public by providing corrective and preventive guidance, thus assisting the offender in finding ways and means of developing socially acceptable habit patterns. Whereas a punitive philosophy is interested only in what an offender has done, treatment philosophy wants to know, in addition, *why* the offender committed the offense. The Federal Youth Correction Act subscribes to the *treatment philosophy* and, therefore, directs the Youth Division and the Federal Bureau of Prisons, through its institutions and diagnostic centers, to explore the personality and life experiences of every new commitment. The program is treatment-oriented and diagnosis may determine a youngster's I.Q., his academic achievement level, and his areas of retardation. It must also discover his personal interests, his strengths, and his weaknesses.

After conviction of a youthful offender, the court may:[21]

1. *Section 5010* (a), suspend disposition or execution of sentence and place the youth offender on probation, for which purpose the Probation Act is available.

[20]A. E. Gottshall, "Sentencing the Youth Offender and Young Adult Offender," *Federal Probation,* Vol. XXVI, No. 2, June 1962, p. 18.

[21]Reed, *op. cit.,* p. 12.

2. *Section 5010* (b), sentence the youth offender, in lieu of a definite term, to the custody of the Attorney General for treatment and supervision until discharged by the Youth Correction Division. Such a committed youthful offender *may* be released under supervision at any time by the Youth Correction Division. He *must* be released under supervision upon expiration of four years from date of conviction and must be unconditionally discharged upon expiration of six years from the date of conviction, as provided by *Section 5017 (c).*
3. *Section 5010 (c),* sentence the youthful offender to the custody of the Attorney General for any term of imprisonment authorized by the statute under which the offender stands convicted if it feels that the youth would not derive the maximum benefit from treatment by the Youth Division before expiration of six years from the date of conviction. Such a committed youth offender *may* be released under supervision at any time by the Youth Correction Division. He *must* be released under supervision not later than two years before expiration of a term imposed by the court. He may be unconditionally discharged one year later and must be unconditionally discharged on or before expiration of the maximum term imposed as provided by *Section 5017(d).*
4. *Section 5010(d)* sentence the youth under any other applicable penalty division if the court finds the offender will not derive benefit from treatment under *Section 5010(a) or (b).* The offender will then be eligible for parole and conditional release under laws applicable to general prisoners.
5. *Section 5010(e)* commits the youth offender to the custody of the Attorney General for observation and study at a classification center if the court desires additional information as to whether the youth offender will benefit from treatment under *Section 5010(b) or (c).* Within 60 days from the date of the order or such additional period the court may grant, the Youth Corrections Division shall report its findings to the court.

When a youth is committed to the Attorney General under any of the above provisions, he will usually be sent to a classification center. There a complete study of the youthful offender will be made. The law requires that in the absence of exceptional circumstances, the study be completed within 30 days. The classification center will then forward to the director of the Bureau of Prisons and to the Youth Division a report of its findings on the youth offender and its recommendation as to treatment.

The Act prescribes that the director of the Bureau of Prisons shall, (1) set aside and adapt institutions[22] under the control of the Depart-

[22]*Institutions specially designed for commitment of Youth offenders include four reformatories*: Peterburg, Va.; Chillicothe, Ohio; El Reno, Okla.; and Lompoc, Calif.; also two corectional institutions: Ashland, Ky., and Englewood, Colo.; one prison camp of Tucson, Ariz.; and two juvenile institutions, namely, National Training School for Boys, Washington, D.C., and Natural Bridge Camp, Natural Bridge, Va.

ment of Justice to be used, as far as possible only for treatment of youth offenders (*Section 5011*), (2) provide classification centers for complete study of the offender upon commitment (*Section 5014*), and (3) cause periodic examinations of each offender to be made and reported to the Youth Corrections Division as provided under *Section 5016*.

The law provides great flexibility and latitude to the Division and to the Director of the Bureau of Prisons in determining the proper type of program which will be accorded to the youth. The youth can be:

(a) released under supervision immediately;
(b) transferred to a small open-type youth institution;
(c) continued for pre-vocational or educational training in the Ashland or Englewood Youth Centers;
(d) transferred to a larger Federal institution with a more general type of program.

Act Extended to Young Adult Offenders

Provisions of the Youth Corrections Act have been extended to the youth adult offenders. One Section of the Act known as *Public Law 85 752*, approved August 25, 1957, authorizes a court, in the case of a convicted offender who has passed his twenty-second birthday, but not his twenty-sixth birthday, to apply the sentencing provisions of the Youth Corrections Act, if, after consideration of the offender's background, health, and capabilities, it finds that he might benefit from the treatment provided by that Act (*72 Stat. 846, Title 18, U.S.C. 4209*).

It was quite apparent soon after the activation of the Youth Corrections Act that some convicted offenders, who were eligible, except in age, for commitment under legislation were ruled ineligible due to the fact that the offenders had passed their twenty-second birthdays. This factor was quite disturbing to both the courts and administrative officers. Therefore, it was proposed that the Act be amended to cover offenders 25 and under. This proposal had received the support of a strong majority of judges. However, it was ultimately concluded that more experience with that Act was desirable before its provisions were changed and opened wide to all offenders under 26 years of age. Consequently, it was decided that the Act may be applied to an offender between the ages of 22 and 26 years only by a special finding of the court.[23]

The reader should be aware that the Youth Corrections Act sentenc-

[23]U. S. Code, *Congressional and Administrative News*, Legislative History, 85th Congress, 1958, Second Session, p. 3902, 3892.

ing provisions are not available when the offender falls in the age group specified by *Section 4209 (22-26)*, if the offender has been convicted of an offense which requires the imposition of a mandatory penalty, in particular, violation of certain narcotic laws.

The provisions mentioned in this chapter make possible a wide variation of custody and treatment to fit the needs of the individual youthful offender. In total, the goal of the Federal Youth Corrections Act is to protect society better and to retrain the youth more effectively.

Review, Control, and Supervision

As previously indicated, the primary objective of the Federal Youth Corrections Act is to re-educate and rehabilitate the individual offender. Therefore, it is necessary that a periodic review of his adjustment be scheduled for evaluation by the professional staff. The Youth Division evaluates all written material and interviews the committed youthful offender at least once annually. However, such an annual review does not preclude the release of the offender at any time during the year that the institutional classification committee feels such release would be not only in the best interest of the minor, but also the community. The youthful offender, therefore, is aware that he is "not just serving time," but is, in fact, himself the one who really determines by his own attitudes and adjustment the date of his release. This procedure permits an earlier-than-usual release date for youths who apply themselves and longer-than-usual release date for youths who are unable to make a positive adjustment in the institution and who are hostile not only toward the program, but toward society in general.

Those youths who are released on parole are supervised by the federal probation system, and periodic reports are submitted to the Youth Corrections Division regarding the adjustment of the parolee.

Furthermore, authority is granted in the Youth Act for the Division to expunge the records of youthful offenders who, after one year of release under supervision, are given an unconditional discharge prior to the expiration of their maximum sentences. Obviously, this is of tremendous value to the youth and serves as a motivating factor for positive adjustment while on parole.

SUMMARY

The Youth Corrections Act does not have any effect on the Juvenile Delinquency Act. Unlike the Federal Juvenile Delinquency Act, which provides for special handling of the offender at the time of arrest until disposition by the court, the Youth Corrections Act contemplates regular criminal procedure. Whereas the Youth Corrections Act deals with youthful offenders under 22 years of age, under the Juvenile Delinquency Act a juvenile is a person who is under his eighteenth birthday at the time of the offense.

Under the Federal Juvenile Delinquency Act, any juvenile who has committed an act in violation of a law in the United States shall be proceeded against as a juvenile delinquent. Three exceptions to this particular Act are as follows:

1. where the offense is punishable by death or by life imprisonment;
2. where the juvenile offender is diverted to state authorities;
3. where the Attorney General, in his discretion, expressly directs adult procedure.

Procedure under the Act prescribes that all district courts of the United States shall have jurisdiction of proceedings of juvenile delinquents. This statute (*Section 5033 of Title 18*) further provides that the court may be convened at any time or any place in the district, in chambers or otherwise. Furthermore, the minor charged with an offense must be fully appraised of his rights, including his right to the assistance of counsel. If a juvenile elects to be treated as a juvenile under the Act, it is incumbent upon the court to explain fully to the minor the effects of his election. If the minor chooses juvenile procedure, he will have no record and if found to be a delinquent, he will have been found guilty of no felony, no misdemeanor, and no petty offense, but will have been adjudged guilty merely of status which attaches no stigma such as accompanies conviction of a crime. Regarding the sentencing of the juvenile offender under the Juvenile Delinquency Act, the juvenile may not be committed for a longer term than the penalty provisions of the substantive statute violated. He may, under no circumstances, be committed beyond his minority.

Under the *Youth Corrections Act,* the youthful offender is a person under the age of 22 years at the time of conviction, and "conviction" means the judgment on a verdict or finding of guilty; a plea of guilty or a plea of *nolo contendere*. After conviction of a youthful offender, the court may (1) suspend the imposition or execution of sentence and place him on probation; (2) in lieu of the penalty of imprisonment authorized by statute violated, sentence him to the custody of the Attorney General for treatment and supervision until discharged by the Youth Corrections Division; (3) in lieu of the penalty of imprisonment authorized by the statute violated, if it considers him incapable of deriving maximum benefit from treatment within six years from the date of conviction, sentence him for a further period authorized by the statute or statutes under which conviction was had or until discharged by the Youth Corrections Division; (4) sentence him under any applicable penalty provision if it is found he will not derive any benefit from treatment; and (5) commit him to the custody of the Attorney General for observation and study if it desires further information as to whether he will derive benefit from treatment and the Youth Corrections Division is required to report their findings to the Court within 60 days unless granted an extension.

The Youth Corrections Act further prescribes that the director of the Bureau of Prisons shall (1) set aside and adapt institutions under the control of the Department of Justice to be used, as far as possible, only for treatment of the youth offenders, (2) provide classification centers for complete studies of the offender upon commitment, and (3) cause periodic examinations of the offender to be reported to the Youth Corrections Division.

QUESTIONS

1. What are the ages applicable to the Federal Juvenile Delinquency Act and The Youth Corrections Act?
2. What are the duties and powers of the Attorney General regarding the Juvenile Delinquency Act?
3. What are the rights of a juvenile who has consented to be tried as a juvenile under the Juvenile Delinquency Act?
4. The Director of the Bureau of Prisons (Youth Corrections Act) in determining the proper type of program for the minor, may do various things. List alternatives.
5. What are the alternatives of the court after a minor is convicted under the Youth Corrections Act?
6. List three (3) exceptions in the applicability of the Federal Juvenile Delinquency Act.
7. Discuss the reaction of the Youth Corrections Act to the Juvenile Delinquency Act.

Chapter 14

Rights and Liabilities of Minors[1]

THE STUDENT SHOULD BE COGNIZANT of the fact that although the laws pertaining to *rights and liabilities of minors* are basic throughout the country, there is a great deal of variation in the area of age, minority and majority. Therefore, *the age limitations* presented here may, or may not, be applicable to the reader's state. Such age variations should be taken into consideration when reading and/or interpreting the laws.

Laws of the United States and each state are divided into major divisions: criminal laws and civil laws. *Civil law* is that body of law contained both in statutes and in the decisions of courts of law which apply to society as a whole and define the rights, duties, obligations, and liabilities of citizens. *Criminal law* is that code of law which defines offenses against the state and provides punishment for individuals convicted of violations of criminal laws. Violation of civil law could be an offense against one or several persons, and not necessarily an offense against the state. To enforce civil law, an individual normally initiates a law suit in the civil courts.

The district attorney can initiate a criminal action. In order to dispose of the criminal and civil actions, there are municipal courts which handle minor crimes and civil law suits under specific sums set up by each state. A superior court handles major crimes (called felonies) and civil law suits *in excess* of the amount designated by the municipal court of each state, as well as family law cases.[2]

TORTS

A tort is a harm done to one's person, property, or reputation by another. A person suffering this harm must show that the party inflict-

[1]For further detailed information see "Rights and Liabilities of Minors," *Department of the California Youth Authority, 1965*, by W. E. Thornton, Attorney, Chief Probation Officer Sacramento County, California.

[2]"Youth and the Law," *Palo Alto Unified School District*, Community Council of Northern Santa Clara County, California, 1962, p. 1.

ing it had a duty to do or refrain from doing it. Furthermore, he must show that this duty was violated in a neglectful or deliberate manner, and that such act was the approximate cause suffered.

The layman always presumes that when harm occurs, someone must be responsible and therefore liable for damages, This is a false assumption, because many accidents do occur in which neither party is negligent. In these unavoidable accidents, no recovery can be obtained. *Many states have the rule of contributory negligence, which provides that if both parties are negligent, neither party can recover.* These two rules may be summed up briefly by saying that if neither party is negligent, there can be no recovery in damages for either; if both parties are negligent there is no recovery for either.

Most of these situations in regard to torts that the probation, parole, or police officer deals with involve a deliberate act. The minor deliberately breaks a window, deliberately steals an automobile, deliberately strikes a person. They are intentional torts, against a person or property of another. The victim of the minor's intentional act has suffered a harm and may be legally entitled to payment for damages.

In order to understand what constitutes damages, it is necessary to analyze the different types briefly:

Compensating Damages. Damages are normally awarded for the express purpose of giving the victim compensation for the actual damage suffered. The theory is to return the victim, as nearly as possible, to his former position. If the window was broken, pay to get it replaced; if the victim was injured, pay for all medical and hospital bills, and so on, etc. Special damages may be awarded for pain and suffering resulting from injury, loss of limbs while hospitalized, and inability to work.

Punitive or Exemplary Damages. Most states allow the victim not only money for actual damages suffered, but where the act is deliberate the victim, in addition, may recover damages for the sake of example and by way of punishing the wrongdoer.

In every crime there is also a tort action when the victim suffers some harm. If the victim is injured deliberately, the wrongdoer is liable for criminal action; if property is stolen and not recovered, civil action will apply; or if an automobile is stolen and subsequently recovered, civil action will apply. Damages in terms of money will usually be awarded for the actual loss suffered, plus punitive damages to teach the wrongdoer a lesson.

There are, then, really two separate actions involved in a crime. The first is represented by the *People of the State versus the Defendant* (or in a juvenile court proceeding a petition is filed on behalf of the minor alleging commission of a particular act specified as a low violation). These proceedings are brought into either criminal court or the juvenile court.

The second is a civil action which may be brought by the victim in a civil court against the defendant for tort. Recovery is in payment of money for loss suffered, and punitive damages if such are allowable.

The two actions are separate and distinct, brought into different courts by different parties, with different causes of action and with different types of judgment. The criminal court is the people against the defendant, while the civil action is a remedy by the victim for loss suffered. A criminal conviction, or a juvenile court proceeding *does not* cancel out the civil action for money damages.

EXAMPLE. *A person steals an automobile. The wrongdoer may be prosecuted in a criminal court for auto theft; the victim may sue the wrongdoer in a civil court for damages in a tort action.*

EXAMPLE. *A person strikes another; the injured party may sign a complaint and have the wrongdoer prosecuted for battery in a criminal court; he may also sue in civil court for money damages in a tort action.*

A recovery in a civil action for tort does not bar criminal action for the same fact any more than a conviction in a criminal case bars a civil action.

Liability of Minor for His Torts

There is much confusion in the general public's mind regarding the liability of the minor for his own deliberate torts. The rule in many states is that a minor is liable for his own torts in the same manner as if he were an adult. This simply means that a minor must face civil liability for his willful misconduct or negligence. There are obvious cases where the child is so young that he does not know the consequences of his wrongful act and to penalize him for his lack of understanding would be unjust. While all children are civilly liable for actual damages caused, they *are not* liable for punitive or exemplary damages unless the child is capable of knowing the act was wrong.

When the minor's civil liability is examined carefully, it is found that the victim has a right to be compensated; however, it is usually ascertained that the minor has no assets to satisfy a judgment. There is a remedy, but once this remedy is reduced to a judgment, there is little the victim can do to recover. Because of this, claimants generally make little effort to seek a judgment, but seek aid in the juvenile court. The juvenile court, of course, as a term of probation, may order the minor to make restitution to the victim. However, the litigation involving civil matters rightfully belongs in the proper civil court, and cannot be litigated in the juvenile court. There is a conflict among juvenile court judges as to whether or not restitution should be a part of juvenile court procedure, and whether the parties should best be left to civil remedies in the proper court.

The procedure to sue a minor in a civil matter will be discussed later, but it is well to examine the process of holding the minor to a judgment once obtained:

1. Sue the minor in tort through guardian ad litem.
2. Obtain judgment award.
3. Execute this judgment on any real or personal property the minor has.
4. Return judgment unsatisfied if minor has no assets, or a deficiency if minor does not have sufficient assets to completely satisfy the total judgment.
5. A judgment may be executed any time *within* 10 years and after that, may be renewed for a like period if execution is not possible;
6. Keep judgment alive and executed when minor does acquire property, even if he has reached a majority.

It is important to realize that mere minority is not a bar to recovery in a civil action. A foolish act on the part of a 15- or 16-year-old child may result in a large money judgment against him. Ten or 20 years later, when the child has grown, married, or has acquired property and assets, he may be subject to an execution of this judgment. The law has provided a remedy for the victim of a minor's deliberate or negligent act, and enforcement of it by execution of judgment may occur many years later.

Parents' Liability for Torts of Their Children

Parental liability for the torts of children is an area that has received wide discussion. For example, *the law in California, prior to a statutory enactment in 1955, had been that parents were usually not liable. It is only by direct statutory provision that the rule is relaxed or modified.*

The rule was that minors themselves were liable for their torts, but the mere relationship of the parent and child did not impute liability.

Most states subscribe to the above California version pertaining to parents' liability for torts of their children. Victims of minors' intentional torts were surprised to learn that they were unable to hold the parents responsible. The exceptions to the rule of no liability by parents were as follows:

1. If the minor acted as an agent of the parents, the parents were liable. The parents actually had to authorize the child to said act and it is doubtful if many parents order a child to steal a car or commit a burglary. One would have to show the child did the wrongful act at the parents' order, or at least implied constructive authorization.
2. If the parents did provide the child with a dangerous instrument, and should have known that damage could be caused. Examples could be: a BB gun in the city, a knife, possibly fire crackers, etc.
3. Where the *parents know* that the child is following a course of careless or intentional acts which may cause harm to others, they must take *reasonable steps* to control his conduct. However, the question of "notice" and what is considered "reasonable", are two areas that generally would bar recovery from parents for willful misconduct of the child.

EXAMPLE. *Parents of a four-year-old child, who had violent propensities, were liable for damages caused when the child attacked the babysitter. Parents had knowledge of this conduct and failed to warn the babysitter.*

It is always difficult to show that parents could reasonably know the minor would commit a law violation which caused damage to another, and more difficult to show what "reasonable steps" should have been taken to prevent it.

It was generally presumed that parents do not authorize, order, or allow their children to steel cars, break and enter, or commit vandalism, and usually cannot be held on notice that their children will do these acts. What the parents can do to prevent these acts is also open to speculation. Thus, in most cases, we see the parents were not liable for the torts of their children.

Statutory Provisions Imputing Liability to Parents for Child's Willful Acts

In several states, including California, there are two specific areas that make parents civilly liable for the intentional torts of their minor children. Both of these sections, however, refer to willful and intentional acts which cause damage to another's property and *not negligent acts.*

Section 16074 of the California Educational Code imputes liability to the parents for any willful act which causes damages to school property. The implication, however, is that the child must be a pupil and that if he willfully breaks windows, cuts chairs or books, or commits any vandalism, the school board may sue the parents. This section also covers parental liability for books and supplies loaned to the child and not returned.

Section 1714.1, a 1955 provision of the Civil Code of California, makes the parent or parents having custody or control over a minor child severally and jointly liable for any damages that a child willfully causes to the property of another. The limitation is $500 that may be recovered for each individual toward the child.

The above section does not mean the minor himself is not liable for the full amount of the damage he caused, but his parents are liable up to $500. If the damage caused was willful and the actual cost for repair was $1,000, the parent is liable for only $500. Obviously, the total amount that can be collected, however, would be actual damages of $1,000. The victim would be wise to join both the parents and the minor in the action and to seek a recovery in the form of a judgment against both.

However, Section 1714.1 probably does not apply where the minor is *not* subject to control of the parents, i.e., he is emancipated and living alone. Examples of this are married minors, minors in the armed forces, minors who, by implication, are declared emancipated and are living alone. This section would also probably not include a parent who, by court decree or actually a fact, has been deprived of custody. Examples of this may be where parents are divorced and the minor is living with the parent who was awarded custody. The other parent would not have custody and control, and thus it would appear he would escape imputed liability. The same would apply to children who have been removed from their parents' custody and placed in foster homes or institutions by the courts.

Many other questions also arise which are at present unanswered. What if the parent having custody or control specifically orders the minor *not* to do a certain act and he nevertheless willfully does this act and causes harm to another's property? Is the victim to hold the parents liable? This section covers damage to "property" and apparently does not cover damages to "person." Suppose a 17-year-old causes physical harm to another. How about the 20-year-old living at home who robs a gas station and spend the money? Does the state hold the parents liable?

What of the 16-year-old who willfully steals a car, but negligently has an accident which damages the stolen car as well as the auto of the third person? The damage caused was not willful, but was accidentally caused by the negligent operation of stolen car. Are the parents liable for the damages to the stolen car? The car of the third person? The medical expenses of an injured third party? These questions, and many more, will arise in future litigation and be answered then.

It must be remembered that this action against the parent is a civil remedy for the plaintiff. The litigation arises in a lower civil court. The proper place for filing the complaint for damages is either in the justice or municipal court, and is not an action to be litigated in the juvenile court. This is purely a civil matter and should not be confused with juvenile court proceedings.

The juvenile court proceedings is one in which a petition is filed on behalf of the child, and jurisdiction is over the child, not the parents. The juvenile court may make reasonable orders over the parents regarding child support, but it has no jurisdiction to litigate a civil issue which concerns the parental liability for the tort of the minor. Much confusion has already arisen as to the fundamental legal principal action versus juvenile court jurisdiction.

Criminal Responsibility of Parents for the Acts of Their Children

Throughout the country there is a growing demand to make the parents responsible in criminal proceedings for willful violations of the law by their children. One of the basic doctrines of criminal law is that the offender must have willfully violated a specific criminal statute; knowing that such act was a violation is not necessary, but he must have intentionally committed the act. There are exceptions to this general rule which involves criminal negligence, but for our purposes the general rule is basic.

Relationship. The basic question is, does the law punish parents with criminal proceedings based on the parent-child relationship for wrongful acts of their children? Is the state going to prosecute parents for being incapable of controlling their children?

At the present time, to this author's knowledge, no state has a statute which attempts to make parents criminally responsible for law violations committed by their children. The civil liability has previously been discussed. The only statute which in many states has implications of criminal liability, relates to the sections pertaining to *contributing to the delinquency of a minor.* Such a section often provide that "a person who commits any act or omits the performance of any duty, which act or omission causes or tends to cause or encourage any person under (age to be deterined by the respective state) become within the jurisdiction of the juvenile court (such jurisdiction refer to provisions for which a minor may be declared a Ward of the court) is guilty of a misdeameanor."

If a minor commits a law violation, what must his parents have done or not done in order to be charged with contributing to his delinquency? Can parents be convicted under the aforementioned section if they are incapable of controlling their children, or if they are doing all a reasonable parent could do, even though their children commit law violations? The answer seems to be that there is nothing in the mere parent-child relationship that makes a parent criminally liable for his child's violations of the law. In order to convict, it would seem that the parent must have aided, counselled, or authorized the child to commit a crime, and not merely have been passible in exercising control.

The only statutes which seem to impute criminal liability are local curfew ordinances. These generally provide that if the minor is on the streets after a certain hour he is guilty of a misdemeanor. It also provides that any parent, guardian, or other adult having custody of the minor is also guilty of a misdemeanor if they allow or permit the minor to be on the streets after a designated hour.

If the parent gave consent for the minor to be out after the designated hour, or actually ordered the child to be on the street, it is quite possible that a case for conspiracy or aiding and abetting the child to violate the ordinance could be shown. Under these circumstances the parent would probably be liable. The problem, of course, comes when the parent has no knowledge that the minor is out after the curfew hour, or has told the minor to be home before that time. If this is the case, can the parent be charged with willfully and unlawfully violating that ordinance? It does not appear that conviction can be sustained unless there was an intentional violation by the parent and if the parent did approve the minor being sent out after the designated hour, or specifically ordered him to be home, the parent is guilty of nothing.

Again, the prosecution of the criminal aspects of these ordinances against the parent is one for the district attorney or city attorney. This is a criminal proceeding against the parents based on their willfull and unlawful violation of the specific ordinance. The action is in the lower court (justice or municipal) and parents are entitled to a jury trial. There have been few commissions under these sections. These curfew ordinances have been an attempt to keep the minors off the streets and, from public places after a designated hour, unless accompanied by an adult or on their way home from some recreational pursuit.

Therefore, taking the above into consideration, it can be concluded that the relationship of parent and child does not, in itself, create criminal liability in the parent for law violations by the child. Incompetent or incapable parents must commit some overt act, or fail to perform some specific legal duty which violates a statute, before they may be prosecuted for their child's misconduct.

CONTRACTS

What is a contract? A contract is an agreement between two or more parties under which each of them agrees to do or to refrain from doing some act. In order to be binding, there must be an offer and an acceptance of the offer. A contract may be made by custom where acceptance is implied. There must also be an exchange of consideration, which means an exchange of cash, property, or some other benefit.[3]

In simple terms a contract is an agreement between competent parties to do or refrain from doing some act which is supported by a consideration. All of us, each day, make contracts. Some are made by mere custom where consent is implied, some are oral, some are written, some executed, and some remain to be executed. A minor's contract, like that of an adult, when all legal prerequisites are met, is valid and binding—with certain exceptions.

However, the law seeks to protect a minor from some of his own imprudent acts. Because of his age, he lacks sound judgment. So that advantage will not be taken of him, the law provides him with a "way out." Even though the contract is otherwise binding, the law gives the minor a voidable option. That is to say, most contracts entered into by a minor (in most states, under 21 years of age) with an adult are voidable. It is voidable at the minor's option, but nevertheless the adult is bound and does not have the same privilege of voidability. Note that most of the contracts of a minor are not *VOID*, but voidable at the minor's option. It may be generally said that adults contracting with minors *do so at their own risk*, and the law discourages such dealings.

There are few situations in which a minor's contract is not voidable, but actually void. A youngster (who is considered a minor; any state legislature can set any specific age as majority) cannot give a delegation of power or make any contract regarding real property or make any contract relative to personal property not in his immediate possession or control. Any such contract is void, not voidable, and no act on the minor's part to disaffirm is necessary.

The general rule, then, is that any contract entered into by a minor is voidable at the minor's option. The minor may refuse to perform his obligations and not be liable in damages for the breach. The adult who contracted with the minor, however, must perform. The minor may, of course, refuse to perform and use his age as a defense.

The minor may intentionally and willfully misrepresent his age, *i.e., falsely stating that he is over the statutory age as set by a state*, and yet this in itself will not prevent him from disaffirming the contract. The law gives him the voidable option and he is not liable in a tort action

[3]*Ibid.*, p. 1.

for false misrepresentation of age, nor will this misrepresentation bind him to a contract even though the other party so relied. These rules apply whether the minor is buyer or seller. The dangers inherit in entering contractual relationships with the minor may well be seen.

In California, for example, there are different rules regarding minors under 18 years and between 18 and 21 years. These are treated below:

1. Minor over 18

The minor may disaffirm his contract by refusing to perform, and he is not liable for the breach. If he has purchased an article on installment, he may refuse to make further payments, recover back any amounts he has already paid, but he must return the purchased article. Both parties should be returned as nearly as possible to the status quo prior to the transaction.

The minor must also pay for any damage, depreciation, or reasonable rental value of the article so restored. The contract, even though already executed, is subject to disaffirming by the minor and a return to prior status by both parties. The minor gets his money back and the adult seller gets his property back, with compensation for any damage inflicted on the property. Misrepresentation of age by a minor still does not bind him. The law seeks to protect the minor from himself as well as from adults who deal with him, even though an innocent yet careless adult has contracted with him. This is true whether the minor is over 18 years of age or under.

2. Minor under 18

The minor under 18 may disaffirm his contract in the same manner as the minor over 18. The one great distinction is that a minor under 18 is not liable for damage done to the article, and if he has lost the article purchased, he is not liable to reimburse the seller. The same rule seems to apply if the minor under 18 is the buyer rather than the seller. He may recover the article sold, and need not return the money received from th sale, if he no longer has it.

He can always recover his property from the buyer—adult, unless the article has passed into the hands of an innocent purchaser from the adult-buyer. The innocent third party is not a party to the minor-seller and the adult-buyer transaction, and to penalize him would be unjust. The law protects this third person who was in no way involved in the voidable contract transaction.

3. Exceptions

There are some exceptions to the voidable aspects of the minor's contract. The voidable ones are as follows:

When a minor is living alone he may contract for necessities of life. It may well be seen that many minors are "on their own" and if their contracts were voidable, it would be almost impossible for them to rent rooms, buy groceries, purchase clothes, and so forth. Adults would be reluctant to deal with them, as their contracts would normally be voidable. The law seeks to give the minor living alone the status of an adult. In contract law, it comes to the things necessary for existence. What these things are is the difficult question. They probably would not include jewelry, watches, automobiles, etc.

A minor who is 18 years of age and married has the same legal rights of contract as an adult. Note that this applies to both male and female, and once the minor has fulfilled both requirements, 18 and married, subsequent divorce and annulment will not disqualify the minor. Once this status has been reached, the minor has forever lost the power to disaffirm any contract on the basis of minority. Of course, the contract must have been entered into subsequent to reaching this status in order to be binding.

Note also that a parent is not liable for contracts entered into by his minor child. If the parent enters into a contractual relationship in behalf of the minor child, he, of course, becomes bound in his individual capacity. A parent can be a co-signer on a note or contract with his minor child, and could not deny his own liability when the minor sought to rescind the contract because of his age. This might result in an unusual situation where the minor could not be bound, but the co-signing parent may be legally liable in event of the minor's breach of contract. Adults contracting with minors would be wise to bind the parent in the transaction, so that the parent accepts liability in case the minor seeks rescission or refuses to perform.

There may be some questions, however, where a minor enters a contract for necessities and fails to pay. It may well be that the parent has an obligation of support under state law and may be liable on the minor's contract for these necessities of life, or at least liable to pay for a fair amount of these necessities.

While the general rules of contracts relating to minors have been discussed, there are specific sections granting consent to minors to enter into binding contracts. These are generally enacted to allow such contracts that are deemed necessary to the minor and thus allow adults to contract with no fear of rescission by the minor. For example:

1. Minors may contract bank deposits allowing minors to open savings accounts and make withdrawals. Similar provisions are made in regard to savings and loan associations and building and loan associations.
2. A female minor may sign relinquishment for the adoption of a child, and also make contract with a hospital for medical or surgical care in regard to pregnancy if she is married.
3. Married minors may contract with a hospital for medical or surgical care. In the event of annulment the right of consent continues.
4. A minor in the armed forces is able to contract for any medical care when necessary for himself.
5. A minor who is married may enter into a property settlement agreement in reference to the marriage.
6. If over 16, a minor may make a contract of insurance for himself, with a member of the family as beneficiary.

CRIMINAL SUITS BY AND AGAINST MINORS

Minor as a Plaintiff

A minor, like an adult, always has a civil remedy when his rights are invaded. He has protection both in tort and contract against adults or other minors. The minor may enforce his rights by civil action, or other legal proceedings, in the same manner as a person of full age, except that a guardian must initiate the proceeding. The theory behind this is that the minor lacks sound discretion and good judgment, so the law seeks to protect from his own imprudent acts. The requirement that he proceed through a guardian is intended to more fully protect his rights. The parents of a minor unmarried child are his natural general guardians and are such by their parent-child relationship.

The minor, if he is the plaintiff in an action, must appear by and with his guardian. The complaint should clearly indicate this so that the defendant is put on notice as to the plaintiff's status. If the minor fails to proceed through his guardian, and does obtain a judgment, it will not be void because of failure to have a guardian appointed. The best procedure is to have a guardian appointed by the court for the proceedings, even though the guardian is the natural parent and by law the general guardian.

In California, if the minor is over 14 years of age, he must nominate and approve of his own guardian. This permits the 14-year-old minor to choose whom ever he pleases to assist in representing his interests and the courts will appoint this nominee, unless he is not a fit and proper person. These appointments are generally done on affadavit of the minor and the guardian ad litem before issuance of a complaint and summons upon the defendant. A guardian ad litem is an adult appointed by the court for the express purpose of the litigation and the jurisdiction of the guardian is limited to the litigation. The guardian ad litem appointed by the court for a 14-year-old or older minor must be so appointed on the nomination of the minor, or at least his appointment must be ratified by the minor. If either of these are not done, the judgment by the court is without the jurisdiction and the judgment may be disaffimed by the minor. This, again, is to permit the minor over 14 to choose his own guardian and to protect his right given him by the statute.

The point to remember is that, although the ages differ in different states, the basic premise as indicated above is similar.

The plaintiff minor under 14 years does not have the right to select his guardian *ad litem.* A friend or relative may apply to the court for appointment, and after being duly appointed may proceed with the complaint and summons on the minor's behalf. Even though the minor has a general guardian the court in which an action or proceeding is prosecuted, may appoint a guardian *ad litem* if the court feels that it is expedient even if the minor appears with his general guardian. The court, representing the minor's best interests, may require a guardian *ad litem* even though the parent objects.

A minor in the United States may have a right to prosecute a civil action through a guardian *ad litem*, but situations arise where his suits may be settled without court action. The law again attempts to protect the minor against himself, and requires that his compromise be handled by those who are competent. A disputed claim of the minor must be approved by the superior court. This also brings the whole matter before the court, and does not permit the parents to give a release of the action which might be unjust to the minor. The parents may have the approval of the superior court to compromise, and the funds may be held by them in trust for the minor. The funds, however, are the child's not the parents', and they may be required to post bond and account to the court. The court may require that a guardian be appointed to administer the funds. This guardian would in most instances be the parents, although the normal rule is that minors over 14 years may choose their own guardians. The parents have a right to be appointed guardian if the minor is under 14, and unless there is some very compelling reason, the court will appoint the parent guardian of the minor over 14 years. The parents are, by the very nature of the parent-child relationship, the natural guardian of their child, and their interest is almost the same as an invested property right. Therefore, parents, when available, have almost a right to be appointed their child's guardian in any matter that requires such appointments.

Minor as a Defendant

The minor who is being sued, i.e., the defendant in an action, must also be protected. State laws recognize that a minor defendant does not have the knowledge or experience to protect himself against suits, and he may well have a legal defense to the action. It would be unjust to allow the plaintiff to take advantage of a minor's inexperience, and possibly to obtain a default judgment against him.

The plaintiff, when suing a minor, must serve the defendant personally if he is over 14 years of age—age varies from state to state—and if the minor is under 14 years in addition to serving the summons on him personally, he must serve the father, mother, or guardian. If there is no father, mother, or guardian in the state, service must be made on the person having the care, custody, and control of the minor, or on the person with whom he resides or in whose service he is employed.

Should the plaintiff fail to make this service as required, the court in which the action is filed lacks jurisdiction and a judgment is voidable. The plaintiff should name the parents, if there are parents, as the general guardians when bringing the suit against the minor defendant, and serve all the parties named.

The defendant minor over 14 must apply for appointment of a guardian *ad litem* within 10 days after receiving a service of summons. If the defendant is under 14 (if over 14 and he fails to apply for appointment of guardian *ad litem*, a relative, friend, or any other party to the action may apply for the Court to appoint a guardian *ad litem* to assist in defending the action), the court on its own motion may also appoint a guardian *ad litem* to protect the interests of the child.

The plaintiff suing a defendant minor often makes application to the court for the appointment of the guardian *ad litem* so that the action may proceed. A judgment obtained against a minor defendant by default, unless a guardian *ad litem* was appointed, may be set aside. Thus plaintiffs have the burden of proper service, as well as making certain that a guardian *ad litem* is appointed. The court acquires jurisdiction over a minor defendant, to authorize the appointment of a guardian *ad litem*, only when service of summons on the defendant minor has been made.

Note that when the minor is the plaintiff and fails to have a guardian *ad litem* appointed but obtains a judgment, a judgment is not voidable by the defendant because of a failure to appoint a guardian. However, if the minor is the defendant and a judgment is obtained without a guardian *ad litem* being appointed, the situation is not the same. The judgment may be set aside. The minor in both cases may have the judgment set aside, but in neither case can the adverse adult party to the action do the same.

The apparent liability statute imputes liability from child to parent for $500 on each tort. As previously discussed the minor is liable for full damages of his tort, but the parent is restricted to $500 for each tort. The plaintiff may now proceed against the minor child and the parents. The plaintiff may join both parents and child in the action and seek a judgment against both. The factual issues against both parent and child are the same, so that they may be severally and jointly liable. The parents, however, have a $500 limitation while the minor has an unlimited amount for his own torts. If the total situation is under $500, the plaintiff could join the parent and child in the same action.

PARENT AND CHILD

This action on the parent and child relationship will cover only the more perplexing problems. It is not an attempt to outline the voluminous material on the subject.

Domicile and Residence

Domicile and residence become important in deciding the proper court for action, eligibility for various county services, and juvenile court jurisdiction. *Domicile* means physical presence and intention to make a place a home. *Residence* may be merely a temporary place of abode. The terms, however, are many times used synonymously and, for our own purposes here, they will be so used. The child's residence is controlled by his parents. Neither parent of a legitimate child has any greater right than the other over the custody of the child. The husband selects the location of the home. It is a general rule of law that the residence of the wife and children is that of the husband-father. The residence of the father determines that of the child during the father's lifetime. However, if he has abandoned the child, or if a court has awarded custody to the mother, the child's residence becomes that of the mother. If the parents are separated and living apart, the residence of the child becomes that of the parent actually having physical custody of the child. This may not be true if the custody order of the court vests custody in one parent, while the other parent or third person in fact has physical custody and is caring for the child.

A child who has been abandoned is a foundling. He gains residence in the state and county where he is found. Subsequent finding of either parent may change the child's residence, but not in such a manner so that the child will suffer from this change of residence. An unmarried minor who has a parent living, may not obtain a residence by acts of his own. This is subject to the rules of emancipation which will be discussed later.

The adopted child, of course, acquires the residence of his adopting parents and loses that of his natural parents. Once adopted, the same rule applies as if his adoptive parents were his natural parents. The child on adoption relinquishes all rights to his natural parents, and may inherit from and through his adoptive parents. The natural parents are no longer liable for the child's support and are relieved from all parental duties.

Parental Authority

A parent may use reasonable physical force to discipline his children, but this may not be done to excess. The parent has a duty to care for his children, to support them, and be responsible for any of their acts which are imputed to him by the law. The courts will seldom intervene, either through the criminal or juvenile court, to interfere with the way parents rear their children unless the conditions are severely unacceptable. Social agencies and probation officers may on occasions, seek to have children removed from their natural parents through "neglect" or "dependency" petitions in juvenile court, and placed in foster homes. The line between neglect and the rights of parents to rear their children in the manner they see fit is a very narrow on. The rights of parents must be balanced against the state's interests in the rights the children have in being provided with substantial opportunity, and a chance for a successful future life.

The juvenile Court law does not contemplate the taking of children from their parents and breaking up of family ties merely because, in the estimation of probation officers and courts, the children can be better provided for or more wisely trained as wards of the state. Probably from mere consideration of helpful and hygenic living and systematic education and training, this would be true in the case of thousands of families of wealth and respectability. It is only in instances where there is demonstrated incapacity, akin to criminal neglect, that the state is justified in interfering with the natural relationship of parent and child.

The evidence to support the allegation that the child is being neglected by his parents must be clear and convincing before the juvenile court can intervene. Each case must, of course, be examined on its own merits, and while it may be clearly in the best interests of the child to be removed from his parents, the vested interests of the parents' authority over their children must be heavily considered. The supremacy of the parents in their own home in regard to the control of their children is generally recognized.

The child may expect support and education from his parents. The father is primarily responsible for this, but the mother must assist to the extent of her ability. This is, of course, subject to the "station in life rule," and the ability of the respective parents. The father is under no legal duty to send his children to college, no matter what his financial condition may be. The father, unless his parental authority has been taken away by the courts, is the one to decide the extent of the education of his children beyond what is provided by the school system of the state. His duty to support is reciprocal between parent and child. The adult child has a duty to support his parents if they are unable to support themselves. If a parent abandoned his child while the child was under 16 years, and this abandonment continued for over two years, the adult child may be relieved of any responsibility to support his parent.

Should the father fail to provide the necessities for his minor children, and if a third party assumes this responsibility, the third party may hold the father liable for the funds expended upon this minor child for the necessities of life. This applies when this third party is the county, relative, or some charitable agency. The father is not liable for compensation to the other parent or relative without an agreement for compensation when the child has abandoned the father without just cause.

Parents' Right in Property of the Child

A minor child, like an adult, may own and dispose of his own property. The mere fact of being a parent gives no right over property owned by the child. Parents may not exercise control over property of their children by sale, lease, or destruction. This, of course, is subject to the common-sense rule that the parent may restrict the child in the use of his property when such restriction is for the best interest of the child. The relationship of parent gives a certain control over the custody and conduct of the minor child, but nothing inherent in this relationship makes the property of the child that of the parents. The minor having a right to own and dispose of his own property is usually handicapped because of the voidable nature of his contracts, and adult buyers are very cautious concerning their dealings with him. Generally, the minor is prohibited from making a contract dealing with his real property when he is under 18 years (remember, minor age varies in states) and cannot give a valid power of attorney. A minor may dispose of his property by will only if he is over 18, and if under 18 his property will be distributed by the law of intestate succession at his death.

The father and mother are equally entitled to the custody and services of their minor children. They are entitled to have their children work for them without compensation. However, if the minor chooses to work for someone else for wages, the parents are entitled to the child's wages. This simply means that all earnings of the minor legally belong to the parents, and the child has no right to keep any part of these earnings. If either parent is dead, the other is entitled to these earnings; and if the parents are separated, the parent having legal or physical custody is entitled to the earnings. The mother of an illegitimate child is entitled to that child's earnings.

The employer of a minor must have some protection for compensating the minor directly for services performed, so the law permits an employer to pay wages directly to the minor *until notified to pay only to parents.* The parents of an unemployed minor may notify the employer to pay them for the child's employment, and if the employer refuses and pays the child instead, the parents still may collect from the employer.

These earnings are not similar to property the minor receives as a gift, inheritance, will, and etc., as this type of property belongs only to the minor child. Earnings of a minor child are part of the services the parent is entitled to receive from the parent-child relationship, and earnings belong only to the parents. However, parents may relinquish their rights to the earnings of a child and permit the child to keep them. If this occurs, in fact or by implication, the earnings then belong to the child and the parent has no further control over the money.

Emancipation

Upon reaching the age of majority, or entering into a lawful marriage, a child is emancipated (set on his own) by operation of the law, and the right of the parent to control him and to receive his earnings ceases.

A parent may emancipate his child by voluntarily relinquishing the right to control him and to receive his earnings. This emancipation may be accomplished by express agreement, by involuntary agreement of parent and child as to the child's freedom from control, or it may be implied from such acts as reasonably indicate consent on the part of the parent and child. After complete emancipation, the child is in every respect his own person and may claim his earnings as against the parents, and may bring court action for personal injuries resulting from the parents' ordinary negligence; however, the child must obviously be old enough to work and care for himself.[4]

This *voluntary emancipation* on the part of the parents is not as extensive a doctrine as most presume. Such a voluntary emancipation of minors *under the majority age* does not enlarge a minor's right to contract, except for his right to contract for necessities, as previously discussed, nor does it permit suit without a guardian, or enlarge his political rights, or release him from the jurisdiction of any court orders.

It is doubtful that the parents may escape liability for the child's support by releasing the child from their control. The primary liability to support a minor child lies with the father, and it would be counter to sound logic to permit the father to evade this responsibility by an agreement with a minor child. Certainly the county or some third person who assumes support of the child could have looked to the father

[4]*Ibid.*, p. 18.

for reimbursement. However, a third party cannot expect reimbursement from the father of an emancipated child when the father has been abandoned by the child. It appears logical, however, that a criminal action of failure to provide could be instigated against the father if he refused to support his minor child. This would not apply if the father is willing to have the child returned home to live and the child refuses.

Emancipation or release from parental authority may result even without the consent of the parents. A minor when enlisting in the armed forces is no longer under the control of his parents. A lawful court order either in a civil court or in the juvenile court may release the child from one or both parents. These orders may or may not release the parents from the liability of support. A guardianship procedure may completely divest the parents from any control over the child, or a juvenile court action may also deprive the parents of all control. A step-parent adoption relieves the natural father or mother of all control and interests in the child, and places control with the step-parent.

The marriage of a minor child emancipates the child from control of his parents. This appears true even in the case of a voidable marriage and until the parent proceeds with annulment action, the child is not under the control of his parents. There is no case law as a guide, but it would appear that if the annulment is granted, the minor once again would be under the control of his parents. Emancipation would only be temporary, and the parental control would resume when the marriage is declared not to have existed. However, if the marriage is dissolved by divorce, it may be that the dissolution does not return the minor to parents' control.

The above question remains unanswered by statute or case law. It would appear that the parents no longer are liable to support a married minor child. This obligation is assumed by the spouse of the married minor child. Mutuality of support between husband and wife is the controlling factor in such a case, and the parental obligation of support would cease. This may not apply to annulment of an under-age marriage, and it may well be that the parents of the minor child assume this liability of support and the spouse of the minor child is relieved of this support obligation.

SUMMARY

There are two types of laws in the United States: *criminal law* and *civil law*. Civil law is that body of law contained in both statutes and in decisions of courts of law which apply to society as a whole and define the rights, duties, obligations, and liabilities of citizens. Criminal law is that code of law which defines offenses against the state and provides punishment for individuals convicted of violations of criminal law.

What is a contract? A contract is an agreement between two or more parties under which each of them agree to do or to refrain from doing some act. In order to be binding, there must be an offer and acceptance of the offer.

Is a minor's contract valid? A minor's contract, when all legal presumptions are met, is valid and binding with certain exceptions. The reason for having certain exceptions is that the law seeks to protect a minor from his own lack of sound judgment, and to prevent adults from taking advantage of him.

Another division of civil law deals with torts. What is a tort? A tort is a harm done to a person, property, or reputation of another person by a person who had a legal duty to refrain from doing that act. The harm may be caused by a deliberate act or negligence or lack of care of the actor.

The minor is liable for all of his torts in the same manner as if he were an adult. On occasion there may be cases where the minor is too young to realize the consequences of his wrong act, but children as young as five years of age have been held liable for their torts.

Upon reaching majority, the adult child has a duty to support his parents if they are unable to support themselves. The child, however, is not liable for such support if the parents abandoned the child.

The parents have a legal right to all earnings of their child. Such earnings may be paid directly to the parents or indirectly to the child and channeled to the parents. However, if the parents inform the minor's employer that all wages should be paid to them and the employer does not respond to their request, he is liable for a duplication of wages—one to the minor and one to the parents if it is so requested. Except for the earnings and services of the child, the minor's property is his own and not that of his parents. The parents cannot take possession of the child's property, unless they are appointed guardians for that purpose.

A minor child is liable for his or her own wrongful acts (torts) which result in injury to another person or damage to property, or both, unless the child is so young that he is incapable of knowing the consequences of his acts. These acts may involve both a civil wrong and a criminal act. Parents are normally not liable for the wrongful acts of their children except in certain circumstances. If the minor child is acting as an agent of the parents, or if the parents have authorized the act, the parents become liable. If the parents provide the child with a dangerous instrument such as BB gun (in the city), a knife, firecrackers, and so on, where it can reasonably be expected that some injury or damage could result to a third person, the parent may be held liable. If the parents know that a child is engaged in a course of careless or intentional acts which may cause harm to others, they may be held liable if they do not take reasonable steps to control this child.

QUESTIONS

1. *True* or *False* . . . A tort is a harm done to one's person.
2. *True* or *False* . . . When harm occurs, someone must be responsible and, therefore, liable for damages.
3. *True* or *False* . . . It may generally be concluded that the relationship of parent and child does not, in itself, create criminal liability in the parent for law violations of the child.
4. What is the process of "holding" the minor to a judgment once obtained? List.
5. List the exception to the rule on "no liability" by parents.
6. Discuss "criminal responsibility" of parents for the acts of their children.
7. Define the term contract as used in the text.
8. What is the rule regarding contracts for a minor under 18 and between 18 and 21.
9. Define and discuss *domicile* and *residence.*
10. When is a child emancipated?

Chapter 15

Special Problems

ALTHOUGH LAW ENFORCEMENT AGENCIES are accustomed to handling anti-social behavior pertaining to law violators, there are *special problems* which require considerably more flexibility and, due to their uniqueness, a great deal of cogitation. These are not the type of problems the police can handle in a more or less unvarying customary manner. Procedures for handling *juvenile gangs, use of narcotics and alcoholic beverages by juveniles, sex offenses,* and the perplexing problem of *schools and delinquents,* cannot be considered routine. Therefore, the prospective police officer should have some understanding of such problems.

JUVENILE GANGS

The word *gang* has a long history in the United States, and some of that history sheds light on contemporary use of the term and on present social attitudes toward designated groups of adolescents throughout the country. In early English usage, *gang* was often employed as a synonym for "a going," "a walking," or "a journey." In this sense, it traces its origin to the Scandinavian languages. As early as 1340, there was an Anglo-Saxon derivation which had a common meaning of "a number of things used together or forming a complete set." The above meanings were shortly combined so that *gang* came to stand for a crew of a ship or companies of mariners.

Although the word *gang* is usually associated with anti-social behavior or rebelling against authority, the gang in itself is not inherently vicious. Group activity is a necessary part of a growing child's life. The gang becomes dangerous if the street life from which it springs offers opportunities for delinquency, and if the leader of a gang is a bad influence. To the youngster who is in danger of becoming a delinquent, gang life often becomes particularly attractive. With others of his own age who may be as neglected as he is, he may get recognition and acceptance by adopting the ways of the gang. In such a manner, the goal he seeks—satisfaction—is obtained.

The influence of the gang, whether negative or positive, is particularly effective because it often completely answers the boy's needs. His desire for companionship and adventure is satisfied. He gets the feeling of belonging and of loyalty to the group. If the gang is delinquently orientated, the tougher he is the more recognition he gets. Furthermore, he may also find the discipline he needs. Gangs develop their own codes and rules of behavior, and demand that their members rigidly abide by them. Because a gang's control over boys' conduct often becomes stronger than that of their families or of the larger social group, attitudes and behavior patterns may result in delinquent activities.[1]

The etymology of the word *gang* provides a starting point from which to examine contemporary social views about juvenile gangs. The social views are constructed from an amalgam of fact, myth, and stereotype and, like all other such views, they tend to elicit and to preserve the process that they seek to describe. It is one of the noteworthy insights of social science that the isolation and labeling of forms of behavior tend to solidify, and sometimes increase, such behavior. Labeling provides a definitional framework in its recognition of a phenomenon, adding a further dimension to its previous characteristics. It is one thing to drink intoxicating beverages, but it is often quite another to violate the law by such behavior. It is one thing to hang around with a group of boys, but another thing to be a member of a gang; and the particular self and social definition imparted to the behavior may sometimes greatly affect the behavior itself.[2]

Many attempts to indicate policies and lines of action that appear to offer the greatest hope for effective intervention with gangs whose activities have been defined as antisocial, or whose members appear to be caught up in a self-defeating way of life, have been extremely difficult. For one thing, generalizations derived from work with groups in particular areas are not necessarily applicable to other geographical areas. Gangs in Los Angeles, for instance, are notably more mobile, more automobile orientated, than gangs in New York or Chicago; therefore, programs directed toward a particular gang must take these factors into consideration.

Attempts to assess and to summarize even a fractional part of the literature, and to elicit training guidelines, must almost of necessity be tentative. As a first step, before looking at the issues involved directly with intervention work with gangs, an attempt will be made to review popular studies dealing with gangs so that the practitioner can famil-

[1] J. E. Winters, *Crime and Kids*, Charles C Thomas, Springfield, Illinois, 1959, p. 96.
[2] G. Geis, *Juvenile Gangs*, President's Committee on Juvenile Delinquency and Youth Crime, Government Printing Office, Washington, D.C., June, 1965, p. 2.

iarize himself with the present state of the field and place his own work into clear perspective.[3]

Gang Studies

A popular presentation of a delinquent gang as perceived by a layman was written by *Harrison Salisbury*, Pulitzer Prize winner, in a book, *The Shook-Up Generation*, after observing for a period of three months some of the juvenile gangs in New York. Salisbury pointed out that gangs often are "pitiful, tragic, dangerous," and that youth within them find it hard, if not impossible, to break away once a member.[4]

According to Salisbury, gangs are products of social deterioration and are mainly found in slum areas in the community. Lack of basic security in families, neighborhoods, and community life are experienced by the adolescent in these settings. The gang offers a dubious substitute for security which does not exist in the present and for which there is no promise in the future.

Salisbury indicated that there are means for working out the problems which have created delinquent gangs. He feels that the universal education principle is unrealistic in that youths learn at different rates and this creates great difficulty for the slow learner. Different children have different capacities and different chronological ages for maturation.

He also feels that social disorganization, which has occurred in many housing projects in the "slum" areas, may be improved by making the income requirements more flexible. This would help prevent mobility which is created by having families move when they reach a certain income bracket. Active social work would help to reduce conflict in the housing area and create more stability. Social programs would improve the housekeeping and family life habits of housing tenants and make such developments better places in which to live.

Schools, Salisbury insists, are in most instances the only place for security and refuge for the lower-class youth who is buffeted by poverty, family inadequacy, lack of formal, and informal neighborhood organization.

Walter Miller, in his paper, "Lower-Class Culture as a Generating Milieu of Gang Delinquency,"[5] dealt with one type of delinquency that consisted of law-violating acts committed by members of adolescent street-corner groups in lower-class communities, and attributed this behavior to lower-class values. Miller attempted to show that the domi-

[3] *Ibid.*, p. 3.

[4] H. E. Salisbury, *The Shook-Up Generation*, Harper & Row, New York, 1958, p. 42.

[5] W. B. Miller, "Lower-Class Culture as a Generating Milieu of Gang Delinquency," *Journal of Social Issue*, Vol. XIV, University of Michigan, Ann Arbor, Michigan, p. 5.

nant component of motivation underlying these acts consisted in a direct attempt by the adolescent to adhere to forms of behavior, and to achieve standards of values as they are defined within the lower-class community itself. It is a long-established, distinctively patterned tradition with an integrity of its own rather than a so-called "delinquent subculture" which has arisen through conflict with the middle-class culture.

Miller presented six of the major concerns of lower-class culture, listed in degrees of explicit attention.

Trouble is of great concern in the lower-class population in that it results in the unwelcome or complicating involvement with official authorities or agencies of middle-class society. Substantial segments of the lower class, however, feel that "getting into trouble" is not in itself overtly defined as prestige, but as a means to an end.[6]

Toughness is demonstrated by physical prowess in which the lower-class individual exhibits strength and endurance and athletic skill. Masculinity is symbolized by a distinctive complex of acts and avoidance. Tattooing, absence of sentimentality, and non-concern with "art" and "literature" are indications of one's masculinity in the lower class.[7]

Smartness is the capacity of one to outsmart, outfox, outwit, dupe, or "con" another individual through maximum use of mental ability and a minimum use of physical effort. Examples of the individual in the lower class who utilizes this means for "success" is the professional gambler, the "con" artist, and the promoter.[8]

Excitement is an important characteristic feature of lower-class life which is expressed by the "night on the town" involving a pattern of activities in which alcohol, music, and sexual adventure are components.

Fate is a characteristic in which lower-class individuals believe their lives are subject to a set of forces over which they have relatively little control. A distinction is made between two states: being "lucky" or "in luck," and being "unlucky" or jinxed."[9]

Autonomy, according to Miller, is a phenomenon in which the tough, rebellious independence often assumed by the lower-class person frequently conceals a powerful dependency craving. The adolescent street-corner group represents the adolescent variant of the lower-class social group. In many cases, it is the most stable and solidary primary group he has ever belonged to and provides a dependency on the peers faced with similar problems of adjustment.

[6]*Ibid.*, p. 8.
[7]*Ibid.*, p. 9.
[8]*Ibid.*, p. 11.
[9]*Ibid.*, p. 11.

Belonging is an important content of the lower-class group. One achieves "belonging" primarily by demonstrating knowledge of, and a determination to adhere to, the system of standards and valued qualities defined by the group. One maintains membership by acting in conformity with valued aspects of toughness, smartness, autonomy, etc.[10]

In conclusion, Miller states that the commission of crimes by members of adolescent street-corner groups is motivated primarily by the attempt to achieve ends, status, or conditions which are valued, and avoid those that are disvalued by the lower class.

Albert K. Cohen, in describing the development of a delinquent subculture in *Delinquent Boys,* calls attention to the crucial condition for the emergence of a new cultural form, as the existence in effective interaction with one another, of a number of individuals with similar problems of adjustment. These may be the entire membership of a group or only certain members similarly circumscribed within the group.[11] The adjustment problems of the working-class boy, according to Cohen, stem from the fact that he is unable to live in accordance with the middle-class standard of the dominant culture because of a disadvantageous social position.[12]

The working-class boy's problem is one of "status-frustration," the basis for which is created by early exposure to lower-class socialization. For example, middle-class value is to aspire to an occupational position of economic advantage and social prestige.

The working boy's aspirations are not necessarily considered a step toward economic mobility. Eventual "advancement" and "promotion" are not so important in the working class. "Planning" and "foresight" are often outside the range of values. The "pinch" of the present is far more demanding than the promise of the future. "Payoff" is considered an immediate need, not eventual upgrading. The "ethic of responsibility" for the down-and-out in the family is imperative to the extent that one branch of the family will spend all it has for another in need, and the "law of reciprocity" holds, in that the same is expected in return in times of stress.

One is honest with particular persons, not honest in general. Persons in this socioeconomic group feel more at home in their own families and in their immediate neighborhood, and are ill-at-ease in secondary social contacts. Emotions appear to be released more spontaneously and there is free expression of aggression with no hesitancy to right. Little attempt is made to cultivate polish, sophistication, fluency, appearance,

[10] *Ibid.*, p. 14.
[11] A. K. Cohen, *Delinquent Boys,* The Free Press, Glencoe, Illinois, 1955, p. 59.
[12] *Ibid.*, p. 135.

and personality which are considered so necessary in the middle-class world.[13]

In contrast, the middle-class culture values ambition as a virtue and lack of it a serious defect. Responsibility is individual, and reliance and resourcefulness are considered essentials. Skills have to be developed so that there may be tangible achievements through outstanding performances, either in the scholastic, athletic, or the artistic areas. Forethought, conscious planning, and budgeting of time are considered of high value. Manners, courtesy, charm, and other skills in relationships are the basis for "selling of self" to others. Aggression is controlled, and violence and physical combat are frowned upon. Recreation has to be such that it is considered "wholesome," "constructive," and "not a waste of time." Property must be respected. To achieve status and success, Cohen states these are the ground rules of the prevailing culture in the United States.[14]

This socialization to lower-class values handicaps the working-class boy from achievement in the middle-class status system. Nevertheless, he must compete where achievement is judged by middle-class standards of behavior and performance.

The lower-class boy, relates Cohen, *finds the delinquent subculture a solution to his problems. It gives him a chance to belong, to amount to something, to develop his masculinity, to fight middle-class society.*

This solution for the "status-frustration" problem may not appear to be acceptable behavior, but it may appeal more than the already institutionalized solutions. When youngsters find it impossible to achieve status according to middle-class standards, they turn to development of "characteristics they do not possess and the kinds of conduct of which they are capable."[15]

Mob or gang action sets up its own "positive morality," a value structure to justify its conduct with a rapid transition into behavior according to the new "group standards" with emergence of a distinctive subculture.[16] These new values which emerge, according to Cohen, are opposed to the larger cultural structure. The mechanism of "reaction formation" takes place in which the delinquent seeks to obtain unequivocal status by repudiating, once and for all, the norms of the middle-class culture.[17]

There is strong hostility and contempt for those who are not a mem-

[13]*Ibid.*, pp. 94–97.
[14]*Ibid.*, pp. 89–91.
[15]*Ibid.*, p. 66.
[16]*Ibid.*, p. 65.
[17]*Ibid.*, p. 132.

ber of the delinquent subculture. Anti-social behavior is indulged in simply because it is considered disreputable by the dominant class. In order to gain status in the delinquent gang, a member must constantly exhibit his defiance of middle-class norms.

The corner-boy way of life "temporizes" with middle-class morality; the full-fledged delinquent subculture does not. The boy who breaks clean with middle-class morality has no inhibitions against aggressive and hostile behavior toward the sources of his frustration. The corner boy who has not embraced delinquent subculture and still compromises with middle-class norms inhibits his hostility and aggression against the middle class. On the other hand, delinquent subculture legitimatizes aggression.[18]

Cohen contends that the delinquent subculture is non-utilitarian, malicious, and negativistic. By non-utilitarian, he means that the boys really do not want the things they steal. They steal for the glory, for the "hell-of-it," for the status. By malice, he means "an enjoyment in the discomfort of others, a delight in the defiance of taboos." By negativistic, he means that the delinquent subculture negates the values of the middle-class culture. Other characteristics are short-run hedonism, by which he means that the gang has very little interest in long-range goals, planned activity, practice to develop skill and group autonomy in which the gang has an intolerance of restraints, except from the informal pressures within the group itself. Relations with other groups tend to be indifferent, hostile, or rebellious.[19]

According to Cohen, the delinquent subculture is a solution to the problems of status and success for the male rather than the female. Female delinquency is usually involved with establishing a satisfactory relationship with the opposite sex.

Intervention with Gangs

As previously indicated, some difficulty arises from attempts to generate ideas about gangs and work with gangs when the groups themselves differ, often in radical and dramatic fashion, from one geographical locale to another. Experimentation regarding different approaches to the understanding and the control of gang behavior has been carried on in various cities, and it would appear profitable to attempt to delineate some of these efforts against the background of their geographical setting. To do so, gang projects in New York City will be considered and, where appropriate, projects from other cities will be channeled into the presentation.

[18] *Ibid.*, p. 23.
[19] *Ibid.*, pp. 25–28.

Most of the work with gangs in New York City today falls to the *Youth Board.* The efforts of the Board have been primarily directed toward the control of fighting or bopping gangs, a concentration that may indicate the more aggressive nature of gang behavior in New York, or may reflect the city's huge size and limited resources, necessitating a focus on those groups considered to be the most socially hazardous.

The New York City Youth Board was organized in 1947, and its earliest efforts to combat fighting gangs were carried on by means of subsidies to existing social agencies which were designed to encourage expansion of their on-going programs. This tactic proved ineffective, however, primarily because the established agencies were unable to set up the special kinds of undertakings necessary to cope with a problem which had not traditionally been defined as part of their assignment. The lesson concerning the tendency toward inflexibility in some social agencies, their inability to respond readily to new ideas and approaches, is one that must be kept in mind in all novel and imaginative programs. Procedures and paths must be discovered to deal with such institutional inertia—and often this is quite possible—or calculated steps must be taken to bypass such obstacles as expeditiously as possible.[20]

The Youth Board terminated its relationships with private agencies in 1950 and initiated a program of its own. Such programs involved assigning special "detached" workers into territories controlled by gangs, with instructions to the workers to establish a liaison with gang members and to exploit this liaison for the purpose of rechanneling gang activities into acceptable paths. The Youth Board assigned 11 workers to two high-delinquency areas in Brooklyn in 1950. The program proliferated rapidly and a decade later there were some 85 detached workers dealing with more than 100 gangs located throughout the city.[21]

According to the Youth Board, the prime goal of work with anti-social teen-age gangs is the building of a bridge between the members of these groups and the community from which they have cut themselves off. From a handbook published by the Youth Board, entitled, *Reaching the Fighting Gang,* and enumerated in a publication by *Hans W. Mattick* and *Nathan S. Caplan* describing the rationale for the Chicago Youth Development Program, the philosophical aims of the Youth Board action program can be summarized as:[22]

1. To reduce the absolute amount of illegal and anti-social behavior attributable to the target population in the experimental area.
2. To change the behavior of individuals and groups in the contacted part of

[20]Geis, *op. cit.*, pp. 42–43.
[21]*Ibid.*, p. 43.
[22]*Ibid.*, p. 43.

the target population, where necessary, from the more seriously anti-social to the less seriously, and from the less seriously anti-social to the conventional, within the class and the cultural norms of the local population.

3. To help individuals and groups in the contacted part of the target population meet their emotional needs for association, friendship, and status by providing conventionally organized and supervised activities for them, with a view to increasing their capacity for participation and autonomy.
4. To increase the objective opportunities for youth in the external environment, in the field of education, employment, and cultural experiences.
5. To help youth prepare themselves for conventional adult roles by providing guidance in the fields of education, work, family life, and citizenship through direct intervention in their life processes, especially in times of crises.
6. To relate the target population to local adults and institutions in positive ways so that communication channels between youth and adults may be developed through which a shared, conventional system of values may be transmitted.
7. To develop in parents and local adults a concern for local problems affecting youth welfare, and to organize them with a view to having them assume responsibility for the solution of local problems.
8. To create a positive change in attitude in both youth and adults, about the possibility of local self-help efforts to improve the local community, through active and cooperative intervention in community processes, and thus to create a more positive attitude toward the local community itself.[23]

There is a certain similarity between the Chicago goals and a more general operating statement preferred in New York by the Youth Board:[24]

Street club members can be reached and will respond to sympathy, acceptance, affection, and understanding when approached by adults who possess these characteristics and reach out to them on their own level.

The positive relationship that is developed between an adult worker and a street club can serve as a catalytic agent for modifying anti-social attitudes and behavior. This relationship can also be used to help the individual member meet his needs in more positive ways.

According to the Youth Board in New York, there is no single simple formula for establishing initial liaison with gangs, but the most successful approach seems to stem from the suggestion that the particular circumstances be allowed to dictate the opening appeal of the worker to the boys. According to the Youth Board, there are various ways of estab-

[23]*Ibid.*, p. 44.
[24]*Ibid.*, pp. 44–45.

lishing contact. Among these are hanging around, direct introduction, agency referral, referral by a service group, self-referral, and, during an emergency, self-introduction. These initial and beginning relationships are usually developed through marginal participation in group activities and conversation. One develops relationships through offering and providing services, by sharing personal information, by meeting the members' suspicions and tests, and dealing with them understandingly. If the worker can accept the group, their games, new foods, new dress habits or fads, he is moving toward acceptable contact with the group and its members.[25]

Having learned through experience, the Youth Board advises workers to select for initial contact those individuals who seem either to be more amenable, the most important, or the most available. There need be no concern if initial contact is not made with the leader, but instead with individuals more toward the outer fringes of the gang structure. Such persons will, if all goes well, represent channels of access to the upper echelons of the gang hierarchy. There will, of course, be continuous testing of the worker, attempts to determine the sincerity and the particular limits of his tolerance for the group and its behavior, and to establish with some precision the ground rules under which the worker is operating. It is obviously crucial that the worker himself know more or less exactly and establish clearly what these boundaries and principles are so that he can function properly and effectively.[26]

During the many years the youth board has been in operation there have been some conclusions and speculation regarding gang activities in areas falling under its jurisdiction. It is noted that two particular long-run trends merit notice. *The first relates to the apparent change in the nature of youth gangs in New York, and perhaps elsewhere, particularly in relation to the emphasis on aggression and the movement toward the use of narcotic drugs. The second relates to the change in the role of girl auxiliaries to boys' gangs.*

Nationwide surveys by leading authorities suggest that gang fighting is on the decline throughout the United States. There was said to be more than 500 fighting gangs in 29 high-hazard areas in New York City less than five years ago. Today, the number is put at about 130, with these showing quite varying characteristics. The Assassins of Manhattan's Park West area may be taken as a typical example of the transition. In 1959, the Assassins were involved in the worst outbreak of teen-age warfare New York had experienced in years. Because of the outbreak, many of their leaders were taken into custody by the police.

[25]*Ibid.*, pp. 46–47.
[26]*Ibid.*, p. 47.

The police crackdown is said to have contributed to the alleviation of aggression among the Assassins, and the growing number of gangs in more remote areas brought neighboring gangs, formerly intense rivals, into more relaxed relationships in the face of a defined common enemy.[27]

The Assassins changed their name to Socializers, and gradually shifted to more mild-mannered pursuits, keeping in line with their new look as a "cool" group:

> "We're cool because everyone wants to grow up without worrying about it. The guys want to be like grown up. When I was jailed for carrying a zip gun, that was time wasted, man. You can't bring back that lost time. You can waste yourself, man."

Today, investigation reveals that all the boys who replaced the former Assassins in the area, as they outgrew gang membership, smoke marijuana. It is estimated that about 20 per cent use heroin more or less regularly. Use of drugs may, of course, represent even less desirable performance than the former pattern of fighting, which may at least have drained off hatreds and energies which, without outlet now, are turned to escapist stratagems through narcotics. If this is the case, it would be an indication of some of the complex social issues involved in *intervention programs* and the necessity to ascertain that they are directed to deal with basic underlying problems rather than only with manifest issues.

Drug addiction, among other things, usually results in the isolation of the addict from members of the gang partly because of his presumed unreliability in fulfilling group demands, and partly because of his vulnerability to arrest and to police pressures. Entry by a gang worker is a complicated problem because of the all-absorbing life of an addict.[28]

The *second major change in New York gangs* concerns the altered role of girl gangs. Girls affiliated with gangs, either formally or informally, represent a resource for good or bad that probably has not yet been adequately tapped. For one thing, it is believed that marriage, as much as anything else, tends to draw many boys from gang activity, partly from a sense of increased maturity, and partly because the girl offers feminine objections to the expenditure of time and money and to the dangers which may be involved in some gang associations. Girls in this sense become socializing forces. Walter Miller, has also pointed out in *Lower-Class Culture as a Generating Milieu of Gang Delinquency* that some gang members use marriage as an excuse (and one

[27]*Ibid.*, p. 48.
[28]*Ibid.*, p. 48.

which is oddly acceptable) for diminished participation in gang activities:

> "One recently-married corner boy stated, 'Sure, I'd like to go out drinking, but the old lady would kill me! She'd drag me out by my ear if I went into a bar!' She was not, of course, strong enough to do this but the legitimacy of the 'old lady's demand' was recognized by the group."

At the same time, younger girls in New York are said to be more often of late forming gangs of their own, and these gangs have become increasingly handmaidens of male lawbreaking. It is estimated by the Youth Board that some 8,000 New York boys are in gangs and, that the number of girl gang members is now 3,000. There is as yet very little work done by the Youth Board among the girls.[29]

Nearly all the girl gangs constitute units of boy gangs and use a variant of the same name. If the boys call themselves the Dead Beats, for example, the girls may name themselves, the Dead Beats Debs, or Debutantes, or the Dead Beatrices. The girls' roles include those of weapon carriers and weapon concealing, sexual intimacy with the boys, prostitution to obtain money for narcotics for themselves and for their boy friends, and courier and errand-girl chores. Status in girl gangs generally accrues in terms of the rank of the girl's boy friend in his own gang; the higher his standing, the better her position will be. In this respect, the girls are said to be particularly resistive to efforts to work with them because of their special need for gang-derived security. They are also reported to be more responsible for fighting than was true in an earlier period. Sometimes they falsely claim that they were mistreated or approached by members of rival gangs in order to stir up trouble and create excitement about themselves.[30]

Increased aggressiveness of the behavior of girls associated with gangs in New York thus represents one among many new patterns emerging in that city. Some will find their way elsewhere, others have already begun in different areas, and some will remain peculiarly restricted to the city of their origin. Together, they may be blended into a general portrait of gang activity and, as previously indicated, they must be examined with great care in establishing proper procedures for intervention with gangs wherever such work is undertaken.

Experiences from cities other than New York shed additional light and perspective upon work with gangs. *In Los Angeles,* gang intervention programs are under the auspices of the Group Guidance Section of the Los Angeles County Probation Department, respresenting an administrative arrangement different from that usually found elsewhere.

[29]*Ibid.*, pp. 50–51.
[30]*Ibid.*, p. 51.

There has always been a lack of agreement among researchers as to the basic aspects of juvenile gang dynamics, and the fact that what is known about them is based on information collected in other greographical areas prompted the decision of the Los Angeles County Probation Department Research Office to go directly to the gang boys themselves for information about juvenile gangs. The Los Angeles Probation Department assumed that the best method of gaining a better understanding of the etiology and dynamics of the local gangs was to interview in depth several juvenile gang leaders. Such an approach resulted in an excellent publication[31] which will serve as a guide for the following discussion on gang activities in Los Angeles.

Joining the Gang

The Los Angeles Probation Department Research Office ascertained that although there was great variety in the reasons for gang involvement, there were also common elements. Among the diverse reasons were: (1) some boys followed in the footsteps of their brothers; (2) some reactivated dormant gangs; (3) some joined because their friends belonged; (4) some joined as a group from another club or gang; and (5) in one occasion, it was ascertained that one boy helped originate the group.[32]

The common elements included: the proximity of the mothers' residences, the existing personal ties among the members, and the almost accidental character of their involvement. In most cases, it appeared that the boys just "drifted" into gang membership.

One boy described how he met members of the Twenties every morning on the street corner and, finally, started to "hang around" with them. Later, he was "hanging around" when the Twenties became involved in a fight with the Businessmen, and was thereafter considered to be a member. His membership was fully established when he was an accomplice in a robbery of bus transfers worth $1.50. Here is how the boy described it:[33]

> "At first, I cut it loose; I wasn't in any gang, but I used to just associate with them, you know. And so we got into this little fight with this Businessmen, and, you know, I helped; so I might as well considered myself as one of them. And then, we robbed that bus and went to jail and came out. Ever since then, we was big enough, you know."

[31] R. E. Rice, and R. B. Christensen, *The Juvenile Gang: Its Structure, Function ,and Treatment*, Los Angeles County Probation Department Research Office, Report No. 24, 1965.
[32] *Ibid.*, p. 9.
[33] *Ibid.*, pp. 9–10.

Another boy described how he "hung around" with the Caballeros and the Midnight Choppers, two of the gangs attending his high school. However, neither of these groups interested him enough to seek formal membership; instead, he attempted to start his own "social club" which lasted six months and then collapsed due to internal friction. This club was probably a "spontaneous gang" as some of its members were described as taking "some stuff" and were "kind of messed up." After the club broke up, most of the members joined an established gang, the Road Dancers.[34]

Two youngsters who followed in the footsteps of their older brothers gave some hints as to how gangs become traditional. Their descriptions of initial gang involvement are almost identical; here is one:[35]

> "The Rebel Rousers, oh, well, came from our older brothers. They started it, and, when we got old enough, we took it over. I'd say I was about seven years old. I don't know when they first got together but I know when they first called themselves the Rebel Rousers, and my brother was one and I was one. When the club first started, I never run around as much as my brothers did, but I was a member. Most everybody was close together in age ,you know. My brother's only three years older than I am. Since I was 13, I was involved in the fights."

The above quotation reveals one of the ways in which gangs are transmitted from year to year, a procedure which can, and often does, continue for generations.

Interviews with an older gang member who had reactivated a dormant gang revealed that the young inheritors of that traditional gang displayed a great deal of hostility toward "retired" members and attempted to pass themselves off as "tougher" than the older boys. The older member stated:[36]

> "I know quite a few of the fellows in the present gang, but no real connection. They just considered us one of the older fellows. They don't consider anybody one of the greats, they try to tell us older fellows that the present club members are as great as anybody that has ever been in the club; but we don't believe them. Especially one of the younger groups, it's called the Midgets. They keep telling us they are the greatest. They try to say they fight more. Although I can remember when there were just younger fellows, we used to have more or less interclub squabbles, or just free-for-alls, us against them, we'd be in different groups, and I can't see where they're growing any tougher as the years have aged them."

[34]*Ibid.*, p. 10.
[35]*Ibid.*, p. 11.
[33]*Ibid.*, p. 13.

Such competitive toughness is basically attributed to a great deal of tradition within their respective club.

The research completed by the Los Angeles Probation Department further reveals that the boys described above are from the southwest part of Los Angeles, an area of few and more recent gangs. Therefore, it has been only in the past several years that the traditional gang has become a factor in this part of the county; in previous years many spontaneous groups were formed, but they were easily dispersed or would lose momentum and disintegrate by themselves.[37]

In east Los Angeles, according to the Los Angeles Probation Department, the conditions are quite dissimilar and most gangs in this area have been in existence for two or more generations. The density is greater and each gang tends to incorporate a smaller geographical area. Until recently, the groups in this area, along with those in San Fernando Valley, have been the most violent in the county. It was gang activity in east Los Angeles that induced the Board of Supervisors to establish the Delinquency Prevention Unit within the Los Angeles County Probation Department in 1943.

The compact nature of the east Los Angeles gangs, along with the vast network of organized youth, has resulted in the situation which markedly affects the manner in which a boy is inducted into the gang. There is often a pattern of amalgamation of smaller gangs into one or more large groups, and often this territorial expansion leads to the destruction of their rival gangs. These amalgamations and expansions have something of the qualities of international treaties and invasions.[38]

It should be pointed out that there is a propensity for the youths to move from one gang into another. Such movement may be repeated several times during their adolescence. One of the interviewees from the east Los Angeles area describes his membership experience with several gangs as follows:[39]

"I must have been about 15 when I joined a big gang, or 14. But before that, I used to be from the Mariaches, it was small time. . . . I learned about 'em, let's see now, I moved in, you know, I didn't know they existed before. But as soon as I started hanging around with the guys, my neighbor especially, we're the ones that used to be pretty close, and there's this other club we used to belong to, from there we met some guys from the Mariaches and we got in. I was 13 when I went in there. This first one, I didn't last very long 'cause, as I said, it was small time, and we started seeing some bigger ones, so you get interested; I guess I lasted in the Mariaches about six, seven months in there. And when I initiated to get out ('Initiated out' usually

[37] *Ibid.*, p. 14.
[38] *Ibid.*, p. 14.
[39] *Ibid.*, p. 15.

requires a ritualistic beating by the gang members), I wanted to get out . . . and, well, this other guy, me and my neighbor friend, we used to be pretty tight, and he, well, he's the one that introduced us to the Lomitas. I was in there three years. But, before we was the Lomitas, we used to be the Chatos, from Fortieth Street, see, in our group, the Chatos transferred to Lomitas and our 40 guys were Lomitas."

Before the minor mentioned above had reached the age of 15 he had belonged to four separate gangs or groups, and at no time after age 12 was he without a group of organized peers. The minor eventually chose a gang with a reputation for long-standing violence and trouble in the community. After leaving the Lomitas, he joined two sponsored gangs and played an active role in each.

Another youngster who was raised in the vicinity where gangs flourished in the east part of Los Angeles refused to be inducted into a gang for several years. This youngster was subsequently harassed by the gang's membership. At the age of 16, this youngster started a club consisting of 30 boys, called the Diamontes, which met at Laguna Park for recreational and social activities. However, the pressure increased on him to join the Little Valley Gang which he had previously refused. Subsequently, his own club was often attacked by the Little Valley Gang. Unable to defend themselves, the Diamontes solicited the aid of two gangs operating in the same territory, and with whom they were friendly. These gangs, the Varrio Nuevo and the Headhunters, were feuding with the Little Valley at the time, so they took up the defense of the Diamontes. Eventually, this led to the merging of the Diamontes with the Varrio Nuevo. *According to R. E. Rice, and S. Addams, who made a definitive study of this gang in "The Correctional Cost of Service and Unservice Gangs,"* this "harassed youngster" eventually became one of its leaders and, during the next three years the Varrio Nuevo became one of the most notorious in the east Los Angeles area.

The Los Angeles Probation Department researchers obtained five pages of transcript narration regarding the description of the complex story of this particular gang leader's gradual involvement in a gang. The gang leader summed it up as follows:[40]

"Well, the guys from Varrio Nuevo started moving into the park. And the guys from the Little Valley started moving toward the valley. They started pushing 'em back. This was in the summer of '58, and that's when I got into the gang. All of the guys from the park went down to the Estrada Courts, and the guys from the Varrio Nuevo, they said that if the Headhunters didn't break up and join the Varrio Nuevo, well, they would have to, you know, march. At that time, march meant get beat up or somethin'. And, at

[40]*Ibid.*, p. 17.

that time, the headquarters had 150 guys, but they were all young, you know, and the guys from the Varrio Nuevo, they were more, you know, these guys have been fightin' four years, since early '40's. And they're younger boys, well, right now, the youngest guy's from Varrio Nuevo, they're 23. And they said we're goin' to need younger guys and you got to either break up or come in with us or don't come around—move out someplace else, you know, because they said that the Little Valley, we've got 'em on the go now and we want to keep 'em that way. We've already took over the park but we ain't got that many guys, you know. So we got together, the guys from the park, we had 30 guys, and the guys from the Headhunters, they had quite a few guys. So we went down to the court and decided whether we're going to get into the Varrio Nuevo or not. We got to the point, we said okay."

In Los Angeles County, Juvenile Probation Department researchers ascertained that there were two factors in joining a gang, One is the "drifting-in" quality of involvement. This, according to the experts in the gang research field, is considered quite unusual in that it has long been recognized by workers in the field that induction into a structured gang was usually a formal ritualistic event in the lives of its members. This position was subscribed to by such experts as William F. Whyte, author of *Streetcorner Society; the Social Structure of an Italian Slum*, Frederic M. Thrasher, author of *The Gang*, and Robert Summers, author of an article entitled, "Juvenile Gang Activity in Los Angeles County." There was nothing in the interviews conducted by Los Angeles researchers which supported the belief of formal ritualistic initiation.

The other factor is well known to street workers, and deals with the apparently high motivation that gang members have to join a group that is outside the mainstream of the dominant adolescent culture.[41]

There are *many functions* of gangs, most notably the social functions, defensive functions, and fighting.

It appeared that the *social function* were quite important in filling a large void in the lives of its members. Such functions were disorganized and the social activities were summed up by the Rebel Rousers:[42]

"When the club first got started, we didn't have no specific activities, you know, like every day we'd go over to the park and lay down and talk and drink all day. Not many 12-year-old boys go around drinking wine; but 'cause everybody else did it, I did it too. Maybe on weekends, everybody goin' to a swimmin' pool or somethin'. We usually stayed at one another's house, and stayed together most of the time, play cards, something like that. Everybody just stay at home during the day time, and come out at night. We'd go down to the park and talk. At night, them that was goin' to school they'd come down to the park."

[41] *Ibid.*, p. 19.
[42] *Ibid.*, p. 21.

It can be assumed that these types of social and delinquent activities were closely correlated. Considering the activities of gang members, it is not difficult to understand how violence follows the drinking of alcoholic beverages. On numerous occasions, the interviewees mentioned use of intoxicating beverages and the subsequent violent behavior of the indulgent members.

It is difficult to separate the social and defensive purpose of the gang due to the fact that social activities usually resulted in members defending themselves from aggressive acts. According to the researchers, the accounts of interviews made it quite difficult to determine whether fighting associated with dances and party crashing was more important than the social events themselves. The boys, however, mentioned each as a separate and mutually exclusive function of the gang. A Midnight Chopper told of the defensive aspect of the gang in these words:[43]

> "There was really no major purpose for the gang. I think it was just all—everybody gettin' tired of bein' pushed around by other fellows, you know. They were willing to fight for their rights, but they just didn't have enough strength to."

Gang membership, according to certain members, might enhance the possibilities of a member being attacked by another juvenile. The concept that a boy's chances of being attacked are increased, rather than decreased, through gang membership is expressed more colorfully by the non-gang member. His comments were:[44]

> "They know that when they don't get in it (the gang), they know that they're safe. If they do git in it, they know they ain't safe. They know that man gonna' always be on their tail. There's always gonna' be someone lookin' for 'em from another gang, no matter what gang they're in. A lotta guys say they gonna' join for protection, shoot, let 'em go in. Some of 'em do join gangs just for protection, but that's some protection."

Although the above might imply otherwise, the defensive aspect of the group, however, cannot be overlooked, even if there is ambiguity regarding this function in the above statements. The very fact that all the gang leaders described defense as one of the main purposes of the gang makes the concept itself important.

Fighting seemed to permeate all activities. This function, although unmentioned as either a direct or indirect purpose of the gang, had been amplified in activities such as party crashing, expansion of territory, defensive activities, and revenge. It is apparent, however, that the

[43]*Ibid.*, p. 24.
[44]*Ibid.*, p. 24.

violence was not always planned. Over the past years, experience in working with gangs in Los Angeles County reveals that in most instances violence is an unplanned and situational occurrence.

Here is how a Rebel Rouser told of the feelings he had when fighting:[45]

> "The feeling you get in a fight—you could call it excitement. You felt proud 'cause you fightin' for your name, you know. Protect your name, protect your part of town. You know, you be proud to stand up and fight for your name."

This quotation and others not included clearly indicate that violence is apparently one of the primary functions of gangs, and not a secondary one. At the same time, the lack of affect shown by these youths while describing some of their most violent activities may reflect a desire to repress memories of this behavior.

The City of Chicago has had a considerably longer and more intensive experience with gang work programs than Los Angeles. It was there that the *Area Project,* known sometimes as the Back-of-the-Yards Program, was first undertaken by Clifford Shaw in 1929.[46] This effort was designed to involve local residents as deeply as possible in the resolution of problems in their own neighborhoods.

The basic rationale of the Area Project was that the program regards as indispensable to the success of welfare activity in general and delinquency prevention in particular the participation of those who form a significant part of the social world of the recipients of help. This is seen not as a prescription of a panacea, but as a condition for progress in finding a solution. The program has remained experimental in the sense that it has continued to explore the questions: What kind of participation is necessary on the part of which kinds of persons in terms of social role in the local society? But it has rested firmly and consistently on the conviction that no solution of a basic and lasting character is possible in the absence of such participation.

The Chicago Area Project stresses programs for recreation for children of the neighborhood and campaigns for community improvement. The project is also concerned about delinquency prevention and the neighborhood groups assist other agencies with their work, visit boys' community training schools, and provide support for parolees and persons similarly requiring assistance. Twenty-five years after its inception, the impact of the ground-breaking Chicago Area Project must remain

[45] *Ibid.*, p. 28.
[46] C. Shaw, *Delinquency Areas,* Chicago University Press, Chicago, 1929.

somewhat speculative because of the difficulty of careful evaluation of such an endeavor.

It is extremely difficult to reach concrete conclusions as to when the intervention programs are at a point which would guaranty success. Such difficulty is attributed to the diversity of programs directed toward gangs, the complex nature of their ingredients, and the punitive nature of research findings. However, a number of general observations can be safely put forward.

Boys, according to studies, will respond more readily to persons who are not severely detrimental; that is, individuals who do not criticize or condemn the habits and general deportment of the gang member. Standards and values adhered to by the intervention worker are not easily transmitted to persons with whom he works. Training, combined with experience and built upon original qualifications, represents the most desirable amalgam for effective gang work.

There are, generally, two types of programs: formal and informal. *Formal programs* tend to emphasize enhancement of skills, participation and success in relationships with various institutional segments of society, such as the world of employment or that of education, as well as family adaptations. *Informal* arrangements are usually directed toward creating greater ease and comfort in living, with the underlying belief that such items serve to create, besides law-abiding behavior, additional success in adjustment to the institutional structures.[47]

Agencies directing intervention programs will undoubtedly establish general operational guidelines. In all probability, their emphasis will be upon the particular strengths of the staff, the needs of the gang members, and the services and resources available in different geographical areas. Information presented here regarding such programs has endeavored to indicate major themes and patterns in various undertakings so as to provide some indication of what is being done and what might be potentially useful elsewhere, as well as to point out the wide range of approaches possible and the fact that it is not necessary to remain inexorably tied to a procedure which has proven to be a failure.

POLICE ROLE

As this chapter has attempted to point out, neither punitive methods nor adult-sponsored recreational programs are adequate in coping with street gangs. Revenge or simple punishment will not deter anti-social

[47]Geis, *op. cit.*, p. 58.

activities. Such methods only increase tensions and make behavior more hostile and aggressive. The main difficulties facing athletic-recreational and leisure-time programs is that the youngsters who need them the most are usually not participants in adult-sponsored activities of this kind. Such activities usually attract youngsters who have not displayed delinquent tendencies. Furthermore, many agencies that are attempting to organize programs with the delinquent youngster are not equipped to integrate into their total programs those autonomous street gangs which have already developed patterns of aggressive behavior. If the punitive approach is unsound, and if the provision of recreation through agencies tend to be ineffective, what other methods could be utilized and where do the police fit in?

Law enforcement agencies throughout the United States recommend that an area project approach be adopted. The reason for such a recommendation is quite practical. Under the coordinating council program, each area of the community would have a committee composed of a cross section of persons living in that particular neighborhood, including representatives of social agencies, schools, labor unions, churches, police, fraternal, and business organizations. One good example of this approach is the area programs being set up by the Economic Opportunity Commission (a federally subsidized agency) throughout the United States. Such intervention groups would have the objective of developing local resources to meet the needs of street gangs in that particular area. It should stimulate community action toward removing those factors in various neighborhoods which are inimical to the full development of a secure democratic way of life for all residents in the neighborhood.

The area in which the police can be quite helpful would be the identification of potential anti-social gangs and the transmitting of such information to trained workers sent into the streets to work with these gangs. The police should endeavor to obtain information concerning members, background information, prior criminal history, if any, and extensive information on gang leaders. This approach obviously calls for tact on the part of the investigating officer. These groups generally resent those in authority, and it must be impressed upon each group and its leaders that the objective of the officers is not to take the course of punitive action but to assist the area committee in supplying information concerning the gangs, their members, purposes, and desires.[48]

The area committee, with all information obtainable, would then direct the workers to try to direct the clubs along socially constructive

[48]Winters, *op. cit.*, p. 98.

lines. If the members of the gang respond positively to accepting understanding adults,. the relationships with such adults would serve as a powerful force for personal and social adjustment.[49]

It is unfortunate that in many areas the lack of trained workers may make it necessary for someone else to attempt to perform this task. The police, then, have no alternative but to enter this field. Certainly, under most conditions, the police should not become directly involved in intervention work. However, if there is no other agency available, then someone must take the initiative if effective action against undesirable gang conditions is to be instituted. The approach utilized by the police would be that used by trained intervention workers. The police should relinquish this particular role as soon as some other agency can assume this task.

The following are suggestions offered by Inspector John E. Winters, commanding officer, Youth Aide Division, Metropolitan Police Department, Washington, D.C., to police officers assigned to gang investigations:[50]

1. The investigating officer should not approach a gang with predetermined ideas and suggestions. Because the officer may be in a position to suggest rooms for club meetings, halls for dances, or locations for athletic activities, knowledge of the neighborhood and its resources is a must. Such referrals should only be done, however, if the group expresses a desire for such facilities.
2. The officer must become acquainted with members individually. The individual needs of the youngsters must be determined in order to make intelligent referrals to vocational, case-work, or psychiatric services, and seek assistance of the court if necessary.
3. The most important "tool" of an officer investigating gang activities is his ability to relate to gang members. The officer should have the type of personality which would enable him to converse and develop rapport with young people. He should be democratic, and able to accept the difference between his standards and those of the group without imposing his thinking or ideology upon them. Club members should not be protected from their responsibilities for, or the consequences of, their anti-social acts.
4. Understanding of procedures of various social services available in the community is an important part of an officer delegated to gang investigations.
5. The police should work in close cooperation with the area committee, if there is one; consult with specialists in case work, group work, and psychiatry.
6. The ultimate objective would be a self-governing federation of the various clubs in each area. This is important because through federation, the clubs' own leadership can be unified and steered toward constructive goals. In

[49]*Ibid.*, p. 99.
[50]*Ibid.*, p. 99.

short, the police should function to gain the acceptance and confidence of these clubs and then use all the means at their disposal to work toward their objectives. These objectives, according to Inspector Winters, should be:

a. The opportunity for the club to enjoy the normal adolescent group life that the street club potentially offers its members.
b. The gradual development on the part of the club members of the feeling that they are needed and important members of the community and that they have a real part to play in the job of making their neighborhood a happier, more comfortable, more secure place in which to live.
c. The opportunity for club members to develop a close relationship with accepting and understanding police officers, and to create in the minds of these young people that the police want to help, not prosecute.

The above recommendations offered by *Inspector Winters* are made on the premise that when there are other agencies available, the police should not enter the treatment field. Although there is no reason for law enforcement officers not to strike up friendly relationships with these groups, appraise interested citizens of the needs of groups, and provide whatever assistance is possible to those who are in the treatment field, it should be pointed out that treatment should be delegated to those who are trained to assume this role.

According to Inspector Winters, it must be borne in mind that:[51]

"Though this approach has been successful in some communities, there are those hardbitten, sophisticated, and antisocial groups of young adults and teen-agers who would not respond to any reproach. They are believed to consist of only a small percentage of the total. The only action that can be taken against these groups is constant surveillance, arrest, and prosecution for unlawful acts. In any determination of police action in a given situation, the welfare of the community must take precedence over the individual. For this reason, all investigations into group situations, whether designed to provide help for the group or to develop sufficiently for prosecution, should be made a matter of record."

Inspector Winters further states:[52]

"A file should be maintained in the office of the juvenile unit. This file should identify groups by name and location. Cards on individual members should contain information relating to that individual such as any prior record of criminal activity or reports received on misbehavior, truancy, etc., the results of consultations with parents (a good technique that has produced constructive results), the school attended, etc. It has been established that the mere recording of pertinent information concerning a gang member has a deterring effect on the member with relation to antisocial activity. This file should not be a public record and should not be used as a basis for punitive action except where absolutely necessary. Its main purpose would

[51] *Ibid.*, p. 101.
[52] *Ibid.*, p. 101.

be to furnish information to the community's coordinating council and, through that council, to the various area committees."

The fact remains that the police department's first approach to a gang situation should be that of a helping agency; i.e., assisting other agencies and groups to redirect the gang's activities into constructive channels. However, it is the responsibility of the law enforcement agency to utilize aggressive and consistent action if intervention programs fail and the interests of the community are being threatened.

ADOLESCENT DRUG ADDICTION

Since the close of World War II, there has been a continuous increase in the number of adolescents in our society, particularly in the large metropolitan areas, who have become involved in the use of narcotics. This has produced much controversy and discussion in this country, perhaps the most emotionally alarming one has been the nature of its relationship to criminality. This relationship has become the focus of even greater attention in these post war years, as the use of narcotics has spread in almost epidemic proportions among some sectors of our adolescent and young adult population, and as these youthful addicts, in ever-increasing numbers, have become involved in altercations with law enforcement agencies for violations of the narcotic drug laws and for other criminal offenses.

What is the nature of the adolescent who becomes involved in the use of drugs? Although the drug addict is not an individual who has remained aloof from crime, he is rarely many of the sensational things portrayed in the public mind. Those who have worked with the adolescent drug addict recognize him as an emotionally sick individual whose difficulties relate back to a life history of social and emotional maladjustment.

Extent of the Problem

On December 31, 1964, the number of active addicts recorded by the Federal Bureau of Narcotics was 55,899, an increase of 7,364 over the number a year earlier. The number of new addicts reported during 1964, 10,000, represented an increase of 2,544 over the number reported during 1963. This increase may be due to improved reporting methods by some state and local agencies.

Active addicts in the group over 40 years of age showed the greatest increase during the year, from 5,441 to 6,517. Those 31 to 40 years of age increased from 18,482 to 21,247.

The group 21 to 30 years of age, which constitutes the largest number of addicts, increased from 23,033 to 26,106. *Addicts under 21 years of age increased from 1,579 to 2,029. Of this group, those 18-20 years of age increased from 1,504 to 1,872; those 17 years of age and under increased from 75 to 157.*

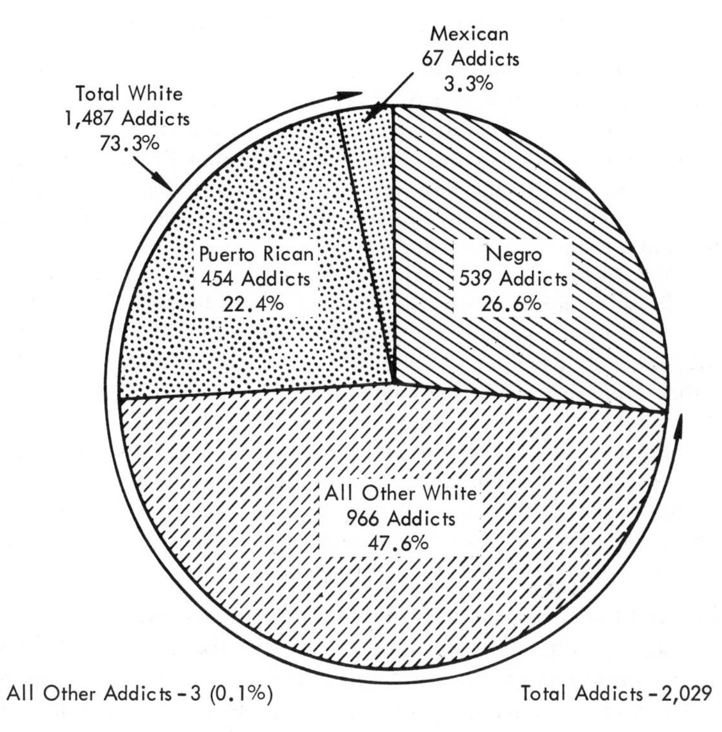

Figure 2 Active narcotic addicts in the United States under 21 years of age as of December 31, 1964. (*Source*: Treasury Department Bureau of Narcotics.)

Apart from narcotic drug law violations for which these addicts have been arrested, what are the types of offenses usually committed by the drug addict adolescent or adult? Is there any credence to the common knowledge that a high proportion of crimes committed by addicts are crimes of violence? The organization of the Narcotic Bureau of the Chicago Police Department in 1950, made possible the collection of data about the arrests of well-known narcotic users which shed some light in this area. From this data, for the year 1951, it has been possible to classify these arrests and to determine the percentage distribution of the more serious types of offenses among addicts as compared to the criminal population at large. The data indicate that the number of arrests for nonviolent property crimes was proportionately higher among addicts. In contrast, however, the number of arrests of addicts for violent offenses against a person, such as rape and aggravated assault, was only a fraction of the proportion constituted by such arrests among the population at large.[53]

In view of the above information, *Harold Finestone* states:[54]

> "To adolescent groups who simultaneously evaluate highly adults who were engaged in a wide variety of criminal activity and adults who were addicted; and these valuations were reflected in both criminal activity and experimentation with narcotics. Thus, both the criminality and experimentation with narcotics stemmed, at least in part, from influences to which the youngsters were exposed, as represented by adult models within the local community. Both criminality and narcotics use came to be prestigeful forms of activity. In this sense, it is irrelevant to ask whether the delinquency preceded the addiction or vice versa. Many of those who became addicted and were forced to engage in crime to support the high cost of their addiction would probably have gone to engage in crime as adolescents regardless of whether or not they had become addicted. . . .
>
> "The impression gained from interviewing adolescent addicts was that these addicts were petty thieves and petty 'operators' who, status-wise, were at the bottom of the criminal population or underworld. It is difficult to see how they could be otherwise. The typical young junkie spent so much of his time in a harried quest for narcotics, dodging the police, and in lockups, that he was hardly in a position to plan major crimes."

The extent of the problem is much more serious than previously indicated (Fig. 2). The statistics pointing out the use of narcotics derived from *only those reported* to the Federal Bureau of Narcotics from local law enforcement agencies. Furthermore, the data represents only those adolescent drug addicts who have been classified as *bona fide addicts.* On many occasions, youngsters who have abused the use of drugs and are in the process of experimenting have not come to the attention of the law enforcement agencies or, when detected, are not viewed as "legitimate addicts." Therefore, the magnitude of the problem is much more extensive than the statistics compiled by the Federal Bureau of Narcotics indicates. In comparison with the great amount of data pertaining to adults in this chapter, juvenile statistics are quite meager. This is unfortunate in one respect since so much public attention has been forcused on the juvenile drug problem. Because of this, if for no

[53]H. Finestone, "Narcotics: Narcotics and Criminality," *Law and Contemporary Problems*, School of Law, Duke University, Vol. XXII, No. 1, Winter, 1957, pp. 74.
[54]*Ibid.*, pp. 75–77.

other reason, the Federal Bureau of Narcotics should be in a position to provide statistics which might answer more vital questions.

It has been estimated that the arrests recorded account for the majority of all adult drug arrests. It is very unlikely that an adult arrest will fail to be recorded since at least one of the many sources available to the study will give some indication of the arrest. This principle does not hold true for juvenile arrestees.

Most juveniles are not fingerprinted, the dispositions of their arrests are not routinely transmitted to the Federal Bureau of Narcotics, and, in fact, many arrests occur without an arrest report being prepared or forwarded to the Bureau. Because of this situation, it must be frankly stated that it is impossible to estimate the number of omissions of data pertaining to adolescent drug addiction. Therefore, their absence from the Bureau's statistics must be considered.

Drug Law[55]

Narcotics (Opiate Type, Cocaine and Marijuana)

FEDERAL. Since 1914, the federal government has imposed a tax on narcotics and, by use of this tax statute (Harrison Act), has regulated the manufacture and distribution of narcotics. Several other laws also give the federal government additional authority. At the present time, all phases of narcotic distribution, including international shipments, are under the regulatory control of the Bureau of Narcotics, a branch of the Treasury Department.

Narcotics made and controlled under these laws include meperidine, coca leaves, opiates, and any derivatives or preparations of these substances. Cannabis (marijuana) and chemically-related substances are also covered. In addition, drugs can be and have been added to this list if they have an addiction-forming or addiction-sustaining liability similar to morphine or cocaine. Many of the additions to the original list are synthetic or "man-made" narcotics. Meperidine (isonipecaine) is an example of a synthetic narcotic.

Important features of the narcotic laws and regulations are: *(1) registration of those dealing in narcotic drugs; (2) special taxes; (3) special order forms and record-keeping provisions; and, (4) prohibitions and severe penalties for illegal possession and trafficking in these drugs.*

Not all narcotic preparations are treated alike. The regulations define certain narcotic-containing medicines as "exempt preparations." The quantity of narcotic drug in these preparations is very low. Under fed-

[55]J. B. Landis, M.D., and Dr. K. K. Fletcher, *Drug Abuse: A Manual for Law Enforcement Officers* Smith, Kline and French Laboratories, Philadelphia, Pa., 1967, pp. 11–12.

eral law, the "exempt" narcotics may be sold without a physician's prescription. However, complete records must be kept. The pharmacist fulfills his part of the record-keeping responsibility by having his patron "sign" for the medicine. Most of these "exempt" preparations are cough syrups.

The penalties under federal narcotic law deserve special mention. For illegal sale or transfer, the penalty is not less than 5 or more than 20 years for the first offense; not less than 10 or more than 40 years for the second or subsequent offense. In either case, a fine of up to $20,000 is permitted. Moreover, the sentence cannot be suspended or probation or parole granted. For most other narcotic offenses the penalty is not less than 2 or more than 10 years for the first offense, not less than 5 or more than 20 years for the second offense, and not less than 10 or more than 40 years for the third or subsequent offense. After the first offense, sentences cannot be suspended or probation or parole granted.

STATE. All but a few states have enacted the Uniform Narcotic Drug Act or similar legislation. This Act follows federal law and is recommended by the Bureau of Narcotics. Some states have variations, but, generally speaking, the important provisions are the same in most states.

Barbiturates and Amphetamine

FEDERAL. From the standpoint of illicit traffic, a beginning has been made toward comprehensive federal control over amphetamine-like compounds and barbiturates. The Food and Drug Administration obtains a certain number of convictions every year on the ground that such drugs were dispensed by pharmacists without a prescription, or sold by unauthorized persons. However, this small weapon was not sufficient to prevent or deter the bulk of the illicit traffic.

There was long a real need for federal legislation that would embody such features as registration of manufacturers and wholesalers; record-keeping by manufacturers, wholesalers, and pharmacists; an illegal possession clause; authority for FDA inspection; and severe penalties for sales to juveniles. The "Drug Abuse Control Amendments of 1965" (H.R. 2), passed by Congress in 1965, has these features and was supported by the Pharmaceutical Manufacturers Association, the Food and Drug Administration, the American Medical Association, organized pharmacy and other groups and individuals.

These amendments provide strict federal controls on the distribution of amphetamine and the barbiturates, including these key provisions:

1. All manufacturers and wholesalers who produce, compound, or sell amphetamine, barbiturates (and other drugs which are found to

have a similar effect on the central nervous system) must register with the FDA.

2. Manufacturers, wholesalers, retailers, and dispensing physicians must keep accurate records, including registration numbers, of all purchases and dispositions of the controlled drugs for three years and make these records available to the FDA inspectors.

3. The definition of who is authorized to possess and sell these drugs is clearly stated.

4. Penalties for illegal sales of these drugs to minors are increased.

5. FDA investigators are authorized to carry firearms, and enforcement powers related to search, seizure, and arrest are expanded.

6. FDA authority to combat counterfeiting of drugs is expanded.

H.R. 2 also gives the Food and Drug Administration the authority to stop *interstate* and *intrastate* illicit traffic in abused drugs.

STATE. State control of the illicit distribution of barbiturates and amphetamine-like compounds is anything but uniform. Although all states have some type of regulation for prescription drugs, some have additional, more stringent regulations covering drugs, such as amphetamine and the barbiturates. The most recent state laws usually have an illegal possession feature and a requirement that records of receipt and delivery be kept for several years. If a law enforcement officer has problems in this area, he should consult the attorney assigned to his agency on the local law. Penalties for violation of the state dangerous drug laws are less than for narcotic violations. In the great majority of the states, violation is a misdemeanor. Sometimes the maximum penalty is a fine as low as $100.

Portrait of an Adolescent Drug Addict

Identification of any drug adict, adolescent or adult, is vague because we usually do not recognize a drug addict until addiction is well established with the attendant personality and social habit regression. The recognition of an addict is, if not impossible, extremely difficult. The clue to the understanding of the adolescent drug addict, therefore, is dependent upon examining both his psychological and social development to see if it is possible to determine what commonalities of background have served to create his current difficulties. Generally, the teen-age drug addict comes from a rather deprived social environment that lacks the necessary resources which might endow him with greater potential for survival. Because of the basic lack of support from his environment in general and his family in particular, the adolescent addict is geared for failure rather than success, and in truth, as we have traced his life pattern, it can be readily seen that he has known failure rather intimately. His initial failure was in relationship to his family toward whom he looked for love and support but, instead, found rejection or lack of understanding. This failure later developed into social failure as he internalized profound feelings of insecurity and worthlessness. Therefore, the youth becomes a rather withdrawn, somewhat isolated individual who seems more of an inactive observer of life than a direct participant in it. He is unable and unwilling to extend himself in the everyday world because the spector of failure is always before him.[56]

This is clearly seen in the educational background of the adolescent drug user, where, despite the fact that his intelligence parallels that of the average population, he soon drops out of school after having completed poor work at a level significantly below his actual capabilities. It is rare to meet an adolescent user who has gone beyond the third or fourth year of high school.

Early in the period of an addict's experience with narcotics, the effect of the drug is dissipated in a few hours and no deviation from his normal routine occurs. The user may seem somewhat subdued, under no particular pressure, perhaps inclined to talk more than usual, and have a somewhat pleased feelings about his surroundings. Close scrutiny of his eyes reveals the tell tale pinpoint pupils. When *high,* he is lethargic, sleepy, perhaps stuporous, dreamy, and with no particular interests but that of going to sleep. He may also be preoccupied with various fantasties of grandiose omnipotent type. Nausea, vomiting, and intense scratching may be temporary side effects. If the individual continues with only occasional *joy pops* (as occasional injections are called) , those probably will be the limit of the observable signs. Needle marks may be found if the individual were examined physically, but there are many users in the adolescent field who don't inject, but *snort* or *sniff* the drug, and among these there are no tell-tale physical marks. The locations of *works,* that is, the eye dropper, the needle, the bent spoon, or little cones that are utilized for inhalation of the drug, would be presumptive evidence.[57]

The adolescent drug user tends to be materialistic since, in a sense, he has ceased to believe that his emotional needs can be met in a positive manner. It is of interest to note that he is an individual who is ordinarily unable to retain whatever material possessions he has because they are needed to maintain a drug supply.

[56]L. Gold, "Toward an Understanding of Adolescent Drug Addition," *Federal Probation,* Vol. XXII, No. 3, September, 1958, p. 43.

[57]The New York Academy of Medicine, *Conference on Drug Addition Among Adolescents,* The Blakiston Company, New York, 1953, pp. 8–9.

The drug user approaches life with a profound sense of inadequacy and helplessness which overwhelms him and causes him to flee from realities of everyday living. He seeks the comfortable vacuum that the drug offers him. The drug has value for the adolescent addict not solely because it can provide pleasurable sensations, but because it becomes a buffer between the user and the society which he fears.

Since he is an escapist, he is unable to relate to othe people in a meaningful, constructive, realistic fashion. He can only take from others in a dependent and passive manner and is unable to give anything in return in either a physical or emotional sense. His basically dependent orientation tends to breed suspicion and resentment to the degree that it blocks the development of positive relationships with another person.[58]

The teen-age drug addict usually is involved in a conflictual relationship with parental figures. He feels that the parent does not understand him, and also anticipates that the parent will act in a manner that will be detrimental to his personal interests.

Many times, the parents of the drug addict are also inadequate people. They are unable to really live up to the criteria expected in a parent-child relationship. This quality of weakness that exists in a parental relationship is not solely a fact that occurs during a period of addiction, but it permeates the entire living situation. Because of his relatively unstable, immature personality structure, the teen-age drug addict perceives his environmental situation out of perspective. As a result, the individual experiences great difficulty where only moderate difficulty should exist.

Because he perceives the adult world as an unstable place, he prefers to seek out the security of an infantile type of relationship. So the infantile behavior may be not only the result of cultural deprivation, but also actually serve as a protection from dealing with the more complex situations and responsibilities that can be expected of one who aspires to be accepted as an adult.

In brief, according to *Conferences on Drug Addiction Among Adolescents,* held by The New York Academy of Medicine, the following are the three phases which a young addict will complete: (a) the early phase, when very little can be observed, in which perhaps the *works* is the only clue; (b) the later stage, in which the personality changes, the social group changes, and the appearance of needle marks (if the person is injecting himself) are the signs which will be detected; (c) later, the phase of physical dependency, in which the obstinence syndrome is the diagnostic clue.[59]

[58]Gold, *op. cit.*, p. 43.

[59]The New York Academy of Medicine, *op. cit.*, p. 43.

Personality is an important factor in the development of abuse. Some individuals seem particularly prone to psychic dependence: a desire for drugs that is entirely independent of physical symptoms or needs. It is not the direct effect of the drug—sedation or stimulation—which influences the development of psychic dependence, but rather the interpretation of this effect as euphoria or "feeling good" and the use of the drug to escape from reality. These people often succumb to alcohol. In fact, abuse of alcohol is often the first step on the road to the abuse of drugs.

The development of abuse is rooted in the repeated use of drugs as a way of solving life's problems. Eventually, the tendency to solve or hide from problems through the use of drugs interferes with normal personality functioning.

Chronic abuse of drugs is generally considered a symptom of mental or emotional illness. This illness does not fall into any one category such as schizophrenia or depression. (However, most drug abusers suffer from personality disorders.) Nor are all drug abusers alike from an emotional standpoint. Perhaps the only common characteristic is that drug abusers use drugs to a point where they feel they can no longer manage without such support.

There is a significant difference between two classes of drug abusers: the adult abuser and the juvenile or "teen-age" abuser. The adult abuser of drugs commonly has a history of social maladjustment. The pressures and demands of society are too much for him to bear. Typically, he has a background of family difficulties, disciplinary problems, and trouble with the police. At some point, he finds that there are artificial ways to escape reality, anxiety, and his feelings of inadequacy in coping with life's problems. In escaping, he may turn to alcohol or drugs and draw a chemical curtain between himself and reality. Association with other drug abusers is an important factor in developing a dependency on drugs.

The juvenile or "teen-ager" presents a more complex picture. Going through adolescence is, under the best of circumstances, a difficult and complex process. Some authorities feel that boredom and lack of definite goals contribute to juvenile troubles. One salient feature of adolescence is the need that all juveniles have to be accepted and "to belong." For many, a juvenile gang fills this need. By conforming to the gang's code of behavior, the youngster gains recognition in his group. Ofter the degree of recognition is in direct proportion to the juvenile's willingness to defy legal, social, and parental authority. Juvenile drug abuse frequently stems from this "gang psychology." It usually begins in a gang or party setting. One member of the group starts, and the rest go along for fear of appearing "chicken."

One aspect of drug abuse is the fact that many abusers will use any substance that gives them a "thrill." "Airplane" glue, lighter fluid, gasoline, nutmeg, and ether have all been used. Because of their easy availability, many of these substances are often used by children and teen-agers.

Drugs Commonly Abused

The drugs commonly abused can be divided into two main groups, the *depressants* and the *stimulants.*

The *depressants* are the pain killers (opiates and their synthetic equivalents) and the sleeping pills (barbiturates). These are the most harmful for their victims are addicts in the exact sense of the word: they think they must have the drug; they need larger and larger doses; and they suffer terribly, even with convulsions, when the drug is stopped abruptly.

The *stimulants* are cocaine, marijuana, and the "pep" pills (amphetamines). The stimulants are habit forming, causing emotional dependence, and continued use may result in a certain degree of tolerance and physical dependence, depending upon the susceptibility of the individual, although not in such a marked degree as with the depressants. The kind of compulsive behavior they form and the damaging effect they have is so serious that their victims are usually called "addicts."

Depressants

OPIATES. Morphine and many other narcotics derived from opium or created in the laboratory are of tremendous value to physicians in treating their patients because they deaden pain and relieve suffering. Heroin is one of the narcotics derived from opium, but it is *not* used in medical practice in the United States.

Aside from their medical use, opiates are usually taken to give a sense of ease and contentment, a pleasant intoxication without the mental confusion and loss of motor control that comes with intoxication from alcohol or barbiturates.

Amounts of barbiturates have to be increased by addicts until almost unbelievable amounts are taken. Then when the drug is suddenly stopped, the symptoms of withdrawal begin. First, drousiness, eyes and nose watering, sweating, dilated pupils, then great restlessness, twitching of the legs and arms, nausea, and vomiting.

Barbiturates. These are the many sleep-producing drugs valuable to medical practice, made from barbiturate acid. Addiction to these drugs is common and is increasing. They produce an intoxication similar to alcohol with mental sluggishness, confusion, slurring of speech, staggering, and shaking.

The barbiturate addicts become tolerant of large doses and these addicts suffer severe and dangerous symptoms of withdrawal, even worse than the opiate addicts. If they have been taking several capsules a day for two months or more, abrupt withdrawal brings on a nervous restlessness, feelings of weakness and fear, followed by vomiting; then, in most cases, severe convulsions. After the convulsions, most patients recover, but some go on into a state like the delirium tremors of alcoholics.

It is estimated that three-fours of all deaths from drugs are from barbiturates.

Stimulants

These are taken for relief of fatigue or to get a temporary sense of increased ability or superiority. COCAINE used to be a commonly abused stimulant, but the AMPHETAMINES ("bennies" and "dexies") and MARIJUANA cost less and are most commonly used now.

The amphetamines are valuable drugs in medical practice, but marijuana has no medical value.

The stimulant drugs are very intoxicating, and some of them produce extreme elation, delusions, "visions," and distortions of space and time.

Tolerance does not develop for the stimulant drugs in the same degree that it does for the depressants, and withdrawing effects may occur when their use is stopped although it is not the rule as with the depressants.

Drug Abuse Is a Law-Enforcement Problem

All the drugs commonly abused are either completely outlawed, as are heroin and marijuana, or they can be obtained only from the underworld peddler or from thieves or diversion of legitimate supplies from physicians, hospitals, or pharmacies. So the drug abuse problem immediately has legal aspects, and law enforcement becomes extremely important.

Crimes of violence are often committed by persons under delusions from stimulant drugs; the delusion that they are being watched or followed is common with stimulant users. Sex parties and violent assaults are rarely committed while under the influence of opiates or barbiturates because these depressants quiet the users and lessen sex drives. However, the use of depressant drugs can lead to violent assaults, holdups, and even murder when approaching withdrawal symptoms lead to desperation and the addict will take any risk to get drugs or the money to buy them.

Part of society's duty is that of passing necessary laws and upholding law-enforcement activities. Problems of enforcement are complicated in metropolitan areas and cities where there is a large import-export maritime business. New York and California's problems in controlling drug abuse are complicated by the smuggling of heroin and marijuana via ships, planes, and land travel, and by the lack of laws to control the importing of barbiturates and other dangerous drugs.

The problem of narcotics will continue and, without doubt, expand as long as there is ineffective control at the source of production. Therefore, law enforcement must seek ways and means of international control. Efforts to increase law-enforcement personnel at points of entry in order to insure closer inspection is probably the first step toward controlling the traffic. Stronger feeling or measures would deter some of the narcotic traffic, thereby lowering the profits inherent in this illegal trade.

Measures to control narcotic traffic depend on the degree of cooperation between nations. There is at the present time little effective control over production of raw materials. This is an area where immediate attention will have to be focused.

International control is only one aspect of the problems confronting law enforcement. As previously stated, as far as the adolescents are concerned, experimentation with the use of drugs is quite prevalent in the school setting. Therefore, the control of narcotic traffic nationally is of paramount importance to law enforcement agencies. Without "customers" narcotic traffic will dissipate. Social institutions can play an important part in the tremendous struggle to prevent narcotic use. Schools are in a position to be able to detect experimentation on the part of youngsters who will utilize such drugs for a "thrill."[60]

Investigative Techniques[61]

Common Methods of Hiding or Disguising Drugs

The search for drugs is one of the most difficult problems faced by an officer. Drugs may be in solid, powder, or liquid form. In its pure state, the "bulk" of a drug may be very small.

One popular way to carry illegally obtained drugs is to keep them in

[60]J. P. Kenney, and D. G. Pursuit, *Police Work with Juveniles*, 2nd ed., Charles C Thomas, Springfield, Illinois, 1959, p. 175.
[61]Landis and Fletcher, *op. cit.*, pp. 13–15.

an old prescription bottle. The officer should be suspicious of any bottle with a worn or dirty label.

Illegally obtained drugs are often hidden in the bottom of a cigarette pack. The cigarettes are cut off and the pack appears normal. Drugs may also be found in fountain pens, cigarette lighters, toothpaste tubes, flashlights ,and lipstick tubes which have had their contents removed. Tablets and capsules may be folded into letters, handkerchiefs, personal papers, books and newspapers, or secreted in the linings of clothing. Occasionally, drugs may be dissolved into innocent-appearing liquids.

Determining the Illegal Possession, Use, and Source of Drugs

There are many ways that a drug abuser comes into contact with the police. The officer may find drugs—or evidence of their use—during a routine check or in the course of an arrest for a totally unconnected offense. He may actually see a person taking drugs, find evidence of unusual behavior, or he may encounter a suicide attempt involving drugs.

In each of these cases, the officer seeks several items of information to build a successful case or save a life. He must be able to answer these questions:

Does the suspect have drugs in his possession?
What are the drugs and where did they come from?
Is the possession legal?
Has he taken doses of the drugs?

There are literally thousands of drugs on the market. Some require a physician's prescription, but many do not.

Prescription drugs can, generally speaking, be purchased only from pharmacists, but non-prescription items are often bought from supermarkets, variety stores, grocery stores, and newsstands. (Some doctors, particularly those in isolated areas, dispense drugs to their patients, rather than write prescriptions.)

The officer's best approach to questioning relies on the principle that a suspect is innocent until proven guilty. Such an attitude is essential in producing evidence that will be admissible in court, and, incidentally, often results in digging out the greatest amount of helpful evidence.

As the questioning proceeds, the officer should remember that many of the subject's answers can be verified later.

Questioning often follows this pattern:

Are you sick now? Have you been ill?
Who is your doctor? Did you receive a prescription?
Is this medicine yours? Does it belong to someone else?

Do you know what it is?
Where was the prescription filled?
When did you last take the medicine?
How long have you been taking the medicine?
What is the medicine being taken for?
Are you under the care of a doctor? Do you take the medicine according to his orders?

By using this questioning pattern, the officer has given the subject a logical alibi and, apparently, believes his story that he is ill. Hopefully, the subject will volunteer that the medicine is his and that he is taking it. The officer is, moreover, protected in case the subject is actually ill and is taking a legally prescribed medicine.

The officer should now attempt to verify the answers to his questions.

1. DOCTOR'S NAME. This should appear on the prescription label, and can be verified by telephoning the doctor.
2. NAME OF PHARMACY. This can be verified by calling the pharmacist.
3. PRESCRIPTION DATE. The pharmacist's records will help there.
4. HOW MEDICINE IS TAKEN. Check number of tablets or capsules left in bottle against the number the pharmacist says he dispensed.
5. IS THE MEDICINE THE SAME AS THAT PRESCRIBED? Check with pharmacist. (Pharmacists give all prescriptions an individual number. This appears on the container which is given to the patient. The pharmacist will need this number to refer back to the original prescription.)

With this procedure, the officer has either confirmed or invalidated the subject's story. Remember that both physicians and pharmacists are generally most helpful and cooperative in such investigations.

TEEN-AGERS, DRINKING, AND THE LAW

During the last several years, there appears to have been an increase in the use of alcoholic beverages by teen-agers to such an extent that in many areas law-enforcement officials are greatly concerned over the problem.

Most state laws make it unlawful for minors to purchase alcoholic beverages. As an example, the state of California, through its legislature, has decided that 21 years is the earliest date of maturity in the average person. Laws have been passed with this limitation in voting and use of alcoholic beverages. The law, as contained in the Alcoholic Beverage Control Act, is clear and concise. *Section 25658(a)* of the Alcoholic Beverage Control Act states:

"Any person who gives, furnishes, sells, or causes to be given, sold, or furnished, any alcoholic beverage to any person under the age of 21 years is guilty of a misdemeanor."

This does not exclude the home of relatives or friends, so that parents or "good neighbors" who give alcoholic beverages to minors at a graduation party, or at any time, commit a misdemeanor and are a real party to the teen-ager drinking problem. Parents or friends who leave alcoholic beverages available or exposed are chargeable under the "causes to be given away" portion of the law.

California also has another section which covers possession by minors in any public place, even schools. There is even a separate section for public school grounds up to and including junior colleges, and there are other laws which cover other situations very adequately. Such laws are not ambiguous or misleading.

Generally speaking, it is quite evident from official records that the general public has an attitude of apathy to enforcement of the Alcoholic Beverage Control laws throughout the states. Most people, even juries, seem to feel that it is only an ABC violation and therefore can't be very serious. The exceptions to this are death or bodily injury, accidents, or crimes of violence. This indifferent attitude of the adult is transmitted to the minor. Most high school and college students would never stoop to commit petty theft or any similar crime, but they wouldn't give a second thought to an ABC violation, even though it is, in fact, a misdemeanor.

The most important single thing in the life of one of these students is status, that is, acceptance by their peers. If their group drinks, it is likely that they will also drink. It is estimated that 80 per cent of high school students throughout the United States consume some alcoholic beverages at some time during their high school career, and, in most cases, they are oblivious to the fact they they have committed a crime, or they just "don't care."

Juvenile delinquency studies reflect a high correlation between alcoholic parents and juvenile delinquents. Juvenile drinking is often a defiance of adult standards and authority, an attempt to prove manliness, to obtain status in their group, or may be mere experimentation and curiosity.

As of this date, there is no scientific proof that alcohol causes crime, but it appears to be a factor in some criminal behavior.[62]

[62]H. Treger, "The Alcoholic and the Probation Officer: A New Relationship," *Federal Probation*, Vol. XXVI, No. 4, December 1962, p. 23.

Extent of the Problem

A search of probation records throughout the states would probably show that somewhere between 50 and 60 per cent of all juvenile crimes are involved with alcoholic beverages. The records would also show that many petty thefts, burglaries, auto thefts, gang fights, vandalism, and crimes of violence were perpetrated after the responsibles had been drinking.[63]

In case of aggravated assault and homicide, alcohol is probably a facilitative factor because there is less inhibition after drinking. Some studies appear to show that there is a higher incidence of assault and violence among alcoholic criminals as compared with non-alcoholic offenders.

In rape and homicide, alcohol may be an important factor not only as it affects the offender, but for the victims as well, inasmuch as their drinking may tacitly invite rape and assault.[64]

Statistics obtained from the *Subcommittee on Alcoholism and Rehabilitation Studies,* which met in Los Angeles on October 21, 1964, showed the following facts pertaining to California:[65]

1. In 1963, there were 15,136 juveniles under 18 arrested for a specific liquor law violation. Of this group, 315 were arrested for the specific offense of drunk driving. Over one-half of this total group of 15,136 were referred to probation departments or other agencies for further disposition.
2. For every 100 youths committed to the Youth Authority from the criminal court of California in 1963, 28 had an excessive drinking problem. From the juvenile court, 12 out of every 100 had an excessive drinking problem. These figures do not take into account, those instances in which a youngster had an occasional or one-time drinking experience. (See Table 8 in Appendix A.)
3. According to statistics compiled by the *Department of Public Health in 1963,* California leads the nation in the number of alcoholics. The number is 185,000 and of this number, 151,000 are females.
4. In 1963, more than one-half of California's 700,000 annual arrests are estimated to be for public intoxication. This figure does not include citations and arrests for drunk driving. Los Angeles figures alone for drunk driving exceed 10,000 annually.
5. Surveys in California reportedly indicate that 700,000 teen-agers consume intoxicating beverages.
6. The State Legislature, in an attempt to "rehabilitate" the ever increasing number of alcoholics has authorized the expenditure of approximately $1,000,-

[63]Assembly Interim Committee on Judiciary, *Subcommittee on Alcoholism and Rehabilitation Studies,* Los Angeles, October 21, 1964, p. 56 (unpublished material).
[64]Treger, *op. cit.,* p. 23.
[65]Assembly Interim Committee on Judiciary, *op. cit.,* p. 63.

000 annually for the past seven years by The Division of Alcoholic Rehabilitation of the State Department of Public Health.

7. Approximately 12,000 "people" reportedly have been "seen" at the seven state-supported clinics during this seven-year-period.

8. Almost $600 per "person" has thus been spent by the Division of the Alcoholic Rehabilitation during this time.

As previously stated, nationally it is estimated that approximately 80 per cent of all high school students at some point in their four-year matriculation in high school will consume some alcoholic beverages. This may be done at home, with the full consent and approval of the parents, at a beach party, or in a bar. In many instances, it's a one-time test. After the first contact with alcoholic beverages, the youngster decides that it has no appeal for him and doesn't want to take the risk of getting involved with the law, so he either discontinues his association with the group he is concerned with, or he decides to associate with the group and discontinue any further use of alcoholic beverages (a very rare thing).

There are approximately 15,000,000 teen-agers in the United States. Five of youth's most pressing problems today are sex, boredom, need for challenge, a search for security, and last, but not least, alcohol. It is estimated that 97 per cent of these teen-agers are honest, law-abiding young men and women, but the remaining 3 per cent who see fit to ignore the rules of common decency and the laws of this country are causing the law-enforcement officers of this nation to assign more and more of their manpower to crime prevention. Respect for the law is breaking down, not only in this country but in all the countries of the world where teen-agers are concerned.

Teen-agers have knowingly been using their age as a crutch to assist them in escaping punishment for their criminal acts and juvenile crime has increased 250 per cent since 1950. This is four times the rate of the juvenile population increase. It is becoming more evident that when juveniles commit anti-social acts there usually has been some contact with "John Barleycorn." When youngsters gather and alcohol is present, the morals of the group are affected. Dares and jibes are tossed back and forth, a dare is taken and some criminal or immoral act is committed.

Causes

What causes the teen-ager drinking problem? Why do teen-agers drink? Most experts are of the opinion that drinking is a status symbol. Teen-agers are striving for understanding, they are striving for acceptance with their peers, and with their own social group. If that particular group tends to drink or leans toward this vice, to stay in and be one of the group, the teen-ager may participate in whatever form of drinking is practiced by his or her particular set of friends.

Most parents are not aware that the law, in most states does not exclude the youngster who might be served alcoholic beverages in his own home. As a matter of fact, there are no exclusions, and if there is a state Alcoholic Beverage Control Act it does not say—nor does it imply—that a father, on a warm afternoon out in the patio listening to the football game, can give his 17- or 18-year-old son a tall, cold glass of beer. If this happens, in reality a misdemeanor is committed.

Here is a situation of poor example and poor judgment on the part of the parents. Many parents leave large amounts of alcoholic beverages available, uncontrolled, about the house. Consequently, when the pressures are put on by their peers, their fellow classmates, to obtain alcoholic beverages, it is much easier to lift a little from the home than it is perhaps to buy it or obtain it in some other way.

In this area of discussion, law enforcement faces a problem, a historic problem, a problem of tradition. Many of the European families that emigrated to America brought historic customs with them. History reveals that in many parts of Europe the water was very poor for drinking purposes, and in place of drinking water the habit of drinking wine became very prominent and was handed down from generation to generation. Thus in many areas of this country wine is still served at home as a regular part of family meals from an early age. This, regardless of the tradition, is a misdemeanor. Some say, "Well, it's a good way to teach the youngster to drink." Law enforcement is of the opinion that there is no way you can teach a youngster to drink. The problem is particularly prevalent around high school graduation time. It is constant, it is regular, and parents do not believe that the law is intended for them. They say, "Well, my son or daughter is now 18; he or she has graduated from high school and is certainly capable of handling a few cocktails." The parents actually participate in giving graduation parties where alcoholic beverages are knowingly served. The same youngsters then drive cars on the highways and dangerous situations are created. Mass media throughout the United States cite many cases where, as a result of these parties, youngsters get into high-powered cars, take off and "fly," and before they have travelled very far they collide with another car or other object, and either loss of life or serious damage to the human body and property occurs.

Although the first source of liquor supply is often the home of the minor or the home of a friend, a similar source is the package liquor store, which is either knowingly the supplier or which has accepted false identification. When the juvenile finds himself without a source, he may resort to the method of approaching strangers in the vicinity of a package store, usually some "wino" or other "questionable characters," and pay that person to purchase alcoholic beverages for him. Often payment is made by sharing in the liquor purchase.

Of all of these, undoubtedly the most troublesome is the alcohol provided by "friends" of the minor. Any person over the age limit dictated by state law may purchase large amounts of liquor legally and share the purchase with a youngster under the legal age. Thus compatible groups of persons at large private gatherings who may be as young as 15 or 16 years of age, with others of 21 or 22 years of age, share in alcoholic beverages.

Police Role

Many youngsters have, on their first contact with law and alcoholic beverages as a combination, received proper guidance and counseling, good motivation and direction. The chances are very good that they will not continue this pattern. Many of them have personality weaknesses that need bolstering. Frequently, those who have the most obvious personality weakness turn out to be the leaders of the particular group, and it does take a tremendous amount of courage for the young person today to say "no" to his friends. If a youngster's father happens to own a liquor store, this boy could run for "president and win unopposed" in school. If he happens to work in a grocery or liquor store, the pressure to push a case of beer out with the old boxes near the incinerator becomes tremendous. Even though the youngster repeatedly ignores the urge, the pressure becomes so great that with just an average young man, the desire to succeed with his own group overcomes what the youngster knows to be right. Law enforcement has experienced numerous cases of this type, and it is always disheartening to see the crushed personality when the young man is caught in the act or subsequent investigation indicates to the owner of a market that his employee was not trustworthy.

In the area of possible cures, law-enforcement agencies, educators, church groups, fraternal club members, service club members, and parents, cooperating in a mass program of communication controls, may become effective. Properly designed and edited literature and handout material should be considered. As a matter of fact, the system should be incorporated in regular law-enforcement, probation, and other community programs. Another method in a long-range prevention program would be to educate adults, especially parents, to conduct themselves in a manner that will give good examples, especially when using alcoholic beverages.

Law-enforcement agencies cannot, alone, eliminate the teen-ager drinking problems. The burden of work, the increase in population, the slow increase in granting of added personnel, and this is true in most agencies, make it impossible to cover all the bases. The most important factor in preventing the use of alcoholic beverage on the part of juveniles is the elimination of the *causes.*

Effective control of the juvenile alcohol problem is not in sight. Any program of control requires considerable positive action by the local police and should include the help and the support of vendors of alcoholic beverages. The assistance of interested lay persons and youth-serving agencies should also be solicited.

SCHOOL DROP-OUTS AND JUVENILE DELINQUENCY

The causes of delinquent behavior are complex. People are concerned because the juvenile delinquency rate is said to be approximately 10 times as high among adolescents who drop out of high school as among high school graduates. Therefore, keeping young people in school is probably the most feasible method to combat delinquency.

It is true that maladjustment in school and rebellion against authority, the chief causes of drop-outs, tend to carry over into anti-social behavior within the community. However, unless the factors that lead the youngster to reject school are rectified, continued school attendance is likely to mean more rebellion.

Certain school experiences contribute to some pupils' desires to leave school as soon as legally possible. These result in negative attitudes, truancy, low achievement, and frustrations. As a result of lack of educational and vocational assets, these students become more amenable to a delinquency orientation.

Extent of the Problem

School enrollments between 1930 and 1953 increased more than six million. The proportion of 16- and 17-year-olds enrolled in schools rose between 1930 and 1953 from about 57 to 75 per cent. The bulk of delinquents come from the age range 10 to 17, a group that will increase 42 per cent by 1970.

Since the schools, in comparison with other community agencies, get the children first and keep them longest, they are, next to the home, the most important line of defense against this growing problem of delinquency. The schools are in a strategic position to do a job of prevention, beginning with the nursery school. Law-enforcement officers and those employed in the correctional field are also fully aware that the

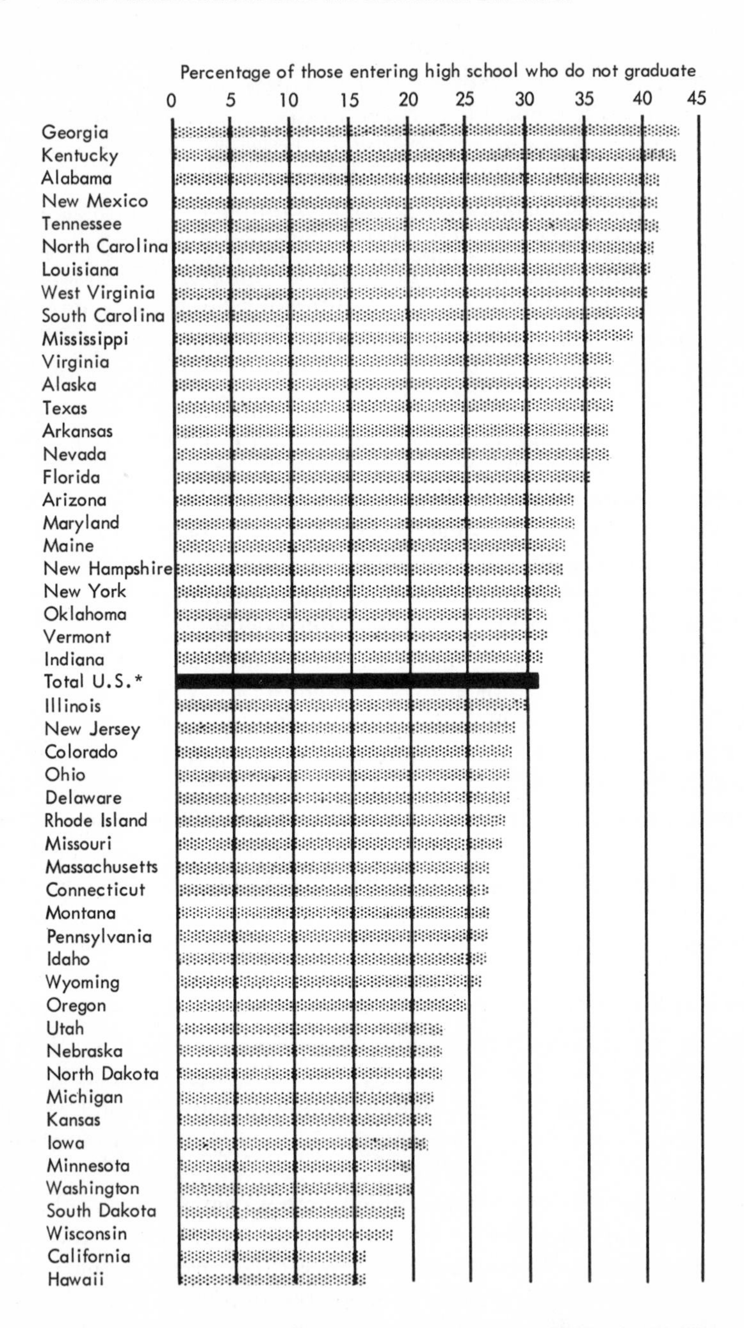

Figure 3 School drop-outs, 1963-64. An average of 1 in 3 entering high school drop out before graduation. (*Source*: Department of Health, Education, and Welfare.)

schools are a reliable source of assistance in investigative and supervisory work in probation and parole.[66]

It is not a coincidence that truancy from school is the most common initial act of delinquency. In 1934, Sheldon and Eleanor Glueck in their book, *One Thousand Juvenile Delinquents,* revealed the results of their investigation of 1,000 boy delinquents who had been brought to the attention of the Boston Juvenile Court. According to Sheldon and Eleanor Glueck, 85 per cent were found to have been retarded to some degree in school. Sixty-two percent were two years or more behind in grade; 85 per cent of the offenders showed anti-social behavior in school, and 64 per cent had been truant. The average age of onset of delinquent behavior was that of the fourth grader in school.

In a more recent study by the Gluecks, entitled *Unraveling Juvenile Delinquency,* 500 delinquent and 500 non-delinquent boys of similar backgrounds were compared. The delinquents were found to be definitely more retarded academically than were the non-delinquents. Furthermore, the delinquents expressed violent dislike of school, resentment at its restriction, and lack of interest in school work. Their school attainment was far below that of the non-delinquents. *Again, truancy was the first and most frequent act of delinquency.*

Relationship between Schools and Delinquency

Educational institutions are concerned about delinquency because it is an important problem in the field of education. The existence of delinquency proves that education, in its broad sense, has not been fully successful—that the combination of home, school, church, and other factors of environment has been unable to prevent the child from doing things which stigmatize him as a delinquent.

It is incumbent upon schools to separate the potential juvenile delinquent from that of the normal child. Attempts to discover the influences which are contributing toward the anti-social activities of youngsters and methods to prevent and eliminate such problems are responsibilities that the educational system must except.

The home, the church, the neighborhood, and the school all influence children. The school, by law, has children under its control roughly five and one-half hours a day for eight or nine months a year, minus the short vacations, or less than one-fifth of the child's waking hours during a 10- or 12-year period. The home and neighborhood control his activities entirely during the formative pre-school age and more than four-fifths of the time during his school years. Schools, therefore, have

[66]S. Miller Brownell, Ph.D., "The Unique Position of the Schools in the Prevention and Control of Delinquency," *Federal Probation,* Vol. XIX, No. 1, March, 1955, p. 14.

definite limitations, as well as challenges, in considering what they can do to strengthen good family and neighborhood influences to offset poor ones.[67]

The above relationship has been pointed out by the *National Society for the Study of Education in their Forty-Seventh Yearbook, entitled, Juvenile Delinquency and the Schools.* These scholars, in 1948, decided that the school is related to juvenile delinquency in three ways: " (1) It may produce delinquency; (2) it may help to prevent delinquency; (3) it may deal with delinquent behavior that is encountered within its walls."

Other causes for school drop-outs can be ascertained from the responses given by juveniles to school officials. Seldom is there one clear-cut reason. *Financial reasons* often involved the youth's need for the clothes that will gain him acceptance of his peers and the reluctance to ask hard-pressed parents for money for all the hidden costs of school attendance.

Participation in many extra-curricular activities that would tend to hold young people in school is often curtailed by meager funds. Lack of money also often discourages participation in the industrial arts and home economics courses, which for many students would give meaning to the whole school program.

Prefer to work is another reason that covers many factors that make youths unhappy in school. Feelings of rejection, constant failures, lack of someone to care, narrow curricula which seem to have no relevance to the students' present interests or future life, retardation which becomes cumulatively greater the longer it is uncorrected, all make the idea of work appealing as a chance to start anew, with some vague hope of success in a rosy future unrelated to the dismal past.[68]

Unrealistic ideas regarding employment opportunities are probably responsible for many decisions to drop school. Parents are often unable to realize the changes which have taken place in job requirements and hiring policies since they themselves left school. Previously, youngsters who were drop-outs from school were able to obtain unskilled jobs in factories. However, such unskilled labor has largely been taken over by machinery. The youngsters are, therefore, discouraged and frustrated. Parents are often critical when they ascertain that the only employment open to the youths is infrequent, poor-paying jobs that often require long and unusual hours.

The typical delinquent boy is of borderline intelligence and about

[67] *Ibid.*, p. 14.
[68] M. Furhman, "School Drop-Outs and Juvenile Delinquency," *Federal Probation*, Vol. XXIV, No. 3, September 1960, p. 35.

three years retarded in reading, writing, and arithmetic. The school frequently does not have the staff or program appropriate for this type of youngster. This particular deficiency is compounded in this day of emphasis on science, mathematics, and college preparatory curricula. The potentially delinquent boy is too bright for the special classes for the mentally retarded and unsuited on many counts for the regular school program with its emphasis on verbal abstractions. Without adequate skill in the three R's, the young student is almost certain to view school as a hindrance and a frustrating episode in his life.

For pupils with school-learning difficulties, the classroom is a very threatening place. The pupil responds to his deficiencies with defense mechanisms in order to hide his difficulties from himself, his classmates, and his teacher. The more common defenses include classroom disruptions, emotional outbreaks, aggression, and withdrawal, including daydreaming and truancy. The typical teacher who is faced with behavior of this type sees it as a threat to himself. He does his utmost to handle it. Initially, the teacher may be sympathetic to the youngster and try to make adjustments. However, when the disturbing behavior does not subside, the teacher will be forced to use threats and other punitive actions. Thus teacher and pupil find themselves on a treadmill from which escape is nearly impossible; the bearings on which it rolls are aggression and counter-aggression.[69]

Taking all these factors into consideration, it is not unusual that the typical delinquent finds success at school unreachable. It is a "chain reaction," the less he learns, the more negative his behavior becomes and the harsher the school treatment. The longer this "tug-of-war" persists, the more likely it is that the pupil will engage in delinquent behavior. The youngster with personal problems, who is a product of a disturbed family, does not leave these problems at the classroom door as he walks into the class. Similarly, neither does a pupil who is frustrated, ridiculed, and harassed in school leave his problems at the school door on his way out. Such a youngster, obviously, is a candidate for juvenile crime.

Although some school conditions may help to motivate delinquency, it is also true that schools may prevent it. Schools aid in preventing delinquency when they set tasks and recognize progress for each child according to his abilities. Such schools ascertain the psychological make-up of each pupil and utilize the information about each child so that all who work with him may act on it. This type of approach maintains close contacts with homes and neighborhoods. By such an association, the

[69]B. Balow, Ph.D., "Delinquency and School Failure," *Federal Probation*, Vol. XXV. No. 2, June, 1961, p. 15.

schools attempt to make up for deficiencies and supply resources otherwise absent. When children are clearly victims of their own or family personality difficulties, appropriate resources are utilized such as Family Service Associations, Adult and Child Guidance Clinics, probation services, medical, and social services. In short, schools endeavor to keep children in school and to achieve worthwhile successes in school. This all takes time, staff, and money. Above all, it takes a desire to see that every child is treated as an important human being, not just as an additional number in the school enrollment.

Police Role

Law enforcement can accomplish a great deal through development of a close-working relationship with the school system in their communities. Most school administrators are keenly interested in the welfare of the children and would, therefore, be pleased to offer help to the law enforcement agency. The following are a number of specific suggestions offered by *John P. Kenney,* and *Dan G. Pursuit,* as to how law enforcement can effectively work with the educational system:[70]

"1. Get acquainted with the school administrator in each school in the district. This key person may be the principal, or he may be the vice-principal or counselor, depending upon the particular school organization. Some administrators may be more cooperative than others and it is therefore logical that the police officer should try to locate the most cooperative school official in the various schools. Approach each school in an individualized manner in order to locate the right person with whom to work. It is quite possible for a police officer to be working with school personnel with four different position titles in four different schools.

"2. Learn as much as possible about the total school program. This information comes in handy when talking with boys and girls about their school adjustment. This valuable information might also enable an officer to make some constructive suggestions to the school authorities regarding a change of program for a boy. The information is also available for interpretation to parents.

"3. Notify the school when a child is taken into custody. This information is naturally important to the school personnel in the keeping of their records. Good cooperation on this point will encourage the school to want to work closely with the police department.

"4. Develop policies and procedures for the use of case information. Some police officers hesitate to inform the school personnel about the behavior of a child. Such information may, on occasion, have been used to stamp a youngster as a 'bad boy' and this designation stayed with him throughout his school career. If a definite set of policies is developed, this type of situation should not occur.

[70] J. P. Kenney, and D. G. Pursuit, *Op. Cit.*, pp. 289–291.

"5. Offer information on cases when requested. If the police are willing to offer information, there is a good possibility that the school authorities will in turn cooperate when the police request further information from them. The amount of information offered by the police department will have to be varied with the individual school authority. The officer will have to use his good judgment as to how much detail he should provide.

"6. Request information from the school regarding cases. If the officer has developed a good relationship with the school personnel, he should be able to get a valuable cumulative story on any child who gets into difficulty. This information is of value because it provides considerable significant material about the child. It might provide information on his physical condition, intelligence quotient, family background information, and general all-around school adjustment. With this information available, the officer should be in much better position to determine what should be done with each case.

"7. Learn about the diagnostic facilities offered by schools. The officer should know how many intensive diagnostic and treatment facilities are available. Some schools have an intensive program of psychological testing and counseling and even psychiatric treatment programs. Many of the children can thus be referred right to the school system for further treatment rather than taking juvenile court action.

"8. Discuss policy and procedures on truancy cases and school burglaries. Many police contacts with the school will be regarding these matters. Very close relations for working on these types of cases should be maintained.

"9. Accept invitations to school affairs. There are frequent school affairs such as open houses, PTA meetings, etc., to which the police juvenile officer might be invited. He should be encouraged to take advantage of these invitations because it gives him a chance to get better acquainted with the teaching personnel of the school. The children see the officer in a different light and this is important in the broad public relations approach.

"10. Invite school officials to juvenile officer meetings. This would present an excellent opportunity for the school personnel to get better acquainted with the objectives of the juvenile office group. They would discover that the two groups have much in common.

"11. Invite the school authorities to accompany you on tours of duty. Although this approach has some drawbacks because of the possible dangers involved, the idea still has some merits. Secondly, the school personnel individually might get a different impression of police work.

"12. Invite school personnel to an open house in the police department. Police departments have much of interest for school personnel to observe. An open house by the department would enable the police department to demonstrate some of the technical phases of their work which ordinarily would catch the interest of school personnel.

"13. Offer to speak and show films to classes in the schools. Most teachers would be pleased to have a police juvenile officer meet with their classes, particularly in the social study courses.

"14. Offer special help to the schools regarding lotteries near the school grounds. Many adult offenders can be apprehended by this type of special service to the schools. It is the type of offer of help which should be keenly appreciated by most school authorities.

"15. Offer police protection at special school events. The school would appreciate special police help at some of their events, such as athletic contests, carnivals, and other activities.

"16. Send a thank you note to the school personnel occasionally. A letter from the chief of police to the school superintendent and a letter from the police juvenile officer to the school person with whom he works most frequently would be a good public relations gesture."

Undoubtedly, there are many other programs which can be developed by local police agencies in order to further strengthen their relationship with schools. The suggestions by *Kenny* and *Pursuit* are but a minute part of the over-all program. Consideration should be accorded to liaison groups, for instance, composed of representatives of the various agencies dealing with youth, such as the schools, the juvenile courts, juvenile police, training schools, public and private social agencies, etc., to coordinate and integrate the necessary programs to meet the needs of maladjusted youth. This step can be taken immediately and will reduce the number of children who fall into gaps and who go without services. Through these groups, the teachers and other school personnel will know community resources, what can be expected, as well as the limitations, and be sure of services when children are referred. This type of program brings about a kindred spirit of partnership in meeting the needs of children, and also strengthens the communication between school and community agencies. This liaison can be achieved through local community groups, such as boards of education, local coordinating councils, community councils, or youth boards.

Whatever type of program developed by a local community, law-enforcement agencies should concentrate on the participation of qualified law-enforcement officials in school curricula utilized for the purpose of helping students understand law, law-enforcement, and their personal responsibilities as citizens. Where this procedure has been developed, students have been able to understand and cope with the problems caused by the deficiencies in state laws. Law-enforcement officials have been utilized in conferences with young people on such subjects as teen-age drinking, teen-age driving, and vandalism.

SEX OFFENSES

Sex offenders are either a danger to the community or a nuisance that the community need not tolerate. Sex offenses include rape, indecent exposure, exhibitionism, incest, child molesting, and homosexuality, as well as a variety of related acts. Legislators have taken the position that sex offenders are different from other types of law violators. Therefore, this has led to legislation that results in placement of sex offenders in a state of limbo, somewhere between the criminal and the mentally ill.

Legislation defining sex psychopaths and establishing administrative procedures for their custody, treatment, and release, was passed by some 13 states between 1937 and 1950, and has been extended to other states since that time. The procedures leading up to legislation were similar in many different jurisdictions. In a review of the development of sex psychopath laws, the late criminologist, *Edwin Sutherland, in an article titled "The Diffusion of Sexual Psychopath Laws,"* noted a sequence characterized by: (a) an upspring of fear within the community as a result of a few serious sex crimes; (b) community response in the form of fear and anxiety, leading to (c) the gathering of information from an appointed committee and recommendations that generally were uncritically accepted by state legislatures. Usually, committees proceeded to make recommendations based largely on the absence of facts. *Sutherland* noted that the laws embodied a set of implicit assumptions that were explicit in much of the popular literature on sex offenses. Such assumptions were largely based on the notion that all sex offenders were potentially dangerous, that they were recidivists, that they can be accurately diagnosed and efficiently treated by psychiatrists. These laws were passed in the name of science, although the scientific method was completely ignored.

Taking various legislative acts into consideration, it can be concluded that the sexual offender is an adult or juvenile who becomes involved in any sexual play (masturbation excluded) that falls outside the socially acceptable scope of normal sexual behavior. Normal sexuality is regarded as heterosexual relations voluntarily and privately practiced in a normal manner by responsible adults, not very closely related. Although such relationships are usually preceded by marriage, there are occasions when marriage does not occur.

Sexual deviation is responsible for the majority of sex crimes. However, although rape and incest are always criminal, such crimes are often committed by sexually deviate people. They are thought of as psychologically abnormal because of our cultural and emotional ties.[71]

[71]S. W. Hartwell, *A Citizen's Handbook of Sexual Abnormalties*, Report to the Committee on Education of the Governor's Study Commission on the Deviate Sex Offender, State of Michigan, 1950, p. 72.

According to Kinsey,[72] a sex offender is a person who violates a law prohibiting some kind of sexual behavior and is apprehended by the authorities. Furthermore, sex offenders make up a very large segment of the population.

There is an almost universal disregard regarding the prohibitions of sex offense laws. The ignoring of such laws motivated the following criticism from *Dr. Kinsey*:

> "All of these and still other types of sexual behavior are illicit activities, each performance of which is punishable as a crime under the law. The persons involved in these activities, taken as a whole constitute more than 95% of the total male population. Only a relatively small proportion of the males who are sent to penal institutions for sex offenses *have been involved in behavior which is materially different from the behavior of most of the males in the population.* But it is the *total 95% of the male population* for which the judge of the board of public safety or church, or civic group demands *apprehension, arrest, and conviction,* when they call for a clean-up of the sex offenders in a community. It is, in fact, *a proposal that 5% of the population should support the other 95% in penal institutions.*"

Morris Ploscowe, in his book *Sex and Law,* has pointed out that the above conclusion (95 per cent of the male population could be jailed because of violations of sex offense laws) is an exaggeration. Such a statement, according to Ploscowe, presupposes that such legislation is uniform throughout the country, that all sexual activity except solitary masturbation and normal marital intercourse is universally prohibited, and that these laws invariably prescribe jail and prison sentences for their violation. This, however, is not so. One of the most remarkable features of American sex offense laws, continues Ploscowe, is their wide disparity in types of sexual behavior prohibited and their extraordinary variation in penalties imposed for similar offenses.

Law and Adolescent Sexual Offenses

Failure to accord the child in the United States a distinct status position that is closely integrated with the larger structure of American society and the resulting minimum institutionalization of norms for governing adolescent behavior has numerous important implications for defining and sanctioning the sexual conduct of youngsters in American society. Because of the lack of transitional status between childhood and adulthood in the United States, numerous problems have developed in the area of the law and sexual offenses. Such a problem has resulted

[72]A. C. Kinsey, W. B. Pomeroy, and G. E. Martin, *Sexual Behavior in the Human Male,* W. B. Saunders, Co., Philadelphia and London, 1948, p. 133.

in the following conclusions of *Albert J. Reiss, in his article entitled "Sex Offenses: The Marginal Status of the Adolescent"*:[73]

"1. The perception of adolescent sex offenders as neither child nor adult tends to (a) encourage considerable variation in definition of their sexual offenses; (b) lead to differential treatment and differential adjudication of their cases of sexual behavior on the basis of age, sex, socioeconomic status, and jurisdictional consideration; and (c) obscure the degree to which they are denied the due process of law.

"2. The age-based status reference point for evaluating adolescent sexual offenses is a factor in the sanctions applied to their deviation. When adolescent sex offenders are viewed as 'not adult,' they are generally overprotected and absolved from moral responsibility for their behavior, thereby weakening the moral integration of the total society. When they are viewed as 'not children' there often is a tendency to deal more punitively with them than with adults who commit similar sex offenses.

"3. The sexual behavior of adolescents is primarily peer-organized and peer-controlled. As such, it reflects the attempt by adolescents to achieve a compromise between being encouraged to behave like adults and being denied the rights and privileges of that status. An examination of the peer-organized basis for adolescent sexual conduct provides a normative basis for evaluating their behavior in relation to the larger social structure in which they are held accountable for their behavior."

Taking these conclusions into consideration, we wonder what acts committed by youngsters would be defined as violations of sexual conduct norms. Furthermore, to what degree does a youngster's status as "not child" and "not adult" encourage misinterpretation in the definition of an adolescent's sexual conduct as a sex offense?

Despite some variation in the legal codes from state to state in American society, the statutes define the acts for which violators are classified as adult sex offenders. Such classification on the part of adults is not complex. However, the problem of defining the juvenile as a sex offender is extremely confusing. Most juvenile court statutes not only define the violation of all criminal statutory codes as sufficient ground for finding of delinquency, but also hold that if the child is growing up in a situation undesirable to his welfare, he or she may be adjudicated a delinquent. For all practical purposes, then, the definition of a juvenile sex offender rests with the standards adhered to in a respective juvenile jurisdiction. The statutes, in fact, prescribe that the finding be that the child is a delinquent, and not a specific type of offender.

[73]A. J. Reiss, "Sex Offenses: The Marginal Status of the Adolescent," *Law and Contemporary Problems,* School of Law, Duke University, Vol. XXV, No. 2, Spring, 1960, p. 310.

Juvenile court law statutes are phrased in such general and inclusive terms that *any sexual* act or conduct can be viewed as a delinquent offense. The general provision pertaining to "lewd, immoral, and lascivious behavior" can be construed to cover all deviations from sexual conduct norms. As previously stated, there is considerable ambiguity as to what sexual conduct is to be defined as a violation and what is permitted sexual behavior for adolescents. Juveniles who are held to be guilty of a sex offense often are not charged with a specific sex conduct violation. Categories such as "incorrigibility," "loitering," "lewd and immoral conduct," "runaway," and similar charges frequently are the preferred allegations, particularly if the juvenile court has a policy to avoid stigmatizing an individual with a sex offense record. In many jurisdictions, minors are charged with "disturbing the peace" and petitions state the offense as such. The terms "sex offense" and "sexual offender" are not clearly defined, then, for adolescents in legal codes or in adjudication of cases involving the violation of sexual conduct norms.[74]

However, according to *Reiss*:[75]

"Adolescents themselves set standards for what is a violation of their sexual codes. The standards in these adolescent codes vary considerably according to the social status position of the adolescent and his family in the larger society. Among young lower-status adolescent boys, perhaps the most common mode of heterosexual intercourse is the 'gang-shag' or 'gang bang." A gang of boys usually knows one or more girls who are easy 'pick-ups' for the group who will consent to serial intercourse with the members of the gang. To understand this behavior several peer normative factors need to be taken into account. First of all, the girl in the 'gang-bank' is almost always one who gives her consent. She is not being sexually exploited in any sense of forcible rape. In fact, when she consents to being picked up, she understands that she is to be a partner in the heterosexual coition. Lower-status boys clearly distinguish between 'putting it to a girl' (she consents) and 'making a girl' (she does not consent). Fewer lower-status boys, particularly delinquent boys, will 'make a girl' although almost all frequently engage in heterosexual intercourse and most have at least participated in a gang-bang. Most lower-status adolescent boys express the view: 'Why should I *make* a girl when I can get all I want without it.' The opportunities for heterosexual coition with consent are ever-present to lower-status boys, so that they negatively sanction forcible rape. This is not to say that some adolescent girls are not forcibly raped by an adolescent boy or even a gang, but the proportion who are is, without doubt, very small."

Regarding the girls' inordinant amount of contacts with the authorities, *Reiss* continues:

[74]*Ibid.*, p. 312.

[75]*Ibid.*, pp. 312-313.

"It is not so much the sexual act of coition that brings the girls to the attention of legal authorities as it is either of these consequences of the act—premarital pregnancy or venereal infection. The couple is seldom caught in the act of coition. Since girls are more likely than boys to be defined as the carries of the venereal disease, a girl who is picked up by police or juvenile authorities is almost always given a physical examination to determine whether she has had sexual intercourse, now has venereal infection or is pregnant. This is particularly true for runaway girls. Boys seldom are given a complete physical examination for venereal infection as are girls. Even less often are they questioned as to their sex experiences. There is a great variation among jurisdictions in this respect, however, personnel in some are more likely than in others to learn about the sexual deviation of girls. The life chances of a girl before police and juvenile authorities, therefore, are more favorable to definition as a sex delinquent than are the life chances of a boy.

"Adolescent boys come to the attention of the court as heterosexual sex offenders usually only when the morality of the girl's family is offended. The most common form of complaint is for the family to define coition as 'rape' of their daughter. Research evidence shows that in most cases the boy is not a rapist in any technical sense that force or coercion was used. The act occurred through common consent. The complaint arises because the girl, under family pressure, charges that she did not consent. Although many complaints arise in this way, it does not follow, of course, that some delinquent boys gangs do not forcibly rape a young girl nor that boys individually do not engage in such acts; it rather to emphasize that available evidence strongly indicates that most heterosexual coition between adolescents occurs through mutual consent. The girl has a reputation. She is sought out or picked up. She knows what is expected of her, consents, and services one or more boys. No money is exchanged."

Classification of Sexual Offenses

Incest. Sexual intercourse between two persons, married or not, who are too closely related by blood affinity to be married is considered incest. The element of age is not considered and want of chastity is no defense. Blood relation, in some states, is not necessary. Furthermore, relations between step-mother and step-son are incest until the death of the natural parent.

Sadomasochism. Sadism is a paraphiliac neurosis in which the will to power is sexually accentuated and masochism is one in which the will to submission is sexually accentuated.

Authorities in the field view masochism as the seeking of what would normally be painful for sexual reasons. Such pain is tied in with domination, humiliation, and degredation.

The attainment of sexual pleasure from acts of cruelty and the infliction of pain is sadism. It is interesting to note that the individual inflicted with this psychological illness is often undersexed rather than oversexed. Sadistic crimes include murder, attempted murder, assault with intent to do bodily harm, battery, bodily injuries, sexual assaults, damage to property, maiming, and other offenses involving bodily harm.

Rape. Rape is defined as an act of sexual intercourse performed with the female, not the wife of the perpetrator, without her consent. Statutory rape is an act of sexual intercourse performed upon the person of a female who is under the age of consent and not the wife of the perpetrator. Regardless how slight the penetration may be, rape is committed if there is penetration.

Necrophilia. Necrophilia (sexual intercourse with a female cadaver) is very uncommon. A necrophiliac either kills a woman and has sexual intercourse with the body or otherwise violates it, or procures corpses which he rapes, mutilates, or uses to commit *necrophagy* (eats the corpse).

Homosexuality. In homosexuality, sexual desires are directed toward an individual of the same sex. Furthermore, the homosexual is often an individual endowed with characteristics and emotional traits of the opposite sex.

Sodomy and Pederasty. Sodomy, according to penal law, refers to any actual sexual relations between men. The penal law includes sodomy under crimes against nature; oral and anal penetration of homosexual or heterosexual nature are included, as well as sex acts with animals and birds.

Anal coitus, with a boy as the passive and adult as the active partner, is referred to as pederasty.

Transvestism. A transvestite utilizes the garments of the opposite sex for sexual gratification.

Pedophilia. Pedophilia is an abnormal craving for a child, whether it be female or male, on the part of an adult. However, such behavior is illegal only when it attains overt proportions.

Obscenity and Pornography. The expression, representation, or display to others in certain contexts or situations of something culturally regarded as shocking or repugnant is considered as obscenity. Such obscenity could take the form of displaying the genitals in public.

Pornography is the utilization of obscene and immodest writing and pictures for purposes of leading to certain sexual feats that take place in actual intercourse.

Indecent Exposure. Indecent exposure and acts of exhibitionism are synonymous with the exposure of genitals to women, girls, or young children. Exhibitionism is the exposure of one's self to obtain sexual gratification. Indecent exposure must be indecent, public, and witnessed by more than one person.

Voyeurism and Scoptophilia. Unusual and excessive interest in the viewing of genitalia, sex acts, etc., as a means of obtaining sexual stimulus is called scoptophilia. Voyeurism is a pathological indulgence in viewing some form of nudity as a source of gratification in place of the normal sex act. It should be pointed out that voyeurism is a crime only when the person observed has not given consent.

Police Role in Prevention and Control

There are many practical programs which could be constructed to prevent and control the inordinant amount of sexual offenses involving adolescents in the United States. The following are suggestions which could be utilized by law-enforcement agencies and communities concerned about the problem:

1. Law enforcement should endeavor to become involved in the selection of potential parolees from institutions who have been involved in sexual offenses.
2. Law enforcement officers experienced in the area of deviant sexual behavior should be organized into a squad capable of coping with sex degenerates. Along these lines, a card-index file should be maintained, cataloging all sexual offenders residing within the community. Fingerprints, photographs, and a *modus operandi* should be included with the cards.
3. Areas where sexual offenses appear to have increased should be kept under special surveillance. Areas such as parks, theaters, zoos, and public lavatories should be kept under careful observation. Over-crowding tends to produce immorality of all kinds. The number of park keepers should be increased; student teachers in training should receive instructions as to how to deal with problems of undesirable conversation and conduct which may arise in school; prospective teachers should be advised how best to give individual help on matters of sex to all the children.
4. The sex offender should be brought under psychiatric observation promptly with minimum contact with police. When possible, he should be committed for psychiatric examination. He should be held in a hospital, not jail. Police authorities and judges should be given instructions in the nature of the sex offender and his psychopathology. There should be a pre-pleading probationary investigation, psychiatric observation, and examination. More serious offenders should not be allowed to plead guilty to lesser offenses. The publicity should be carefully controlled for the sake of the rehabilitation of the individual.[76]
5. More consideration should be accorded to the handling of victims of sex

[76]L. C. Herning, "General Exhibitionism: An Interpretative Study," *Journal of Clinical Psychopathology*, Vol. 8, 1946, pp. 557–564.

crimes, particularly children. The inept handling of victims is often at the root of the reluctance of parents to complain. Separate facilities should be provided for juveniles, according to the degree of seriousness of the behavior problem.

6. Copies of parole and supervisory reports concerning sex degenerates should be filed with the local law-enforcement agency.

Prevention is the area that should be expanded, and a preventative program should include the following:

Organization of a special squad familiar with methods of coping with sex degenerates.

A file should be maintained with complete information on all known sex deviates in the community.

A close working relationship with private and state mental institution personnel is necessary in order to obtain fingerprints, photographs, and other pertinent data pertaining to sex degenerates who are capable of committing sex crimes. If the person in question changes residence, this information should be forwarded to the law-enforcement agency in the community where the person in question plans to reside.

Fingerprinting and photography should be mandatory for all individuals, minor or adult, who are arrested for sexual offenses.

Close surveillance of "known areas" where sex degenerates congregate should be maintained by the local police.

In addition to the points for prevention already mentioned, one of the most important weapons to consider is the use of *education* in combating sex crimes. A specific and detailed educational program should be initiated, directed particularly at: (1) the legislature and other public officials; (2) the public; and (3) the police.[77] To elaborate:

Cooperation of the legislature and other public officials should be secured.

The general public should be enlightened concerning such matters and be accorded specific instructions as to how to help.

Special training should be provided to law-enforcement officers with respect to techniques and methods of investigation.[78]

SUMMARY

The influence of the gang, whether negative or positive, is particularly effective because it often completely answers the boy's needs. His desire for adventure and companionship is satisfied. He gets the feeling of belonging and of loyalty to the group. If the gang is delinquently orientated, the tougher he is, the more recognition he gets. Furthermore, he may also find the discipline he needs. Gangs develop their own

[77]J. P. Kenney and D. G. Pursuit, *op. cit.*, p. 186.
[78]*Ibid.*, p. 186.

codes and rules of behavior and demand that the members rigidly abide by them.

Although the word *gang* is associated with anti-social behavior or rebellion against authority, the gang, in itself, is not inherently vicious. Group activity is a necessary part of a growing child's life. The gang becomes dangerous if the street life from which it springs offers opportunities for delinquency and if the leader is a bad influence.

There are many studies of gangs. Some of the most popular are: *The Shook-Up Generation,* by Harrison Salisbury; Walter Miller's *Lower-Class Culture as a Generating Milieu of Gang Delinquency*; and Albert Cohen's *Delinquent Boys.*

Experimentation regarding different approaches to the understanding and control of gang behavior has been carried on in various cities and it is recommended by law-enforcement agencies throughout the United States that an area approach be adopted. The reason for such a recommendation is quite practical. Under the coordinating council program, each area of the community would have a committee composed of a cross section of persons living in that particular neighborhood, including representatives of social agencies, schools, labor unions, churches, police, and fraternal and business organizations.

What is the nature of the adolescent who becomes involved in the use of drugs? Although the drug addict is not an individual who has remained aloof from crime, he is rarely many of the sensational things portrayed in the public mind. Those who have worked with the adolescent drug addict recognize him as an emotionally sick individual whose difficulties relate back to a life history of social and emotional maladjustment.

Since 1914, the federal government has imposed a tax on narcotics and, by using this tax statute (Harrison Act), has regulated the manufacture and distribution of narcotics. Several laws have followed giving the federal government additional authority. At the present time, all phases of narcotic distribution, including international shipments, are under the regulatory control of the Bureau of Narcotics, a branch of the Treasury Department.

Important features of the narcotic laws and regulations are: (1) registration of those dealing in narcotic drugs; (2) special taxes; (3) special order forms and record-keeping provisions; and, (4) prohibitions and severe penalties for illegal possession and trafficking in these drugs.

All but a few states have enacted the uniform Narcotic Drug Act or similar legislation. This Act follows federal laws and is recommended by the Bureau of Narcotics. Some states have variations, but generally speaking, the important provisions are the same in most states.

The search for drugs is one of the most difficult problems faced by an officer. Drugs may be in solid, powder, or liquid form. In its pure state, the "bulk" of the drug may be very small. One popular way to carry illegally obtained drugs is to keep them in an old prescription bottle. The officer should be suspicious of any bottle with a worn or dirty label.

Illegally-obtained drugs are often hidden in the bottom of a cigarette pack. The cigarettes are cut off and the pack appears normal. Drugs may also be found in fountain pens, cigarette lighters, toothpaste tubes, flashlights, and lipstick tubes which have had their contents removed. Tablets and capsules may be folded into letters, handkerchiefs, personal papers, books, and newspapers, or secreted in the lining of clothing. Occasionally, drugs may be dissolved into innocent-appearing liquids.

Juvenile delinquency studies reflect a high correlation between alcoholic parents and juvenile delinquents. Juvenile drinking is often a defiance of adult standards and authority, an attempt to prove manliness, to obtain status in their group, or may be mere experimentation and curiosity.

Most experts are of the opinion that drinking is a status symbol. Teen-agers are striving for understanding, they are striving for acceptance with their peers, and with their own social group. If that particular group tends to drink or tends toward this vice, to stay in and be one of the group, the teen-ager may participate in whatever form of drinking practiced by his particular set of friends.

Educational institutions are concerned about delinquency because it is an important problem in the field of education. The typical delinquent boy is of borderline intelligence and about three years retarded in reading, writing and arithmetic. The school frequently does not have the staff or program appropriate for this type of youngster. This particular deficiency is compounded in this day of emphasis on science, mathematics, and college preparatory curricula. This potentially delinquent boy is too bright for the special classes for the mentally retarded and unsuited for the regular school program with its emphasis on verbal abstractions. Without adequate skill in the three "R's" the young student is almost certain to view school as a hindrance, and a frustrating episode in his life.

Sex offenses include rape, indecent exposure, exhibitionism, incest, child molesting, and homosexuality, as well as a variety of related acts. Legislators have taken the position that sex offenders are different from other types of law violators. Therefore, this has led to legislation that results in a placement of sex offenders in a state of limbo, somewhere between criminal and the mentally ill.

In review of the development of sex psychopath laws, the late criminologist, *Edwin Sutherland,* noted a sequence characterized by: (a) an upspring of fear within the community as a result of a few serious sex crimes; (b) community response in the form of anxiety, leading to (c) the gathering of information from an appointed committee and recommendations that generally were uncritically accepted by state legislature.

Failure to accord the child in the United States a distinct status that is closely integrated with the larger structure of American society and the resulting minimum institutionalization of norms for governing adolescent behavior has numerous important implications for defining and sanctioning the sexual conduct of youngsters in American society. Because of the lack of emotional status between childhood and adulthood in the United States, numerous problems have evolved in the area of law and sexual offenses.

QUESTIONS

1. Discuss the influence of the gang on a gang member.
2. Discuss Salisbury's perception of a delinquent gang.
3. Miller presented six of the major concerns in his study of the delinquent gang. List the six concerns.
4. Discuss the function and efforts of the New York City Youth Board.
5. Name and discuss the function of gangs.
6. Describe the personality of a typical adolescent drug addict—"Portrait of an adolescent drug addict."
7. What are the drugs commonly abused?
8. Discuss investigative techniques with relation to drug law violations.
9. What causes the teen-ager drinking problem?
10. What is the role of the police in prevention and control of sex crimes?

Bibliography

Adlow, E., *Policemen and People,* William J. Rockford, Boston, 1947.

Advisory Committee on Social Welfare Education, *Social Workers for California,* Regents of University of California, Los Angeles, 1960.

Assembly Interim Committee on Judiciary, *Subcommittee on Alcoholism and Rehabilitation Studies,* Los Angeles, October 21, 1964. (unpublished material)

Balow, B., "Delinquency and School Failure, *Federal Probation,* Vol. XXV, No. 2, June, 1961.

Barnes, H. E., and N. K. Teeters, *New Horizons in Criminology,* 3rd ed., Prentice-Hall, Englewood Cliffs, N.J., 1959.

Block, H. A., and F. T. Flynn, *Delinquency,* Random House, New York 1956.

Boehm, W. W., "Objectives of the Social Work Curriculum of the Future," *Social Work Curriculum Study,* Vol. 1, Council on Social Education, New York, 1959.

Breckenridge, S. P., *Social Work in the Courts,* Chicago University Press, Chicago, 1934.

Breckenridge, S. P., and E. Abbot, *The Delinquent Child and the Home,* Charities Publication Committee, New York, 1912.

Brownell, S. Miller, "The Unique Position of the Schools in the Prevention and Control of Delinquency," *Federal Probation,* Vol. XIX, No. 1, March, 1955.

Burchinal, L. G., *Rural Youth in Crisis,* Children's Bureau, Department of Health, Education, and Welfare, Washington, D.C. 1965.

Burt, C., *The Young Delinquent,* 1st ed., University of London Press, London, 1938.

Byerly, J. F., "Sentencing the Juvenile Offenders," *Federal Probation,* Vol. XXVI, No. 2, June, 1962.

Carr, L. J., "Most Courts Have To Be Substandard," *Federal Probation,* Vol. XIII, No. 29, 1949.

Children and Neglect: Hazardous Home Conditions, Children's Bureau, Department of Health, Education, and Welfare, Washington, D.C. 1962.

Child Welfare Services, Children's Bureau Publication #359, Department of Health, Education, and Welfare, Washington, D.C., 1957.

Clife, R. E., *A Guide to Modern Police Thinking,* The W. H. Anderson Company, Cincinnati, 1956.

Cohen, A. K., *Delinquent Boys,* The Free Press, Glencoe, Illinois 1955.

Dunham, W. H., "Juvenile Court: Contradiction in Processing Offenders," *Law and Contemporary Problems,* Summer, 1958.

Eastman, H. L., Judge, "The Juvenile Court Judge's Job," *National Probation Parole Association,* October, 1959.

Essentials of Adoption Law and Procedure, Children's Bureau, Department of Health, Education and Welfare, Washington, D.C. 1949.

Finestone, H., "Narcotics: Narcotics and Criminality," *Law and Contemporary Problems,* School of Law, Duke University, Vol. XXII, No. 2, Winter, 1957.

Fort, W. S., "The Juvenile Court Examines Itself," *National Probation Parole Association,* Vol. V, No. 4, New York, October, 1959.

Furhman, M., "School Drop-Outs and Juvenile Delinquency," *Federal Probation,* Vol. XXIV, No. 3, September, 1960.

Gardner, G. E., "The Juvenile Court as a Child Care Institution," *Federal Probation,* Vol. XVI, No. 2, June 1952.

Geis, G., *Juvenile Gangs,* President's Committee on Juvenile Delinquency and Youth Crime, Government Printing Office, Washington, D.C., June, 1965.

Geis, G., "Publicity and the Juvenile Court Proceedings," *Facts and Facets,* Children's Bureau, Department of Health, Education, and Welfare, Washington, D.C., 1962

Glueck, S., and E. Glueck, *Unraveling Juvenile Delinquency,* Commonwealth Fund, New York, 1950.

Gold, L., "Toward an Understanding of Adolescent Drug Addiction," *Federal Probation,* Vol. XXII, No. 3, September, 1958.

Gottshall, A. E., "Sentencing the Youth Offender and Youth Adult Offender," *Federal Probation,* Vol. XXVI, No. 2, June, 1962.

Gourley, G. D., *Public Relations and the Police,* Charles C Thomas, Springfield, Illinois, 1953.

"Guide for Police Practices: Departmental Juvenile Inventory," *International Association of Chiefs of Police,* Washington, D.C., (unpublished) .

Hartwell, S. W., *A Citizen's Handbook of Sexual Abnormalities,* report to the Committee on Education of the Governor's Study Commission on Deviate Sex Offender, State of Michigan, 1950.

Healy, W., and A. F. Bronner, *Delinquents and Criminals; Their Making and Unmaking,* Macmillan, New York, 1926.

Hennings, T. C., Jr., "Effectiveness of the Juvenile Court System," *Federal Probation,* Vol. XXXIII, No. 21, June, 1959.

Herning, L. C., "General Exhibitionism: An Interpretation Study," *Journal of Clinical Psychopathology,* Vol. 8, 1946.

Hughs, S. T., "Trial of Juvenile Delinquents in Federal Courts," *Law Enforcement and the Juvenile Offender,* Charles C Thomas, Springfield, Illinois, 1963.

International City Managers' Association, *Municipal Police Administration,* Chicago, 1954.

Jensen, W. W., *Preliminary Image Assessment, Los Angeles County Sheriff's Department,* Special Report, Los Angeles, April 24, 1961.

Juvenile Court Statistics, Statistical Series #831, Children's Bureau, Department of Health, Education, and Welfare, Washington, D.C., 1964.

Kempe, H. C., "The Battered Child Syndrome," *Journal of the American Medical Association,* Vol. CLXXXI, No. 1, July 7, 1962.

Kenney, J. P., and D. G. Pursuit, *Police Work with Juveniles,* 2nd ed., Charles C Thomas, Springfield, Illinois 1959.

Ketcham, O. W., "The Unfulfilled Promise of the Juvenile Court," *National Council on Crime and Delinquency,* Vol. VII, No. 2, April, 1961.

King, E. M., *The Auxiliary Police Unit,* Charles C Thomas, Springfield, Illinois, 1960.

Kinsey, A. C., W. B. Pomeroy, and G. E. Martin, *Sexual Behavior in the Human Male,* W. B. Saunders Co., Philidalephia and London, 1948.

Klein, M. W., and B. G. Myerhoff, *Juvenile Gangs, in Context: Theory, Research and Action,* University of Southern California, Los Angeles, California, 1964.

Kvaraceus, W. C., "Juvenile Delinquency: A Problem for the Modern World," *Federal Probation,* Vol. XXXIII, No. 3, September, 1964.

Kvaraceus, W. C., *The Community and the Delinquent,* World Book Company, Yonkers, N.Y., 1954.

Kvaraceus, W. C., and W. B. Miller, *Delinquent Behavior; Culture and the Individual,* National Education Association of the U. S., Washington, D.C., 1959.

Kvaraceus, W. C., and W. E. Ulrich, *Delinquent Behavior; Principles and Practices,* National Education Association of the U. S., Washington, D.C., 1959.

Landis, J. B., and Dr. K. K. Fletcher, *Drug Abuse: A Manual for Law Enforcement Officers,* Training Bulletin No. 11, November, 1966 (unpublished).

Lejins, P., "Is the Youth Authority Really Paying Off?" *Proceedings of the National Conference of Juvenile Agencies,* Forty-seventh Annual Meeting, 1950.

Linroot, K. F., "Should the Protection of Neglected and Morally Abandoned Children Be Secured by the Judicial Authority or a Nonjudicial Body; Should the Court for Delinquent Children and Juveniles be Maintained?" *Twelfth International Penal and Penitentiary Congress,* 1950, The Hague, Administration of Prisons, Vol. IV, 1950.

Lou, H. H., *Juvenile Courts in the United States,* The University of North Carolina Press, Chapel Hill, N. C., 1927.

Mays, J. B., *Growing Up in The City,* Liverpool University Press, London, England, 1954.

Miller, W. B., "Lower-Class Culture as a Generating Milieu of Gang Delinquency," *Journal of Social Issue,* Vol. XIV, University of Michigan, Ann Arbor, Michigan.

Neglect, Social Deviance, and Community Action, *National Probation Parole Association,* Vol. VI, No. 1, January, 1960.

New York Academy of Medicine, *Conference on Drug Addiction Among Adolescents,* Blakiston, New York, Toronto, 1953.

O'Connor, G. W., and N. E. Watson, *Juvenile Delinquency and Youth Crime: The Police Role,* International Association of Chiefs of Police, Washington, D.C., 1964.

Office of the County Counsel, "Joint Report and Review of the Sheriff, District Attorney, County Counsel and Probation Officer of Existing Legislative

Program Relating to Amendments to the State Narcotics Law," Los Angeles, December 29, 1960 (mimeographed).

Parker, W. H., Chief of Police, Los Angeles Police Department, as quoted in *Los Angeles Mirror*, December, 1954.

Perlman, I.R., "Antisocial Behavior of the Minor in the United States," *Federal Probation*, Vol. XXVIII, No. 4, December, 1964.

Planning for the Protection and Care of Neglected Children in California, preliminary report of a study by National Study Service, New York, 1964.

Police Services for Juveniles, Children's Bureau, Department of Health, Education, and Welfare, Washington, D.C., 1954.

Pomeroy, A., *Treatise on Equity Jurisprudence*, 5th ed., 1307, 1941.

Pope, J. K., *Police-Press Relations*, Academy Literary Guild, Fresno, Calif., 1954.

Pound, R., "Jurisprudence," *Encyclopedia of the Social Sciences*, Macmillan, New York, 8:477–490, 1935.

Pound, R., "The Juvenile Court and the Law," *National Probation Parole Association Yearbook*, New York, 1944.

Pound, R., "The Juvenile Court in the Service State. Current Approaches to Delinquency," *National Probation Parole Association 1949 Yearbook*, New York, 1950.

Pound, R., "Society's Stake in the Offender," *National Probation Parole Association Yearbook*, New York, 1947.

Public Relations Today, *Business Week*, Vol. XXI, No. 7, July 2, 1960.

Reckless, W. C., *The Crime Problem*, 2nd ed., Appleton-Century-Crofts, New York, 1955.

Reed, G., "The Federal Youth Corrections Act in Operation," *Federal Probation*, Vol. XVIII, No. 3, September, 1954.

Reiss, A. J., "Sex Offenses: The Marginal Status of the Adolescent," *Law and Contemporary Problems: Sex Problems*, School of Law, Duke University, Vol. XXV, No. 2, Spring, 1960.

Report on Workshops: Juvenile Delinquency and the Police, International Association of Police Chiefs, Washington, D.C. (unpublished).

Rice, R. E., and R. B. Christensen, *The Juvenile Gang: Its Structure, Function, and Treatment*, Los Angeles County Probation Department Research Office, Report No. 24, 1965.

Roucek, J. S., *Juvenile Delinquency*, Philosophical Library, New York, 1958.

Salisbury, H. E., *The Shook-Up Generation*, Harper & Row, New York, 1958.

Schilder, C. L., "Juvenile Offenders Should Be Fingerprinted," *Federal Probation*, Vol. XI, No. 1, January-March, 1947.

Schramm, G. L., "Philosophy of the Juvenile Court," *The Annals of the American Academy of Political and Social Service*, 261-101-108, 1949.

Sellin, T., *Research Memorandum on Crime in the Depression*, University of London Press, London, 1938.

Shaw, C. R., *Delinquent Areas*, Chicago University Press, Chicago, 1929.

Shaw, C. R., and H. D. McKay, *Juvenile Delinquency in Urban Area*, University of Chicago Press, Chicago, 1942.

Skehaw, J. J., *Modern Police Work,* Francis M. Basuino, New York, 1951.
Smith, B., *Police Systems in the United States,* Harper, New York, 1949.
Solomon, B., "Why We Have Not Solved the Delinquency Problem," *Federal Probation,* Vol. XXVII, No. 4, December, 1958.
Standard Family Court Act, National Probation Parole Association, New York, 1959.
Standard Juvenile Court Act, 6th ed., National Council on Crime and Delinquency, New York, 1959.
Standards for Specialized Courts Dealing With Children, Department of Health, Education, and Welfare, Washington, D.C., 1954.
Swanson, L. D., "Role of the Police in Protection of Children From Neglect and Abuse," *Federal Probation,* Vol. XXI, No. 1, March, 1961.
Taft, D. R., *Criminology,* 3rd ed., Macmillan, New York, 1958.
Tappan, P. W., *Juvenile Delinquency,* McGraw-Hill Book Co., New York, 1949.
The California Juvenile Court, *Stanford Law Review,* Vol. X, No. 3, Stanford University, Stanford, California, May, 1958.
Thornton, W. E., Chief Probation Officer, Sacramento County, California, "Rights and Liabilities of Minors," Department of the California Youth Authority, 1966.
Training for Juvenile Probation Officers, Children's Bureau, Department, of Health, Education, and Welfare, Washington, D.C., 1962.
Treger, H., "The Alcoholic and the Probation Officer: A New Relationship," *Federal Probation,* Vol. XXVI, No. 4, December, 1962.
Tunley, R., *Kids, Crime and Chaos,* Harper & Row, New York, 1964.
Vedder, C. B., *Juvenile Offenders,* Charles C Thomas, Springfield, Illinois, 1963.
Vold, G. B., *Theoretical Criminology,* Oxford University Press, New York, 1958.
Vollmer, A., *The Criminal,* The Foundation Press, Inc., Brooklyn, N.Y., 1949.
Warner, W. L., and P. S. Lunt, *The Social Life of a Modern Community,* Yale University Press, New Haven, Conn., 1941.
Watson, N. A., "Analysis and Self-Criticism in Juvenile Work," *The Police Chief,* Washington, D.C., June, 1964.
Watson, N. A., and R. N. Walker, *Training Police for Work With Juveniles,* International Association of Chiefs of Police, Washington, D.C., 1965.
Welfare and Institutions Code, State of California, Sacramento, Calif., 1965.
Winters, J. E., *Crime and Kids,* Charles C Thomas, Springfield, Illinois, 1959.
Winters, J. E., "The Role of the Police in the Prevention and Control of Delinquency," *Federal Probation,* Vol. XXI, No. 2, June 1957.
Wolfgang, M. E., L. Savitz, and N. Johnston, *The Sociology of Crime and Delinquency,* John Wiley and Sons, New York, London, 1962.
Wylegaig, V. B., Judge, "Juvenile Offenders Should Not Be Fingerprinted," *Federal Probation,* Vol. II, No. 1, January-March, 1947.
Youth and the Law, *Palo Alto Unified School District,* Community Council of Northern Santa Clara County, California, 1962.

Appendix A

Table 1

State Laws Concerning Court Jurisdiction over Juveniles[1]

State	Age Limit of Jurisdiction of Juvenile Courts: Exclusive	Age Limit of Jurisdiction of Juvenile Courts: Concurrent with Criminal Courts	Conditions of Transfer Between Juvenile and Criminal Courts
Alabama[2]	Under 16	...	Juvenile court may waive jurisdiction of children over age 14, and as to any child in Jefferson and Montgomery Counties. Children between 16 and 18 may be transferred by criminal courts to juvenile courts, except in Mobile County. Juvenile court also has exclusive jurisdiction over girls under 18 in Jefferson and Montgomery Counties.
Alaska	Under 18	...	Juvenile court may waive jurisdiction in felony cases.
Arizona	Under 18	...	...
Arkansas	Under 21	...	Juvenile court may transfer children age 21 arrested without warrant to criminal court; if arrested on warrant, criminal court may transfer to juvenile court.
California	Under 18	18–21	Criminal court may transfer children between 18 and 21 to juvenile court. Juvenile court may waive jurisdiction of children between 16 and 21.
Colorado	Under 18	18–21	Juvenile court has exclusive jurisdiction over children under 18 except as to crimes punishable by death or life imprisonment where accused is over 16. Juvenile court jurisdiction is concurrent with criminal court over children between 18 and 21 in Denver only.

Table 1 (Continued)

State	Age Limit of Jurisdiction of Juvenile Courts: Exclusive	Age Limit of Jurisdiction of Juvenile Courts: Concurrent with Criminal Courts	Conditions of Transfer Between Juvenile and Criminal Courts
Connecticut	Under 16	...	Criminal court may transfer children between 16 and 18 to juvenile court.
Delaware	Under 18	...	At discretion of attorney general and criminal court judge, children over 16 may be tried in criminal court on recommendation of judge of juvenile court. Juvenile court has exclusive jurisdiction over children under the age of 18 except for capital offenses.
Florida	...	Under 18	...
Georgia[2]	Under 16	...	Juvenile court has exclusive jurisdiction over children under the age of 16 in counties of 60,000 population and over. Jurisdiction over felonies is concurrent.
Hawaii	Between 12-18	...	Juvenile court may waive jurisdiction over children between 14 and 18 years in felony cases.
Idaho	Under 18	...	Jurisdiction over felonies is concurrent.
Illinois[2]	Boys under 17; girls under 18	...	Juvenile court may waive jurisdiction in any case. Jurisdiction is exclusive in Cook County; concurrent elsewhere in state.
Indiana	Under 18	...	Juvenile court may waive jurisdiction of children over 16 charged with a crime. Juvenile court has exclusive jurisdiction over children under the age of 18 except as to crimes punishable by death or life imprisonment, and children over 16 charged with traffic violations.
Iowa	Under 18	...	Except when punishment is death or life imprisonment, criminal court may transfer case to juvenile court. Juvenile court has exclusive jurisdiction over children under

Table 1 (Continued)

State	Age Limit of Jurisdiction of Juvenile Courts: Exclusive	Concurrent with Criminal Courts	Conditions of Transfer Between Juvenile and Criminal Courts
			the age of 18, except as to crimes punishable by death or life imprisonment.
Kansas	Under 16	...	In felony cases juvenile court may transfer case to criminal court for trial, after which juvenile court again takes jurisdiction.
Kentucky	Boys under 17; girls under 18	...	Juvenile court, after hearing, may waive jurisdiction and permit criminal prosecution if juvenile court believes child has committed a crime.
Louisiana	Under 17	...	Juvenile court has exclusive jurisdiction also over children between 17 and 21 charged with an offense committed before 17, except children charged with having committed while 15 or older a capital offense or an assault with intent to commit aggravated rape.
Maine	Under 17	...	Juvenile court has exclusive jurisdiction over children under the age of 17 with the exception of capital or other infamous crimes.
Maryland[2]	Under 18	...	Juvenile court may waive jurisdiction except in Montgomery and Washington Counties; in Washington County as to felonies if child is over 14. Juvenile court has exclusive jurisdiction over children under 18 with certain exceptions: in Baltimore and Washington County under 16; except crimes punishable by death or life imprisonment in all counties except Washington; except traffic violations in Allegany County. In Montgomery County criminal court has concurrent jurisdiction over children 16 to 18.

Table 1 (Continued)

State	Age Limit of Jurisdiction of Juvenile Courts: Exclusive	Age Limit of Jurisdiction of Juvenile Courts: Concurrent with Criminal Courts	Conditions of Transfer Between Juvenile and Criminal Courts
North Carolina	Under 16	...	Juvenile court may waive jurisdiction over children between 14 and 16 charged with felonies the punishment for which cannot exceed 10 years imprisonment. Juvenile court has exclusive jurisdiction over children under 16 except children 14 and older charged with felonies the punishment for which may exceed 10 years' imprisonment.
North Dakota	Under 18	18–21	Juvenile court may waive jurisdiction over children 14 or older. Juvenile court has exclusive jurisdiction over children under 18 and older minors charged with offenses committed under such age.
Ohio	Under 18	...	Juvenile court has exclusive jurisdiction over children under 18, but child may waive right to juvenile court.
Oklahoma[2]	Boys under 16; girls under 18		Juvenile court may transfer serious cases to criminal court in certain circumstances. In Tulsa the age limit is 18 for both boys and girls.
Oregon	...	Under 18	Criminal court may transfer case to juvenile court, or after trial refer case to juvenile court for disposition.
Pennsylvania	Under 16	16–18	Juvenile court may transfer to criminal court case of any child over 14 charged with a crime (other than murder) punishable by imprisonment in a state penitentiary. Age limits for exclusive and concurrent jurisdiction prevail except in charges of murder under 18.
Rhode Island	Under 18	...	Juvenile court may waive jurisdiction of children 16 or older charged with an indictable offense. Juvenile court has exclusive jurisdiction over children under 18

Table 1 (Continued)

State	Age Limit of Jurisdiction of Juvenile Courts: Exclusive	Concurrent with Criminal Courts	Conditions of Transfer Between Juvenile and Criminal Courts
			and older minors charged with offenses committed under such age.
South Carolina[2]	Under 18	[2]	Juvenile court may waive jurisdiction under specified conditions varying in the several counties. Concurrent jurisdiction varies within the state. In Greenville County, exclusive jurisdiction of children under 16, except in cases of murder, manslaughter, rape, attempted rape, arson, burglary, bribery or perjury; in Charleston County, juvenile court has exclusive jurisdiction under 16 and minors charged with offenses committed under such age; in Spartanburg County, exclusive jurisdiction under 16; in Richland County, jurisdiction is concurrent between 7 and 18, except in capital offenses, and applies to persons under age 18 at time of committing offense.
South Dakota	Under 18	...	Juvenile court may transfer to criminal court. Juvenile court has exclusive jurisdiction of children under 18 and older minors charged with offenses committed under such age.
Tennessee[2]	Under 17	...	Juvenile court has exclusive jurisdiction over children under 18 in Carter County; under 16 in Kingsport City and Knox County. Child of juvenile court age who has been committed as a delinquent and later is found by the court to be incorrigible or dangerous may be remanded for criminal proceedings. Under various special acts offenses punishable by death or life imprisonment are excepted from jurisdiction of most juvenile courts.

Table 1 (Continued)

State	Age Limit of Jurisdiction of Juvenile Courts: Exclusive	Concurrent with Criminal Courts	Conditions of Transfer Between Juvenile and Criminal Courts
Texas	Boys, 10 to 17; girls, 10 to 18	. . .	. . .
Utah	Under 18	. . .	Juvenile court may waive jurisdiction in felony cases between 14 and 18. Criminal court may retransfer such felony cases to juvenile court. Juvenile court has exclusive jurisdiction over children under 18 and older minors charged with offenses committed under such age. Jurisdiction is concurrent over children between 14 and 18 charged with a felony.
Vermont	Under 16	. . .	Juvenile court has exclusive jurisdiction over children under 16, except for capital offenses.
Virginia	Under 18	. . .	Criminal courts may transfer to juvenile court. Juvenile court may transfer child 14 or over to criminal court if charged with offense punishable by 20 years or more in penitentiary, or death. Juvenile court has jurisdiction except as to crimes punishable by death or life imprisonment where accused is over 16. Juvenile court has exclusive jurisdiction over children under 18 and older minors charged with offenses committed under such age.
Washington	Under 18	. . .	Juvenile court may transfer to criminal court children arrested for any crimes.
West Virginia	Under 18	. . .	Juvenile court may waive jurisdiction of children over 16. Juvenile court has exclusive jurisdiction of children under 18 except for capital offenses and over older minors charged with offenses committed under such age.

Table 1 (Continued)

State	Age Limit of Jurisdiction of Juvenile Courts: Exclusive	Concurrent with Criminal Courts	Conditions of Transfer Between Juvenile and Criminal Courts
Wisconsin	Under 16	16–18	Juvenile court has concurrent jurisdiction also over boys under 21 committing certain sex offenses with girls under 18. Criminal court may transfer to juvenile court boys under 21 charged with certain sex offenses with girls under 18.
Wyoming	Boys 8-19 Girls 8-21	...	...
District of Columbia	Under 18	...	Juvenile court may waive jurisdiction in cases of children 16 or over charged with felony or any child charged with offense punishable by life imprisonment or death. Juvenile court has exclusive jurisdiction of children under 18 and older minors charged with offenses committed under such age.
Puerto Rico	Under 16	...	...

[1]Adapted from "Schools Help Prevent Delinquency," Research Bulletin, XXXI, No. 3, National Education Association, State Law on Court Jurisdiction Over Juveniles, pp. 129–130.
[2]Variations within state.

Table 2

Juvenile Delinquency Arrest Rates Per 100,000 Population Aged 10-17, 1960-1964, in California by Type of Arrest

	Arrest Rates			
Year	Total Arrests	Major law Violation	Minor law Violation	Delinquent Tendencies
1960	8,758	1,576	1,940	5,062
1961	8,393	1,464	1,932	4,997
1962	8,812	1,527	2,095	5,190
1963	9,623	1,596	2,174	5,853
1964	10,059	1,724	2,305	6,030
Percent increase in rate				
1964 over 1960	17.3	9.4	18.8	19.1
1964 over 1963	4.5	8.0	6.0	3.0

Source: "Division of Criminal Law In California," *Crime in California, 1964*, State Printing Office, Sacramento, Calif., p. 52.

Table 3

Juvenile Arrests by Sex in California

	Boys		Girls
All arrests	4.1	to	1
Major law violation arrests	15.3	to	1
Minor law violation arrests	3.8	to	1
Delinquent tendency arrests	3.3	to	1

Source: "Division of Criminal Law In California," *Crime In California, 1964*, State Printing Office, Sacramento, Calif., p. 53.

Table 4

Projected Population Increases for Various Age Groups Most Vulnerable to Delinquency and Crime

Age Group	Percentage Increase 1960-1970
All ages	+19%
10-14	+20%
15-19	+41%
20-44	+12%
45 and over	+18%

Sources: Children's Bureau, Federal Bureau of Investigation, and Bureau of the Census.

Table 5

Number and Rate of Dependency and Neglect Cases Disposed of by Juvenile Courts, United States, 1964[a]

Type of Court	Number of Cases	Rate per 1,000 Child Population[b] All Courts	Age Jurisdiction of Court Under 16	Under 17	Under 18[c]
Urban	103,000	2.9	2.3	3.7	2.6
Semi-urban	34,000	2.5	1.6	3.0	2.6
Rural	13,000	1.7	1.1	1.7	2.0

[a]Estimates based on data from 1,735 courts whose jurisdictions include about three-fourths percent of the child population under 18 years of age.
[b]Calculated on basis of the 1960 child population at risk; that is, the child population under 16 for courts whose age jurisdiction is under 16, etc.
[c]A small number of courts having jurisdiction under 21 years of age are included here. The number of cases involved does not seriously affect the rates of the courts in this column.
Source: Children's Bureau, "Juvenile Court Statistics—1964," Department of Health, Education, and Welfare, Washington, D.C., p. 13.

Table 6

Percentage Change in Dependency and Neglect Cases Disposed of by Juvenile Courts, United States, 1963-1964[a]

Type of Court	Total	Judicial Cases	Non-Judicial Cases
Total	+3	+1	+6
Urban	+2	(b)	+7
Semi-urban	(b)	+1	−2
Rural	+17	+11	+48

[a]Estimates based on data from 1,593 courts reporting both years whose jurisdiction include over two-thirds of the child population under 18 years of age.
[b]Less than 0.5 per cent change.
Source: Children's Bureau, "Juvenile Court Statistics—1964," Department of Health, Education, and Welfare, Washington, D.C., p. 14.

Table 7

Trend in Dependency and Neglect Cases Disposed of by Juvenile Courts, United States, 1946-1964

Year	Dependency and neglect cases[a]	Child population of U.S. (under 18 years of age)[b]
1946	101,000	41,759,000
1947	104,000	43,301,000
1948	103,000	44,512,000
1949	98,000	45,775,000
1950	93,000	47,017,000
1951	97,000	48,598,000
1952	98,000	50,296,000
1953	103,000	51,987,000
1954	103,000	53,737,000
1955	106,000	55,568,000
1956	105,000	57,377,000
1957	114,000	59,336,000
1958	124,000	61,238,000
1959	128,000	63,038,000
1960	131,000	64,553,000
1961	140,000	65,940,000
1962	141,500	67,377,000
1963	146,000	68,707,000
1964	150,000	70,054,000

[a]Data for 1955-64 estimated from courts serving about two-thirds of the child population under 18 years of age in the United States. Data prior to 1955 estimated by the Children's Bureau, based on reports from a smaller but comparable group of courts. Inclusion of estimates for Alaska and Hawaii beginning in 1960 does not materially affect the trend.

[b]Data based on estimates from Bureau of Census, U.S. Department of Commerce (Current Population Report, Series P-25) .

Source: Children's Bureau, "Juvenile Court Statistics—1964," U.S. Department of Health, Education and Welfare, Washington, D.C., p. 14.

Table 8

*Juvenile Arrests for Liquor Law Violations in California 1960-1963**

Year	Offense	Total Arrested	Type of Arrest		Police Disposition		Juv. Crt. Or Prob. Depart-ment	New cases ref. to Prob.
			De-tained	Not de-tained	Handled within department	Other juris-diction		
1960	Total	13,774	5,375	9,499	6,343	792	6,639	5,262
	Drunk driving	339	228	111	50	22	267	
	Other liquor laws	13,435	4,147	9,288	6,293	770	6,372	
1961	Total	13,427	3,978	9,449	6,068	663	6,696	5,282
	Drunk Driving	308	178	130	41	15	252	
	Other liquor laws	13,119	3,825	9,294	6,027	648	6,444	
1962	Total	13,700	4,369	9,331	6,769	616	6,315	5,654
	Drunk Driving	310	165	145	48	8	254	
	Other liquor laws	13,390	4,204	9,186	6,721	608	6,061	
1963	Total	15,136	5,325	9,813	7,381	724	7,031	N/A
	Drunk Driving	315	181	134	44	10	261	
	Other liquor laws	14,821	5,142	9,679	7,337	714	6,770	

Source: California Youth Authority's Division of Research and Statistics, 1963, (unpublished)

*Current data not available.

Appendix B

CALIFORNIA JUVENILE COURT LAW[1]

The new Juvenile Court Act covering nearly 200 sections has been rewritten with many significant changes. This section on Juvenile Law is not intended to analyze all of the changes, but it is an attempt to spell out the significant areas that would be applicable to *law-enforcement officers in California.*

Jurisdiction

Jurisdiction of the Juvenile Court *may* extend to any person under 21 who comes within any of the following descriptions (this does not apply to traffic matters) :

600 *Dependents*	*Sec. 600(a):*	Who is in need of proper and effective care or control and who has no guardian willing to exercise or capable of exercising such care or control, or has no parent or guardian actually exercising such care or control.
Sec. 600(b):		Who is destitute, or who is not provided with a home or suitable place of abode, or whose home is an unfit place for him by reason of neglect, cruelty, or depravity of either of his parents, or of his guardian or other person in whose custody he is.
Sec. 600(c):		Who is physically dangerous to the public because of a mental or physical deficiency, disorder or abnormality.
601 *Predelinquents*	*Sec. 601:*	Any person under the age of 21 years who persistently or habitually refuses to obey the reasonable and proper orders or directions of his parents, guardian, or school authorities, or who is beyond the control of such person, or any person who is a habitual truant from school within the meaning of the law of this State or who from any cause is in danger of leading an idle, dissolute, lewd, or immoral life, is within the jurisdiction of the juvenile court which may adjudge such person to be a ward of the court.
602 *Law Violators*	*Sec. 602:*	Any person under the age of 21 years who violates any law of this State or of the United States or any ordinance of any city or county of this State defining crime, or who, after having been found by the juvenile court to be a person described by Section 601, fails to obey any lawful order of the juvenile court, is within the jurisdiction of

[1]*Welfare and Institutions Code*, State of California, Sacramento, Calif., 1965, pp. 168–214.

the juvenile court, which may adjudge such person to be a ward of the court.

Original Jurisdiction

Original jurisdiction is delegated to the juvenile court for those who are under 18 years of age and who come within the above sections. If the minor is between 18 and 21, it is discretionary with the juvenile court to accept jurisdiction. It is common practice not to accept jurisdiction on those minors 18 years and over. Seldom will a petition be filed, or will the Probation Officer accept a referral on any minor over 18 years of age.

The 1961 statutes also require the lower courts to process a law violator under 18 years when his true age is known. Section 650 clearly defines the manner in which proceedings are commenced when a minor under 18 violates the law. This commencement of action is by the filing of a petition in the juvenile court by the Probation Officer, and by no one else (other than the juvenile court judge). It makes no difference where the act takes place, but the court may take jurisdiction if *one* of the following conditions is present:

1. If the act took place in the county where petition is filed.
2. If the child resides in the county.
3. If the minor is physically present in the county (651).

No other court has authority to conduct a preliminary examination or to try the case of any person who was under the age of 18 at the time the alleged offense was committed (603). The juvenile court has original jurisdiction and only it has authority to remand cases for criminal prosecution, and only then when the offense is a felony and the minor is over 16 (707). Thus if by inadvertence a case arrives before a magistrate of a court other than the juvenile court, proceedings must be suspended, and the matter certified to the proper court, i.e., the juvenile court (W&I 604). When a petition is filed in the juvenile court, the minor cannot be subjected to criminal proceeding until and unless the juvenile court remands the case as unfit for juvenile court disposition (604). Thus no law-enforcement officer should request a criminal complaint via the lower court.

Consequently, the district attorney, city prosecutor, or clerk of a lower court has no authority or jurisdiction to accept a criminal complaint commencing proceeding against a minor under the age of 18 when his true age is known. Procedure for the arresting officer is outlined above under 625-628, and under 653 the procedure is outlined for the making of an application for a petition by anyone to the Probation Officer. From a practicable view, the Probation Officer will request a criminal complaint where it appears that the case may be considered unfit by the court. This will permit the court to remand for prosecution under the general law as an adult in the criminal court those cases where the minor is over 16, the act is felonious, and the court feels the minor is unfit for juvenile court proceedings. This is a judicial determination, and while the Probation Officer may anticipate and recommend, the final decision is for the court.

Responsibilities and Procedure by Officer Following Arrest

The 1961 legislation now specifically gives peace officers authority to take into custody any minor under 18 without a warrant when he has "reasonable cause" for believing that the person comes under Section 600, 601, or 602 (625). This arrest may be for a violation of any federal, state, county, or city statute, as well as for being a dependent or neglected child.

Arrest Without Warrant

Simply defined, a minor under 18 may now be arrested without a warrant, if reasonable cause is shown that he violated a law, regardless of whether it be a felony or misdemeanor, as defined by the Penal Code (625 W&I). Adults and minors in California now have different statutory rights involving their arrest, and officers are given much greater powers to arrest minors. Additional powers are given to arresting officers in making a disposition after arrest of a minor.

Procedure by Officer after Arrest

If a minor under 18 is arrested, the procedure for disposition is prescribed by Section 626. This section states that the arresting officer has the following choices of procedure:

1. He may release the minor.

2. He may cite the minor to appear before the Probation Officer. The procedure for citing is as follows:

a. Prepare in duplicate a written notice to appear before the Probation Officer.

b. The notice should contain a concise statement of the violation and the reason why the minor was taken into custody (facts making up a violation of the law).

c. A copy of this notice is to be given to the minor or his parent, and each may be required to sign a promise to appear, and the minor must then be immediately released.

d. As soon as practicable, one copy of the notice to appear, including the facts of the offense, shall be filed with the Probation Officer.

3. The arresting officer may take the minor without unnecessary delay before the Probation Officer of the

county and deliver custody of such minor to the Probation Officer.

In determining which of the three dispositions he will make, the arresting officer shall select the one which least restricts the minor's freedom of movement, provided such is compatible with the best interests of the minor and the community (625).

Notify Parents

If the minor is taken to the juvenile hall, or to any other place of confinement, the arresting officer shall take immediate steps to notify the minor's parents, guardian, or custodian that the minor is in custody and specify the place where he is being held (627).

P.O. Not Involved

If the arresting agency choose under 626(a) to release a minor without referral to the Probation Officer, the Probation Officer is not involved in the disposition or proceeding. It is suggested, however, that CJI (County Juvenile Index) be advised on the proper field investigation card.

Concise Statement of Facts on Citations

Should the arresting agency release the minor under 626(b) and cite the minor to the Probation Officer, the citation notices must be prepared by the arresting agency and proper notice given to the parents and the Probation Officer. The Probation Officer must have a concise statement of the facts that constitute a violation of the law, as well as names, dates, and places concerning the violation. If there were damages, these should also be ascertained so the Probation Officer can determine restitution. All this material is essential so that the Probation Officer can make an intelligent determination as to how the case should be handled. These facts must be obtained *prior* to the date set for the minor's appearance before the Probation Officer.

Should the arresting officer choose under 626(c) to take the minor before the Probation Officer at the juvenile hall, the Probation Officer, in taking the minor's custody, must carry out 628 immediately. Law enforcement must notify parents per 627.

Corpus Deliciti Must Be Available upon Admission to Juvenile Hall

In order for the Probation Officer to determine the necessity of detention as specified in 628 and 629, he must have the facts concerning the offense *at the time the minor is delivered to his custody*. The arresting agency must provide the Probation Officer with all these facts that make up the *corpus delicti* of the offense, including times, dates, places, parties, and the specific penal code section violated to bring the minor under Section 602 of the Welfare & Institutions Code. Section 602 states "The court may take jurisdiction of a minor who violates any law of the state, or United States, or any ordinance of any city or county defining a crime."

Evidence and Reports Necessary to File Petition

The specific law violated and the evidence supporting the allegations must be provided in order for a proper determination to be made. The same evidence would be required for an arrest under 600 or 601 if custody is given to the Probation Officer.

The Probation Officer must also have these reports of the investigating officer in order to prepare the petition. The items which must be provided by law enforcement would be exactly the same as given the district attorney in an adult criminal matter for a complaint.

The Petitioning Process

Proceeding in the juvenile court to declare a minor a ward or a dependent child of the court is commenced by the filing of a petition *by the Probation Officer* (650).

Petitions

The Probation Officer shall make an investigation to determine whether proceedings in the juvenile court should be commenced (652). It appears that the Probation Officer is vested with wide discretion as to whether or not the case should be brought before the court by petition. He has dispositions available other than the filing of a petition.

Six Months' Informal Supervision

He may conclude that a minor is a person coming under 600, 601, or 602, but may in lieu of filing a petition, and with consent of the minor's parents, place the minor under a program of supervision by the Probation Department (654). The maximum length of time is for six months, but at anytime during this period the Probation Officer may still file the petition.

He may also dismiss the matter at intake with no further action.

Referrals to the Probation Officer for the filing of a petition may come from several sources:

1. Informal referrals from various agencies or persons (652). These matters would generally be referred to the proper law enforcement agency for a police investigation.

2. A minor cited by a law enforcement agency for a law violation under 602, or acts which bring the minor under 600 or 601 (626b).

3. A minor taken into custody by a peace officer and his custody delivered to the Probation Officer at the juvenile hall or elsewhere as designated by the Probation Officer (626c).

4. Any person may make an application for a petition to the Probation Officer alleging that a minor comes within the jurisdiction of the juvenile court under 600, 601, or 602. The person must make an affidavit to all jurisdictional facts.

What the P.O. Must Do with Request for Petition

If the Probation Officer does not file a petition pursuant to the application, he must, within 21 days, notify the applicant of this action. He must endorse upon the affidavit of application his decision not to file a petition and his reasons therefor; retaining the affidavit for 30 days after notice to the applicant (653).

The applicant may apply to the juvenile court for a review of the Probation Officer's decision not to file a petition within one month after the application was made (655).

Only the P.O. Can File Petition

It appears from the procedure outlined above that no petition can be filed except by the Probation Officer, or unless he is ordered to do so by the juvenile court (655).

When P.O. Must File

There are two other situations, however, which make it mandatory that a petition be filed by the Probation Officer. They are:

1. If a person appears in an adult criminal court and it seems or it is suggested to the court that the person was under 18 at the time the alleged offense was committed, the court *must* suspend proceedings and certify the matter to the juvenile court (604a). The Probation Officer *must* file a petition as provided in 656 (604d).

2. If a person appears before an adult criminal court, and the person is under 21 (but over 18), the court *may* suspend proceedings and certify the case to juvenile court (604b). The Probation Officer *must* file a petition as provided in 656 (604d).

Certification—Criminal Court Cannot Proceed Until

It is noted that the criminal court, having certified the case to juvenile court, cannot proceed *until* the juvenile court finds the minor unfit to be dealt with under the juvenile court law, and orders criminal proceedings to be resumed (606). The juvenile court *must* accept them.

Regardless of which of the various methods are used to refer the case to the Probation Officer, he must follow 656 in filing the petition. If the minor is in custody, a petition *must* be filed immediately (630). The minor *must* be released if the petition is not filed within 48 hours after having been taken into custody (631).

If P.O. Retains Minor

Upon the filing of a petition, a date for a hearing must be set within 30 days. However, if the minor is in custody at the time the petition is filed, the hearing must be set within 15 judicial days from date of the order of detention (657).

Time Schedule for Notices and Hearing

The parents must be served with notice of the hearing and must also receive a copy of the petition (658). They are entitled to receive notice at least 24 hours before the time of the hearing if they reside in the county, or be given five days' notice either in person or by certified mail if the parents reside outside the county. Service may be waived by the parents, or a voluntary appearance entered in the court minutes is sufficient (660).

Attorney

The parents must receive a statement in writing that they or the minor are entitled to have their attorney present at the hearing on the petition, and that, if the parent or guardian is indigent and cannot afford an attorney, *and the minor or his parent* desires to be represented by an attorney, such parent or guardian shall promptly notify the clerk of the juvenile court (659).

Warrants and Subpoenas

Whenever the petition has been filed and it appears to the court that the conduct or behavior of the minor may endanger the health, welfare, property, or person of himself or others, or that circumstances of his home may endanger his health welfare, property, or person, a warrant of arrest may be issued for said minor (663). The parents, minor, or the Probation Officer may also have the clerk of the court issue subpoenas requiring attendance and testimony of the witnesses and production of papers at any hearings (664).

The Juvenile Court Petition—The Document

The juvenile court petition is the document that gets the case before the court. It is the only document that legally frames the issues for the court and the parties. This is the legal pleading that commences the proceeding in the juvenile courts (650).

Contents of a Petition

The statutes state that the verified petition must contain (656):

1. Name of the court.
2. Title of proceeding.
3. The code sections and subdivision(s) under which the proceedings are instituted.
4. The name, age, and address of the minor upon whose behalf the action is brought.
5. Name and address of parents or guardian.
6. A concise statement of facts, separately stated, to support the conclusion that the minor upon whose behalf the petition is being brought is a person within the definition of each of the sections and subsections under which proceedings are being instigated.
7. The fact whether the minor is in custody and the date ordered detained.

Petition Must Be Filed within 48 Hours

This document must be filed within 48 hours after the minor is taken into custody (630) and a copy of it must be served on the parents prior to the jurisdictional disposition hearing (660). The petition and Probation Officer's report are confidential and may only be inspected by the minor, his parents, or counsel, and the court personnel and by such other persons designated by the judge of the juvenile court (827).

Petition Must Contain Concise Statement of Facts

The concise statement of facts required under 656f means the elements of the offense that make up the violation. If the allegation is under 602, "any person who violates any law of the state, United States, or any ordinance of any city or county defining crime," the specific statute in the penal code, or other specific statute defining a crime, must be quoted, the times, dates, places, and elements of the specific offense must be alleged with clarity. *These are the same kinds of allegations that are contained in a criminal complaint.*

Same Kind of Evidence as in Adult Cases

The law enforcement agency making these allegations is responsible to obtain the facts and evidence and present them to the Probation Officer *much in the same manner that evidence of law violations are presented to the district attorney in adult criminal cases. The same kind of evidence is necessary in juvenile cases as in adult cases.*

Preponderance of Evidence

The juvenile court must find a "preponderance of evidence legally admissible in the trial of criminal cases to support a finding under 602 (701) and a preponderance of evidence legally admissible in civil cases to support a finding under 600 and 601 (701)."

It is the duty of the investigating law enforcement agency to prepare the evidence in advance of requesting a petition from the Probation Officer. The Probation Officer *cannot file a petition without the evidence to support it.*

The allegations in the petition are the facts to be proven at the hearing. This pleading is subject to all the rules relating to variance and amendments of pleadings in civil actions, and with the same effect as if the proceeding were civil action (678).

Petition Subject to Demur. Has to Be in Fact an Offense. A Corpus Delicti

The petition is subject to *demur* by counsel, and it must be specific and carefully drawn to state a legal course of action. Every element of the violation must be alleged to constitute a course of action, and each element must be provable. There has to be in fact an offense; that is, a "corpus delicti," before an allegation can be made that the minor did violate the law when the pleading is 602. Even pleadings under 600, neglected and dependent, and 601, beyond control, must contain allegations of specific acts; facts with time, dates, and places that constitute behavior or conditions that bring the minor under 600 and 601.

The Detention Hearing

A minor taken into custody shall be brought before the juvenile court for a hearing to determine whether he shall be further detained, *as soon as possible,* but in any event before the expiration of the next judicial day following the filing of the petition, *or he must be released* (632).

Detention Hearing Must Be Held the Next Judicial Day after Petition Filed

The petition *must* be filed before 48 hours are up, and a detention hearing held on the next judicial day following this filing.

The Probation Officer shall notify the parents of the minor of the time, date, and place of the detention hearing. This may be done orally (630).

At the detention hearing, the following procedure is mandatory by Section 633-639. *This hearing is to determine continued detention* (632):

What the Judge Must Do

1. The court must inform the minor and his parents of the reasons why the minor was taken into custody (633).

2. The nature of the hearing and of the juvenile court proceedings (633).

Right to Counsel

3. The rights of the minor and his parents to be represented at every stage of the proceedings by counsel (634).

4. If the court determines that the minor or his parents desire counsel, but are indigent and cannot employ counsel, the court *may* appoint counsel. However, if the misconduct alleged is such that it would constitute a felony if committed by an adult, the court *must* appoint counsel if they desire such and are indigent.

If it appears there is conflict of interests between parents and child, the court *may* appoint each counsel (634).

5. The court will examine the minor, his parents, or other persons having relevant knowledge, and hear such relevant evidence as the minor, his parents, or counsel desire to present concerning whether the minor should continue in detention.

The court shall order the minor released from custody unless it finds that:

Must Release Unless

1. The minor has violated an order of the juvenile court, or has escaped from the commitment of the juvenile court.

2. It is a matter of immediate or urgent necessity for the protection of said minor or the person or property of another that he be detained.

3. The minor is likely to flee the jurisdiction of the court.

It should be noted that these three reasons for detention are the same ones that the intake Probation Officer has already used under 628 when the minor was delivered to his custody. The court of the detention hearing is in fact having a judicial review of the Probation Officer's findings as reason for detention. This, then, assures the minor of two determinations as to the need for detention; one by the Probation Officer (628) and one by the Court (635), both using the same statutory criteria for continued detention. The court may hold a detention hearing if the parents are not present, but the absent parents may file an affidavit with the court clerk and a rehearing shall be held within twenty-four hours (637). Upon the motion of the minor or his parents, the court may continue a detention hearing for one judicial day (638).

Rehearing If Parents Not Notified and Not Present

Time Schedule for Notices and Hearing

If the court finds the minor should be detained under one of the three reasons outlined above under Section 635, it shall make its order together with its findings of facts in support thereof in the records of the court. *The order of detention shall not exceed 15 judicial days (636).* The dispositional hearing must be calendared for no longer than 15 judicial days when the minor is in custody (657).

Court Reporter

If the detention hearing is conducted by the judge, it is mandatory that a court reporter be present to take down the proceedings. However, if the hearing is conducted by the referee (as it generally is), it is not mandatory that a court reporter be present.

No one under 18 may be detained elsewhere than in juvenile hall, except on order of the court (502). No minor may be detained under 600 with minors who are in custody under 601 and 602 (506).

The Jurisdictional Hearing

The statutes now provide that this hearing must be held within 15 judicial days of the order directing detention (if the minor is in custody) and within 30 days if the minor is not in custody (657).

Closed Session

This hearing shall be at a special session, closed to the public and only the minor, parents, relatives, counsel shall be permitted (675). Witnesses and court attaches are, of course, present.

Exceptions

The judge or referee may admit persons he deems to have a direct and legitimate interest in the particular case or work of the court (676).

Reporter Mandatory in Juvenile Court Hearings

Proceedings conducted by the judge must be taken down by an official court reporter. They *may* be taken down in proceedings conducted by a referee, but it is not mandatory (677). However, if proceedings are not taken down before the referee, the parents may appeal the referee's order within 10 days, and may have as a right a rehearing before the judge (558). The cost of transcribing the proceedings must be paid by the party requesting them (677).

Policy

The court shall control the hearing with a view to the expeditious and effective ascertainment of the jurisdictional facts and all information relative to the present conditions and future welfare of the minor (*except where there is a contested issue of fact or law*). *The proceeding shall be conducted in an informal non-adversary atmosphere with a view of obtaining the maximum cooperation of the minor and all persons interested in his welfare* (680).

Judge's Duties at Hearing

Section 700-703 provides how the court shall proceed:

1. The clerk or judge shall read the petition to those present.
2. Upon the request of the minor, parents, or guardian, the court shall explain:
   a. Any term of allegation in the petition.
   b. The nature of the hearing.
   c. The procedures.
   d. Possible consequences.
3. The court shall ascertain whether the minor and his parents have been notified of their right to counsel; if not, he shall advise them.

Appointment of Counsel

4. If the parents are indigent and desire counsel, and if the misconduct alleged would constitute a felony if committed by an adult, the court *must* appoint counsel if the parents so desire and they are indigent.

(Note: This is the same test and requirement as provided by 634 at the detention hearing except under that provision the minor himself may request counsel if indigent. The parent only is mentioned in 700 for requesting counsel; nothing is said about the minor being indigent and requesting counsel.)

Public Defender

Section 27706 Government Code has ben amended to authorize the public defender to represent persons entitled to be represented by counsel, but who are not financially able to employ counsel, when ordered by the court in proceedings under the Juvenile Court Law when a person is alleged to come under 600, 601, or 602. The court may continue the case for seven days to appoint counsel or to enable counsel to acquaint himself with the case or to determine whether the parent is indigent and unable to afford counsel.

Finding of Jurisdictional Fact

5. The court shall first consider only the question of whether the minor is a person under 600, 601, or 602 (701). This is known as the jurisdictional hearing. This may be likened to a criminal case where the defendant's guilt is first established before any disposition is considered. This is currently the procedure in adult probation matters where the issues of guilt are established *before* the probation officer makes a written report recommending disposition or sentence. This jurisdic-

tional hearing is to simply establish at the commencement of the case all those requirements that give the court authority to dispose of the matter.

Things Which Must Be Found

The court must establish that the minor is of the age described by Sections 600, 601, or 602; i.e., under 21, that a petition has been filed pursuant to 656, that parents have had due notice as required by 660, and that the minor is within the county, resides within the county, or committed an act within the county coming under 600, 601, or 602, as required by 652.

The basic issue the court must first determine is whether the allegations made that the minor comes within 600, 601, or 602 are such to constitute court jurisdiction, and if they are enough, that they are in fact true.

Minor's Admission in Open Court

An admission in the presence of the court is sufficient for the court to make a finding that the allegations are true, and to sustain the petition giving the court jurisdiction to proceed on disposition.

However, if there is no admission of the allegations, or in fact a denial, the court must proceed to hear evidence if the petition is to be sustained. Section 701 provides that if the minor had previously admitted the allegations, but at the hearing he denies same to the court, the probation officer may subpoena witnesses to prove the allegations of the petition.

Continuance of Seven Days

A continuance of seven days may be granted by the court to enable the probation officer to produce those witnesses necessary to prove the allegations.

To prove the disputed allegations of the petition, the probation officer may present any matter or information relevant and material to the circumstances or acts which are alleged to bring the minor within the juvenile court jurisdiction. This information is admissible and may be received by the court as evidence; however a preponderance of evidence, legally admissible in the trial of criminal cases, must be adduced to support a finding that the minor comes under 602.

If the minor is not represented by counsel, it shall be deemed that objections that could have been made (by counsel) to the evidence were made (701). Prior cases in law indicate that a minor need not testify against himself, and may refuse to answer questions relative to the allegations asked by the court.

If No Facts to Sustain Jurisdiction, Must Release

After hearing the evidence, the court shall make a finding, noted in the minutes of the court, whether or not the minor is a person described by 600, 601, or 602. If the court finds that the minor is not such a person, it shall order the petition dismissed and the minor released from all detention and restrictions (702).

If Unfit, Return to Criminal Court

At any time during a hearing upon the petition alleging that a minor is a person described in Section 602 when evidence has been adduced *indicating that the offense alleged is punishable as a felony under the general law, and the minor was 16 years or older at the time of the commission of the offense, and that the minor would not be amendable to care, treatment and training available through the facilities of the juvenile court, the court may make a finding noted in the minutes that the minor is not a fit and proper subject, and direct the district attorney to prosecute the person under the general law and thereafter dismiss the petition.*

A denial of the allegations of the petition is not in itself sufficient to support a finding of unfitness (707).

The Disposition Hearing

If the court finds the minor is a person described by Section 600, 601, or 602, it shall make and enter its finding or judgment accordingly, and shall then proceed to hear evidence on the proper disposition to be made of the minor (702).

Social Study in Evidence

The court may, however, continue the case to receive the social study of the probation officer. However, if the minor is in custody, the case may be continued for *no longer than 10 judicial days, and for no more than 5 days if the minor has been detained more than 10 days prior to the hearing*. Should the minor not be in custody, the case may be continued for 30 days counting from the date the petition was filed, but for good cause shown the court may continue the matter for an additional 15 days (702).

After the finding that the minor comes under 600, 601, or 602, the court shall hear evidence on the question of the proper disposition to be made of the minor. The court shall receive in evidence the social study of the probation officer and such other relevant and material evidence as may be offered, and in any judgment and order of disposition, shall state the social study by the probation officer has been read and considered by the court (706).

After receiving and considering the evidence on the proper disposition of the case, the court may enter judgment as follows (725):

1. If the court finds the minor to be a person coming under 601 or 602, the court, without making the minor a ward, places the minor on probation for a period not to exceed six months.
2. If a finding is made under 601 or 602, the court may adjudge the minor a ward of the court.

3. If a finding is made under 600, the minor may be adjudged a dependent child of the court.

Summary of Court Jurisdiction and Disposition Hearing

The court actually makes three determinations in each case: (1) *the jurisdictional*; (2) *dispositional status*; and (3) *dispositional care.*

1. *The Jurisdictional Aspect.* The court finds whether or not the allegations of the petition are true and that the person is a minor coming under 600, 601, or 602 (701 and 702).

Where Mental Hearing Ordered in Other Court

a. *After* the finding the court may, if in doubt as to the mental health or mental condition of the minor, commit to Department of Mental Hygiene for a period not to exceed 90 days for observation (703). The Department of Mental Hygiene must submit to the Court a written report on the state of the minor's mental condition, a diagnosis, and recommendation concerning his future care, supervision and treatment.

Juvenile Court Jurisdiction Suspended

The court may make this referral and commitment *without* declaring the minor a ward or dependent child of the court. The case is *continued* for 90 days for a declaration of status and disposition. This commitment is for observation and recommendation to help the court make a proper disposition *after* the report is received and is *not in itself* a disposition (703).

b. After a finding of the jurisdictional facts, the court may use the same procedure as (a) above in an observational commitment to the Youth Authority for 90 days (704).

California Youth Authority Diagnostic Center

The county, however, must have a contract with the Youth Authority for this service. This procedure, again, is an observational period for the Youth Authority clinic teams to make a recommendation for disposition of the case. This in itself is not a final disposition and the case is continued without making the minor a ward or a dependent child of the court (704).

These two procedures are for diagnosis and recommendation, *the continuance is for a period of 90 days or less*, to permit the court to receive this before making a disposition and order for the minor's case.

2. *The Disposition Aspect—Status of Minor.* After finding under 1, above, that the minor comes under 600, 601, or 602, the court establishes the minor's status (706). The court may:

a. Place minor on probation without declaring him a ward of the court if he comes under 601 or 602 (725).

b. Make minor a ward of the court under 601 or 602.

c. Declare child a dependent child of the court.

d. Reprimand and dismiss the case and the petition under 600, 601, or 602.

The court, without a finding under 602, may declare the minor not a fit and proper subject to be processed in the juvenile court and direct the District Attorney to process the matter as an adult. The offense alleged in the petition must be a felonious act and the minor must be 16 or older (707).

3. *Disposition Aspect—Care of Minor.* After court has found minor comes under 600, 601 or 602, and establishes the minor's status, it then proceeds to make a disposition concerning the ward's care:

a. May return child to own home under supervision of the probation office under 600, 601, or 602.

Disposition of 600 Child

b. A dependent child under *600* (726):

(1) Care, custody, control, and conduct of the minor under the probation office, or to be placed in a suitable foster home by the probation office (727).

c. Comitment of minor to some reputable person or to some public or private association that cares for needy or neglected children.

The court may require that the private or public agency caring for children who are dependents of the court make regular prescribed visits and periodical reports to the court (728).

Annual Review

Any order declaring a minor a dependent child of the court under 600 must be reviewed at least every year. No order is valid for longer than one year, unless a supplemental petition is filed and a rehearing is held in the same manner as the original proceeding. This simply means that all dependent child cases under 600 must have a new hearing each year with a petition, service on parents, etc. (729). *The purpose of this is to give parents a judicial review of their case at least once a year, so that dependent crildren are not being kept away from their parents by administrative officers.*

Disposition of 601 Child

c. The incorrigible/beyond-control minor under *601* (730):

(1) The same disposition as dependent children under 600; i.e., to foster home, probation office case, etc. (727).

(2) Commit to a county facility such as a boys' ranch or girls' school.

(3) Commit to some private institution or school.

(4) Commit to the CYA *only* after a supplemental petition has been filed (730) and a hearing with

facts to support the conclusion "that the previous disposition has not been effective in the rehabilitation of the minor." (777)

This means no minor can be committed to the YA under 601 (as an incorrigible/beyond-control case) *until* he has first been placed under jurisdiction of the court as a ward under 601, or on probation under 601, and his conduct has been such during this period to indicate that he has not rehabilitated (777). His conduct must be alleged and proved through the filing of a supplemental petition in the same manner as the original hearing.

Disposition of 602 Child

d. The violation of a criminal statute under *602*.

This is the section must commonly used for boy cases where there is criminal statute violated. Proceedings in the juvenile court are not criminal, however, and a finding under 602 does *not* constitute conviction of a crime by the minor (503).

This is the only section under which a commitment to the YA can be made *except* there can be such under 601, *after* the minor has failed to adjust under supervision and then had a rehearing on this failure (777).

The court may make orders concerning the care of a 602 in the same manner and the same things as ordered both under 600 and 601 cases; i.e., supervision of probation office, placed in private or public agency for placement in foster home, placed with a private person in a foster home, to the probation office for placement in a foster home, private or public institution, or in a county boys' or girls' school.

In all placements out of a child's own home by the court, there must be a finding first that one of the following exists (726):

Placement Out of Own Home

(1) That the parent or guardian is incapable of providing or has failed or neglected to provide proper maintenance, training, and education for the minor.

(2) That the minor has been tried on probation in such custody and has failed to reform.

(3) That the welfare of the minor requires that his custody be taken from his parent or guardian.

Index